The BIG Book
of
NLP Techniques

ISBN: 1-4392-0793-3
ISBN-13: 9781439207932

Visit www.booksurge.com to order additional copies.

The **BIG** Book
of
NLP Techniques

200+ Patterns
Methods & Strategies of
Neuro Linguistic Programming

Shlomo Vaknin

Table of Contents

Acknowledgments	xiii
Disclaimer	xv
Introduction	xvii
How To Use This Book	1
Applying NLP — What, How & When	3
NLP Patterns & Strategies	33
1. The Swish Pattern	35
2. The Failure Into Feedback Pattern	38
3. Well Defined Outcomes	43
4. The E & E.P. Formation Pattern	49
5. Pacing & Matching	52
6. Finding Positive Intention	54
7. Behavior Appreciation	57
8. Mirroring	60
9. The As-If Pattern	68
10. Eliciting Subconscious Responses	71
11. Ecology Check	73
12. Physiomental State Interruption	76
13. State Induction	78
14. Accessing Resourceful States	81
15. The Kinesthetic Swish Pattern	84
16. Anchoring	86
17. A Script For Self Anchoring	94
18. Downtime	95
19. Collapsing Anchors	98
20. Perceptual Positions	102

21. Conflicting Beliefs Integration 108
22. Belief Out-Framing 115
23. Colliding & Colluding Beliefs 118
24. Parts Negotiation 121
25. Dis-Identification 124
26. Resolving Internal Conflicts 127
27. Making Peace With Your Parents 129
28. Six Steps Reframing 134
29. Content Reframing 136
30. Context Reframing 140
31. Reframing Beliefs & Opinions – Examples 142
32. Basic Inner Conflict Integration 145
33. Mistakes Into Experience 149
34. Hierarchy Of Criteria 153
35. Aligning Perceptual Positions 162
36. The Allergy Pattern 170
37. Calibration 174
38. The Autobiography Pattern 176
39. Congruence 182
40. The Phobia Cure Pattern 184
41. Pleasure Installation 188
42. Exploring Causes & Effects 191
43. Applying Logical Levels 193
44. Pleasure Reduction 196
45. Developing Sensory Acuity 199
46. The Loving Yourself Pattern 200
47. Abandoned Predisposition 203
48, Chaining States 205
49. Pragmagraphic Swish Design 207
50. Collecting Resources 211
51. Advanced Visual Squash 213
52. Digital Vs. Analogue Submodalities 216
53. Submodality Overlapping 218
54. External Stimulus Threshold 220

55. Decision Destroyer 224

56. The Godiva Chocolate Pattern 228

57. Using Rep Systems 232

58. Auditory Rep. System Development 238

59. Visual Rep. System Development 240

60. State Of Consciousness Awareness 243

61. Non-Verbal Cues Recognition 245

62. Compulsion Blow-Out 249

63. Creating Positive Expectations 252

64. Breaking Limiting Associations 254

65. Secondary Gain and Personal Ecology 258

66. Whole System Ecology 259

67. Meta-Model Challenging 260

68. Meta-Model Intentional Usage 262

69. De-Nominalizing 264

70. The Forgiveness Pattern 266

71. Aligned Self 268

72. Circle Of Excellence 272

73. Assertiveness Installation 275

74. Self Esteem Quick Fix 280

75. The Smart Eating Pattern 286

76. Boundaries Installation 290

77. Criticism Analyzer 294

78. The Excuse Blow-Out Pattern 300

79. The Basic Motivation Pattern 304

80. The Winning Over Internal War Zone Pattern 306

81. Inducing Amnesia 310

82. Thought Virus Inoculation 311

83. The Inner Peace Questionnaire 314

84. The Relationship Clarifying Pattern 315

85. Building & Maintaining Rapport 317

86. The Falling In-Love Pattern 322

87. Avoiding Counter-Productive Suggestions 325

88. The Cyber-Porn Addiction Removal Pattern 326

89.	The Spelling Strategy	332
90.	Elicitation Of Learning Strategies	334
91.	New Language Rapid Learning	339
92.	Rhythmic Learning	342
93.	Commitment	344
94.	The (Accelerated) Learning Chain	345
95.	Apposition (Of Opposites)	348
96.	Identifying Self Sabotage Elements	349
97.	Problem Definition	352
98.	Problem Solving Strategy (I)	355
99.	Problem Solving Strategy (II)	358
100.	The Walt Disney Strategy	362
101.	The Binary Code Of Forgetfulness	365
102.	Conflict Resolution	374
103.	Co-Dependency Resolution	377
104.	Meta-Programs Identification	382
105.	Limiting Meta-Programs Challenging	384
106.	The Meta-Programs Change Pattern	386
107.	The Analogical Marking Method	389
108.	Persuasion By Chunking Up/Down	392
109.	The Classic Confusion Method	394
110.	Applying The Law of Reversed Effect	396
111.	The Nested Loops Method	398
112.	A Sample Nested Loops Story	404
113.	Subliminal Persuasion	407
114.	Intonation	410
115.	The Embedded Command (I) Method	411
116.	The Embedded Command (II) – Advanced Method	414
117.	Erickson's 55 Hypnotic Phrases	417
118.	The Frame Of Agreement	422
119.	TDS Manipulation	425
120.	Values Hierarchy Identification	427
121.	New Behavior Generator	430
122.	Active Dreaming	433

123. Emotional Pain Management   435

124. The Inner Hero Pattern   437

125. The Wholeness Pattern   442

126. The SCORE Pattern   448

127. Life Transitions Tracking   451

128. Transformation Archetype Identification   454

129. The Grief Pattern   457

130. The Pre-Grieving Pattern   460

131. Self-Nurturing   463

132. Awakening To Freedom   466

133. The Longevity Pattern   470

134. Change Personal History   475

135. The End-Of-Day Pattern   480

136. Negative Associated Emotions Dissolving   483

137. Core Transformation   486

138. Mapping Anyone's Brain   496

139. Undetermined State Integration   499

140. Choice Expansion   502

141. The F/B Pattern   504

142. Memory De-Energizing   509

143. Somatic Fractal   511

144. Resource Fractal   513

145. Changing Beliefs – The Logic Approach   515

146. Logical Levels Co-Alignment   518

147. The Embedded Command In A Question Method   521

148. The Double Bind Method   523

149. The Ambiguity Method   526

150. The Presupposition Method   528

151. The Metaphor Method   530

152. Shared Resource   532

153. The Dancing SCORE Pattern   534

154. Advantageous NLP Beliefs   538

155. The D.V.P Pattern   549

156. Belief Systems Dis-Integration   553

157. Criteria Installation 555

158. Kinesthetic Criteria 559

159. The Spinning Icons Pattern 562

160. Basic Belief Chaining 565

161. Advanced Belief Chaining 567

162. Gentling 571

163. Meta Transformation 574

164. Re-Imprinting 577

Modeling Excellence With NLP 581

Introduction To NLP Modeling 583

The Key Elements of Modeling 586

Once You Have a Model, What Do You Do With It? 588

165. Basic 2nd Position Modeling 589

166. 2nd Position Intuitive Modeling 591

167. Basic 3rd Position Modeling 593

168. Basic States Of Excellence Modeling 595

The NLP Meta-Model 597

Introduction 597

169. Generalizations 600

170. Universal Quantifiers 601

171. Lost Performatives 602

172. Modal Operators 603

173. Deletions 604

174. Lack of Referential Index 606

175. Comparative Deletions 607

176. Distortions 608

177. Nominalization 609

178. Mind Reading 611

179. Cause and Effect Distortions 612

180. Presuppositions 613

181. Complex Equivalence 614

How to Use the Meta-Model for Therapeutic Purposes? 615

The Milton-Model 617

Why Use Hypnosis in NLP? 617

Milton Erickson	617
Your Subconscious	618
What is Hypnosis?	620
Defining A Trance	621
Experiencing Rapid Trances	622
Conversational Hypnosis	622
Benefits Of The Milton Model	623
Transderivational Search	623
182. Meta-Model Violations	625
183. Pacing Current Experience	626
184. Pacing and Leading	627
185. Linking Words	628
186. Disjunction	630
187. Implied Causes	631
188. Tag Questions	632
189. Double Binds	633
190. Embedded Commands	634
191. Analogue Marking	635
192. Utilization	636
193. Nesting	638
194. Extended Quotes	639
195. Spell Out Words	640
196. Conversational Postulate	641
197. Selectional Restriction Violations	642
198. Ambiguities	643
199. Phonological Ambiguities	644
200. Syntactic Ambiguities	635
201. Scope Ambiguities	646
202. Punctuation Ambiguities	647
203. Metaphors	648
The Satir Model	651
Introduction	651
Satir categories	652
204. The Blamer	653

205. The Placater   654

206. The Computer   655

207. The Distracter   656

208. The Leveler   657

209. Utilizing Flexibility   658

210. Category Rapport-Building   659

Meta Programs   661

Introduction To The NLP Meta-Programs   661

How Does A Meta-Program Work?   663

How to Learn and Practice the Meta-Programs   668

Perception and Interest Styles Meta Programs   669

Behavior Styles Meta Programs   670

Outcomes Alignment Styles Meta Programs   671

Additional Resources   673

Appendix A: Modalities Abbreviations   677

Appendix B: The Submodalities   679

Visual Submodalities   679

Auditory Submodalities   687

Kinesthetic Submodalities   689

NLP Contributors   693

Appendix C: Logical Levels   695

Begin!   697

Acknowledgments

FIRST AND FOREMOST, big thanks to my friends and colleagues at the NLP Weekly Community. Their support and encouragement are the main reasons this book exists, and it is written with their needs and suggestions in mind.

Special thanks to Robert A. Yourell, who has contributed his considerable editorial and psychological talents to this project. His experience in the mental health field began in the 1970's, and his training includes NLP, Ericksonian hypnosis, somatic psychotherapy, and other areas. He provides writing and editorial assistance to a variety of psychological and grant-related projects. His current biographical information, including organizations he has presented or provided clinical services to, is available at his website, Yourell.com. Robert shares our vision that NLP training materials can be greatly improved, and worked tirelessly with us to ensure a readable and practical result.

The author and editor drew from many sources, so we wish to offer a limitless thank you to all the trainers named as originators of the patterns, as well as the many others who have influenced the development of NLP.

We have made every effort to ensure that all the patterns give proper credit to their developers. Refer to the Resources section at the end of the book to get in touch with any of these contributors.

Last, but not least, to Tad & Adriana James, two of the most fruitful and hard working NLP Master Trainers. Tad and Adriana are the biggest supporters of the NLP Weekly Community, and they have been an inspiration and a resource for the creation of this book.

And, of course, many thanks to you! For buying this book, for reading it, for trying out a pattern and reporting back to us, so that the next edition will be even better.

Disclaimer

NLP Is Not An Alternative To Professional Help...

THIS BOOK DOES NOT provide medical, psychiatric or psychological diagnosis, treatment, or advice. It is for informational purposes only. The material is not intended to substitute for professional medical advice or professional clinical training. Never disregard professional clinical advice and never delay in seeking it because of anything you read in this book. It is the responsibility of the reader to gain competent consultation as to their fitness to utilize the techniques disclosed in this book for any purpose, and as to what training, certification or licensure the reader may need for any application of the techniques.

The author has attempted to accurately represent the opinions and techniques expressed by NLP trainers and their documentation in a useful manner, however, the author provides the material on an "AS-IS" basis. The author disclaims all warranties, either express or implied, including fitness for a particular purpose. The author does not warrant that this book can be relied upon for complete accuracy or applicability to any purpose or situation, including those resembling any listed as typical applications for any given technique.

Although this material is believed to accurately reflect the techniques of the NLP community at the time of publication, the possibility of human error and changing standards for utilization of such techniques, the individuals involved in the production of this book do not warrant that the information contained herein is in every respect accurate or complete, and thus are not responsible for any errors or omissions or for the results obtained from the use of such information. The author makes no representation or warranties, express or implied.

In no event shall the author, any contributors or editors, or anyone referenced as a source or authority be liable for any claims or damages (including, without limitation, direct, incidental and consequential damages, personal injury/wrongful death, lost profits, resulting from the use of or inability to use this book, whether based on warranty, contract, tort, or any other legal theory, and whether or not the author is advised of the possibility of such damages. The author is not liable for any personal injury, including death, caused by your use or misuse of this book.

Attributions

We apologize in advance for any errors or omissions regarding the persons responsible for the NLP patterns. Because of the large community of NLP developers, and the rapid rate of development of the techniques, it can be difficult to be certain who originated a specific pattern. We relied on documentation from various dates, and members of the community familiar with the work of many developers.

Introduction

If there was one really useful book on NLP...
...it would be full of NLP patterns. Everyone who learns Neuro Linguistic Programming knows the power of the patterns and strategies that employ the skills and knowledge of NLP. Whether you have just been introduced to the basics, or you have mastered advanced material and patterns, this work provides you with more than 100 patterns in a concise reference format.

I have selected each pattern for its value and relevance. If you know the pattern, you can refresh your memory; if you want to learn it, you can do so without wading through any "fluff" such as ridiculously long explanations of NLP terms, or "magical stories" of healing and success. I chose to make this book clean of theories and fiction stories, and packed it with the most practical guidelines and advice.

I have selected patterns that you can use for your personal development, coaching sessions, clinical work, and business applications such as persuasion, sales, leadership and management. If you would like to use these patterns on yourself, you can follow the steps, or use your own voice to create a recording with gaps that you feel are the right duration for you to work through the procedure; or you can pause your player for the exact time that you need. I would recommend the latter approach. It also saves time in recording.

A very serious problem with quite a lot of the published materials on NLP is that they are poorly written or contain an enormous amount of "fluff". I have read more than 90% of the books in this field by now. Much of the material presented in those books is vague, makes a lot of assumptions about what the reader knows and what he or she can interpret, and even contradicts itself at times.

Since NLP developed for the most part outside of an academic or scientifically informed process, many of the contributors to NLP developed their patterns without necessarily knowing about already existing interventions, or without making use of information available from clinical or research communities and literature. On the other hand, it's a bit of an irony that much of what is now taken for granted by psychotherapists originated or was successfully developed into training by NLP developers, but without those developers receiving any credit from the mainstream for their revolutionary research and contributions.

The power of NLP lies in its base of presuppositions and practical experience. NLP developers have leveraged this base to create powerfully effective patterns. However, these writers often neglect to tell the reader whether they have successfully applied a pattern with a large number of people. This work attempts to improve the situation:

1) by carefully selecting patterns that have solid reputations in the NLP community, and which the author knows of first-hand,

2) with the help of a team of professional editors, painstakingly and unambiguously writing the patterns with very specific steps, so that they can be followed by a broad readership that includes people with only a basic understanding of NLP, and

3) re-engineering the patterns liberally, to take advantage of current knowledge in areas such as psychotherapy and learning theory. In many patterns, significant changes are made, simply by applying existing knowledge and the experience of the author and consultants. However, they remain very much in alignment with the presuppositions of NLP and the intent of the pattern.

This is certainly not the end of my outcome in creating this book. It is, by all means, a published work in process. It is also where your involvement and contribution can be seen—while you read this book, practice the concepts and methods and apply them on yourself and others, keep an open mind. Find what works best, when and how, and write back to us.

Tell us about your successes with these patterns or others you have come across, and by that you will help us make future editions of this book even more useful and powerful.

Feel free to email me at *editor@bigbookofnlp.com* with any question, suggestion or comment. You can also visit the largest and most affectionate NLP community online at BigBookOfNLP.com.

Enjoy the experience!

— Shlomo Vaknin, C.Ht

How To Use This Book

The Big Book is only a modest beginning...

Highly experienced NLP practitioners will have no trouble making immediate use of this book. They will recognize many of the patterns, and be curious about the ones they haven't learned seen before. We recommend that these practitioners eventually work their way through all the patterns, at least by looking them over, because they will see some improvements to many of the patterns, and may even get a clearer understanding of the pattern because of how the steps are laid out.

The beginner will appreciate the structure of this book because the first section has the more fundamental NLP patterns. These will round out their repertoire and build confidence. The patterns come in three main flavors. Those that you can easily try out on yourself, those that you can try on clients or other people that you interact with, and those that require some structured participation of two or more people. Each pattern states what is needed early on.

All readers will appreciate that credit is given for each pattern whenever possible. Each pattern has an introduction that explains its purpose, and is divided into steps. Once you know a pattern, the titles of the steps will be enough to guide you in practicing or in refreshing your memory of the exact steps.

As you build mastery with these patterns, we encourage you to also build flexibility and creativity. In performing these patterns, you are, most importantly, applying the presuppositions and knowledge of NLP and every other source that is available to you.

This ultimately transcends steps, because your mastery will enable you to improvise as you encounter new challenges and opportunities with clients. A pattern should never keep you back from overcoming an obstacle, and it should never blind you to an opportunity. Just as a jazz musician practices scales and time signatures to support improvisation that goes well beyond those structures, NLP practitioners are informed by the principles of NLP as they gain subconscious mastery.

As you get started with this book, have a pen or highlighter handy and mark the patterns that you want to learn or review. Highlight any words in the steps that will help you gain mastery. Be sure to stay connected with life, and have a good time. Joy and humor are great facilitators of learning and creativity.

And one last advice, perhaps the most important of all—learn with others. NLP has been around for more than three decades now, and there are surely peo-ple around you who are excited about learning NLP as you are. Find new colleagues and practice with them, share resources and knowledge, challenge and inspire each other. Join the largest international NLP community forum at BigBookOfNLP.com (free access, always!) to meet thousands of like-minded individuals and enjoy the success that comes from learning and growing together.

"Two basic rules of life are these:
(1) change is inevitable.
(2) everybody resists change.
The only person who likes change
is a wet baby".
— Roy Blitzer

Applying NLP – What, How & When

MAKING a change is as easy as 1, 2, 3... 10...

The first and most important lesson I learned in the Hypnotherapy College is this: "Accept and use whatever happens and make it work for your outcome." Here's an example of what this means. Let's say that you're with a client, and someone interrupts your session. Act as if it was all planned in advance. When you're a therapist, a coach, a consultant, a motivational speaker, or any other "agent of change," your outcome is to get the client the outcome he's paying you to help him achieve. Therefore, anything that happens during the process you two are going through is OK! I have learned this lesson in the Hypnotherapy context, but it applies for NLP change-work as well.

You have to understand, that it is not YOU who is making new understandings for your client, it is your client's brain that is making them. You are not changing your client's behavior. Your job is to direct the client's mind through a certain process and let "it" do the work.

To make NLP work for your client, you must assume that your client's mind is already in the process of changing that discouraging thought pattern or disabling set of behaviors. Once you assume that, all you have to do is to choose the right pattern, work with your client through that pattern, accept and use whatever happens and make it work for your outcome (sounds familiar?), compare the feedback to the given outcome, and proceed accordingly.

If the feedback and the outcome are aligned, which means the client has achieved what they asked for, then your job is done. If not, you re-evaluate the session, choose a better (or stronger) pattern, perhaps also induce hypnosis in the client to reduce subconscious secondary gain based objections, and you aim for the same outcome again.

But you have to remember to keep a high level of sensory acuity while you're with the client.

Be "out there," observe, absorb, constantly evaluate the direct and indirect messages coming from the client, and work with whatever it is to facilitate the change your client is paying you for.

Another lesson I learned quite early in my training is that you should never make your client a friend. Yes, of course, you can have social relationships with your clients, but AFTER you've done the change-work. It is much better not to accept relatives, close family members or friends as clients, because of many reasons. The main reason is that no matter how well your intentions are, your relationship with them is in the way of their therapy and progress.

On the other hand, it is also not for the client's benefit if you become friendly with them early on in the sessions. Stay formal. Be the authority they might need to be "commended" and lead, in order to change themselves. Avoid humor in the first session at least, and never ever tell jokes or lose control over the session. You are paid to help the person produce new or renewed results, not to be a comedian or just another friend. Even subconsciously, if the client suspects that your lack of skill is covered by humor and needy be-havior, your prospects of success with them will be dim.

Stay focused on one outcome at a time. Don't spread yourself too thin or work on 10 different issues in one session. Give their mind some time for processing, for re-organizing, for venting, for recovering, for grieving (usual with ex-addicts) and so on. Give them the time to see results from one or two outcomes first, so that when they return to you their motivation and confidence in your skills are high and strong.

How to work with a pattern

This book lists over 100 NLP patterns. You cannot realistically memorize them all, and frankly, you don't need to memorize them at all.

When you choose a pattern to work with, go through the steps carefully and make sure you understand the process. There's wisdom behind every procedure in Neuro Linguistic Programming. There's a logic to the way steps are organized. Try to uncover and understand that logic. Because it is a reference work for NLP patterns this book does not cover NLP theory, but we encourage you to grasp the "why" behind the patterns. The best way to do this is by reading the steps and imagining yourself saying them out loud to a client, and remaining in your imagination as an observer. That's the perceptual position you want to be in as you learn what makes a pattern work.

Once you have the gestalt of that pattern, you actually own the process! Now you can work with it comfortably and with confidence without memorizing steps or scripts. You can allow yourself to experiment with a pattern, change a few things and see how it works out. You cannot harm your client if you ask him to Swish an image from bottom right to bottom left instead of the actual written instruction, so feel free to experiment and explore. In addition, you might want to record your trials and errors and successes, and make this a part of your work journal.

NLP is ever-changing, just like our world, our societies and cultures. NLP evolves all the time, and you need to make sure you're always informed of the new developments. We can help you with that. Just sign up to our free newsletter at BigBookOfNLP.com.

Secrets Of Successful NLP Interventions

There are many reasons for why a change-work session succeeds. NLP has the reputation of a "one time therapy", which usually means that a client will only have to see you (and pay) once for resolving a specific issue.

From my experience in private practice, the one and most important factor of session success is the client's cooperation. If the client is not cooperative, there is no use to keep the session going. If they refuse to "do" things in their imagination, as an NLP pattern dictates, you ought to make it clear to them that without their full participation it is not going to work well.

In other words, you are not a magician or a therapist that is forcing his clients to get better. You could, in a way, but that would leave you exhausted, frustrated and distressed, which will lead you… into therapy yourself.

Now, full cooperation is the success secret on the surface. In the deeper realm lies a very interesting therapeutic "fact": in many cases, as I've seen in my practice and noticed in more than a handful of other people's case studies, the change the client desires starts to take place as soon as he or she becomes aware of the purpose or structure of their undesired behaviors or thought patterns. In fact, I've been a witness to the whole process being completed and sealed in that phase alone!

The most common example is the client who comes in suffering from severe pain, which every physician concludes to be a "phantom pain", and before you even complete a "chunk down" exercise, the pain disappears.

By facing the pain, by describing its modalities and submodalities, its subtle characteristics, and most importantly—its "message" or "intention", it is as if that subconscious process (inducing pain to protect the core or get attention) has been "caught" and revealed, and therefore has no longer control over the nervous system's responses to its signals.

In other words, once you see how a trick is being done (what the pain was for), there's no power to the illusion (the pain without the physiological reason).

This is a "fact" that you need to remember when you work with clients. Expect it to work, anticipate it, and you will soon notice that your work is much easier this way. Yes, you need to make your work as easy as possible, because your clients expect to get results and get them fast. NLP is a rapid change-work, not a tool you use when you're done with listening for hundred of hours to your client's issues.

Content Vs. Content Free

Another secret that would work well for you as an active practitioner is to avoid working with content as much as possible. As an NLP practitioner, your job is not to provide your client a setting in which he or she can vent out their troubles and miseries. That's what good friends are for, and you are being paid for something completely different.

In fact, it would be more helpful for your session if you prevent your client from venting out the negative emotions. One reason for this is, that you want your client to be fully absorbed in the process, for example if you use the States Chaining pattern or even the Swish pattern. You want their minds to be influenced and sometimes akin to make the resolution that lies within each NLP process.

With most of my clients I spent 10–15 minutes, and not more than 45 minutes. I do not let them dwell on the details of the issue, certainly I would not be willing to hear gossip stories, interpretations of reality and endless amount of sorrow. I am not a psychologist and in my training I was educated to be dealing with the end result, not with what happened when they were 3 years and 10 months old, on a rainy day in Boston.

The best setting for a successful NLP procedure is content free. That is, without taking actual details unless you need them. Most of the patterns and method you can find in this book are content free style. Their mind knows why they're there, and in a subconscious level all the details are being figured out as you move ahead with the process. So your control over which detail goes where and why has no meaning.

More than so, dwelling on details might prevent the client from actually getting results. You cannot perform the Swish pattern, for example, by letting your client telling you the meaning of the color blue in the negative image or the reason that his hand looks dim in the positive one. These details have no meaning and if you give your client's brain a chance to doubt the process, there's a very high chance it will fail.

Your Level Of NLP Experience

This work assumes that the reader knows the basics of NLP. We're referring to words like "state" "pattern" and "outcome."

Our website and online NLP Community, BigBookOfNLP.com, is an excellent and detailed, but fun, introduction to NLP that includes powerful guided experiences, resources and support that will help you learn much more.

It does not end here...

We know that NLP is more than just a collection of techniques. We know that we cannot contain its spirit in a cook book. But we have done our best and beyond to make sure that this reference work has selected from the best of hundreds of NLP patterns and strategies. This work will help you add to your abilities.

Beyond that, it is up to you to continue developing the personal abilities that bring NLP to life: your own ability to size up a situation and choose your approach and timing; your ability to recognize what thoughts and behaviors that appear troubling, but can be utilized; your own flexibility, creativity and ability to connect the dots.

This equates to a flexible, innovative attitude that takes you beyond blindly applying instructions. The more you practice this, the more you will intuitively create or modify patterns in response to new situations. After all, that is how the patterns in this work were created.

An overview of the NLP patterns, strategies and methods listed in this book:

1. The Swish Pattern

Break an automatic thought or behavior pattern, and replace it with a resourceful one. Use the Swish pattern for problems such as smoking cessation, anger management, public speaking, nervousness, self-confidence, and self esteem.

಄಄

2. The Failure Into Feedback Pattern

Change an attitude or belief into one that supports your excellence and success. Turn "failure" into valuable feedback and into a winning state that includes curiosity and motivation.

಄಄

3. Well Defined Outcomes

Since most of our behavior is designed to achieve certain outcomes (goals and desires), it is very important to define these outcomes in advance. If you know where you want to be, you will be in a better position to construct the right maps to guide you. Better yet, you will be able to come up with new, easier, or faster ways to get there.

಄಄

4. The E & E.P. Formation Pattern

Determine when you have achieved a desired outcome by watching for the indications or clues that tell you. We'll call these "evidence." Develop a procedure for making sure that you perceive the evidence when it arises.

಄಄

5. Pacing & Matching

Pacing and matching are important to modeling and rapport-building. Practicing this pattern sharpens your awareness of people and their unconscious communications

಄಄

6. Finding Positive Intention

Transforming self sabotage into success. By discovering the positive intent behind a negative behavior or attitude, you can release tremendous energy and positive commitment.

಄಄

7. Behavior Appreciation

Improve your performance and self care by developing a positive approach to change and personal development.

౸

8. Mirroring

Enhance your ability to establish rapport and to model excellence. This pattern builds a useful "second position" with another person. This skill is key in modeling others and for becoming intuitive in understanding the internal experiences of those you model.

౸

9. The As-If Pattern

Create useful states by envisioning excellence. It is a way to use imagination for success in the spirit of Milton Erickson's famous quote, "You can pretend anything and master it." This is an important skill for using modeling to achieve excellence and success.

౸

10. Eliciting Subconscious Responses

Become a master communicator by learning to recognize and utilize subtle changes in others' physiology. This pattern involves the valuable skill of eliciting unconscious resources, a skill that serves you best when it, too, is unconscious.

౸

11. Ecology Check

Induce change with this flexible and important pattern. It prevents self sabotage by making sure a change will be acceptable to all parts.

౸

12. Physiomental State Interruption

Master the art of change by learning to clear a space for a new state. You can do this by breaking or interrupting the current state. You can guide a person to the state of your choosing much more easily from a state of confusion than any other.

౸

13. State Induction

Apply one of the most fundamental NLP skills; state induction. This tool helps us induce a needed state such as confidence, prepare for an event, or take steps in many NLP patterns.

౸

14. Accessing Resourceful States

Learn state mastery. Elicit resourceful states such as confidence and creativity that will move you toward your goals.

౸

15. The Kinesthetic Swish Pattern

Utilize feelings to generate constructive motivation and drive.

☙☙

16. Anchoring

Anchoring is how we get into the right state for what we want to do. You connect a symbol with the desired state, or resource state.

☙☙

17. A Script For Self Anchoring

A helpful word by word anchoring script you can record and listen to.

☙☙

18. Downtime

Learn to create a light, momentary trance in people for various uses. When your conscious awareness is focused entirely on internal experience, NLP refers to this as downtime.

☙☙

19. Collapsing Anchors

This pattern helps in changing a dysfunctional response.

☙☙

20. Perceptual Positions

Perceptual positions are a bit like the persons in grammar, but, of course, these positions are used in NLP for visualization.

☙☙

21. Conflicting Beliefs Integration

Conflicting beliefs can cause self-sabotage and prevent people from assertively pursuing their goals. They can undermine relationships of all kinds. This pattern assists in aligning beliefs so that they are accurate and synergistic.

☙☙

22. Belief Out-Framing

Question a limiting belief or assumption and consider alternative opinions. This pattern uses the law of requisite variety to accomplish this create excellence in this skill.

☙☙

23. Colliding & Colluding Beliefs

Replace stress and frustration with empowerment and confidence, by resolving conflicting and colluding beliefs. This pattern is primarily for interpersonal situations.

☙☙

24. Parts Negotiation

Win the battle for will power and succeed with inner alignment. Eliminate self-sabotage and liberate energy for commitment and innovative problem solving. Enjoy the pleasures of life, knowing that you are leading a balanced life.

This happens when your parts are working together effectively.

⌘

25. Dis-Identification

Gain new freedom and capacity by dis-identifying with limiting beliefs. Sometimes we over-identify with some facet of our life experiences-our beliefs, body, gender, race, etc. This is limiting in itself, but we may also over-identify with even more seriously limited aspects of ourselves. This pattern serves to correct over-identification.

⌘

26. Resolving Internal Conflicts

This pattern helps with the very common problem of disagreement between parts. When you struggle with yourself to do or not do something, when you procrastinate and seem to be arguing with yourself in your mind, this is the pattern to use.

⌘

27. Making Peace With Your Parents

Liberate a great deal of energy, creativity, and personal development by resolving old issues with your parents. This is done IN your mind, not necessarily in direct contact with your parents.

⌘

28. Six Steps Reframing

Elicit subconscious resources in order to change a habit by producing alternative behaviors.

⌘

29. Content Reframing

Create dramatic improvements in yourself and others by applying one of the most fundamental methods for getting a change in perspective.

⌘

30. Context Reframing

Build awareness of context, and build mental flexibility and creativity. It helps you imagine "importing" a behavior, state, belief, or other aspect of yourself into various contexts.

⌘

31. Reframing Beliefs & Opinions – Examples

A real life example of a conversational reframing (content and context).

⌘

32. Basic Inner Conflict Integration

Improve mood, motivation, and success by resolving internal conflicts between states. Generate resourceful states more consistently by resolving habitual (automatic) negative states.

11

❧

33. Mistakes Into Experience

Update a behavior that has not been re-evaluated, but that is not working optimally, or is dysfunctional.

❧

34. Hierarchy Of Criteria

Resolve inner conflicts so you can engage consistently in a desired behavior. This pattern uses logical levels and NLP resources in an interweave that deserves some explaining.

❧

35. Aligning Perceptual Positions

Get dramatic improvements in your relationships with others and with yourself by correcting bad habits in perception. This pattern addresses the tendency for people to become stuck in a particular perceptual position.

❧

36. The Allergy Pattern

This pattern has a reputation for reducing or eliminating symptoms of allergies.

❧

37. Calibration

Improve your ability to observe and respond to the physiological and behavioral cues of others. "Calibration" involves linking behavioral cues to internal cognitive and emotional responses.

❧

38. The Autobiography Pattern

Build deep self acceptance with this hypnotic script, by experiencing it through multiple perspectives and sensory channels.

❧

39. Congruence

Alignment, as occurs when your parts are aligned, brings much value to NLP, because it empowers our resources.

❧

40. The Phobia Cure Pattern

Eliminate unrealistic, habitual fears (such as the fear of flying) that can limit people's lives. It can even serve for trauma recovery, reducing or eliminating symptoms of post traumatic stress. This is also known as the visual-kinesthetic dissociation pattern.

❧

41. Pleasure Installation

Rebuild your happiness. Many of us have lost our connection to happiness. It may be because we need to recover from something that was psychologically over-whelming, or from the frog-in-a-kettle death of happiness that creeps up on us as we become over-invested in superficial things.

❦

42. Exploring Causes & Effects

When a client comes in and seems to have a hard time to pinpoint the triggers or causes to unwanted be-haviors or thought patterns.

❦

43. Applying Logical Levels

The Logical Levels concept in NLP was first introduced to the field by Robert Dilts, one of the most productive NLP master train-ers and researcher. Dilts devel-oped his logical levels to guide the process of intervention.

❦

44. Pleasure Reduction

Break out of addictions, com-pulsions, and obsessions by re-ducing the pleasure they create. It is for behaviors that are based on real needs, but that have become excessive.

❦

45. Developing Sensory Acuity

When you learn to observe people well you will notice that they make minute subconscious changes.

❦

46. The Loving Yourself Pattern

Enhance your ego strength and self esteem by improving your abil-ity to love and appreciate yourself.

❦

47. Abandoned Predisposition

A predisposition is a tendency which is not yet a habit. It is when you hold a particular thought pat-tern and can't let go of it or when you act in a particular way and catch yourself "too late." This pat-tern helps you to abandon the predisposition by turning the com-pulsion into an aversion. In other words, it turns a specific thing or action you "like" into a "dislike."

❦

48. Chaining States

Make yourself immune to neg-ative states. Create an automatic reaction that creates a resourceful and positive state instead.

❦

49. Pragmagraphic Swish Design

Resolve compulsive patterns; the acts that a person feels compelled to do, despite knowing better. This can include addiction, blurting out thing you thought only your parents would say, eating comfort food, switching on the television when you have paperwork to do, and many other behaviors.

❧

50. Collecting Resources

When you're in the process of achieving an outcome or goal, you are "consuming" or using resources.

❧

51. Advanced Visual Squash

Build your congruence and success by resolving parts conflicts. Integrate parts that are not aligned.

❧

52. Digital Vs. Analogue Submodalities

Utilizing digital or analogue submodalities and the differences between the two.

❧

53. Submodality Overlapping

Build up weaker submodalities to improve creativity and problem solving though as you represent things in a richer way.

❧

54. External Stimulus Threshold

A threshold is a line between two states of mind: bearable and unbearable. Sometimes, in order to change a behavior, you have to induce the triggers and resourceful states at the same time, making sure that the resourceful states win in each "threshold battle".

❧

55. Decision Destroyer

Exchange limiting decisions for constructive ones in order to improve success and mood.

❧

56. The Godiva Choccolate Pattern

Increase your motivation by associating intense pleasure with a desired behavior.

❧

57. Using Rep. Systems

Thorough information on using rep. systems in communication and persuasion.

❧

58. Auditory Rep. System Development

Improve your auditory rep system in order to better perceive sound, its meanings, and subtleties. This can enhance your modeling and communication.

⊙⊘

59. Visual Rep. System Development

This pattern will help you refine the subtleties and perceptions of your visual representational system. It will improve your abilities to distinguish submodalities, which is a necessary skill when working with NLP patterns. It will also freshen-up your creativity and problem solving capabilities.

⊙⊘

60. State Of Consciousness Awareness

This pattern increases your awareness of your states and how they affect your perspective. This awareness is valuable in nearly every aspect of Neuro Linguistic Programming and life in general.

⊙⊘

61. Non-Verbal Cues Recognition

Practice recognizing non-verbal cues and getting to know you're your own face expresses emotions that you experience, even when you are not trying to show them. This skill will help you function almost like you can read minds.

⊙⊘

62. Compulsion Blow Out

This pattern desensitizes compulsions that range from fingernail chewing to obsessing about being jilted.

⊙⊘

63. Creating Positive Expectations

How to utilize a very important tool for helping people to change faster.

⊙⊘

64. Breaking Limiting Associations

One of the most important ways out of stuck thought patterns is to develop a better-articulated sense of how our minds work. That is, to develop a more subtle and detailed recognition of our thoughts and rep systems and how they form interlocking patterns.

⊙⊘

65. Secondary Gain And Personal Ecology

Personal ecology means that you consider your personal needs, aspirations, and values in the outcome. Personal ecology gives an important edge to your plans because it brings about inner alignment.

ળ

66. Whole System Ecology

Much like in personal ecology, applied to systems. By systems, we mean families, schools, regulatory government agencies, businesses and so on.

ળ

67. Meta-Model Challenging

With this pattern, you will practice the fundamental skill that assists with modeling and with ensuring adequate communication. Refer to Appendix C for a full explanation of the meta-model and its violations in language.

ળ

68. Meta-Model Intentional Usage

Produce constructive change as efficiently as possible with the very structured questioning of this pattern. It includes presuppositions in the course of asking meta-model questions.

ળ

69. De-Nominalizing

Get much more control over your mind and your life, by resolving the meta-model violation known as nominalization. This works because nominalizations remove the actor from the scene.

ળ

70. The Forgiveness Pattern

Rid yourself of the brooding resentments that can sap your creative energies.

ળ

71. Aligned Self

Aligned self means heading in a strong direction because your values, beliefs, sense of identity and purpose in life are all working together. This pattern helps you achieve or reclaim that state.

ળ

72. Circle Of Excellence

With this pattern, you can produce high-performance states. It helps you become more aware of the internal sensations and the behaviors that can help you produce a positive state.

ળ

73. Assertiveness Installation

Assertiveness is a very important trait, yet people often fall into habits of being too passive or aggressive. These habits can be subconscious, and people often fail to realize how much they are losing and how many bad experiences come from poor assertiveness.

❧

74. Self Esteem Quick Fix

This pattern can help you rapidly recover from an attack of bad self esteem. It is excellent for recovering from a failure, or from someone who had a toxic effect on your self esteem.

❧

75. The Smart Eating Pattern

One of the key causes of excessive eating is poor awareness of when one is one is actually hungry as opposed to simply being tempted or using food as an antidote to stress.

❧

76. Boundaries Installation

Personal boundaries are the borders that we maintain between what is acceptable and what it not in how we are treated. This pattern helps people define and strengthen boundaries that are too weak or unclear.

❧

77. Criticism Analyzer

This pattern let's you experience criticism without taking it too personally. It uses the concept that words are not real.

❧

78. The Excuse Blow Out Pattern

This pattern helps you get things done by turning subconscious excuses into alignment. This stops procrastination.

❧

79. The Basic Motivation Pattern

The following strategy demonstrates how the various elements of imagination, expectation, criteria, submodalities and association can be combined into a simple strategy to help people better inspire and motivate themselves to take actions which will lead them to desired outcomes.

❧

80. The Winning Over Internal War Zone Pattern

Resolve a problem that nearly everyone suffers from; inner wars. These are wars of internal self talk that turn your mind into a battle field. Often, this self talk explodes into vivid imaginings of worst-case scenarios. This kind of visualization all to often churns out self-fulfilling prophecies.

❀

81. Inducing Amnesia

Amnesia is a very useful tool when you work with clients. Milton Erickson used to induce amnesia from the very first contact with the client. The idea is that if the client "forgets" (the client's mind actually pushes the given time period into the subconscious) a certain part of the change work, they will be less likely to interfere with the results consciously.

❀

82. Thought Virus Inculation

This pattern creates a defense against destructive (toxic) thought patterns, conceived by Dilts as "thought viruses".

❀

83. The Inner Peace Questionnaire

A useful tool for exploring self sabotage patterns.

❀

84. The Relationship Clarifying Pattern

Getting to the essence of a dyadic relationship opens the gateway to understanding the dynamics of the relationship and how the two parties contribute to enduring patterns, including patterns that are dysfunctional.

❀

85. Building and Maintaining Rapport

Rapport is a positive connection between you and another person, or you and a group.

❀

86. The Falling In-Love Pattern

This pattern shows how surprisingly easy it is to enhance your feelings of love and affection toward your loved one, to extend infinitely a familiar and endearing intimacy. These exciting results are produced with nothing more than anchoring.

❀

87. Avoiding Counter-Productive Suggestions

Whatever it is you want the client to not think about, do not mention it at all in a suggestion, and definitely not in its negative form.

∞

88. The Cyber-Porn Addiction Removal Pattern

This is another version of the swish pattern, formulated to eliminate cyber-porn addiction, a widespread problem that has a tremendous impact on productivity and peace of mind.

∞

89. The Spelling Strategy

This pattern improves your spelling.

∞

90. Elicitation Of Learning Strategies

Learning is the process of acquiring new thinking patterns and behavioral capabilities. In NLP, a learning strategy is the syntax of steps one takes in order to learn. There are many learning strategies, of course, and some of them are not very effective.

∞

91. New Language Rapid Learning

This pattern will help you memorize words in a foreign language very quickly. It uses the power of submodalities.

∞

92. Rhythmic Learning

Here is a strategy that you can explore and adapt to your own learning adventures. It uses the power of rhythm to create attention and involvement.

∞

93. Commitment

Making a statement of intention (i.e. Making a commitment) is extremely important when you want your client to see immediate progress and improvement.

∞

94. The (Accelerated) Learning Chain

This pattern installs strategies for efficient learning. It uses chaining, a way to link experiences into a sequence that leads to a useful state.

∞

95. Apposition (Of Opposites)

Apposition of opposites is a hypnotic suggestion used to enhance the quality of trance or deepen the client into hypnosis.

෴

96. Identifying Self Sabotage Elements

This is a list that I usually give to every client I accept. It will guide you to answer the most disturbing question: "Why does it always happen to me?".

෴

97. Problem Definition

This pattern helps you find your way out of a problem that you are stuck in. It addresses our tendency to define a problem in a way that makes it seem impossible to solve.

෴

98. Problem Solving Strategy (I)

This pattern is the first of a series of innovative problem-solving strategies. This one uses the power of metaphor.

෴

99. Problem Solving Strategy (II)

This pattern helps a team of 2 or more people resolve a problem by creating a shared experience of an appropriate resource.

෴

100. The Walt Disney Strategy

This pattern helps you use the creative idea-generating talent of the famous animator, Walt Disney.

෴

101. The Binary Code Of Forgetfulness

If you can forget, and you can cause other people to forget (no matter what), you are in a very powerful position to change yourself to any degree. Your complete list of non-useful behaviors and destructive subconscious thought pattern issues can all be solved with the simplest skill of all: forgetting.

෴

102. Conflict Resolution

This pattern helps resolve conflict while generating commitments to fulfilling higher-order goals and values.

෴

103. Co-Dependency Resolution

This pattern helps people think and act more independently by eliminating codependent behavior.

⚯

104. Meta-Programs Identification

This pattern makes you into a more effective communicator by helping your pace the meta-programs of another person.

⚯

105. Limiting Meta-Programs Challenging

This pattern will help solve communication patterns by revealing the meta-program mismatch or meta-program violations (see appendix) involved.

⚯

106. The Meta-Programs Change Pattern

This pattern helps us improve the scope and flexibility of our meta-program use by directing our attention in a way that is somehow opposed to or expanded beyond the current meta-model.

⚯

107. The Analogical Marking Method

Best known as a way to imbed commands into communication, analogical marking means that a portion of the communication is "marked" for greater attention by the subconscious.

⚯

108. Persuasion By Chunking Up/Down

Whatever you say or hear can be marked as a point on that Chunk Up -> Chunk Down range. From that point, you can either chunk up and generalize or chunk down and be more specific.

⚯

109. The Classic Confusion Method

Confusion is useful for breaking state and producing "downtime," a very internal state that promotes hypnosis, reprocessing, patience, and introspection. The classic method, as demonstrated originally by Milton Erickson, is to use vague or otherwise confusing language.

⚯

110. Applying The Law Of Reversed Effect

This law simply states, that the harder you focus on something to do, the harder it becomes or even worst.

❧

111. The Nested Loops Method

Influence and persuade others merely by telling them stories.

❧

112. A Sample Nested Loops Story

Here is an example for a Nested Loops story.

❧

113. Subliminal Persuasion

Subliminal refers to things that you do not consciously perceive. Although you don't perceive subliminals, they may have an effect on you.

❧

114. Intonation

In NLP we recognize 3 patterns of intonation, which assist in persuasion and trance induction.

❧

115. The Embedded Command (I) Method

Embedded commands are typically marked out with analogical marking. This pattern and the next give more opportunity to practice this aspect of communication.

❧

116. The Embedded Command (II) Method

This is a more advanced embedded command pattern that extends the previous Embedded Command (I) and Analogical Marking. This one involves embedding the command in sections, spaced over a larger communication.

❧

117. Erickson's 55 Hypnotic Phrases

Erickson used to combine numerous hypnotic suggestions while he spoke to his patients. Here we list a few dozens of them.

❧

118. The Frame Of Agreement

An ongoing disagreement, or a style of conflictual communication between two people can often be resolved be taking the discussion to a higher logical level (see appendix). This pattern uses logical levels to facilitate agreements. It can be useful in mediation and with groups.

119. TDS Manipulation

TDS stands for "Trance-Derivational Search". This is a natural phenomenon, that is obvious in children when they play or learn. It is also very obvious in adults while they meditate or day dream.

120. Values Hierarchy Identification

Identify the values you're holding currently and the hierarchy in which they are organized.

121. New Behavior Generator

Develop a new and more adaptive behavior; a cohesive, outcome-based strategy. The power of parts makes this pattern effective.

122. Active Dreaming

Get ideas, answers, solutions, and information through active dreaming.

123. Emotional Pain Management

Resolve excessive emotional reactions to gain control, objectivity, and poise. This is also known as the "emo" pattern.

124. The Inner Hero Pattern

Bring out the best in people who are not aligned with their higher values. This pattern is very important for working with people who act in ways that can get them into trouble, such as through violence or problems with authority or with social systems.

125. The Wholeness Pattern

Experience symptoms in a profoundly new way.

126. The SCORE Pattern

Solve problems more effectively by organizing information in a more useful way. The SCORE model drives this pattern with a flexible, multifaceted style of thinking.

127. Life Transitions Tracking

This pattern uses archetypes to help us come to terms with a major change or perceived threat, and to leverage that new relationship in service of our well being.

128. Transformation Archetype Identification

Continue the Life Transitions Tracking Pattern (above) by determining which process archetype is most important in your development at this time. Before doing this exercise, do The Life Transitions Tracking Pattern.

☙☙

129. The Grief Pattern

Resolve grief in a comforting, healing way.

☙☙

130. The Pre-Grieving Pattern

Resolve fears of future losses, eliminating many worries.

☙☙

131. Self-Nurturing

Accelerate your maturation and emotional strength by drawing upon your adult resources to resolve unfinished emotional development. The value of good paren ting resources as conceptualized by NLP drives this pattern.

☙☙

132. Awakening To Freedom

Give and receive support for awakening through personal growth in this dyadic (pair) exercise. Enhance your vision, mission and spirit through this support for awakening.

☙☙

133. The Longevity Pattern

Develop positive beliefs and resources for almost any kind of issue. Directly install the beliefs and strategies of the vital elderly models.

☙☙

134. Change Personal History

Modify negatively-coded memories so that you can realize your potential unfettered by such memories.

☙☙

135. The End-Of-Day Pattern

Make a daily habit of generating behavior and attitudes that are ever more effective and fulfilling with the power of the new behavior generator.

☙☙

136. Negative Associated Emotions Dissolving

Transform any mistakes you make from sources of shame and recrimination to sources of learning and empowerment.

☙☙

137. Core Transformation

Live from a new center that comes from a practical, yet spiritual or expanded experience of life. By discovering the core state at the center of each part, overcome serious limitations.

ᏨᎩ

138. Mapping Anyone's Brain

Build your modeling skill with this form of analysis.

ᏨᎩ

139. Undetermined State Integration

Help your subject describe his or her state.

ᏨᎩ

140. Choice Expansion

Generate motivation by harnessing the power of choice points. You could say that choice points occur when you consciously or unconsciously make a commitment of some kind.

ᏨᎩ

141. The F/B Pattern

Create resource states in people who tend to focus on the negative or disabling aspect of a situation.

ᏨᎩ

142. Memory De-Energizing

Free yourself from troubling memories. Turn them into sources of wisdom.

ᏨᎩ

143. Somatic Fractal

Practice intuiting deep structure, and explore how this is a useful skill and understanding. This pattern draws upon Somatic Syntax.

ᏨᎩ

144. Resource Fractal

Enhance your problem solving, creativity, or simply your enjoyment of life by creating a synesthetic (multi representational system) expression of an optimal state.

ᏨᎩ

145. Changing Beliefs – The Logic Approach

A common sense format to change another person's belief without working with them traditionally through a pattern.

ᏨᎩ

146. Logical Levels Co-Alignment

Discover and align with your vision and values through the power of metaphor and logical levels. Help your team succeed when you form a common identity together through this kind of alignment.

෴

147. The Embedded Command In A Question Method

When embedded commands appear in questions, they have the added benefit of priming a more open, curious state.

෴

148. The Double Bind Method

Improve cooperation in many situations. The double bind is a basic communication pattern that requires that the person you are communicating with accepts a presupposition. This is followed with choices.

෴

149. The Ambiguity Method

Learn to use ambiguity for motivational and healing purposes.

෴

150. The Presupposition Method

Learn to make your communication more persuasive with presuppositions. A presupposition is an assumption that your listener perceives from your communication.

෴

151. The Metaphor Method

Practice using metaphors to achieve therapeutic ends. Metaphor is essentially the use of symbolic events or items to symbolize something else

෴

152. Shared Resource

Improve the value of resourceful states by using various perceptual positions to experience and explore them.

෴

153. The Dancing SCORE Pattern

Solve problems by enhancing your intuition and body wisdom through movement. This pattern promotes the mind-body relationship in a way that accesses and mobilizes deep resources, creating a self-organizing pathway toward a resourceful and relevant state.

෴

154. Advantageous NLP Beliefs

The NLP presuppositions (or core beliefs) are the most important guidelines for learning and doing NLP, and for being successful in life.

෴

155. The D.V.P Pattern

D.V.P stands for Distillation Plus Vision Plus Passion. This process allows you to take a cloud of reactions and ideas, and turn them into very tight talking points, like the ones politicians and sales people have, in order to communicate in a compelling way.

❧

156. Belief Systems Dis-Integration

Improve automatic reactions that come from multiple rep systems firing off a negative state. This pattern separates the parts of a negative synesthesia pattern so that it can be addressed.

❧

157. Criteria Installation

Clarify your values to bring more alignment to an area of your life that seems unclear. Resolve indecisiveness, procrastination, and waffling that stems from unclear or misaligned criteria.

❧

158. Kinesthetic Criteria

Start taking action by overcoming the criteria that get in the way.

❧

159. The Spinning Icons Pattern

Prevent or escape negative states. Solve problems and be creative. This pattern draws upon the power of imagery to create a valuable meta-state.

❧

160. Basic Belief Chaining

Shift a belief from an unresourceful one to a resourceful one.

❧

161. Advanced Belief Chaining

Carry out the Belief Chaining Pattern with a Guide and in a more advanced form.

❧

162. Gentling

Build your inner "good parent" experience by bringing your adult wisdom into your timeline.

❧

163. Meta Transformation

Create personality-wide changes by taking transformation to a meta level.

❧

164. Re-Imprinting

Upgrade your deeper beliefs and your behaviors by changing the influence of role models. Improve the effect of negative role models, and create a stronger influence from positive role models.

❧

NLP Modeling Methods:

165. Basic 2nd Position Modeling

Improve your ability to model excellence. For completing this pattern, you need four people.

❧

166. 2nd Position Intuitive Modeling

Take more advanced steps in developing your ability to model. You need three people for this pattern: the Person Being Modeled, and two Modelers.

❧

167. Basic 3rd Position Modeling

Improve your capacity to model by using the third position. This pattern requires three people: The Person Being Modeled and two Modelers.

❧

168. Basic States Of Excellence Modeling

Model states of excellence. This pattern requires three people: The Person Being Modeled and two Modelers.

❧

The NLP Meta-Model Of Language:

169. Generalizations

Generalizations happen when someone translates some experiences into a rule that applies to all similar experiences.

❧

170. Universal Quantifiers

Universal quantifiers are an all or nothing kind of generalization.

❧

171. Lost Performatives

Lost performatives make a rule without anybody having responsibility for it.

❧

172. Modal Operators

Modal operators make a must out of a preference.

❧

173. Deletions

Deletions happen when the speaker leaves something out. When a person is being too vague or manipulative, deletion may be the culprit.

❧

174. Lack Of Referential Index

Lack of referential index is a deletion where there's an unspecified party or an unknown "they".

⊘⊘

175. Comparative Deletions

Comparative deletions happen when the speaker fails to say what they are comparing something to.

⊘⊘

176. Distortions

Distortions are based on real sensory data, but they twist it in some way to create the wrong conclusion. If it's extreme enough, it's a delusion in psychological language.

⊘⊘

177. Nominalization

Nominalization happens when we transform a verb or adjective into a noun. It also has to be something that isn't a real thing in the world.

⊘⊘

178. Mind Reading

Mind reading is an irritating distortion. This happens when someone decides they know what you are thinking. For some reason, it's usually something pretty bad.

⊘⊘

179. Cause & Effect Distortions

This happens when someone thinks they know what causes something, simply because the two things happened together

⊘⊘

180. Presuppositions

Presuppositions are the hidden ideas in a statement.

⊘⊘

181. Complex Equivalence

Complex equivalence connects two ideas that don't belong together.

⊘⊘

The Milton-Model Or Conversational Hypnosis

182. Meta-Model Violations

⊘⊘

183. Pacing Current Experience

⊘⊘

184. Pacing and Leading

Once you have done enough pacing, the person is ready for you to not merely MATCH their state with pacing, but to LEAD them into whatever state is necessary for what you are doing.

❦

185. Linking Words

Erickson used words called conjunctions, words such as "and" in pacing and leading. He linked the pacing with the leading in a way that made it all seem to belong together, and this gave his leading commands a lot of impact.

❦

186. Disjunction

Disjunction is a lot like linking, but it makes a contrast or choice while it slips in an embedded command or leading statement.

❦

187. Implied Causes

Implied Causes is a technique that uses words that imply that one thing will lead to another.

❦

188. Tag Questions

Tag questions help the statement get by the conscious mind by occupying the mind with the tag question.

❦

189. Double Binds

In double binds that are therapeutic or motivational, you give the person a choice between two forms of the very same presupposition.

❦

190. Embedded Commands

Embedded commands are statements that are inserted into larger sentences.

❦

191. Analogue Marking

❦

192. Utilization

Utilization is a technique that has opened up entirely new vistas in mental health treatment and personal life.

❦

193. Nesting

Nesting means that an idea is contained within another. That can happen in the form of a story that occurs within a another story.

❦

194. Extended Quotes

Extended quotes are a type of nesting where you have nested quotations.

❦

195. Spell Out Words

❦

196. Conversational Postulate

When someone asks you if you can pass the salt, they are actually asking you to pass the salt, but they're being nice about it. NLP calls this a conversational postulate.

❀

197. Selectional Restriction Violation

In the course of eliciting a state or creating a metaphor, you can ascribe feelings to things.

❀

198. Ambiguities

The double meaning of a vague phrase can contribute to trance, because of the transderivational searching that results.

❀

199. Phonological Ambiguities

Phonological ambiguity is uncertainty created by similar-sounding words.

❀

200. Syntactic Ambiguities

You can create ambiguity through violations of syntax. Now we're talking about actual grammar syntax, meaning word order.

❀

201. Scope Ambiguities

In scope ambiguities, you wonder what part of the sentence applies to what other part.

❀

202. Punctual Ambiguities

It is a sentence where the word "physically" does double duty in the middle of two clauses.

❀

203. Metaphors

Metaphor means creating a story or idea that symbolizes something.

❀

The Satir Model

204. The Blamer

Blamer's externalize blame, and appear to be always ready to place the blame in a harsh or judgmental way.

❀

205. The Placater

The placater is also one for displacing blame, but they do it more diplomatically.

❀

206. The Computer

The computer style can be pretty unemotional. They cover up possible emotions with extra words.

❧

207. The Distracter

They are seen as a mix of blamer, computer, and placater.

❧

208. The Leveler

The leveler has high congruence and does not blanch at being factual.

❧

209. Utilizing Flexibility

An important part of the Satir model is that people need to develop flexibility in their styles, so that they are not locked into one.

❧

210. Category Rapport Building

How to establish and maintain rapport with the Satir categories characters.

❧

NLP
Patterns & Strategies

1.

The Swish Pattern

"The man who looks for security, even in the mind, is like a man who would chop off his limbs in order to have artificial ones which will give him no pain or trouble".

— Henry Miller

CREDITS FOR THE CREATION of this NLP pattern belong to Richard Bandler and John Grinder.

Break an automatic thought or behavior pattern, and replace it with a resourceful one. Use the Swish pattern for problems such as smoking cessation, anger management, public speaking, nervousness, self-confidence, and self esteem. The Swish pattern is the most famous and frequently applied Neuro Linguistic Programming technique.

Overview: The Swish Pattern:

Step #1. Recognize the automatic reaction

Step #2. Determine the trigger of the negative image

Step #3. Place the replacement

Step #4. Swish the two images

Step #5. Repeat

Step #6. Test

Step #1. Recognize the automatic reaction

Recognize the automatic reaction (the thoughts, feelings or images that occur to you when you think of the challenging situation).

Select a replacement image (something inspiring, such as a really good outcome), that helps create a positive state.

Imagine yourself in a dissociated image (the third perceptual position, as if you are watching yourself in a movie).

Enhance the qualities, such as submodalities, of the scene until it is as compelling as possible.

Step #2. Determine the trigger of the negative image

Discover what tells your mind to produce the negative image or behavior. Ask yourself what occurs just before this negative or unwanted state begins?

This time, you want an associated scene (first position, looking through your own eyes) of what is going on immediately before you engage in the unwanted activity.

Remember to think in terms of submodalities to get a detailed sense of the scene. It functions as a trigger for the unresourceful state.

Step #3. Place the replacement

Put the replacement off in the corner of the negative image.

Imagine a small, postage-stamp-sized version of your replacement scene in the bottom corner of the negative scene.

Step #4. Swish the two images

Swish the two images.

You will be making both images change simultaneously and with increasing speed. (If you are experienced, you can select two critical submodalities for this.)

When you swish, have the negative scene become smaller and shoot off into the distance.

At the same time, have the positive replacement image zip in closer and larger, rapidly and completely replacing the negative scene.

Imagine it making a whoosh sound as it zips into place. At first, you'll probably do this slowly, taking a few seconds to complete the swish.

As you repeat the process, you will be able to do it faster and faster, until you swish nearly instantaneously.

Step #5. Repeat

Clear your mind after each Swish.

This is very important. Do this by thinking of something else, such as your favorite color or what you need to do later.

Remember to breathe easily during the swish and the breaks.

Do the swish five to seven times, repeating steps three to five each time.

You know you have a good outcome when you have some difficulty maintaining the negative image.

Step #6. Test

Now try to use the limiting thought or behavior again.

Notice how hard, if not impossible, it is for you to act it out.

Notice that you actually have to think about how to do it first; it is not as automatic as it used to be.

If you feel that you could relapse, use the Swish again in a day or two, and again after a week.

Additional Advice

You can also Swish the two images by using other submodalities instead of the ones used here.

You could Swish a full color image with a black & white one; you could Swish by going from 3D to Flat or vice versa; you could Swish a snapshot with a movie or any other contradicting submodalities.

The main key here is to explore and investigate the options.

Some people will respond immediately to the Size/Location forms of Swish, and it is known that these are driver submodalities.

But others may differ, so keep an open minded, and if the Swish pattern by-the-book does not produce the results you seek, experiment with other driver submodalities.

Here is what other NLP trainers had to say about the Swish pattern in the book **"NLP – The New Technology Of Achievement"** by *NLP Comprehensive, Steve Andreas and Charles Faulkner*:

"The Swish pattern is a very simple and effective way to create an objective and favorable image of yourself that produces immediate results in specific troublesome situations... you won't know ahead of time exactly what you will do the next time you encounter a situation that is similar to one that used to be troublesome".

☙❧

2.

The Failure Into Feedback Pattern

"Your philosophy determines whether you will go for the disciplines or continue the errors".

— Jim Rohn

CREDITS for the creation of this NLP pattern belong to Robert Dilts.

Change an attitude or belief into one that supports your excellence and success. Turn "failure" into valuable feedback and into a winning state that includes curiosity and motivation. Imagine feeling positive and motivated after the ninety-ninth failure. As with Edison and his many "failures" on the way to the light bulb, you are on your way to success with this kind of attitude. This pattern makes room for a success state by "dismantling" the failure.

Overview: The Failure Into Feedback Pattern

Step #1. Identify the problem attitude or belief; identify its physiology and rep system activity.

Step #2. Sort the problematic belief by rep systems into their eye positions.

Step #3. Create the images of your desired capability and goal, and place them in the visual constructed space.

Step #4. Distinguish between representations of the capable image and the failure memories.

Step #5. Normalize the failure elements (feelings, memories and self talk) with positive ones.

Step #6. Create an anchor for a positive reference experience.

Step #7. Trigger the positive reference state in connection with your goal.

Step #8. Test.

Step #1. Identify the problem attitude or belief; identify its physiology and rep system activity

Select an attitude or belief that makes you feel defeated, hopeless, or like a failure. It should be associated with a difficulty that you are having in acquiring or expressing a capability, and in achieving a goal that would come from that capability.

For example, let's say Carl is not making very many sales, and he feels like a failure over it. He feels that he is not communicating in a compelling way, and feels very disappointed in himself.

In this example, the capability would be compelling communication. The goal that depends on that capability would be making more sales. The belief coming from it would be something like, "I can't sell."

Next, observe the physiology and eye positions associated with your failure belief. You can use a mirror, a friend or a video-camera if you find it hard to observe yourself while you represent an idea in your mind.

Note what is happening internally in each of the representational systems (VAK) during the mental representation of the belief. What do you see, hear and feel on the inside?

Step #2. Sort the problematic belief by rep systems into the corresponding eye positions

Use your imagination to take each of these sensory representations and slide it into the corresponding eye position, if it isn't there already.

Look (physically, consciously and deliberately turn your eyes) towards that direction at the same time as you put the representation there.

For many people, the kinesthetic sense of failure is so strong, that their internal (self) talk and other representational systems are pulled down into a sort of muddy pool of feelings. The result of putting your representational systems in their respective eye positions is to clear up that muddy conglomeration and achieve a state that is much more workable.

Once you have moved these representations into their positions to each side, notice how this clears up the "space" in front of your for you visual perception of reality.

Open your eyes, if they are closed and see for yourself.

Step #3. Create the images of your desired capability and goal, and place them in the visual constructed space

Think of the *frustrated* capability and goal that your *failure* belief is about.

Create a clear image of that capability in action and in terms of its positive intended results (your goal).

Use imagery that is very positive.

Place this image up and to your right (visual constructed), and look at it in your mental space, moving your eyes up and to the right.

Step #4. Distinguish between representations of the capable image and the failure memories

As you focus on the desired capability, sense the main feeling associated with it. Identify the positive intention underlying that feeling.

Do the same for your self talk around that capability.

Notice how these are different from the representations of your failure belief. The feelings and self talk are represented differently.

Step #5. Normalize the failure elements (feelings, memories and self talk) with positive ones

Look at the memories associated with the belief.

Build a more realistic perspective of the total situation by mixing your positive memories with the memories associated with the problem.

Have them fit on your timeline in the appropriate time sequence.

Note what useful knowledge (warnings, learning, and so forth) can come from your memories of the situation, even though those memories may be associated with frustrating outcomes or feelings.

Note how that useful knowledge can lead you directly to the desired goal.

Modify or add elements to the desired goal based on what you learned from looking at the memories.

Notice what steps can take you from those memories to the positive goal.

Step #6. Create an anchor for a positive reference experience

Think of something positive that you are very certain you can achieve in the future. It can be something that you have done competently and reliably many times. It does not have to be something big. Showing up to work on time is an achievement, even though it is considered basic and mundane.

Establish an anchor for that reference experience.

Step #7. Trigger the positive reference state in connection with your goal

Adjust the structure of the desired state's resource synesthesia so that it matches the positive reference experience. In other words, remember the qualities of the submodalities, including where they occurred in your mental space.

Change the resource state of the goal so that it's elements are laid out in the same way and with the same emphasis and submodalities such as size and brightness.

To help this process, fire the anchor for the positive reference experience while looking at the desired goal.

Step #8. Test

You'll know this pattern is helpful when you experience one or more of the following:

1) Fresh ideas for achieving your goal,

2) A more hopeful and constructive attitude,

3) A clearer sense of your goal and how to achieve it, so that you experience compelling imagery, feelings, and self talk.

જ્જૉ

3.

Well Defined Outcomes

"The reason most people never reach their goals is that they don't define them, or ever seriously consider them as believable or achievable. Winners can tell you where they are going, what they plan to do along the way, and who will be sharing the adventure with them".

— Denis Watley

CREDITS FOR THE creation of this NLP pattern belong to various contributors.

Take an essential step toward success by creating well-defined outcomes. A well-defined outcome answers the question, "What do you really want?"

Remember the model of Be —> Do —> Have? According to this model, you must first become the kind of person who is able to achieve your outcome, and then do the actions that are required to enjoy the fruits of your efforts.

Since most of our behavior is designed to achieve certain outcomes (goals and desires), it is very important to define these outcomes in advance. If you know where you want to be, you will be in a better position to construct the right maps to guide you. Better yet, you will be able to come up with new, easier, or faster ways to get there.

What is the difference between a goal and an outcome?

Goals can go a long way in helping you achieve excellence. Your goal may be to have a great time at a party, or become a billionaire within three years. There are many different kinds of goals.

43

Put your mind into that outcome as if you have achieved it, and open your thinking to means of improving that outcome. The time to rework your outcomes comes before you start investing a lot of resources. The way to align with your highest goals is to stay flexible about your outcome; to rework the outcome as needed; to shape the outcome into something even better. Now you are developing one of the hallmarks of NLP: ecology; where all parts of you agree with the outcome; where your desires, your values, and your needs are all aligned into one powerful direction.

Here's what *Anthony Robbins* has to say about goals and outcomes in his masterpiece book, **Awaken The Giant Within**: "All goal setting must be immediately followed by both the development of a plan, and massive and consistent action toward its fulfillment. You already have this power to act. If you haven't been able to summon it, it's merely because you have failed to set goals that inspire you".

Overview: The Well Defined Outcome Pattern

Step #1. Create a positive, specific goal.

Step #2. State your outcome in terms of ability, not lack of ability.

Step #3. Context

Step #4. Sense Modalities

Step #5. Objectives

Step #6. Support

Step #7. Perform an ecology check

Step #8. Create your milestones.

Step #9. Write down your goals.

Step #10. Test

Step #1. Create a positive, specific goal.

State your outcome/goal in positive, specific terms.

Take the time to describe exactly what you want. A negative goal does not take you in this positive direction. Avoid goals such as, "I do not want to be a perfectionist." A "not frame" encourages the subconscious mind to create what you think you are resisting.

If you erase a problem and replace it with something positive and resourceful, what would it be?

Describe it. Include all key sense modes.

Step #2. State your outcome in terms of ability, not lack of ability.

Consider, *"I want others to support me."* That is not a well-formed outcome. Actually, thinking this way will stop you from making progress!

Make sure your outcome is formed by actions you are doing, not something others are supposed to do. Plus, it should and must be within your own responsibility and ability to act upon.

Ask yourself or your client:

What could you do on your own to make it happen?

What actions would you take to increase your chances this week?

Step #3. Context

Meaning is usually defined by context.

Describe your well-formed outcome in the context of the environment it will be in. This makes your goal more specific and motivational. It also helps to make sure that you have created an ecological goal.

A more well formed, context-related outcome would be: *"I want to make $65,000 within the next 12 months, starting July 1st, by selling my NLP skills to insurance agencies as a sales trainer for their telemarketing team."*

Add places, locations, geography, people and their titles, a budget, time frames and more. By making it specific and context related, you're making it real for your brain.

Another thought on context:

Where wouldn't you want that behavior to be acted upon?

For example, would you want to play like a child with your kids everyday to make them feel more joyful with you?

Great. You wouldn't want to act the same way with your spouse in bed, right? That's why context is extremely important.

You can make a goal of talking with more passion and sexiness to your wife, but if you forget the context being "with the wife, you might slip the wrong tonality talking with your boss.

Step #4. Sense Modalities

Describe your outcome by using your five senses. A well-formed outcome is specific. By adding all senses, you are being more specific and, again, motivational. Add impact to your subconscious.

If you have to use a word such as love, appreciated, or passionate, be sure to include the senses that form that emotion. From a sensory point of view, what does it mean for you to feel more appreciated.

How does 'appreciated' feel?

In what part of your body do you feel it?

Who is appreciating you, and what kind of expression is on their face?

Step #5. Objectives

Break down your goal into manageable objectives (pieces), so that you will feel more motivation, and do better problem solving.

Be sure to define the objectives in achievable terms. Smaller steps feel more achievable. This adds subconscious motivation. In NLP we call this breakdown "chunking down."

How do you feel when you think about writing a whole book? Or losing 60 pounds?

Compare that to smaller pieces. *"I will write a page a day to complete a 240 pages book. Today I will concentrate only on that one page."*

How do you eat an elephant? One piece at a time.

Step #6. Support

Arrange the help you need in order to make this outcome a reality. What resources do you need?

Make a list of the resources you will use in attaining your goal.

Again, be specific:

* *Who are the people who can assist you?*

* *What are their names?*

* *What is their profession?*

* *How about their phone numbers?*

* *What, exactly, should you ask them?*

* *What emotions will you need to develop within yourself?*

Do you need more confidence, resilience, joyfulness, or assertiveness?

How much money?

What information will be important? What questions must be answered ahead of time?

What else do you need?

Step #7: Perform an ecology check

What might be interfering with your goal?

Are there any values, other goals, people, or laws that may be challenging?

How might you accommodate or mitigate now in order to make your dream a reality?

Consider any internal obstacles you may have. Is a part of you interfering with your goal?

Step #8: Create your milestones.

Determine how you will know that you are progressing in the right direction and at the right pace. You must know what signs of progress you will be observing along the way.

One way to create milestones is to place the resources from your checklist onto a timeline. Vagueness about milestones is a warning sign.

Mark on your calendar the dates that you will be checking each milestone. Note in your plan exactly what you want to see by that date.

Being a great lover is an awesome goal. But what about learning to read body language of the person you're with? That would be excellent progress toward your goal. Even something that seems insignificant can be a good milestone. If you want to become rich, balancing your checkbook is part of your master plan, as trivial as it seems.

Step #9: Write down your goals.

There are many benefits to writing down your goals, objectives and milestones. Having a notebook or file for this gives you a place for problem solving and innovation. Sometimes a stray thought will turn into a gold mine when you come across it later.

Having separate sections for these elements gives you a working reference for checking milestones, refining your goals, and working toward your objectives.

Unwritten goals aren't worth the paper they're written on. Also, the written word has commanding power.

Wouldn't it worse to see your name on a "Most Wanted" poster than to hear about it?

Step #10. Test

Monitor your progress on the goal and its milestones.

Keep this in a conspicuous place to remind you.

Notice any ways that this pattern has helped you make progress toward achieving your goal.

Do this pattern as needed for other goals and for refining this goal.

Notice any ways that this pattern has improved your willingness to be more conscious of your goals and milestones, and to commit yourself to them. Not all obstacles that you encounter and decide which NLP patterns might help you with them. Part of the beauty of this pattern is making obstacles more obvious so you can handle them.

Additional Advice

In this modern world, with all the technology and comfort, it is quite easy to become a master procrastinator. My advice, as a major procrastinator myself, is that you do not fight with yourself when it comes to taking action on your goals and outcomes.

Simply remember to keep the outcome in mind as a direction and not as a "to do" list. Make it a big outcome so it inspires you, and then let it be as you take small actions and celebrate each milestone.

Treating outcomes as the end results is not much motivating. Thinking that all you need to do is to "get there" is not going to motivate you to really get there. You should accept your outcome as "means to an end", which means you are about to use them to express or fulfill a greater purpose! That's a true motivational force. Try to change your perspective and notice how it feels much better.

☺☺

4.

The E & E.P. Formation Pattern

"Everyone wants to be a millionaire or a multimillionaire. The only question is whether or not you are willing to do everything necessary and invest all the years required to achieve that financial goal. If you are, there is virtually nothing that can stop you".

— Brian Tracy, Goals! How to Get
Everything You Want–Faster Than You
Ever Thought Possible

CREDITS FOR THE CREATION of this NLP pattern belong to various contributors.

Determine when you have achieved a desired outcome by watching for the indications or clues that tell you. We'll call these "evidence." Develop a procedure for making sure that you perceive the evidence when it arises. We'll call this an "evidence procedure." For example, evidence in a learning situation is typically a test score. The evidence procedure would be the test design and the procedures for giving and grading the test.

Overview: The E & E.P. Formation Pattern

Step #1. Determine the goals of the assessment.
Step #2. Note the purpose of the procedure.
Step #3. Define the evidence in a concrete way
Step #4. Specify who is appropriate for establishing and continuing to carry out the procedure.
Step #5. Develop the timeframes and milestones that indicate progress.
Step #6. Specify what situations could be troublesome.
Step #7. Test

Step #1. Determine the goals of the assessment.

Determine the goals of the assessment. (E.g., to determine how well the student has learned a topic.)

State them in positive terms. (E.g., to establish a score and grade that accurately reflect the student's level of learning.)

Give examples of ideal performance. (E.g., 100%, which equals an "A" grade.)

Step #2. Note the purpose of the procedure.

What are its benefits? That is, why do you need the procedure? (E.g., students who learn Neuro Linguistic Programming concepts can communicate more effectively with other NLP practitioners, and they can learn from the literature and teachers more effectively.)

Step #3. Define the evidence in a concrete way

Define the evidence in a concrete way as, for example, observable behaviors and other outcomes. How will you know when you have achieved the goal? (E.g., students who achieve 85% are reasonably conversant with NLP, and fairly well prepared to benefit from teachers and the literature.)

Step #4. Specify what is appropriate for establishing and continuing to carry out the procedure.

Make sure that any instructions or training for the procedure are complete and understandable. (E.g., trainers with at least five years of successful practice with NLP and achieve at least a 90% score.)

Step #5. Develop the time-frames and milestones that indicate progress.

This can include the points at which progress should be assessed and when the goal is expected to be achieved.

Indicate what your criteria are for each step you specify. (E.g., a weekly quiz will help us determine how well the student mastered the most recent lessons.)

Step #6. Specify what situations could be troublesome.

For example, what problems might come up for someone attempting to administer the evidence procedure?

This can include resistance and positive intentions that might give rise to resistance. (E.g., a trainer may have time management difficulties and forget to administer the quiz. A deeper look tells the trainer that he or she needs the ego boost that they get from teaching, so they

unconsciously avoid the tedium of administering the test. It is a big change from how they did things when they weren't affiliated with a grade-giving institution.)

Step #7. Test

Establish times and responsibilities for evaluating the effectiveness of the testing, the teaching, and the materials used. (E.g., at the end of each quarter, trainers will review student satisfaction with an assessment instrument and a discussion. The trainers will review this at a quarterly staff meeting set aside for improving the program. It will include the opinions gathered from students as well as the opinions of all staff).

"Winners, leaders, masters—people with personal power—all understand that if you try something and do not get the outcome you want, it's simply feedback. You use that information to make finer distinctions about what you need to do to produce the results you desire".

Anthony Robbins, Unlimited Power

❀

51

5.

Pacing & Matching

"You MEET people at their own level, just as you don't discuss philosophy with a baby learning to talk . . . you make NOISES at the baby".

— Dr. Milton H. Erickson

CREDITS FOR THE creation of this NLP pattern belong to John Grinder and Richard Bandler.

Pacing and matching are important to modeling and rapport-building. Practicing this pattern sharpens your awareness of people and their subconscious communications. When you specifically pace a person's model of the world, you can better understand their perspective, as well as be much better able to build rapport.

Pacing involves matching elements of another person's body language and speech in ways that tend to improve rapport. Pacing is not mirroring, because you are not attempting to fully imitate the person. Rather, you are integrating various elements of their style into your own.

For example, if you use the same levels of vocabulary, the person will feel more comfortable with you. If you fake their accent, however, they will feel offended.

Because of the way this can help you build empathy and understanding of other people, you could say that you are pacing the person's model of the world. The other person's sense or intuition that you understand them and can relate to them obviously improves rapport. This improvement in rapport also occurs unconsciously.

Pacing could be compared with method acting, in which the actor enters another person's reality, by finding it within him or herself. This takes pacing to a higher level, in which you are able to embrace the other person's frame of reference.

Bandler and Grinder have found that you can enhance pacing by matching predicates, that is, their primary rep system references. If they "see" your point, you would appreciate them "viewing" it favorably, because they are referring to their visual rep system.

Practice pacing with people as you go about your day. Try it anywhere and everywhere. Start by erring toward being too subtle, and work your way into more complete pacing. That way, you won't offend anyone. If you are in an anonymous situation, where it doesn't matter if you appear eccentric, try more extreme pacing and see what it takes for people to actually give you a funny look. **You may be surprised at how fully you can pace without a problem.** Instead of following steps, you can practice this pattern by improvising from these instructions.

The most influential hypnotherapist, the late Dr. Milton H. Erickson,

described one of the classical examples of the Pacing & Matching pattern. Check out the quote in the beginning of this chapter, I chose this one on purpose.

Dr. Milton H. Erickson tells about a client he had, an autistic child. In his words, from the book **Phoenix Therapeutic Patterns Of Milton H Erickson**, written by *David Gordon*:

"And she brought the girl in, and introduced the girl to me and me to the girl. And the girl made a number of weird sounds and so I REPLIED with weird sounds, and we grunted and groaned and squeaked and squawked for about half an hour. And then the girl answered a few simple questions and very promptly returned to her autistic behavior. And we really had a good time squeaking and squawking and grunting and groaning at each other. And then she took the patient back to the hospital. In the night time she took the patient for a walk. She told me later, "that girl almost pulled my arm off, yanking me down the street, she wanted to see you. . . *the one man who could really talk her language*".

6.

Finding Positive Intention

*"If you can change your mind, you can change your life.
What you believe creates the actual fact. The greatest
revolution of my generation is to discover that individuals,
by changing their inner attitudes of mind, can change the
outer aspects of their lives."*

— William James

CREDITS FOR THE creation of this NLP pattern belong to various contributors.

Transforming self sabotage into success. By discovering the positive intent behind a negative behavior or attitude, you can release tremendous energy and positive commitment. Other NLP patterns, such as The Parts Negotiation Pattern and The Behavior Appreciation Pattern, depend on this insight.

In his outstanding book **Sleight Of Mouth – The Magic Of Conversational Belief Change**, master trainer and famous NLP developer Robert Dilts says:

"At some level all behavior is (or at one time was) "positively intended". It is or was perceived as appropriate given the context in which it was established, from the point of view of the person whose behavior it is. It is easier and more productive to respond to the intention rather than the expression of a problematic behavior".

54

> ## *Overview: The Finding Positive Intention Pattern*
>
> *Step #1. Define the problem.*
>
> *Step #2. Reveal the Underlying Motives*
>
> *Step #3. Get to the core motives.*

Step #1. Define the problem.

Briefly state the problem with enough detail so that it is clear in your mind. It may primarily be a situation, personal problem or a challenge. But focus on defining the unproductive behavior. Get clear on why the behavior is not useful.

Step #2. Reveal the Underlying Motives

Take a few moments to relax, breathe deeply and lay back. Now, go inside, imagine your mind has special internal messengers. In NLP, we call them "parts." These are parts of your personality, which have characteristic tendencies or habitual behaviors.

Find the part that is responsible for generating the unproductive behavior. Bring this part into awareness as though it were a complete personality. Remember that a part is an aspect of you. It is a collection of aligned motivations.

A part is like a little personality inside of you. In order to be aligned and successful, you must not work at cross purposes with yourself. This requires negotiating or working with your parts.

Now imagine that you can do a role playing game with this part. Ask the part what it wanted to have, do or become, through the negative behavior or attitude. What value or benefit was to come from this.

Ask directly, *"What did you wish for me to accomplish by doing this?"*

Take as much time as you need to imagine and listen to the part's responses.

Step #3. Get to the core motives.

Keep asking "why" and "what" questions to clarify the motives.

Recycle each answer by into a new question.

Continue this until you feel that you have gotten to the core motives. You should identify a core belief along with the core value and core reasons for the behaviors or attitudes that, at first glance, seem to be unsupportive of you.

☙❧

7.

Behavior Appreciation

"Live as if you were to die tomorrow. Learn as if you were to live forever".

— Mahatma Gandhi

CREDITS FOR the creation of this NLP pattern belong to various contributors.

Improve your performance and self care by developing a positive approach to change and personal development.

This pattern uses anchors to find the positive intention (the underlying positive outcome-seeking pattern) underlying a negative behavior.

For example, if you burst into tears at times, you have better options than feeling inferior.

Instead, this positive approach might help you decide to accept your need to release an emotional burden, and might help you find ways to live without unnecessary stress.

Overview: The Behavior Appreciation Pattern

Step #1. Identify the behavior.

Step #2. Anchor the context space.

Step #3. Access your underlying positive motivation.

Step #4. Part Space

Step #5. Test.

Step #1. Identify the behavior.

Select a negative behavior. It may be primarily a feeling, a thought pattern, or physical actions.

Include the context in which you carry out the behavior.

Step #2. Anchor the context space.

a. Where in your visual field or body does this experience seem to belong?

Imagine that this spot is a location that you can step into, and that when you step into it, you will see the location around you where the behavior has occurred. This spot now represents the behavior and its context, like a location or a space where you can stand in your imagination. We'll call this the "context space."

b. Step into this space, imagining that it is the location where the behavior took place.

Begin thinking of the behavior in its context.

Recall this as vividly as possible. Anchor the behavior and its context to this spot.

Step #3. Access your underlying positive motivation.

Even the most negative or unwanted behaviors actually have a positive underlying purpose.

Think of the negative behavior that you selected as coming from a part that has a positive underlying motivation. This dramatic change of frame can liberate your creativity and motivation.

However, set aside your first ideas as to these underlying motives.

Get into the "mind" of the part that is responsible for the behavior. This can provide insights that will make this pattern more powerful.

Step #4. Part Space

a. Imagine that there can be a space that is just for the part; a space that does not include the behavior and its context. We will call this the part space.

Step out of the context space, taking this part with you to the part space. You might want to visualize this space as being next to the context space.

Remember to leave the behavior and context behind. This leaves you with the part dissociated from the context, so that you may have easier access to its underlying motives.

b. Now you will clarify the part's motives with questions. At times, speak as if you are the part, speaking in first person. This will help you get an associated experience of the part's motives.

When referring to the negative behavior, point to the previous (context) spot anchor as if it were an actual physical location. This helps you *dis*-identify from the prior behavior.

"What to I really want to get out of what I had been doing (referring to the negative behavior)?"

Note: the past perfect tense of *"had been doing"* helps you mentally distance from the behavior by making it seem to be in the distant past, and implying that you have changed already.

"How do I feel when that desired outcome does or does not occur?"

"When I get the desired outcome, what do I want to do with it?"

"When I get the undesirable parts of the outcome, how to I react to them?"

Typical reactions include: blaming others, rationalization, spacing out or ignoring it, manipulating others to escape the consequences, isolating, self-soothing such as comfort food, distractions, etc.

Continue asking questions such as these until you feel that you have brought out responses that are valuable to you and your part.

c. Imagine yourself in the future, looking back upon the situation from a meta-state, at peace, fully able to enjoy the positive outcomes.

Step #5. Test.

In the coming days and weeks, notice any changes in your behavior when this kind of situation arises.

Notice any ways that you are more resourceful or have more options.

☙❧

8.

Mirroring

"The most effective way to achieve right relations with any living thing is to look for the best in it, and then help that best into the fullest expression".

— Allen J. Boone

CREDITS FOR THE creation of this NLP pattern belong to Richard Bandler and John Grinder.

Enhance your ability to establish rapport and to model excellence. This pattern builds a useful "second position" with another person. This skill is key in modeling others and for becoming intuitive in understanding the internal experiences of those you model.

Behavioral Mirroring

In behavioral mirroring, you match behaviors that have symbolic meaning. They are mostly subconscious. In fact, the more subconscious they are, the better they

are to mirror. After all, no one can think you're imitating them if you are imitating something they don't know they're doing, can they?

But what about being either masculine or feminine with the opposite sex. I mean, aren't you supposed to be different? Doesn't the opposite sex expect this? Well, yes and no. Remember, you are not completely giving up your actual personality. You are just adjusting certain things.

Did you know that when men talk to women, many tend to use a somewhat higher voice?

Apparently many people already do a certain amount of mirroring, whether they know it or not. It makes sense that we would evolve with some subconscious rapport-building instincts. After all, these abilities have contributed to our ability to survive and to procreate.

We know that the brain's neurons that are in charge of empathy and connecting with other feelings are called mirror neurons. Autistic people have difficulty with rapport building because they have less mirror neurons. Autistic people that are high-functioning enough to be concerned about rapport-building have to work extra hard at learning these skills because they are not as good with this kind of sensory acuity on an instinctual level. It has to start out as a much more conscious process.

Getting back to the idea of how we are supposed to be different across genders, consider this. Let's say a man is talking with a woman. She is a purchaser for a clothing company and the man is a sales rep for a textile mill.

He picks up from her behavior that she has worked her way up, she did not get her job because she was a college graduate with an impressive grade point average. He also sees from her skin tone and scent that, although she tries to hide it, she smokes. Her accent tells him that she is from a conservative and religious part of the country.

She happens to make a couple comments that are a little judgmental about people, comments that tell you she feels that people who are different are that way because they want to be eccentric or difficult, or just irresponsible. This is not someone you admit to that you are taking antidepressants.

The man matches her by displaying the qualities that she obviously respects, and mentioning items of personal history that match what she believes in. If he earned something through hard work, that gets mentioned in passing.

If he has a degree, he completely drops the big words and abstract ideas from his speech, except for ideas that he can communicate in a very plain way.

She is from the south of the United States, and he knows that there is a literary tradition of commenting on things with dry humor, like Mark Twain did. He uses his humor in a plain but insightful and a little bit cynical way. His humor is at the expense of the rich, not the poor, and at the expense of marginal people, not regular people.

If he is church going, he drops a comment about his involvement. He may share things about going to visit family with his immediate family members so she knows he values family.

Although he uses similar body movements, he does it with the kind of masculine quality that she expects, but in a gentle way that allows her to feel relaxed and connected.

While he's at it, he does the other physical mirroring that we have talked about, such as posture and breathing.

Symbolic Mirroring

Notice how we have gone beyond physical mirroring to include things of symbolic value. This is symbolic mirroring, and the symbolic behavior is often subconscious behavior. And we have seen that you can combine symbolic and physical mirroring.

This combination of symbolic and physical mirroring is very powerful. This same sales person probably has a wardrobe that is quite different for each area of the country that he visits.

There is an engineer who happens to have autism and who works in the cattle industry. She wears western clothes, complete with the trimming and pearl buttons. This helps her have rapport with the cattle industry people that she works with.

Since she is autistic, it is important for her to do what she can to improve her rapport. But it is an odd idea, an autistic person in a western getup.

Yet, this person became so good with rapport skills, that she was able to get the cattle industry to adopt a very stringent set of rules for humane treatment of animals. Her name is Temple Grandin. She used her leverage with the McDonalds Corporation, which does business with so many of the vendors, as a powerful strategy for inducing change.

This is a person who knows how to create well-formed outcomes.

As an engineer with an analytical mind, she got a head start on how to do a well-formed outcome. Isn't it interesting how she has serious weaknesses as well as powerful strengths. She chose to go with her strengths to create a career and even engage in transformational leadership.

Anyone who saw her as a child, unable to speak for years, and throwing tantrums because of her frustrations, would never have predicted her success.

We know of an individual who wanted to become more persuasive to conservative people. So he wrote a piece that expressed some of his liberal ideas, but using the same language as the conservatives.

The result was that some liberals became angry at him for writing conservative rubbish. That symbolic aspect of the words he used was more powerful than the actual meaning of the words. Never underestimate the power of subconscious symbols and how they play with rep systems.

For practice in looking for subconscious symbols, look to advertisements. For example, when there is an ad for a drug on television, notice how the commercial changes when they talk about the possible side effects of the medication. Notice how the music, acting, body language, colors and other aspects change to make that portion less memorable.

Notice how they give the impression that the drug is highly effective, whether it actually is or not. In one commercial, the main character is a cartoon of a bee with large eyes. During the part about side effects, his eyes get very droopy.

Exchanged Matches

Not all your mirroring has to use the same parts of the body, just as your symbolic mirroring does not necessarily use exactly the same words.

For example, NLP teaches that you can make a motion such as finger taps that match the rhythm of the breath, rather than breathing to the breath timing yourself. This is called an exchanged match. You are exchanging body parts, but matching the rhythm or other mirroring aspect.

If you are a man and you're matching a woman in front of you, avoid looking at her breasts, trying to figure out her breathing pattern! You will get caught, and using the excuse "I was trying to match your breathing" will not work in this case, I believe. Look at her shoulders instead; those tiny movement up and down will give you a hint on the breathing pattern she is using, and by applying exchanged matching you can move your leg or hand up and down accordingly.

You will be surprised to find out that in such a case of exchanged matching a breathing pattern, if you increase the speed of your matched movement, their breathing becomes faster! And if you slow it down, their breathing also becomes deeper and slower. Did you notice that sometimes when there's an angry person shouting and making a fuss, someone will try to come him down by moving their hands palms-down in a rhythmic motion, "hey, slow down, it's Ok, we can find a solution to this problem…"

Here's a quote about Mirroring and Rapport from the book **NLP: The New Technology of Achievement**, by *NLP Comprehensive, Steve Andreas and Charles Faulkner* "Fitting in is a powerful human need. We all have many examples of these behaviors, because we do them already. They are all based on some form of being similar, familiar or alike. Finding ways to be alike reduces our differences, and so we find the common ground upon which to base a relationship".

Overview: The Mirroring Pattern

Step #1. Select the subject.

Step #2. Conduct the conversation while mirroring the person.

Step #3. Exercise your rapport: Test your intuition and understanding of the person.

Step #4. Exercise your influence by shifting your attitude and physiology.

Step #5. Test.

Step #1. Select the subject.

Select someone for a conversation. Don't tell them that you will be mirroring them.

Step #2. Conduct the conversation while mirroring the person.

During the conversation, ask their opinions on various topics.

Mirror their physiology, including factors such as the tenor and cadence of their speech, and body language such as gestures. Do this subtly.

If you need help maintaining the dialog, use active listening. This involves showing that you understand what they are saying by rephrasing their contributions. Beginning with a phrase such as, *"You mean..."* or *"So you're saying..."* As you mirror, add elements such as their breathing as much as possible. Notice how you feel as rapport between you two develops.

Step #3. Exercise your rapport: Test your intuition and understanding of the person.

Test your ability to understand through rapport. Try out your intuitions about what they are saying. *Can you guess their opinion before they express it?*

If you agree, try expressing the opinion yourself, and see how this affects rapport. If you express the opinion in a less certain manner, the person may gain pleasure from holding forth to reassure you that the opinion is correct, and to demonstrate their mastery of the subject.

This helps establish you as a positive anchor. Highly effective rapport can gain information about the other person that you can learn to pull out of your subconscious, making you feel as though you are psychic. This is very useful in modeling.

Step #4. Exercise your influence by shifting your attitude and physiology.

Test your ability to influence others through rapport.

Try shifting your attitude and physiology (e.g., breath pace, facial expression, body language) in what you consider to be a desirable or possible direction.

For example, shifting from a resentful or angry state gradually into a more constructive or powerful state. If you do this with some care, the other party is likely to shift with you. This has enormous value in areas such as sales, leadership and coaching.

Step #5. Test.

Explore these skills of "pacing and leading" in your relationships.

Think of situations in which you could use these skills to improve your personal life or career performance.

Notice what outcomes you get, and refine these skills as you go.

Additional Advice

When NOT to Mirror or Match

There are things that you should not mirror. For example, if someone is getting aggressive and trying to be the alpha dog, you need to be more creative than just acting aggressive.

However, if you show an aggressive attitude about something that the other person is judgmental about, this can form a very powerful bond, plus, it can be fun to shout.

If you are comfortable with your aggressive side, you can adopt a posture that reflects that you are basically an aggressive person, yet not display aggression toward the person.

Adopt a quality that is more like you are both on the same team.

This is a little bit like dealing with people who need attention very badly and don't have very good emotional control, such as people with borderline personality disorder. Mirroring people with very intense needs is much more of an art form and not a good place to start practicing.

If you need to, though, you can do mild mirroring of body language without giving the impression that you think your needs are greater than theirs. You can also, on the symbolic level, share the kinds of resentments and other things that the person tends to focus on.

By staying within the world that they mentally live in, you do not alienate them by intimidating them with a larger world.

These individuals can easily collapse into feeling very threatened or inferior, and this can cause them to go out of their way to undermine you. This can include something called triangulation, where they pit other people against you. This can even include your boss, or legal authorities. Rapport is very important with these individuals, as well as being well-protected against any ways they might try to undermine you.

After you have general rapport-building skills, you will be ready do use them with people who have needs that are more intense than average, if you are so inclined. This is especially the area of psychotherapists, physicians, and other professionals who tend to deal with people in distress.

For example, you will learn that once you can gain rapport, you can use this to lead people or alter their state in positive ways. The pattern or mirroring and changing behavior of others is called pacing and leading.

With people who are suffering, you do not mirror their suffering, you just stick with mirroring the general physical and symbolic items that make them comfortable with you, so that they can feel okay about expressing themselves.

If you feel some of the state they are in, that is enough to you to feel more empathy, and for them to know that you do.

Some of you listeners, however, are already highly empathic, and can even be overwhelmed by others feelings.

This can go two ways.

You may find that mirroring is technical enough that it helps keep you from being overwhelmed or distracted by the other person's feelings when they are in distress.

On the other hand, if this is not so; if you still feel too much of their feelings, then you are probably already mirroring them so much that you are inducing their state in yourself too strongly.

In that case, you will actually need to learn how to tone down your mirroring in at least some aspects, especially the physical aspects. Better yet, you can use NLP to find and change your strategy for feeling overwhelmed. You can start with what internal representations you have about the suffering of others.

Nurses, therapists and social workers are often people who do a lot of subconscious mirroring without any training in it.

But what if someone catches you mimicking him or her?

If someone feels that you are mimicking him or her, they are probably aware of NLP and mirroring. If they seem uncomfortable or offended, the best response is typically to back off of the physical mirroring, but maintain the symbolic mirroring without getting carried away.

☯

9.

The As-If Pattern

"We are all what we pretend to be, so, we had better be very careful what we pretend"

— Kurt Vonnegut

CREDITS FOR THE creation of this NLP pattern belong to John Grinder.

Create useful states by envisioning excellence. It is a way to use imagination for success in the spirit of Milton Erickson's famous quote, *"You can pretend anything and master it."* This is an important skill for using modeling to achieve excellence and success.

An excellent first step in modeling is to place yourself into the second perceptual position (the other person's position) and imagine what it is like to be that person, carrying out the excellence strategies that you wish to model.

This strategy contributes to your intuitive understanding of their thoughts and actions. Of course, one must practice one's craft in order to master it. After all, you wouldn't expect to fly an airplane without sufficient practice.

Overview: The As-If Pattern

Step #1. Select the goal you are doubtful about.

Step #2. Select your imaginary mentor.

Step #3. Specify your limiting belief.

Step #4. Share this situation and belief with your chosen mentor.

Step #5. Imagine Encouragement from Your Mentor

Step #6. Act as if the Outcomes are Coming True

Step #7. Handle Leftover Objections

Step #8. Test

Step #1. Select the goal you are doubtful about.

Think of a personal goal or circumstance about which you feel doubtful. If you're new to this pattern, choose a small goal, such as producing more creative solutions for something you need to brainstorm about.

Step #2. Select your imaginary mentor.

Pick a person, living or dead, whom you feel would make an excellent mentor for you and who could help you believe in your ability to achieve this goal. The person should be very insightful.

You should know enough about them to really imagine how they might relate to you. If you have time, you can learn more about them to better do this pattern.

Step #3. Specify your limiting belief.

Express your limiting belief in terms of the limits that it expresses.

Try beginning with a phrase such as, "I am incapable of (finding a good solution)," or "I don't deserve (a smooth, creative experience)."

Step #4. Share this situation and belief with your chosen mentor.

Imagine that you are speaking to your mentor, explaining the situation as well as your limiting belief.

Step #5. Imagine Encouragement from Your Mentor

Imagine your mentor respectfully encouraging you to explore a positive "as if" perspective, with questions such as, *"What would happen if you could..."* Respond to these questions as they are asked.

Have your mentor ask follow up "as if" questions based on your responses.

Step #6. Act as if the Outcomes are Coming True

Imagine that your mentor is having you act as if the doubtful outcomes were coming true. For example, *"Imagine that you have successfully resolved all the issues you had about this. With full confidence about it now, what will you be thinking or doing that is different?"*

Step #7. Handle Leftover Objections

Notice any leftover objections or resistance you have. Continue steps two and three, focusing them on these residual issues.

Step #8. Test

As you go about pursuing your goal, notice any improvements in your state, behavior, or outcomes. What can you learn from the results?

If the results are disappointing, are there ways you can improve your use of this pattern? For example, do you understand the imaginary mentor well enough?

Additional Advice

This pattern is best done for a small skill or small margin of improvement. It is a good pattern for getting your foot in the door as a prelude to making major improvements in mastery.

☙❧

10.

Eliciting Subconscious Responses

"The important thing is not to stop questioning. Curiosity has its own reason for existing. One cannot help but be in awe when he contemplates the mysteries of eternity, of life, of the marvelous structure of reality. It is enough if one tries merely to comprehend a little of this mystery every day. Never lose a holy curiosity."

— Albert Einstein

CREDITS FOR THE creation of this NLP pattern belong to various contributors.

Become a master communicator by learning to recognize and utilize subtle changes in others' physiology. This pattern involves the valuable skill of eliciting subconscious resources, a skill that serves you best when it, too, is subconscious. This skill deserves serious study, so resist any temptation to treat it like a magic trick.

We recommend that you practice this pattern with a partner until you find yourself using it unconsciously.

Overview: Eliciting Subconscious Responses

Step #1. Get your partner to think about a pleasant memory in the first perceptual position.

Step #2. Have your partner focus on the visual rep system.

Step #3. Have your partner clear their mind and focus on the auditory.

Step #4. Have your partner focus on the kinesthetic.

Step #1. Get your partner to think about a pleasant memory in the first perceptual position.

Find someone who will allow you to practice this exercise with them.

Ask them to think about a pleasant memory.

Encourage them to do this with eyes closed, and in the first perceptual position, as though they are experiencing it first hand.

Step #2. Have your partner focus on the visual rep system.

Once your subject has a pleasant memory in mind, have your subject focus exclusively on the visual aspect of the memory.

Note all of your subject's reactions, including changes in posture, facial expression, changes in skin color, pattern of breathing, and so forth.

Step #3. Have your partner clear their mind and focus on the auditory.

Have your subject clear their mind and open their eyes.

Have them bring up only the auditory aspect of the memory.

Continue making your observations.

Step #4. Have your partner focus on the kinesthetic.

Once they have done this, have them bring up the kinesthetic aspect as you continue to observe.

Additional Advice

You might want to record your observations on a form that you prepare.

Use three titles to divide your operations into *"Visual Reactions,"* *"Auditory Reactions,"* and *"Kinesthetic Reactions."*

Once you have done this exercise, you can improve your powers of observations "in the wild," by being aware of subtle physiological signals, and how they are influenced by factors such as primary sense mode, emotional arousal, rapport, and anything else of importance. This power of observation will be valuable in many NLP patterns, even the ones you don't know you're |using.

☙❧

11.

Ecology Check

"Be careful about reading health books. You may die of a misprint."

— Mark Twain

CREDITS FOR THE creation of this NLP pattern belong to John Grinder and Richard Bandler.

Induce change with this flexible and important pattern. It prevents self sabotage by making sure a change will be acceptable to all parts. You can even apply this ecological approach to multiple systems, such those you notice in politics.

This is an important pattern to use in some form whenever you induce change. It ensures that that change will be acceptable to all parts. This prevents self-sabotage. On a larger scale, you can apply ecological thinking to multiple systems, such as in politics.

When you think "ecologically" you are taking every aspect of your outcome into account. You check to make sure that you are not going to achieve X on the expense of Y, if both are important to you. For example, an Ecology Check is in place when you help a client to stop smoking. Some people gain a lot of weight as a reaction to such a change. You want to make sure that your client is completely congruent about the upcoming change, and this pattern helps you do discover possible obstacles or disadvantages that must be addressed.

Overview: The Ecology Check Pattern

Step #1. Get into an objective state.

Step #2. Ask good questions to do an ecology check.

Step #3. Give this pattern "mind share," by making it an ongoing, recurring pattern in your mind.

Step #4. Evaluate

Step #1. Get into an objective state.

This pattern assumes you already have a pattern such as a behavior pattern that you are working to change. We will frame this pattern for a person problem in your life.

To begin the ecology check, use any method that helps you gain objectivity, such as thinking like a journalist who must adhere to the facts of the situation. You may need to dissociate into the third perceptual position.

From this objective frame of mind, think about your life as a whole, perhaps as if you could look down at your timeline.

Step #2. Ask good questions to do an ecology check.

A key to balance in your life is asking good questions.

As a part of the ecology check ask:

- *"What areas in my life are being benefited from having this belief/behavior?"*

- *"What areas in my life may get hurt because of it?"*

- *"Am I feeling completely assured that this is something I want to generate in my life?"*

- *"What are the specific immediate results of it?"*

- *"What are the specific long term results?"*

- *"Who else is being affected by these outcomes?"*

Step #3. Give this pattern "mind share," by making it an ongoing, recurring pattern in your mind.

This pattern can be even more powerful by maintaining it over a good period of time, even making it a recurring theme in your life.

Keep these questions alive, entraining your creative energies

74

through means such as writing them in your journal. (You do have a journal, don't you?)

Read the questions before you go to sleep so that they will be on your mind.

Once you have recruited enough creative resources, you'll get dreams, songs, words, flashes, memories, and voices... Don't ignore them. It's important to notice, and acknowledge them. Your brain is highly motivated to solve riddles.

Asking good questions and giving it time to find the answers with no pressure, is one the greatest talents you can develop. As answers emerge, note them down. Have a note pad or device at the ready so you can collect them in one place.

Step #4. Evaluate

Once you have accumulated answers, evaluate them.

Realize that, right now, you have many valuable clues to success. What do they mean about the outcomes you appear to be headed for? Do you need to change course?

As you can see, new questions can emerge from these answers. These new questions are even more directly valuable, because they are like tools that are more refined and designed for experts to use.

Additional Advice

You can apply **Cartesian coordinates** to decisions in order to check your ecology and refine your outcomes. You can try this on a decision you're considering. Here they are:

If I do X, what will happen?

If I do X, what won't happen?

If I don't do X, what will happen?

If I don't do X, what won't happen?

Note anything that you hadn't thought of, or any way that these questions help you put things into perspective.

☙❧

12.

Physiomental State Interruption

"The truth is that our finest moments are most likely to occur when we are feeling deeply uncomfortable, unhappy, or unfulfilled. For it is only in such moments, propelled by our discomfort, that we are likely to step out of our ruts and start searching for different ways or truer answers".

— Morgan Scott Peck, M.D., author of The Road Less Traveled

CREDITS FOR THE creation of this NLP pattern belong to various contributors.

Master the art of change by learning to clear a space for a new state. You can do this by breaking or interrupting the current state. You can guide a person to the state of your choosing much more easily from a state of confusion than any other.

As you'll recall, state in NLP refers to your state of mind and body at any given time. States may be functional or dysfunctional. NLP makes extensive use of breaking state, and it has many ways to do it. Confusion is a guaranteed state breaker. You can guide a person to the state of your choosing much more easily from a state of confusion than any other.

Overview: The Physiomental State Interruption Pattern

Step #1. Identify the state you experience

Step #2. Initiate an interruption by exaggerating a driving submodality

Step #3. Test

Step #1. Identify the state you experience.

Recognize what state you are in, and name it. It may not be a clear-cut as depression, boredom, or anger, but you can come up with a name that captures the essence of the state. To help you find a name, notice the feeling of the state or the direction it carries your thoughts.

Step #2. Initiate an interruption by exaggerating a driving submodality.

Notice how this state is represented in your sense modalities.

Identify a submodality feature that is important to this state.

Change that feature to make it absurd. For example, if you hear a voice that says "I am not worthy of love", change that tone of voice into that of a cartoon character. Or if you feel a throb of depression when you have a certain thought, take a break to do a rational procedure such as serial sevens (7, 14, 21, 28...)

Step #3. Test.

Notice whether your state has changed significantly. If not, the problem may be in your choice of submodality feature. You may not have found an impactful one. You also may need to experiment with how you change the submodality to make it absurd.

∞

13.

State Induction

"The emotions aren't always immediately subject to reason, but they are always immediately subject to action".

— William James

CREDITS FOR THE creation of this NLP pattern belong to various contributors.

Apply one of the most fundamental NLP skills; state induction. This tool helps us induce a needed state such as confidence, prepare for an event, or take steps in many NLP patterns.

For example, once you have induced a helpful state, you will find it is easier to do mental rehearsal in preparing for a challenge.

Here are a few useful states you might want to experience and experiment with while working with this pattern, besides the obvious passion and motivation: Acceptance, Alignment, Appreciation, Balance, Artsy, Forgiveness, Grounded, Purified, Purposeful, Chosen, Confessed, Humorist or foolish, Enlighten, Curiosity, Inhibition, Compassion and my favorite – being joyful in solitude.

As you work with states and learn to manage them effectively, make yourself a list of your most favorite ones. Making such a list will actually encourage your mind to explore those states even further, when you're on "auto-pilot".

Overview: The State Induction Pattern

Step #1. Define a desired state

Step #2. Kindle the State

Step #3. Amplify the state with more Rep System Kindling

Step #4. Expand the State kinesthetically (Kv)

Step #1. Define a desired state

Think of a state that you would like to experience.

Pick one that is positive, and feels like a nice alternative to any negative feelings you've had lately.

Think of how you would know you were in that state.

Describe something about it in the four primary sense modes: visual, auditory, verbal-auditory, and kinesthetic.

Step #2. Kindle the State

Recall a variety of situations, in which you have felt some aspect of that state. If this state is not very typical for you, it is okay to think of situation where you felt only a hint of it, or where you could only sense it in one modality.

But remember, when people think something is only in one modality, they are usually just not aware of how it is occurring in one or two others.

As you do this, encourage the feelings of the state to collect and amplify.

Step #3. Amplify the state with more Rep System Kindling

Notice what sense modes are beginning to "kindle" into this state.

As you peruse your memories, work on collecting and amplifying the state in the weaker submodality.

Include the verbal (auditory-digital, as it is called) mode, by saying to your self some phrases that are in line with the state.

For confidence, it might be, *"Piece of cake, this is easy,"* or, *"The folks at the party I'm going to really want me to have a good time."*

Repeating one or more phrases for a while can help strengthen the state.

Step #4. Expand the State kinesthetically (Kv)

Once you have begun to sense the state in all submodalities, encourage the feelings to spread throughout your body, as though energy is flowing through you and carrying the state through you on all of its currents.

Additional Advice

You can rate your state in terms of its completeness or intensity on a scale of zero to ten. This can help you compare methods, and get a sense of what level a state must reach to be of value.

States don't have to reach a nine or ten in order to be valuable.

You can add constructed submodalities, as when you picture yourself walking or talking and gesturing in the desired state. This can be very powerful.

Adjusting submodalities can amplify a state. For example, turning up the volume of the verbal aspect, or increasing the brightness of the visual.

With practice, you will become intuitive and natural at this.

Discovering which submodaility is most powerful in *"driving"* the state can help you use your resources more efficiently.

❧

14.

Accessing Resourceful States

"In bed my real love has always been the sleep that rescued me by allowing me to dream".

— Luigi Pirandello

CREDITS FOR THE creation of this NLP pattern belong to Steve Andreas.

Learn state mastery. Elicit resourceful states such as confidence and creativity that will move you toward your goals.

Managing states is one of the most fundamental skills in Neuro Linguistic Programming.

Overview: The Accessing Resourceful States Pattern

Step #1. Choose a situation that calls on you to be in an excellent state

Step #2. Name the most valuable qualities

Step #3. Select a memory of the resource state

Step #4. Step into the resource state

Step #5. Pick a model for this state. Experience it from second position

Step #6. Anchor

Step #7. Test

Step #1. Choose a situation that calls on you to be in an excellent state.

What resources do you need to have in that situation?

For example, if you are going to a job interview, eagerness, charisma, and confidence are valuable. If you are in a difficult negotiation, emotional buoyancy, charisma, and strategic thinking are important.

Step #2. Name the most valuable qualities.

Name the qualities that you feel are most valuable for the challenge that you have chosen for this pattern.

Step #3. Select a memory of the resource state.

Think of a time when you have experienced and expressed at least one of these qualities.

Bring to mind all the rep systems for this memory (VAK, at least), until the memory is very rich. Go for the sense of actually going back into the memory. This means you need to be in the first position, as yourself.

Step #4. Step into the resource state.

Imagine that this resource (the resource state that this memory is bringing up) is a force field that you can step into.

Step into it and imagine in all rep systems what it is like for you to be fully in this state. This way, you are amplifying the state in the memory.

You can spend some time in the third perceptual position, seeing your posture, facial expression, and behavior as you fully express this state.

Do whatever you need to amplify this state, especially in regards to how it can be most relevant to the challenge that you have in mind.

Step #5. Pick a model for this state. Experience it from second position.

Think of someone that you feel has an abundance of this resource state. It can be anyone from a character from a movie to someone that you know well.

From third position, look at them and notice what in their physiology expresses this state.

Move into second position so that you experience the state from inside that person, as that person.

Access all rep systems.

Step #6. Anchor.

Anchor this resource.

Step #7. Test.

When the situation or challenge comes up, see how this pattern has changed how you handle it.

Repeat this pattern, improving it based on what you learn.

For example, how can you make the resource state a more intense experience for re-anchoring? What submodalities do you need to add to make it more relevant to the challenge?

☙

15.

The Kinesthetic Swish Pattern

"Happiness can be defined, in part at least, as the fruit of the desire and ability to sacrifice what we want now for what we want eventually".

— Stephen Covey, The 7 Habits Of Highly Effective People

CREDITS FOR THE creation of this NLP pattern belong to Robert Dee McDonald.

Utilize feelings to generate constructive motivation and drive.

Ultimately, feelings are the force behind success and failure.

We move away from negative feelings and toward good feelings.

This pattern builds a mind-body strategy for overcoming negativity in the face of challenges that have been daunting until now.

Overview: The Kinesthetic Swish

Step #1. Associate them into the feeling.

Step #2. Break state.

Step #3. Have them associate into and amplify a positive state.

Step #4. Define the submodalities and amplify the feeling.

Step #5. Break state.

Step #6. Map across to modify the negative feeling.

Step #7. Test.

Step #1. Associate them into the feeling.

Have the person think of the situation or thoughts that produce a negative state. Ask them to specify the details of the feeling, especially submodalities such as movement and temperature, and the location of the feeling.

Step #2. Break state.

Step #3. Have them associate into and amplify a positive state.

Have them specify how they would like to feel.

Step #4. Define the submodalities and amplify the feeling.

Have them associate into this feeling, amplifying it through the most effective submodalities.

Step #5. Break state.

Step #6. Map across to modify the negative feeling.

Have them recall the negative feeling and it's location.

Have them move it into the positive feeling's location and get it to conform to the submodalities of the other feeling. **Note**: unlike the visual swish, the kinesthetic swish tends to be slower, so give the pattern time.

Step #7. Test.

In the coming days and weeks, see if your person relates to the situation or thoughts differently, getting improved results in life.

❧❧

16.

Anchoring

"Never let formal education get in the way of your learning".

— Mark Twain

CREDITS FOR THE creation of this NLP pattern belong to John Grinder and Richard Bandler.

Anchoring is how we get into the right state for what we want to do. You connect a symbol with the desired state, or resource state. It's called a resource state, because you are more resourceful when you are in that state.

Of course, we mean resourceful for certain things. If you have intense confidence and desire for opportunity as a resource state, it would be very good for a job interview, and maybe not so good for being a grief counselor.

You'd want to be in a somewhat different state for that. And you would benefit from yet an-

other state to fully enjoy a Greek wedding.

Once you have your symbol, you fire the anchor in order to trigger the associated resource state. This will be very clear once we have covered some examples. Perhaps the most commonly used anchor for personal use is a hand position, but you can get very creative will all aspects of anchoring.

You can quickly induce a state when you have anchored that state in advance. Firing an anchor that you have established in connection with the state activates the anchor and, as a result, the anchored state.

Anchoring is one of the most well-known NLP techniques, and it is used in many patterns.

How Does Anchoring Work?

Anchoring is related to something called behaviorism. Behaviorism tells us how to do behavior modification. This is the collection of methods used to train animals to do tricks; animals like dolphins in a water park that do back flips, and dogs in movies that put their paws up over their eyes. The amazing thing about behavior modification is that it does not require a conscious mind in order to work.

After all, it works on all sorts of animals. This means that it uses very powerful and primitive aspects of your nervous system in order to work. Yes, it works very well on human beings as well, because we have the same brain components as animals do, though we have more. That's why were training them instead of the other way around.

When an anchor is fired each time you are in a certain state, your body associates that state with the anchor.

At first, the anchor is a neutral stimulus. It doesn't do anything much. But once that anchor is associated with the state, you can trigger that state by firing the anchor. The trick, as you will see, is to get that anchor associated with the right state.

In behavior modification, this is called associative conditioning. Conditioning means that you create a response that happens every time there is a certain stimulus.

Associative conditioning means that the response comes to be associated with another stimulus, in this case, an anchor that you can use to your own benefit.

Behavior modification is at the heart of problems like procrastination. That's why we combine communication with understanding the nervous system. With that, we can create solutions that run themselves. If you had to think about every strategy that you use for excellence, you'd run out of brain power very fast. That's why people don't usually get very amazing changes out of a self help book or TV show.

What people don't realize, is that anchors are constantly influencing our behavior. Being in your workplace becomes an anchor for workplace behavior. Being downtown may trigger your desire to visit a favorite watering hole or ice cream parlor. Parents help their children get to bed and fall asleep by having certain things like music happen at certain times of the evening. It's called the evening ritual.

That's a good choice of words, since rituals are anchors that help to trigger states. The soldier who pulls out the locket from his girlfriend back home and looks at her picture is firing an anchor. It gives him some feelings of security and warmth. The non-technical word here is solace. It gives solace.

So an object can be an anchor. There is the action or ritual of manipulating it, there is the visual impression, the kinesthetic aspect of how it feels, and perhaps the sound.

Can Anchors Be in Any Sense Mode?

Yes, visual, auditory, and kinesthetic anchors are all used in NLP. Kinesthetic anchors involving a physical position or point to touch are very common, because you don't have to have anything with you in order to use it. Mental visual symbols or mental pictures are also convenient, as are inner verbal statements. Anchors can be external or internal.

External visual anchors can include a ring or bracelet. However, they may be diluted by the fact that you may look at them a lot without being in the desired state. So when it comes to visual symbols, we recommend using an internal one. If you need to feel grounded, you might visualize a circle that appears to have been created by a Zen calligrapher.

The nature of the symbol makes it easy to establish and recall, and it is not one that you would think of at random; it has a special purpose. A person such as a great historical or religious figure might serve the purpose. You would put them in a special frame or something so that the image is specialized just for this purpose. You might come up with special objects or places that have sentimental or symbolic value.

When using sound as an anchor, again we recommend internal use. You can imagine any sound that you would not normally hear.

If you go digital, a special phrase can do the trick. Prior to doing something that arouses anxiety, you might say, "Piece of Cake!" meaning, it's as easy as eating a piece of cake.

Kinesthetic anchors can be especially powerful. When you are going into a situation where you need to feel supported, you might imagine a hand on your shoulder, a hand that belongs to a historical or religious figure who is significant for compassionate leadership.

You can lace your fingers opposite to the way you would normally do it, so that it feels different. You can make a pattern such as a circle with your fingers. You can touch a specific point that is not too awkward-looking to reach.

You can even create combinations such as having a phrase and a hand position at the same time.

Is Ice Cream an Anchor?

This brings up the difference between a direct physical effect of a substance, and the associative conditioning involved in an anchor. You might be doing both with ice cream.

Certain foods, including ice cream, trigger a reward center in the brain and create other physiological rewards directly. Chocolate contains a very pleasant stimulant, and the rise in blood sugar and the fat can be very satisfying. When a stimulus, like ice cream or a loud noise, cause an innate response, the behaviorists call this an unconditioned response. But an anchor is a conditioned response, so if someone jumps when they hear a loud noise, the loud noise is not an anchor.

Then again, there is a way ice cream can also be an anchor. Let's say your mother gave you ice cream when you had a sore throat, or you had ice cream with birthday parties and friends. Associations like this mean that ice cream, as an anchor, can trigger feelings of being nurtured, of being loved, or of celebrating.

The main difference is that an anchor works because it is associated with a certain state, not because it chemically causes that state or because it triggers a natural response that is typical without creating an anchor, like an animal hearing an loud noise and startling.

It's too bad more people don't know about creating anchors. Instead of using food or drugs to create feelings of an improved mood, there are many alternatives, and anchoring is one of them. The less resources people have to manage their states, the more risk there is of food addiction or drug abuse. In psychology, self-soothing is considered an ability that many people lack.

Those people are at risk for addictions. Therapists attempt to help these people learn to self-soothe. Many therapists use anchoring to help this population.

In addition to ice cream being high in fat and sugar, ice cream is hard to carry around with you. That alone makes it a poor anchor. NLP highly values independence.

Anchoring With Intention

Intention is an important aspect of anchoring. Intention can amplify the effect of anchoring. When rats were conditioned to associate a light with a loud, frightening noise, they learned to startle when the light went on.

But when they became used to the loud noise and no longer startled, they stopped reacting to the light. This means that the significance of the stimulus carries a lot of weight. Your intention adds power to the anchor. When you trigger an anchor, be sure to use your intention to amplify the state.

Don't just do the anchor and passively let it work on its own. Another reason for using your intention is that this helps to prevent extinction, because you are guaranteeing that each time you fire the anchor, the connection with the right state is reinforced.

Anchors can go as far as your inventiveness can.

NLP trained people have come up with countless patterns that use anchoring. Many of them are simply variations that practitioners, sales people, motivational speakers, ministers, supervisors, politicians and other people have come up with on the fly, to use as needed. Many of them have actually been published.

Speakers and other who must use state presence can actually use their position on stage or their gestures or other things as anchors to promote the needed state in the audience as a whole.

Not only are anchors being used in such a case, but emotions or states tend to be infectious in a group setting. If the speaker or presenter can just get that state going, it will kindle as part of the group process.

You can even use positions on a stage to chain anchors. Imagine moving an audience from skepticism or apathy, to motivation and wanting more. Add to this your ability to model the desired state by triggering it in yourself, and you can have a profound effect on an audience.

This method of positioning on stage has even been imported to the television environment. There is a famous political ad in which a frightening criminal was established on one part of the screen, with the politician on the other side.

Then the politician he was competing against appeared in the same spot as the criminal. This is the famous Willie Horton ad used by George Bush Senior against Michael Dukakis in 1988.

In this case, they went beyond anchoring as NLP teaches it, and used human neurology in a cynical move to damage another person. This is a big reason why the public should understand NLP, they need to recognize when neurology is being used to manipulate people in negative ways.

How long is an anchor effective?

Anchors can be effective for the rest of your life. The better formed they are, the longer they last. The better you maintain them, the longer they last.

If you only use an anchor when you feel bad, it can lose it's power to help you feel good.

A good way to maintain an anchor is to use it when you are in the state it is intended to t rigger.

You will learn how to do this during the next section where we teach you how to anchor. Behaviorism uses the word *extinction* for when a conditioned response fades out.

Overview: The Anchoring Pattern

Step #1. Select a state and and decide which trigger to use.

Step #2. Elicit the state.

Step #3. Calibrate.

Step #4. Anchor the state.

Step #5. Test.

Step #1. Select a state and and decide which trigger to use.

Select a state that you want to have access to in the future. Select the anchor trigger you would like to use. As you'll recall, this can be a hand position, a point on your body that you touch, or a word or phrase that you say mentally, among many others or some other UNIQUE action that you can dedicate to this state. That means it must be specific, such as pulling on you little finger.

Step #2. Elicit the state.

For instructions on how to elicit the state, see the State Elicitation pattern.) Make the state fairly strong.

Step #3. Calibrate.

If you are doing this for someone else, have them tell you when they are in the state, and observe their physical cues such as body language, so that you can better calibrate them.

Step #4. Anchor the state.

Once the state is fully active and at its PEAK, anchor the state.

Anchor it by doing the behavior that you selected in step one as your trigger.

At this point, you are associating the trigger with the state, that is, anchoring the state to the trigger.

In the future, activating this trigger will help you activate the state.

Never use this trigger for anything other than this state from now on, and when you activate this state in the future, continue the practice of associating the trigger with the state in order to make this association even stronger.

Step #5. Test.

Think of situations in which you will want to trigger this state, and make a reminder to yourself in your calendar so that you'll remember to practice using it and reaping it's benefits.

Additional Advise

It is important to remember the basic principles. Be sure that your anchor is **unique** so that other states and situations don't dilute it.

Make sure that when you create an anchor, that the state is as **intense** as you can get it. An intense state creates the strongest anchor. The more **pure** the state is, without other things going, the better. The more **precisely** you focus that state, the better.

You can use redundancy in order to make triggering more powerful. Do this by anchoring in multiple sense modalities.

You can fire them simultaneously or in close succession.

If your first efforts do not work adequately, you may need to sharpen your observational or problem-solving skills as you seek the reason.

Does the anchor have another meaning?

Did you adequately associate the anchor with the state?

Repetition may help. Although some NLP materials make it sound like magic, it is a behavioral method that utilizes our nervous systems to create an enduring change. In many people, this may require experience and creativity.

Since one way of creating an anchor involves touching the client in order to establish the anchor, remember to explain this and get the client's permission first, so they aren't surprised.

And, of course, you will want to use spots that aren't too intimate.

∞

17.

A Script For Self Anchoring

DECIDE WHAT *state you want to create an anchor for.*

Maybe you would like an anchor for that meeting and negotiation state.

Maybe you have something else you'd like to anchor.

Whatever it is, chose one…

Now recall all the times that you felt some aspect of that state. Watch yourself like you are in a movie, in third position.

Every time you feel some aspect of the desired state, amplify it and expand it.

Keep doing that until you feel as strong a state as you can…

Each time you think of a time in which you felt some aspect of that state, see what is most visually positive and compelling…

Hear what is most audibly positive and compelling… Hear any

words that others said or that you could say that are most mentally positive and compelling…

Feel what is most palpably positive and compelling…

Feel whatever internal sensations are most positive and compelling, like feeling very up or expansive…

See yourself now, standing in a nice place, fully feeling that state, and see how you look in that state; your facial expression, your posture, you can even add cosmic energy of just the right color streaming into your aura.

Now create a sign with your hand such as an okay sign, one that you would not do very often, or interlace your fingers in the opposite way from normal, and hold that position while you savor the state…

☙❧

94

18.

Downtime

"One reason so few of us achieve what we truly want is that we never direct our focus; we never concentrate our power. Most people dabble their way through life, never deciding to master anything in particular".

— Anthony Robbins, author of Awaen The Giant Within

CREDITS FOR THE creation of this NLP pattern belong to various contributors.

Learn to create a light, momentary trance in people for various uses. When your conscious awareness is focused entirely on internal experience, NLP refers to this as downtime.

The **Downtime** state is a subset type of trance phenomenon, and can help initiate or deepen trance. It can help you manage an interac-

tion as a brief, light trance as occurs in a transderivational search.

Many techniques are used to stimulate downtime, and they are used not only to produce trance, but also patience, introspection, and receptiveness.

Uptime, on the other hand, refers to a more worldly state of awareness that emphasizes external awareness that is effectively informed by internal awareness.

Overview: The Downtime Pattern

Step #1. Restrict your environment

Step #2. Internalize focus with Rep Systems

Step #1. Restrict your environment

Arrange a distraction-free environment, because this specific pattern requires concentration.

Step #2. Internalize focus with Rep Systems

Direct your attention inward, attending to each of your internal representational systems (the substeps below will help you).

Attend to each of the modes as fully and as separately as possible.

a. Notice your audio sense, including your inner voice, the sound of any memories or fantasies that arise. Remember something, and focus totally on the sounds involved.

b. Direct your mental focus to the visual mode.

Include memories and fantasies that arise. Choose a memory and focus all your awareness on the visual aspect.

c. Attend to emotional and physical senses as they arise for a while. Now think of a memory, and direct your attention to your emotional and physical feelings as they occur in the memory.

Notice the difference between those feelings compared to what you feel ABOUT the memory, and what you body physically feels right now as you recall the memory. For example, how hard is the surface you are on right now?

d. Become aware of tastes. Come up with a memory of eating something tasty. Notice that you have various senses involved in the memory. Focus your mind entirely on remembering the taste. Notice how taste is more than one sensation, since much of what we associate with food has to do with its consistency, such as chewiness.

e. Shift your awareness of this memory to smell. Notice how you can separate taste and smell.

Additional Advice

You can anchor the experience of effective downtime. A good way to do this is to fold your hands and, as you experience all rep systems more fully, gradually increase the pressure of your palms pressing together.

Once you have established palm pressure as an anchor, try using it for patterns requiring internal awareness, or with creating a basic trance or awareness meditation.

You can get better with internal sensory awareness by doing the above tip, but by focusing on rep systems in sequence.

Imagine running through an imaginary sequence of behavior, rotating through the above rep systems. You could first try this on a simple task, such as walking.

Notice what rep system is your weakest one, and do this exercise additional times with your focus on that system.

To enhance your ability to integrate your senses, go through this exercise while practicing attending to all systems at once. You might start with rotating through very rapidly, or explore dialing them in as a blend much as you would adjust submodalities.

∽

19.

Collapsing Anchors

*"Whatever you do, you need courage. Whatever course
you decide upon, there is always someone to tell you that
you are wrong. There are always difficulties arising that tempt
you to believe your critics are right. To map out a course of action
and follow it to an end requires some of the same courage that
a soldier needs. Peace has its victories, but it takes brave
men and women to win them".*

— Ralph Waldo Emerson

CREDITS FOR THE creation of this NLP pattern belong to various contributors.

This pattern helps in changing a dysfunctional response.

It involves triggering an anchor for a negative state and one for a positive state simultaneously. The result is an opportunity to reprocess the stuck pattern involved.

The Collapsing Anchors Pattern may help resolve dysfunctional thought / behavioral patterns that have been difficult to change.

The result is greater ease in bypassing the dysfunctional state, and spontaneous generation of more appropriate states for coping with the challenging situation that has been reprocessed.

Many people say that the anchor collapse kind of strange; but in a good way. The collapsing anchors pattern serves to free you from negative feelings that a situation or memory triggers in you.

The pattern starts by establishing an anchor for the negative feeling. Then you create a different anchor that is loaded with positive states. Once the positive anchor is more powerful than the negative one, you fire both anchors at one time.

The result, at first, feels strange. The person's eyes may dart around, as if their mind is trying to restore some kind of order or make sense of things. The end result is that the person is freed from the association between the trigger situation and the negative feelings.

The anchors are usually on opposite sides of the body, such as one spot on each knee. Placing the feelings in the palm of each hand, and then bringing the palms together also collapses the anchors.

Overview: The Collapsing Anchors Pattern

Step #1. Select a problem involving a spontaneous negative state, and establish an anchor for inducing it

Step #2. Break state

Step #3. Elicit a positive state.

Step #4. Amplify the state.

Step #5. Elaborate on the state.

Step #6. Anchor the resourceful state.

Step #7. Break state.

Step #8. Trigger the states.

Step #9. Release the anchors.

Step #10. Test your work.

Step #11. Strengthen the anchor.

Step #1. Select a problem involving a spontaneous negative state, and establish an anchor for inducing it.

Choose a problem that is part of a stuck, dysfunctional pattern.

Create an anchor for the negative state.

Step #2. Break state

Break the negative state. (For instructions, see the State Interrupt pattern.)

Step #3. Elicit a positive state.

Elicit a resourceful, positive state.

Step #4. Amplify the state.

Amplify the state with methods such as enhancing submodalities.

Step #5. Elaborate on the state.

Elaborate on that state, for example, by talking about what you would like to experience in that situation in each rep system.

Step #6. Anchor the resourceful state.

Once the state is firmly established, anchor it.

Step #7. Break state.

Break the resourceful state by clearing your mental screen, opening your eyes and moving around for a moment.

Step #8. Trigger the states.

Fire the anchor for the unresourceful state, then the resourceful state immediately after. Hold both anchors. This supports continued processing. It also helps to periodically remind the person to fully experience their current state. You are likely to observe physiological changes, including facial expressions and eye movements that suggest confusion or processing.

Step #9. Release the anchors.

Once you feel that adequate time to process has take place (halting of the physiological changes usually occurs at that time), release the negative anchor first, then the positive anchor after a brief delay.

Step #10. Test your work.

a. Break state.

b. Fire the anchor of the unresourceful state, or ask the person to attempt to call up their unresourceful state by thinking of the issue. If they are unable to easily experience the unresourceful state, then the pattern was successful.

Step #11. Strengthen the anchor.

a. Break state.

b. Trigger the resourceful state anchor.

c. Enhance the positive state with submodality work and any other appropriate methods.

d. Re-anchor the resourceful state.

Additional Advice

You may need to repeat this a number of times. If so, consider this to be a learning experience that is helping you develop mastery.

ೞ

20.

Perceptual Positions

*"No amount of experimentation can ever prove me right;
a single experiment can prove me wrong".*

— Albert Einstein

PERCEPTUAL POSITIONS CAN really help you with visualization as a tool for excellence.

Perceptual positions are a bit like the persons in grammar, but, of course, these positions are used in NLP for visualization. Let's take a look at each one.

The first position can really help you feel down to earth or grounded. It can help you tune into your own power as a person and feel whole. This first position is seeing the scene through your own eyes. It is called the *"fully associated"* position, because any other position is disconnected from your normal sensory experiences and your thoughts.

In the first position, your seeing, hearing, and feeling are all where they should be when you are 100% in your body and in touch with your senses.

The second position can help you create a more convincing communication strategy. It can help you develop more empathy, understanding people's feelings in a richer way, by walking in the other person's shoes.

In the second position, you see and hear yourself through someone else's eyes, and you imagine experiencing their reaction to you.

The third position is a great way to see things more objectively; without emotions distracting you. In the third position you see yourself as if you are watching a movie of yourself. We have already done a process from the third position. Now you know what to call it. You also see any other people from that more distant position. You can build inner resources from the third position, and you can analyze what's going on from a cool-headed point of view.

"How would this conversation or event look to someone totally uninvolved?" Imagine yourself being out of your body and off to the side of the conversation between you and the other person. You can see both yourself and the other person. The third position allows you to step back, to gain a sense of distance, to observe, to witness, to feel neutral and to appreciate both positions fully.

The fourth position can give you a view of the systems that are involved; systems like the family or organizations that are part of the situation; that are connected with it in some way. The fourth position can help you explore how the situation came to be as it is. This perspective can open up a new channel of creative solutions for any situation; even for situations that appear to involve only one person. That's because every individual is in a cultural and social reality. Remember the NLP presupposition that every communication derives its meaning

from its context. You could say that about every life as well.

In the fourth position, you take on the collective point of view. It's a little like being the sap flowing through all the branches of a tree, you aren't just looking at the tree. As you look at the situation, try saying things like, "The kind of outcomes that would work for us are…" or "The way we should discuss this is…" As you can tell, the fourth position is about us; it's about the collective good and the motives that run through the system, whether it's two people or a global corporation.

The fifth position can give you a cosmic view that is like being enlightened and beyond the whole situation. This cosmic view comes about because the fifth position is more dissociated that any of other positions. Sometimes it can be healing simply because it gives you a transcendent perspective that can bring a sense of peace that you have not experienced in that situation. It can permanently change your experience and your reactions to it.

Getting into the fifth position may take some practice, because it is so foreign to most cultures. Experienced meditators, though, may have already been there and will appreciate seeing how it can be used in NLP.

One way to get a sense of the fifth position is to come from the God place. This is where you imagine being the source of what is going on, whether it's an argument, cancer, or a law suit.

At the same time, you hold the people involved, including yourself, in pure, loving compassion. Then you beam healing and hope into the situation, where that healing and hope are resources that those involved can absorb as they are ready.

If you feel that the universe is a threatening place, or you hate your idea of God, you might appreciate getting a vacation from that state of mind.

What Can I Do with Perceptual Positions?

Here is an example of how you can use perceptual positions. Sometimes you need to imagine a situation without a lot of emotion distracting you. When you get out of first position you can get some of that distance. Sometimes the emotional charge can hold a person back.

They may feel confused, or intimidated. They be close to a creative solution, but see nothing but desire for revenge. They may need to build confidence, but be limited because someone else's voice is in the foreground of their mind, a voice that attacks their identity and confidence.

But that's just the beginning. I'm going to share with you an easy, but powerful way that the second position can help you generate a positive state; a state that can win you a job, a contract, or a date. By getting into the third position, and imagining how you look in a positive state, you can build and amplify that positive state.

You can try this simple process right now.

Imagine watching a movie of yourself walking to a meeting where you need a lot of charisma. While you watch yourself walking, feed a lot of golden charisma energy into yourself. Give yourself great posture and a swinging stride. See the energized confidence on your face.

Remember, this is not to cast a magic spell. This is to help you generate a very positive state that is good for meetings and discussions.

Now imagine yourself in that meeting. But keep the sound turned off so that you can concentrate on the image and the state. See yourself really wowing them with your charisma. Your gestures, your face, your body language, everything. How do you feel doing this? Is it helping you generate a positive state within your real self?

Now see the other people really responding well to everything you do. You can add handshakes, signing of contracts, whatever you like.

Take a moment to enjoy the improvements to your state.

The Aligning Perceptual Positions Pattern (which you can also find in this book) takes perceptual positions to another level.

Here's what we mean by aligned perceptual positions: it means that all three major rep systems are in the same perceptual position at the same time. This ability allows people to do things with NLP that they were unable to do before they learned it.

While some people get stuck in a perceptual position, most of us get our rep systems split out across more than one perceptual position.

How do I know if My Perceptual Positions are Not Aligned?

Let's actually imagine something and see if you get the same thing; the same sense of properly placed senses as you did in real life. Let's see if, in a visualization, you are the center of properly placed senses.

First, pick a situation that is challenging for you, and involves another person, like having an argument with someone...

Imagine yourself in that challenging situation. First, consider what you are seeing. Is your vision 100% exactly where it would be if you were really there, or would you say it is placed a little off from where it should be? Or do you find yourself looking at yourself?

That kind of thing is not aligned with the first perceptual position is it? If vision is not coming from the right place, then it is not coming to you in the way that you experience vision in real life.

Let's try this with hearing. In the imaginary and challenging situation, imagine the sounds you might hear in the situation or add some appropriate sounds... Do they feel that they are coming to you in the same position for real hearing does?

Imagine what the person might say to you… If they are saying what you are thinking, or saying things that are really how YOU feel about yourself, or what YOU feel insecure about, then you are hearing your own thoughts from a different perceptual position. But in the first position, your thoughts should come from where they normally would, not from someone else.

But this can be tricky, especially if you tend to project, that is, if you tend to feel like other people are thinking things ABOUT you that actually come FROM you. If you are very self-conscious, that's probably what's happening, but without you knowing it; it's a subconscious habit.

When people discover this, NLP has just given them a huge gift; the gift of regaining their powers in relationships; power that comes from owning their own thoughts. When you are fully aligned, your internal auditory digital, that is, your verbal thoughts, will be placed so that they very much belong to you and help you feel connected and grounded. You can't feel shy or self-conscious in that state; a fully aligned state.

You can do the same thing with feelings. Do you have emotions in this challenging situation? Tension? And any other feelings?

If you are aligned, they are coming from the part of your body that they should come from. But if your kinesthetic rep system is not aligned, then your feelings may seem to be coming from elsewhere. They might be a little off, or way off, like when you project feelings onto someone else.

A more common problem, though, is when people pick up other people's feelings as their own. This makes a person too easy to manipulate. Con artists, addicts, and other destructive people are drawn to these overly empathic individuals. Codependency involves this problem of being at the mercy of other people's feelings.

How does this work in other perceptual positions?

Other aligned perceptual positions work in pretty much the same way, except from a different point of view. Let's consider the third perceptual position, where you are looking at yourself.

Let's use the movie theater again. You're seeing yourself in that challenging situation, while seated in the seat in the movie theater. When the other person speaks to you in the movie, you don't hear them talking directly to you in your theater seat. Their voice is over near the you that is in the movie.

Your vision of the movie as you watch it should be aligned with your eyes as they would be sitting in the theater. If you are emotional in the movie, you do not feel the emotions, but you might feel empathy.

If you are upset in the movie, you might feel sad about it. Audiences feel all sorts of feelings while they watch movies, of course. You might even feel the same kind of feeling, but from your observer point of view.

If you get as angry as your movie self, the anger probably has a little different quality. You might feel something more like wanting to see revenge or wanting to protect your movie self somehow.

This is a very important point, this idea that you can't feel the feelings of your movie self. If you are truly in third position, you will not feel those exact feelings. Can you see how this could be useful for processes in which the person needs some distance from their feelings?

When a person is not associated into their feelings, they will be less distracted. We use the word "dissociated" for not being associated into your feelings or thoughts.

When people experience extreme dissociation, they feel very disconnected.

With perceptual positions, you can kind of regulate your amount of dissociation so that it's just right for whatever you're doing.

Now here is an advanced secret. When it comes to challenging situations, very few people find that their perceptual positions are aligned. This is true no matter which perceptual position they explore. This is the secret to the power of perceptual position alignment. Once you align your perceptual position, you will have an edge that is rare for people in challenging situations.

Very often, it is the misalignment itself that is the cause of the challenge in the first place. You could say that once you have aligned perceptual positions, you have drained the swamp so you can see whether there really are any alligators to worry about.

☙❧

107

21.

Conflicting Beliefs Integration

"Nothing is so firmly believed as what we least know."

— Michel Eyquem de Montaigne

CREDITS FOR THE creation of this NLP pattern belong to Robert Dilts.

NOTE: Unless you are already a highly experienced NLP practitioner, this pattern may inappropriate for you to try on your own. We suggest that you work with a very competent NLP practitioner who is very mature in his or her own personal work.

Conflicting beliefs can cause self-sabotage and prevent people from assertively pursuing their goals. They can undermine relationships of all kinds. This pattern assists in aligning beliefs so that they are accurate and synergistic.

Overview: The Conflicting Beliefs Integration Pattern

Step #1. Select and state an issue that involves conflicting beliefs.

Step #2. Identify the ideal outcome for this issue.

Step #3. Step into a meta-position

Step #4. Elicit the opposing divisive beliefs.

Step #5. Identify the shared mission of the parts.

Step #6. Explore the resources of each part that can help create the positive future.

Step #7. Re-Anchor the resource state, and work with the anchor.

Step #8. Step into a meta-position opposite (across the timeline) from the first meta-position that you created.

Step #9. Test

Step #1. Select and state an issue that involves conflicting beliefs.

a. Examine your personal issues, and identify one that has conflicting beliefs. State the beliefs as specifically as you can. One of the beliefs is likely to be irrational, so it may be a little embarrassing to express it.

For example, you might, deep down at a gut level, believe that an intimidating person that you have to deal with is capable of destroying your self esteem. Your increased heart rate when you encounter this person is a good sign that there is an irrational fear.

b. State the beliefs as specifically as you can, starting with the words *"I believe that _____ , but at the same time I also believe that _____"*. State any irrational beliefs without censoring or altering it. The more irrational it sounds, the better.

Step #2. Identify the ideal outcome for this issue.

a. Identify an ideal future outcome and time frame for it.

Clearly identify the ideal future outcome of this issue. The best outcome for this purpose is an outcome that one of the beliefs is interfering with.

Select a good time in the future for the ideal outcome to take place.

b. Generate and anchor a related resource state.

Imagine that you are stepping into that point in the future.

What are you like, as the person experiencing that outcome?

What other changes have taken place?

Especially notice what it is like to have the more successful belief fully liberated and engaged. Select a trigger for this state and anchor it.

c. Imagine what you overcame to achieve the outcome.

Now look back and see what obstacles you overcame to reach that successful point in time.

d. Identify the point of origination of the obstacles.

Look back even farther to the time or times that the obstacles originated. Imagine stepping back into the most significant point in time.

Notice especially what it is like to have the more unsuccessful belief inflamed and active at that time.

For many of us, it is better to think of a point at which a number of negative patterns came into focus as a belief that could be put into words. A history of patterned abuse or neglect, developmental problems, drug abuse, chronic difficulties such as ADD, a serious career crash, or a toxic relationship that ruptured your self-esteem over time can be considered a theme.

You can identify a point at which a dysfunctional or unresourceful belief and physiology emerged as an identifiable state. The point at which things were at their worst and it was difficult to see a positive outcome might be a good point to select on your timeline in this case.

e. Notice the polarity comprised by the two beliefs.

Notice how the future successful belief, and the past, less successful belief comprise two opposing elements, such as logic versus emotion, or rationality versus intuition, immature versus mature beliefs, and so forth.

For example, the belief *"I can't succeed or people will expect too much from me,"* versus, *"I thrive on meaningful challenges and enjoy expressing my drive to succeed,"* could be divided into drives for security and avoiding embarrassment versus adventure and risk.

f. Identify the two beliefs as parts with states.

Notice the differing physiologic manifestations of each conflicting belief. Your thought patterns, emotional feelings and other physiology comprise two different, conflicting states.

Pay special attention to asymmetry in the feelings or related body language such as gestures you would make differently in these two states. Think of them as two "parts" for this NLP pattern.

Step #3. Step into a meta-position

Select a meta-position located off your timeline and dissociated from the beliefs and identities.

Step into this position.

Step #4. Elicit the opposing divisive beliefs.

Have each part express its beliefs regarding the other part. They are likely to express distrust, disgust, and other charged judgments.

a. Have the parts face each other.

Have the parts turn to face each other. Notice how this causes the perception of each part to shift.

You might notice, for example, that the future part can see the past part as reacting to inappropriate judgments by adults that as a child you were highly motivated to avoid.

This suggests a part that needs help unfolding its potential, rather than a part that is disgusting or just a threat to success.

b. Identify the positive motivations of each part.

Identify for each part the underlying positive motivations.

Have each part recognize the positive intentions of the other.

Step #5. Identify the shared mission of the parts.

Still in your meta-position, identify the mission that these parts share according to your higher values. For example, achieving success with adequate preparation and effective strategies. This example captures the positive essence of both parts.

Step #6. Explore the resources of each part that can help create the positive future.

Think about the resources and capacities that each part has to offer, and that can help the other part in achieving the positive future that you already explored in this process.

Reviewing the positive motivations and common mission of the two parts can help you come up with more of these resources and capacities. For example, your future scenario will rely upon your analytical skills as well as your passion for the most meaningful elements of the positive outcome and the path to that outcome.

a. Gain an agreement from the parts to work together.

Gain an ecologically sound agreement from the two parts to combine their resources and accomplish their common mission. You have already harmonized their resources, so your previously conflicting parts are ready for a new, powerful alignment.

b. Work with deeper limiting beliefs as needed.

This is the point at which you may discover limiting beliefs that are even deeper or more neglected than the ones you have unearthed so far. If this process has good momentum for you, it may be possible to refine and update these beliefs. If they are challenging, then you may want to subject them to this process from step one at another time. The anchor you have established can help you do this more effectively.

Step #7. Re-Anchor the resource state, and work with the anchor.

Return to the point on your timeline representing your desired future identity. Re-anchor the state that is aligned with this identity. This state includes your positive intent and the sense of your parts' common mission.

The state you are re-anchoring is actually an expanded and enhanced version of the first future state that you anchored.

a. Holding the anchor, move to a point prior to the less successful identity.

Hold the anchor, moving off of the timeline and back to a point that is just behind (earlier than) the past, less successful, identity.

b. Move your future successful self to that point, and act as a mentor.

Have your future successful self step back along your timeline to that past point.

Have this successful self act as a mentor to you in that past point, providing any needed support and resources.

c. Receive this mentoring in the first perceptual position.

CONFLICTING BELIEFS INTEGRATION

Associate into that past identity and experience that point in time while receiving mentoring and resources from your future, successful self.

d. Take the resources into the future point, causing the parts to contain the resources of both parts.

Maintain your focus on the resources of the two identities and the positive changes that are taking place now.

Slowly move forward in the timeline, carrying these resources, until you step into the point that you established in the future. This way, each part has the resources of both parts within it.

Notice all changes in you that result from the integration taking place.

Step #8. Step into a meta-position opposite (across the timeline) from the first meta-position that you created.

Recall the meta-position that you established off of your timeline.

Create a new meta-position on the opposite side of the timeline from that one.

Step into this new meta-position.

a. Have yourself (from your meta-position) and the two parts walk together.

Imagine the past and future parts walking towards each other along the timeline, as you move from your meta-position toward your timeline at the same pace as the parts.

b. Bring the identities into you.

When the two parts meet, reach out with your hands and gather both identities, bringing them into you.

c. Step into your timeline and face forward in first perceptual position, perceiving things with your parts fully integrated as a single entity.

Step into the timeline, in the first perceptual position (associated), and associate the two parts into your perceptual position, so that you are facing forward, fully integrated as a single rich identity.

d. Walk forward in time to the desired state you had established.

Walk forward until you reach the point at which you had established the desired state.

Step #9. Test

Notice what it's like to think about the conflicting beliefs that you started with.

You should feel much more resourceful and unified that you did in the past.

Additional Advice

If the conflict involves more that two parts or issues, you can include those issues or do these integrations in sequence, one pair at a time.

Remember that this is an advanced pattern that may require further training and assistance before it is appropriate to carry out.

☙

22.

Belief Out-Framing

"The idea that seeing life means going from place to place and doing a great variety of obvious things is an illusion natural to dull minds."

— Charles Horton Cooley

CREDITS FOR THE creation of this NLP pattern belong to Robert Dilts.

Question a limiting belief or assumption and consider alternative opinions. This pattern uses the law of requisite variety to accomplish this create excellence in this skill.

Introduced to the cybernetics field by *W. Ross Ashby*, the **"Law Of Requisite Variety"** says – *"If a system is to be stable the number of states of its control mechanism must be greater than or equal to the number of states in the system being controlled"*.

Ashby states the Law as *"only variety can destroy variety"*.

In NLP we use the Out-Framing approach to doubt an existing non-resourceful belief and loosen its neurological "fibers". By doing so, we weaken the belief and make room for a more resourceful one.

Overview: The Belief Out-framing Pattern

Step #1. Create the grid.

Step #2. Move into First Position (Self).

Step #3. Move out of the grid.

Step #4. Repeat with the remaining cells.

Step #5. From The Other Cells

Step #6. From the First Cell, integrate the valuable new information.

Step #1. Create the grid.

Imagine a two-dimensional grid with Past, Present, and Future timeframes on one axis, and Self, Other and Observer perceptual positions on the other axis.

Step #2. Move into First Position (Self).

Associate into the Self position, Present timeframe cell on the grid.

Note any limiting beliefs pertaining to your goals that arise in this cell.

Step #3. Move out of the grid.

Move outside of the grid, leaving the limiting beliefs in their cell.

Step #4. Repeat with the remaining cells.

Do steps two and three for each of the surrounding cells.

Unless the situation dictates a different order, use the one offered below.

Before you proceed, become familiar with the meaning of each cell.

a. First Position, Future:

Treat it as a future in which the limiting beliefs and related issues are resolved.

b. Second Position, Future:

Imagine a mentor that fosters your resourcefulness and totally believes in you and your ability to transform.

c. Third Position, Future:

Picture a wise, compassionate being who is observing your future.

d. Second Position, Present:

Imagine a mentor in the present.

e. Third Position, Present:

Picture a wise, compassionate observer with a detailed but big-picture grasp of your present.

f. First Position, Past:

Imagine yourself in the past, with a positive perspective of your accomplishments, gifts, and skills, as well as the dreams that had already come true for you by that time.

g. Second Position, Past:

Think of a real or imaginary person who is a past and significant mentor.

Imagine this person as having a valuable perspective of your situation now.

h. Third Position, Past:

Think of an observer who has an objective, compassionate perspective on your past and how it is connected to your future.

Step #5. From The Other Cells

From each cell, see yourself and the limiting beliefs you found in the First Position, Present, but from the perspective of each of the other cells, described above.

From each of those perspectives, provide an alternative belief

or meaningful message to help the "you" in First Position, Present become better able to doubt the limiting beliefs you found in that position, and to become more open to alternative beliefs.

Step #6. From the First Cell, integrate the valuable new information.

Associate into your First Person, Present, along with those limiting beliefs.

This time, receive the alternative beliefs and meaningful messages from each cell.

Notice how this alters your experience of these limiting beliefs and your state in that cell.

Directly state that you are experiencing more openness to these alternative perspectives, and describe them as you receive them. *"I am open to the idea that..."*

Additional Advice

You will need to create the grid in order to keep track of these alternatives, resourceful messages. If you are prolific, just write them as you go, preceding them with the name of the cell you are in at the time. Start with your limiting beliefs.

❧

23.

Colliding & Colluding Beliefs

*"The opinion prevailed among advanced minds that it was
time that belief should be replaced increasingly by knowledge;
belief that did not itself rest on knowledge was superstition,
and as such had to be opposed".*

— Albert Einstein

CREDITS FOR THE creation of this NLP pattern belong to Robert Dilts.

Replace stress and frustration with empowerment and confidence, by resolving conflicting and colluding beliefs. This pattern is primarily for interpersonal situations. By *colluding*, we mean beliefs that unconsciously interfere with our success in a way that is interlaced with other beliefs.

Overview: The Colliding and Colluding Beliefs Pattern

Step #1. The Situation

Step #2. Your Belief

Step #3. Their Belief

Step #3. Colluding Belief

Step #4. Meta-Position

Step #5. Positive Foundation

Step #6. Resourceful State

Step #1. The Situation

Identify a situation in which your beliefs conflict with those of another person.

Step #2. Your Belief

Describe your beliefs that collide with this person's beliefs.

Step #3. Their Belief

Describe the other person's beliefs that collide with yours. Associate fully into these beliefs.

Identify which belief is the primary focus of the conflict.

Below are generic beliefs. One of these is likely to apply here.

Mark it with "OT" for "other" (meaning the other party's conflicting belief), and circle the word choice that applies (i.e. "is/is not"). Remember, you are identifying the other party's limiting belief.

a. The objective is/is not desirable and worthwhile.

b. This goal can/cannot be achieved.

c. The actions necessary to achieve this goal are/are not sufficiently detailed, understandable, appropriate, or ecologically sound.

d. I do/don't have the skills or talents that I would need in order to reach this goal.

e. I do/don't deserve to attain this goal.

f. I am/am not responsible for this goal.

Step #3. Colluding Belief

Move out of your conflicting belief state.

Look for colluding beliefs, that is, beliefs of YOURS that in some way reinforce the OTHER person's limiting belief that you perceive as troublesome.

Use the list above.

Mark the applicable belief with a "CL" for "colluding."

Step #4. Meta-Position

Move out to a meta-position where you can be free of the conflict/collusion reality.

From this fresh position, find alternative frames of reference and concepts that can help you find innovative and practical solutions. The following steps are helpful Neuro Linguistic Programming maneuvers intended for transformational processes such as this one.

a. Presuppositions

Note the presuppositions that underlie the beliefs. Typically, these are not conscious, so you will need to be sure you are thinking outside of your current, conventional frame. The following presuppositions can help you here.

1) *"There is no single correct map,"* versus, *"I have the one true map."*

2) *"There is a positive intention behind every behavior and belief,"* versus, *"The behavior (or belief) is negative and must be eliminated."*

3) *"People have the capabilities they need,"* versus, *"Some people are just defective."*

4) *"We are all part of the larger ecosystem,"* versus, *"We are independent entities, and context does not matter."*

b. Positive Intentions

Associate back into the three belief states, and clarify the positive intentions underlying each of them.

c. Meta-Program Level

Move back into the meta-position that you established, and identify the similarities and differences at the meta-program level that exist between these beliefs. Refer to the meta-program appendix as needed.

d. Supportive State

Associate into each belief position again, this time identifying the state that most supports each of the beliefs.

Step #5. Positive Foundation

Return to your first meta-position, and answer these questions for each of the beliefs you have identified:

How could you fill in the missing NLP presupposition?

How could you realize the positive intentions of the beliefs in a constructive manner?

How could you align and balance the meta program patterns?

How could you alter your state or that of the other party so that it is more open to a constructive and ecologically sound resolution?

Step #6. Resourceful State

Develop a resourceful state that embraces the emerging positive beliefs. Maintain that state as you step into your first position. From there, mentally role play new ways of responding to the other party.

24.

Parts Negotiation

"But I do nothing upon myself, and yet I am my own executioner".

— John Donne

CREDITS FOR THE creation of this NLP pattern belong to various contributors.

Win the battle for will power and succeed with inner alignment. Eliminate self-sabotage and liberate energy for commitment and innovative problem solving. Enjoy the pleasures of life, knowing that you are leading a balanced life.

This happens when your parts are working together effectively.

A part is a constellation of motives and attitudes, and can be largely subconscious. It may be irrational according to your consciously-held standards. It includes a state that you can recall experiencing and associate into when needed.

Overview: The Parts Negotiation Pattern

Step #1. Select the behavior.

Step #2. Identify the parts.

Step #3. Specify the outcomes that the parts desire.

Step #4. Identify the meta-outcomes that the part is contributing to.

Step #5. Create inter-part understanding.

Step #6. Negotiate an agreement.

Step #7. Seal the deal.

Step #8. Test.

THE BIG BOOK OF NLP TECHNIQUES

Step #1. Select the behavior.

Select a behavior that you feel is detracting from your success or excellence, and that represents to aspects or parts of you.

Step #2. Identify the parts.

Determine what part primarily supports this behavior and prevents alternative behaviors.

Also identify the part that creates your concern about this behavior. This second part is expressing your distress at not achieving something or at being poorly aligned with your higher values.

Step #3. Specify the outcomes that the parts desire.

Describe what each part wants. Think in terms of outcomes. You can identify with (or associate into) a part, and speak from its point of view to get a rich expression of outcomes in terms of VAK, values, and situations that trigger the part.

Do this for one part at a time.

What outcomes is it supporting? This can include positive outcomes, even if it is failing to produce them.

Don't assume that a part actually intends to produce negative outcomes. They may merely be side effects. However, if there are gains (like avoiding effort or

confrontation of some kind) from the negative outcomes, then that is a clue as that the part may be causing (or at least failing to prevent) these negative outcomes.

Step #4. Identify the meta-outcomes that the part is contributing to.

As you'll recall, a meta-outcome is a higher-level outcome. For example, if a part wants an outcome of eating carbohydrate-rich food before bedtime, the meta-outcome might be that it has learned that this will reduce your anxiety from having unstructured time at night, and even help you sleep.

If you thought the meta-outcome was to make you fat, this is probably actually an unintended out-come. On the other hand, some people feel vulnerable when they lose weight. In that case, the meta-outcome for getting or staying fat would be to feel less vulnerable, and perhaps attract less interest from the opposite sex as an immature means of being protected from child abuse that actually ended a long time ago.

Step #5. Create inter-part understanding.

Make sure each part understands the positive values and roles that the other part is responsible for.

Convey to each part how their behavior interferes with the activity of the other part, and how this lies at the heart of the problem.

Step #6. Negotiate an agreement.

Negotiate an agreement between the parts. Start with a question such as, *"If the other part agrees to refrain from interfering with you, will you refrain from interfering with the other part?"*

Get an internal sense of the response.

Work with these parts until they reach an agreement.

The better you understand the needs that these parts fill (by understanding their positive intentions and roles), the for effective

you will be at facilitating this negotiation.

Step #7. Seal the deal.

Ask each part for a trial period during which it will commit to cooperating. Also, get a commitment to signal you if it is dissatisfied for any reason. That will be a point at which negotiation will be needed again.

Step #8. Test.

In the coming days and weeks, see if your problem behavior improves and if you have new, more resourceful behaviors.

Notice any ecological problems or other nuances that require you to do more parts negotiation.

Notice if there are any additional parts that need to be involved in negotiating on this issue.

☟

25.

Dis-Identification

"Memory is a way of holding on to the things you love, the things you are, the things you never want to lose".

— Kevin Arnold

CREDITS FOR THE creation of this NLP pattern belong to various contributors.

Gain new freedom and capacity by *dis*-identifying with limiting beliefs. Sometimes we over-identify with some facet of our life experiences-our beliefs, body, gender, race, etc. This is limiting in itself, but we may also over-identify with even more seriously limited aspects of ourselves.

For example, we may identify with behavior or thought patterns that construct a victim, dependent, or otherwise unsuccessful self. Terror organizations are known to be very thorough in their propaganda, leading individuals into a state of over-identification with the organization's distorted values, perspectives and beliefs. No wonder that young somnambulistic individuals are willing to strap a suicide bomb to themselves and kill innocent people only to keep their learned deformed identification in tact.

This pattern serves to correct over-identification.

Overview: The Dis-Identification Pattern

Step #1. Supporting Belief
Step #2. Dis-Identify with language.
Step #3. Dis-Identify through trance.
Step #4. Alternate Self & Function
Step #5. Transcendental Identity
Step #6. Amplify in Higher Self

Step #1. Supporting Belief

Try this belief on for size:

"You have a self that is beyond your circumstances, your familiar abilities, behaviors, creative expression, speech, strivings, and even your thoughts".

Step #2. Dis-Identify with language.

Change the frame for all the things about you, such as those in step one.

Use this phrase, "I have (say the thing about you, such as "talent"), but I am not (the same thing, e.g. "talent").

Include thoughts, ("I am not my thoughts.")

Step #3. Dis-Identify through trance.

By accessing a deeply relaxed state, sense yourself as bigger than the things in step one. *"If I lost (fill it in), my core self would remain".*

Step #4. Alternate Self & Function

Notice how you can think about these traits of yours as being functions; a way of getting a result or making your way through the world.

Notice how you have a sense of self that transcends functions.

Step #5. Transcendental Identity

Tune into your sense of a greater self that exists beyond the things that you identify with.

Notice how you can sense a state of pure consciousness, as you have in trance or meditation.

Represent this with a word or phrase that captures the essence of that experience, or see what symbol comes to mind. The words or symbol that emerge spontaneously may be the most significant.

Step #6. Amplify in Higher Self

Notice the submodalities of this sense of higher self and amplify them in any way that enhances it and strengthens your connection with and identification with it.

Move it to the center of your existence and place your consciousness in the center of this higher self Imagine what it's like to live and express yourself from this sense of higher self.

ര∕ാ

26.

Resolving Internal Conflicts

"It's important to realize that we define ourselves not only by who we are, but by who we are not".

— Anthony Robbins, Awaken The Giant Within

CREDITS FOR THE creation of this NLP pattern belong to various contributors.

This pattern helps with the very common problem of disagreement between parts. When you struggle with yourself to do or not do something, when you procrastinate and seem to be arguing with yourself in your mind, this is the pattern to use.

Overview: The Resolving Internal Conflict Pattern

Step #1. The Conflict

Step #2. A Memory

Step #3. Take a Side

Step #4. Positive Intention

Step #5. Switch

Step #6. Repeat

Step #7. Meta-Position

Step #8. New Part

Step #9. Future Pace and Test

Step #1. The Conflict

Select a personal conflict. It may be something you're ambivalent about, or some way that you sabotage yourself or cannot accept yourself.

Step #2. A Memory

Recall a memory of experiencing this inner conflict. View it from the observer position.

Step #3. Take a Side

Get into the first perceptual position with one side of the conflict.

Step into the experience.

Review the OTHER side of the conflict from this position.

Notice what comes up during this in all sense modes.

Step #4. Positive Intention

Still on that side, ask the other side to express all of its positive intentions, including any beliefs and goals that it can express to your side.

Step #5. Switch

Now step into the other part.

From this position, repeat steps three and four.

Step#6. Repeat

Repeat this switching and receiving until both sides have a good understanding of each other.

Be sure to include beliefs, values, and objectives.

Step #7. Meta-Position

Move to a meta-position above both parts.

From there, ask the parts to propose solutions or outcomes that they expect to be satisfactory to both sides. Elicit concerns from either side about these ideas, and note any ecological issues.

Do as much brain-storming as you need to in order to come up with a good collection of ideas.

Step #8. New Part

Notice how this new collection of ideas is an amalgam of the values and higher intentions of the two parts. It is also an agenda.

Experience how it could be considered a part all on its own.

Bring this part into your body and accept it as an important part.

Step #9. Future Pace and Test

Imagine a future with this part creating results for you.

Redo this process as needed for any ecological concerns or problems.

Test it out in real life and come back to this process as needed.

❀

27.

Making Peace With Your Parents

"Everybody knows how to raise children, except the people who have them".

— P. J. O'Rourke

CREDITS FOR THE creation of this NLP pattern belong to Robert McDonald .

Liberate a great deal of energy, creativity, and personal development by resolving old issues with your parents. This is done IN your mind, not necessarily in direct contact with your parents.

This may go on quite unconsciously, but it is no less harmful that way. A deeper issue is that many of us have absorbed the attitude that a parent (or other caretaker) held toward us as children.

This not only limits us directly, but also makes it difficult to fully express the resources that our parents gave us.

Many people continue to struggle with their parents, either in real life or internally as representations. Some notice that they speak to their children with the same content and in the same tone of voice as their parents did with them, but they cannot control it. Even though they promised themselves many times to "never be like my father" or "never be like my mother", they get caught again and again in the same thought patterns and behaviors as their parents did with them.

The first strategy you will notice in your client's behavior, as they come to you with such an issue, is that they use their will power to control their automatic behavioral responses. They may succeed from time to time, but eventually our "programming" (which some people mistakingly call, "genes")

129

wins over. They cannot avoid it because they keep thinking about it.

You should first explain to your client that their parents must have done the best they could, given their limited resources in education, competence, knowledge on parenthood and finances. Their parents must have treated the children (your client) the same as their parents (your client's grandparents) did with them. The heritage of conflict and poisonous criticism and harsh discipline does not have to move on to their children.

The most elegant and mind easing way to help them overcome this situation is if they agree to forgive their parents for mistakes they could not control.

Overview: The Making Peace With Your Parents Pattern

Step #1. Select a conflict with your parents for this pattern.

Step #2. Tune into your negative maternal representations.

Step #3. Concentrate these representations.

Step #4. Constellate these into a shape.

Step #5. Break state.

Step #6. Do steps two through five for your father representations.

Step #7. Elicit your maternal and paternal positive intentions.

Step #8. Thank the parts.

Step #9. Have the parts appreciate each other.

Step #10. Combine the parts.

Step #11. Store the new part.

Step #12. Future pace.

Step #13. Test.

Step #1. Select a conflict with your parents for this pattern.

Think of a conflict with one or both parents or caretakers. The conflict does not have to be current, and your parent does not have to be living.

Pick a conflict that you would like to resolve, or that you feel is limiting you in some way. For example, it may be absorbing your mental or emotional energy.

In these steps, we will work with your internal representation of a male and female parent.

If your situation does not match, you can select an appropriate childhood authority figure or influence for the missing gender parent.

Step #2. Tune into your negative maternal representations.

Focus on the areas in your body and mental space where you find feelings and other representations related to the conflict and negative aspects of your mother figure.

Step #3. Concentrate these representations.

Imagine these feelings and other representations flowing from your body and mind into the palm of your left hand.

Continue until you have them all represented in your palm.

Step #4. Constellate these into a shape.

Invite these representations to function like energy that can coalesce into a solid, visible shape.

Step #5. Break state.

Distract yourself with an activity such as thinking about a travel route or by tying your shoes in order to break your state.

Step #6. Do steps two through five for your father representations.

Tune into your negative paternal representations, concentrate them into the palm of your RIGHT hand, and constellate them into a solid shape. Break state.

Step #7. Elicit your maternal and paternal positive intentions.

Ask your mother image what positive intentions she had underneath the negative actions that led to your representations.

Continue to solicit these meta-intentions until you feel that you have a complete sense of this.

The intentions may not have been rational, but you have many hints from your childhood as to her underlying positive intentions.

You might phrase your question as, *"What good thing were you trying to do for me with these behaviors and attitudes?"*

Repeat this with your father representation.

Step #8. Thank the parts.

Directly thank the parts for participating in this pattern, and validate their positive intentions for you.

Step #9. Have the parts appreciate each other.

Have the parts face each other and express appreciation of each other's participation in this pattern, and their positive intentions.

Step #10. Combine the parts.

Tell the parts that they can not become a single, more positive and powerful force by combining into a single entity.

Ask them if they are willing to proceed with this. If not, resolve any ecological issues.

Then slowly bring your hands together and allow the images to merge into a single entity.

Keep your hands closed together until you have had some time to integrate this change.

Then open your hands to reveal the new entity.

Step #11. Store the new part.

Discover where in your body or mental space that you would like to place this new part so that it can become an integrated aspect of your resources.

Touch the area where you will store these re-sources.

Maintain contact with it to establish an anchor as you bring the image into that area.

Allow the feelings to carry you back through your childhood and into your mother's womb and infused with these positive feelings.

Now allow these resourceful feelings that are resonating throughout your body and mind to carry you through your live, literally growing you up to this present moment in your adulthood.

Step #12. Future pace.

Continue to touch the anchor and step into the future so you can imagine your future with these re-sources.

Step #13. Test.

In the coming days and weeks, notice any changes in your relationship with your parents if they are alive, and any authority figures or intimate relationships.

Notice any ways that you feel yourself powered by these resources.

☜☞

28.

Six Steps Reframing

"I am a world-class weenie when it comes to letting people stick needles into me. My subconscious mind firmly believes that if God had wanted us to have direct access to our bloodstream, He would have equipped our skin with small, clearly marked doors".

— Dave Barry, Author of Dave Barry's History of the Millennium (So Far)

CREDITS FOR THE creation of this NLP pattern belong to John Grinder.

Elicit subconscious resources in order to change a habit by producing alternative behaviors.

Overview: The Six Steps Reframing Pattern

Step #1. Select the behavior.

Step #2. Establish the signal.

Step #3. Elicit the positive intentions.

Step #4. Produce alternative behaviors.

Step #5. Solicit the signal that the behaviors are selected.

Step #6. Future pace and ecology check.

Step #1. Select the behavior.

Select a behavior of yours that you would like to stop or change.

The behavior should be one for which you can say, *"I need to stop (behavior)'ing,"* or *"I want do to (behavior) but I just can seem to do it."*

Step #2. Establish the signal.

Ask the part that creates the behavior to give you a signal (such as lifting a finger) that will mean yes. If the part does not provide a signal, trust for now that there are positive underlying motives for the problem behavior.

Step #3. Elicit the positive intentions.

Ask the part to bring to mind the positive intentions of the behavior that you'd like to change.

Step #4. Produce alternative behaviors.

Ask your creative part to produce three alternative behaviors that would fulfill the needs revealed in the prior step.

Step #5. Solicit the signal that the behaviors are selected.

Ask your part that produces the problem behavior to give the signal when it is satisfied that there are three behaviors that will fill the needs it revealed in step three.

If the part did not cooperate in step two, then ask it now if it will participate by providing a yes signal. If not, then assume for now that you have come up with good alternatives that you will test in the next step.

Step #6. Future pace and ecology check.

a. Future pace the behaviors several times each.

Detect and mitigate for any ecological difficulties.

Re-run this pattern as needed.

b. Try out the behaviors in real life and see if the behavior change you desire takes place. If not, think in terms of ecology (such as parts conflicts) and re-try this pattern in order to refine your behavior change work.

Additional Advice

If you would like to do a version of this pattern that is more conscious (less "new code") because of the circumstances or because you'd like to do more intensive brainstorming, then you can write down the motives (from step two) and alternatives (in step three) as quickly as possible until you feel you have satisfied each step.

As soon as you are done with the basic pattern, you should jot down the new behaviors and place the note someplace where it will remind you to try them out. Perhaps it belongs in your appointment book or on the refrigerator.

29.

Content Reframing

"How many of you have broken no laws this month? That's the kind of society I want to build. I want a guarantee — with physics and mathematics, not with laws — that we can give ourselves real privacy of personal communications".

— John Gilmore

CREATE DRAMATIC improvements in yourself and others by applying one of the most fundamental methods for getting a change in perspective.

As you'll recall, a frame in NLP is the way you limit what you consider. It's impossible to consider every piece of information in your world in order to made a decision, so no matter what you think about anything, there is a frame.

In Neuro Linguistic Programming we do reframing in order to change the existing frame and get a better outcome as a result.

Let's use a reframe to help someone who feels very 'defective'. They tell you that they hate getting out of bed in the morning and their self esteem is terrible because they have no motivation.

Let's say that the person needs to realize that they are in the wrong job. You could ask if they'd have trouble getting out of bed if they were about to go on a vacation to their favorite place in the world. They would say that would be no problem.

Your response: *"So it isn't that you can't get out of bed, it's that your still in that crappy job."*

Now the issue is not that the person is defective, but that they need to mobilize their resources for job or career change. We got there by expanding the frame to include situations in which they could easily get out of bed.

Here is another example. In this one, we actually state the bad frame out loud, and let the person recognize what's wrong with it: A smoker says he thinks he doesn't need to be a purist, even though he has been quitting smoking. He feels there's no harm in a few drags once in a while. He needs to recognize that he has created a false frame of control to under-define a deadly addiction.

If you say, *"So you have complete control over tobacco now, then,"* he is likely to say something like, *"No way, I'm all or nothing, that would get me smoking again in no time!"*

It's helpful when the person states the reframe on their own, since they feel ownership.

For the following steps, we are going to use a pattern of behavior of yours that you don't care for, but you can reframe anything.

Overview: The Content Reframing Pattern

Step #1. Select a behavior you dislike.

Step #2. Identify the part.

Step #3. Identify the positive intention.

Step #4. Identify the frame.

Step #5. De-frame the part.

Step #6. Reframe the behavior and intention (content).

Step #7. Reframe the usefulness in terms of situations (context).

Step #8. Integrate the reframe.

Step #9. Test the reframe.

Step #1. Select a behavior you dislike.

Select a pattern of behavior of yours that you don't care for.

Step #2. Identify the part.

Note the aspect of you that produces this behavior.

Think in terms of parts. Name that part.

Step #3. Identify the positive intention.

Figure out the part's positive intent in producing this behavior.

Step #4. Identify the frame.

What is the frame around the intention and behavior?

You can see this by discovering the presuppositions behind the part's sense of mission and it's behavior in service of that mission. (In the examples we provided, one person thought he was defective because he couldn't get out of bed, and another seemed to think he had complete control over tobacco in order to justify a small amount of smoking.)

Step #5. De-frame the part.

As we ask in the De-framing pattern, how can you expand the part's perspective?

Try to find submodality shifts that will have an impact on this. You can also ask what the behavior and intentions mean to you. You can simply ask, "What else could this mean?"

Step #6. Reframe the behavior and intention (content).

Find the way, however slight, that you can react positively to the part's intentions or to the behavior.

Step #7. Reframe the usefulness in terms of situations (context).

How might this behavior actually serve you in some situation? Connect with how this might feel good or appropriate.

Remember that the behavior may need to take a different form, or even cease, depending on what it is.

You may also find that the underlying motivations can be expressed very differently, so that the behavior is easy to change or eliminate once you learn to satisfy the underlying motivation.

Step #8. Integrate the reframe.

Give yourself permission to make use of this new reframe. Although you may not approve of the way the intention is expressed in some situations, you can now make a good connection with the reframe, because it highlights the positive aspect of the behavior.

Think of ways that you can express the motivation in a more useful way, or that you can direct the behavior in a more useful way.

Step #9. Test the reframe.

How do you feel now when you think of the behavior? How do you feel about the part?

If your self esteem has improved or you feel less in conflict with yourself, that is a good sign that the pattern has been useful. If you have actually come up with a revolutionary and positive way to utilize the underlying motivations, that's even better.

☙❧

30.

Context Reframing

*"When man learns to understand and control his own behavior
as well as he is learning to understand and control the behavior
of crop plants and domestic animals, he may be justified in believing that he has become civilized".*

— Ayn Rand

BUILD AWARENESS of context, and build mental flexibility and creativity. It helps you imagine "importing" a behavior, state, belief, or other aspect of yourself into various contexts.

Overview: The Context Reframing Pattern

Step #1. Identify a resourceful state

Step #2. Ask context questions.

*Step #3. Vividly imagine yourself expressing this aspect in a
typical appropriate context.*

*Step #4. Pick a variety of contexts at random and imagine
yourself expressing this aspect in each of them.*

Step #5. Test

Step #1. Identify a resourceful state

Choose a state, behavior, belief, emotion, aspect of commitment, or some other aspect of yourself that might be helpful for building context awareness.

Step #2. Ask context questions.

Ask yourself where this aspect would be useful. Where would it be an expression of your higher values or self interest?

Step #3. Vividly imagine yourself expressing this aspect in a typical appropriate context.

Step #4. Pick a variety of contexts at random and imagine yourself expressing this aspect in each of them.

Imagine what results are likely to come from expressing this aspect in each context. *What are the effects?* For example, what would come from you taking a negotiat-ing mindset and applying it to a loving relationship.

If at first it seems awkward or objectionable, ask yourself how you would fold it into your other, more typical, forms of self expression as you express this aspect.

For example, negotiating very skillfully, but in a fully loving way. Another example, what would it be like to use highly evolved NLP skills as a prison counselor with a kidnapper?

Step #5. Test

In the next days or weeks, notice any ways that you are thinking more creatively about what aspects of yourself to express in various situations.

Are you more flexible or creative?

Are you more conscious of how you use yourself as a resource for outcomes in any situations?

☯

31.

Reframing Beliefs & Opinions – Examples

"Stiff in opinion, always in the wrong".

— John Dryden

HERE ARE A FEW examples of reframing. When you read the conversation below, notice how one simple shifting of perception can change a person's belief or opinion. This script is a transcript of a recorded conversation between two of my friends in one of our NLP practice group meeting. We recorded all meetings, and luckily for us, we got some great materials out of. This is one:

George: *"I can't imagine living in China, everything there is disgusting!"*

Natasha: *"What do you mean, disgusting? Have you been there?"*

George: *"No, but I read a touristic article about China, and they*

had quite a lot of warnings on the Chinese strange habits"

Natasha: *"What kind of strange habits?"*

George: *"Well, they spit everywhere, in front of you, on the street, in restaurants, on the bus…"*

Natasha: *"They spit everywhere. And you know why?"*

George: *"The article didn't say"*

Natasha: *"I've been in China. I lived in Beijing for about a year. I started spitting everywhere myself after a few weeks"*

George: *"WHY?!"*

Natasha: *"Too much rapport, I guess" (laughing)*

George: *"No, seriously, why do they spit? That's a disgusting* manner, certainly not some-thing tourists would be happy to experience"

Natasha: "Well, I'm sure your article mentioned the extremely polluted air in China. Yes, the Chinese government is the source for this hazard, but the Chinese people are there to suffer it. In such a high polluted environment, you get quite a lot of mucus in your throat... what should they do, swallow it?"

George: "There's no Kleenex in China?!"

Natasha: "There are more than 1,500 million people in China! Can you imagine how many tissue pa-pers they would consume in a day this way?! There would be no trees left after a year!"

George: "Alright, so maybe that's reasonable... still disgust-ing, but reasonable. I guess that's why they don't use diapers..."

Natasha: "Exactly why! You'd have million of dirty diapers stand-ing around"

George: "Alright, toilet paper is one thing. But the article said they eat blood! And bones!"

Natasha: "Of animals, George! Not of human..."

George: "Yes, of course, but why?!"

Natasha: "Same reason as be-fore, it's really economical. Imagine how many animals would have to be butchered if they only ate the animal parts that we eat... they use the blood, by the way, for hot-dogs, and they don't really eat the bones, they put them as extra fla-vor in soups"

George: "Yes, I can imagine how it saves money, and it's prob-ably better without all the biologi-cal waste"

Natasha: "Indeed. Did you change your mind yet?"

George: "A bit. Still strange though. They don't have normal toilets... they have holes instead of a bowl?"

Natasha: "Yes, and this is for hygienic purposes. This way even the public toilets are relatively safe because there is no contact between your skin and the toilet.. You don't need to worry who was there before you. Even the handle for water is operated by foot"

George: "Alright, so many itv's not that disgusting there".

Did you make note of the sim-ple reframing Natasha used here? She didn't even use "facts" as the basis for convincing George. She used known shared values, such as saving the environment, reducing excessive waste and so on. Did you notice the presupposition Natasha gave George in the middle of their short conversation?

෧෧

32.

Basic Inner Conflict Integration

*"If a cluttered desk is the sign of a cluttered mind, what
is the significance of a clean desk?".*

— Laurence J. Peter

CREDITS FOR THE creation of this NLP pattern belong to Richard Bandler/John Grinder.

Improve mood, motivation, and success by resolving internal conflicts between states. Generate resourceful states more consistently by resolving habitual (automatic) negative states.

Robert Dilts, a well-known NLP researcher and master trainer, explains the issue of inner conflict:

"In a typical situation, if we are prevented from reaching a goal due to an external impasse, we maintain our focus on the outcome, inhibit any "antithetical ideas" and continue to attempt other avenues or strategies in order to attain the goal. If there is an internal conflict, however, the "debate ground" shifts inward, and a battle begins between the two parts of one's self. As Freud points out, the external frustration is supplemented by internal frustration. It is as if the person is "caught between a rock and a hard place." And when the fight is between two parts of one's self, one can never 'win'".

Overview: The Basic Inner Conflict Integration Pattern

*Step #1. Notice incongruencies between conscious and
    subconscious communication.*

Step #2. Sort into polarities

Step #3. Integrate the incongruencies.

Step #1. Notice incongruencies between conscious and subconscious communication.

This is done while working with a client on an issue that involves conflict between two directions, but has poor awareness of one of the opposing states.

When exploring the conflict, observe incongruence between the person's conscious and subconscious communication. By this we mean what the person says versus what their body is giving away.

For example, if the person shows anger but denies being angry, you will see body language that contradicts their denial. Anger physiology will show as jaw and lip stiffness, squinting of the eyes, shoulder tension, and maybe even resentment or tension in the voice.

Step #2. Sort into polarities

Some of these incongruencies will have something in common with other incongruencies. If the person really was not angry, they would have relaxed shoulders and other physiology of a "not angry" state.

This observations provides you with a polarity involving two states.

On one end of the polarity is shoulder tension, and, on the other, is relaxed shoulders. The polarity is that of a range of shoulder tension from high to low. Simmering anger is high tension, not being angry is low tension.

Discover more incongruities between these two states, and sort them into polarities as we did with shoulder tension.

To find these incongruities, you are seeking physiology clues.

A good way to detect them, is to have the client enter the very state that their body language is telling you they are not really in.

For example, with the "not angry" state that the angry client insists that they are in, you could help them align with that state by remembering, in first person, what it is like to watch a child play with a very friendly dog.

Once they are fully in the "not angry" state, find out what is happening with every submodality associated with that state. In other words, what they are experiencing in that state.

Now you have moved beyond body language to include submodalities that the client is able to describe for you. This would not have been possible with a client who is not aligned with the state they claim to be in.

This technique is important, because, when people are out of alignment, they can have difficulty being verbal or detailed, or, instead, unconsciously create distractions in order to evade being aware of their schism. The subconscious mind is very creative when it is tasked with this kind of deception.

Sort these incongruencies into their polarities through means such as spatial sorting, symbolic sorting, rep systems, roles, and Satir Categories (i.e., blaming, placating, or rationalizing).

If you don't know about all of these, stick with what is more obvious too you, such as how the client positions them in their mental space and what submodalities they associate with each state.

How the state feels is often the easiest one to elicit. As the client talks about what these states mean to them, note what beliefs appear to drive each state. Thinking of the states as parts may help you derive beliefs that are empowering or limiting.

You are likely to find more than a few negative or limiting beliefs.

To summarize by using an example, fix "depression" in its "space" by having the client recall a recent time that they felt de-pressed, and enter into that state for a few moments.

During that time, elicit submodalities and any other aspects that distinguish these states from each other.

For example, list the predicates, key words, eye accessing cues, and physiology that they use in connection with that state.

As you explore the original issue, you will discover additional states with aspects that can be placed onto polarities.

As you do the sorting, you eventually get to states that do not share enough polarities or similar attributes. At this point, you begin resorting.

On the other hand, some states, such as depression and passion, will be competitive, that is, so incompatible that they cannot be placed on the kind of polarity that we are working with here, because they would be too incongruent.

Step #3. Integrate the incongruencies.

Put each state where it belongs. For example, place depression and happiness in their unique spots, (i.e., their respective spatial locations). Then group similar states in these locations.

a. Make a connection between the polarities.

Have your client group the sensations of the states. To do this, the client must focus on the kinesthetic aspect of the state, bringing it to the foreground, rather than the imagery, sound, and concepts.

In doing this, the client is moving all of the feeling of depression, for example, into a limited space, thereby experiencing it as something that they can control. This makes these states and their feelings less overwhelming and builds in the client a sense of empowerment and hope.

b. Be sure that the client is in a very positive state before proceeding. Your client should be in a very confident state.

Be sure that their positive states are stronger and collectively larger than the other polarities.

Have the client move into a meta position. From there, bring the polarities together in a way what can create new solutions.

◑◐

33.

Mistakes Into Experience

*"The biggest mistake is believing there is one right way to listen,
to talk, to have a conversation — or a relationship".*

— Deborah Tannen

CREDITS FOR THE creation of this NLP pattern belong to Robert Dilts.

Update a behavior that has not been re-evaluated, but that is not working optimally, or is dysfunctional.

Overview: The Mistakes Into Experience Pattern

Step #1.   Select a behavior that needs to be updated.

Step #2.   Elicit the limited beliefs that are part of the behavior.

Step #3.   Think of a negative outcome of this behavior.

Step #4.   Compare the negative outcome to a worse potential outcome.

Step #5.   Identify positive things that resulted from the negative outcome that you identified in step three.

Step #6.   Express the positive intentions underlying the negative behavior.

Step #7.   Discover the positive significance of the bad outcomes.

Step #8.   Re-experience the negative events while in the positive insight state.

Step #9.   Mark and store the wisdom gained from this pattern.

Step #10. Test

Step #1. Select a behavior that needs to be updated.

Choose a recurring behavior pattern that causes some kind of bad outcome. An example: attracting people who violate your boundaries (like someone who shows up to your birthday drunk and starts a fight--it ends up being all about them instead of your birthday).

Step #2. Elicit the limited beliefs that are part of the behavior.

What beliefs encourage this behavior, or limit you from alternative behaviors or outcomes?

Example: "Believing" that you should ask "Why?" over and over instead of coming up with a solution such as setting definite limits with a person who violates your boundaries.

Step #3. Think of a negative outcome of this behavior.

What is a bad outcome of the behavior that has a lot in common with other bad outcomes of the behavior. In other words, it is a fairly predictable type of bad outcome.

For example, having a special day ruined by a person that you have not set limits with.

Step #4. Compare the negative outcome to a worse potential outcome.

Think of something that is even worse, and that actually could have happened as a result of your behavior pattern, but didn't happen.

Step #5. Identify positive things that resulted from the negative outcome that you identified in step three.

Although the negative experience from step three was unfortunate, ask yourself what positive outcomes you can identify.

For example, you may have discovered which one of your friends is the most insightful, because they clearly saw what was going on.

Or perhaps you have gained a lot of knowledge through experience that, once you have put it into action, will constitute tremendous wisdom that you can use to enhance your life and the lives of others.

Step #6. Express the positive intentions underlying the negative behavior.

Your behavior pattern is based on positive intentions of some kind, despite the bad outcomes that have been resulting from it.

Clarify these positive intentions and find a way to express them. They are worth writing down.

Come up with positive intentions of the other people involved, even if they create negative outcomes or intervened in a way that you did not like.

Step #7. Discover the positive significance of the bad outcomes.

What meaning can you take from the bad outcomes that have come from the unresourceful behavior pattern?

For example, you may have realized that you have some very good resources that, once they are used for the right purposes, will serve you well.

You may have realized that there are limits to your stamina or capacity for boundary violations that are worthy of your respect and assertive protection. You may have realized that, once put into action, this wisdom will prevent a tremendous amount of suffering.

Step #8. Re-experience the negative events while in the positive insight state.

Connect fully with the sense of wisdom, putting any feelings of hopelessness or cynicism aside for now.

Realize that this is a positive state. Imagine taking that positive state through the memories you have of those bad experiences, seeing them from a new, resourceful perspective.

Step #9. Mark and store the wisdom gained from this pattern.

Take all the good energy of the positive state, and everything that you have learned from these experiences, and imagine transporting this to the place in your mind where you store the elements of your wisdom.

Tag them in some way that makes them available to you when you encounter situations for which they are relevant, so that you can prevent bad outcomes and generate excellent outcomes.

Step #10. Test

Over the next days or weeks, notice any ways that the problem behavior changes.

For example, do you have better ways to prevent the typical bad outcomes that would come from the behavior.

Example strategies might include being more effective at managing the expectations of others, being more realistic about what you can do, sensing risk factors early enough to take evasive action, and responding more objectively to a situation by keeping things in perspective.

෧෨

34.

Hierarchy Of Criteria

"The whole idea of motivation is a trap. Forget motivation. Just do it. Exercise, lose weight, test your blood sugar, or whatever. Do it without motivation. And then, guess what? After you start doing the thing, that's when the motivation comes and makes it easy for you to keep on doing it".

–John C. Maxwell, author of Talent Is Never Enough

CREDITS FOR THE creation of this NLP pattern belong to Robert Dilts.

Resolve inner conflicts so you can engage consistently in a desired behavior. This pattern uses logical levels and NLP resources in an interweave that deserves some explaining. We encourage you to study this thoroughly. In essence, you will learn to leverage higher levels of criteria in order to produce your desired behavior, despite the resistance, distractions and temptations that have typically sabotaged your efforts in the past.

The Hierarchy Of Criteria pattern addresses a fundamental problem.

Often inner conflict arises from the way higher logical levels override lower ones. This is possible because a desire often gets its drive from more than one level. When these levels work at cross purposes, we can end up sabotaging our higher intentions though procrastination, misplaced priorities, and other self-defeating behavior.

Consider this example:

If you derive personal meaning from helping others, and you have made a career of it, then your Identity level (one of the logical levels) provides much of the drive for your career choice. At the same

153

time, you desire to express your skills and knowledge and to act on habitual behavior. These desires drive your career actions on a day-to-day basis. This example shows three different logical levels driving behavior: Identity (as a helper), Skills/Knowledge (applied to helping), and Behavior (helping).

But what if you want to get a better job so that you can make more money and contribute more by gaining more responsibility in your chosen field? Let's say the answer is that you need to return to school to learn more and get an advanced certification or degree. Although you may be able to say that this goal is connected to your Identity level, it is not enough if that understanding is only an intellectual, conscious one.

If you're strongest connection with going to school is only happening at the skills/knowledge level, then you'll have a problem. That's because your identity level is currently filled with actually carrying out helping behaviors on a day-to-day basis.

This "Identity override" (the Identity level overriding the Behavior level) leaves you procrastinating on going back to school, while your current work absorbs the lion's share of your energies and creativity.

The Hierarchy of Criteria Pattern is designed to help you connect a higher level, such as your identity level, to an important goal, such as going back to school. This creates a strong subconscious drive that causes you to move forward much more easily and creatively.

As you'll see, the power of this pattern comes from its clever integration of several different NLP resources. In addition to logical levels, this pattern can use spatial sorting and the counterexample process.

The Hierarchy Of Criteria pattern will also sharpen your awareness of rep systems and cognitive strategies. It has broad applicability and much flexibility in the hands of an experienced Neuro Linguistic Programming practitioner.

Overview: The Hierarchy Of Criteria Pattern

Step #1. Prepare the page

Step #2. Note the desired behavior.

Step #3. Note the motivating factors.

Step #4. Note the preventing factors.

Step #5. Note the Override criteria.

Step #6. Leverage the process by anchoring the behavioral content from Override.

Step #7. Apply the highest Override criterion.

Step #8. Engineer the desired behavior so that it is in harmony with all criteria levels, and fulfill the objectives of the desired behavior.

Step #9. Map and adjust the Override criteria and limiting beliefs.

Step #10. Test

Step #1. Prepare the page

On a piece of paper, in landscape (sideways) position, create five columns with the following headings.

Leave room at the top of the page for two items: *Behavior* and *Override*.

Column 1) Capability
Column 2) Belief
Column 3) Identity
Column 4) Identity

Step #2. Note the desired behavior.

At the top of the page, write down a behavior that you want to engage in, but that you somehow prevent yourself from carrying out.

For example, studying as much as you need to.

Step #3. Note the motivating factors.

In column #1, Capability, list the factors that give you the most motivation to engage in the positive behavior.

Emphasize factors related to skills, possessions, and knowledge that build and result from your capability to do this behavior.

For example, getting into a top-notch grad program, getting into a great career, or having a nice house.

Note the strategy, meta-program patterns, and submodalities that tell you that each criterion is motivational.

For example, the idea of a great career goes along with the eager excitement in the solar plexus.

The things that feed into that positive feeling include the desirable challenge and desire for prestige.

Refer to the meta-programs appendix as needed.

Step #4. Note the preventing factors.

In column #2, Belief, list the factors that prevent you from carrying out the desired behavior.

Emphasize thoughts, beliefs, attitudes, and values, including any that seem irrational.

Include any resistance or objections that pop up and take you away from your desired behavior, even if you have never put them in words before.

Take yourself through the process of getting pulled away from your desired behavior and analyze it as though it was a formal decision-making process.

Look for strategies, meta-programs, and submodalities that drive these decisions.

Look for the criteria that the decisions are based on.

For example, *"I do not study as much as I need to because it is stressful and I run out of time."*

Another would be, *"When I study and the phone rings, it seems important to answer, even though I know it will be a friend who will distract me from studying. The submodalities are that the ring is in the center of my attention (auditory), and gives rise to feelings (kinesthetic) of relief and excitement that are a very attractive alternative to studying. This creates a sense (kinesthetic) of urgency, so I fail to think (self talk) about setting limits on this. I don't think of myself turning off the ringer (visual)."*

Step #5. Note the Override criteria.

Carefully think about your criteria for your desired behavior from column #1. Think about how these criteria make you aware of criteria at higher levels, including the Identity level.

Jot down any ideas that occur to you in the appropriate column or on a separate sheet if you like.

Continue until you are able to select one criterion that is the highest and most powerful of all.

Write this one down in the space just below the behavior and put a big star beside it or highlight it.

In seeking this high criterion, it might be helpful to ask, *"What strikes me as being so important that I would always have time for it, and that stress would not prevent me from doing?"*

Note what personal value of yours that it satisfies so that it achieves this superior level of importance, (e.g. "preventing tooth decay is a value that means I never forget to brush my teeth twice a day.").

Elicit the strategy, meta-programs, and submodalities that drive this criterion.

For example, preventing tooth decay is represented as seeing bad teeth (visual constructed) and getting a bad feeling about it (kinesthetic). Refer to the meta-programs appendix as needed.

Let's discuss how these levels play out in the example of the student. His problem was that his context contained a convenient temptation (phone calls from friends)

and an aversive (the discipline required for studying).

As a result, the student's behavior appears to be at odds with his identity as a student, and even with his higher values and vision.

Since the conflict is coming from the lowest levels (behavior and context), you can intervene at any of several higher levels, and at the same levels.

For example, students often intervene at the behavioral level by using behavior modification to "outgun" the effects of temptations in their environment.

For example, one student made a rule that he could not leave his study area without doing twenty chin-ups. The chin-ups served as an "aversive stimulus" that reduced his drive to escape to the kitchen for snacks. He enjoyed the side benefits of losing weight and building up his arms.

Prior to this intervention, the snacks tempted him away from his studies too often and he gained weight.

This intervention uses context (the chin up bar and the requirement to do chin ups) to affect behavior, just as the problem caused context to affect behavior.

However, unlike the problem, the solution was driven by his identity as a student and as a physically fit person. You could say that he used leverage from his identity level in order to produce success at the behavioral level.

In this case, he did not directly confront his behavior with beliefs about the value of studying. Instead, he used the identity level, and a rather superficial version of it, pertaining to his physique and attractiveness, in service of his desired behavior, which was actually studying, not building up biceps.

It doesn't matter much where the motivation comes from, so long as you are able to engineer the behavior you desire. Also note that, by using behavior modification principles, the student gained leverage over his behavior at the subconscious level. You will see in the remaining steps how to engineer the most effective behavior, because we're getting a little ahead of ourselves here.

Step #6. Leverage the process by anchoring the behavioral content from Override.

Go back to column #1, Capability, and anchor the behavioral content there.

Really get in touch with carrying out the behavior in a positive state (use the Override criteria to help you).

Anchor that positive state.

Step #7. Apply the highest Override criterion.

In column #4 (Identity), use the highest level criterion that you found by applying it at the Identity level.

With the school example, you might say for the Identity level, *"My identity as a helping professional is expanding and becoming more meaningful because I am attending the program I have chosen."*

On the belief level, you might say, *"I believe in life-long education, and I believe in the craft I am learning."*

Brainstorm, and review what you have done so far to determine how your high-level, override criterion applies to your Identity level.

Step #8. Engineer the desired behavior so that it is in harmony with all criteria levels, and fulfill the objectives of the desired behavior.

This step may mean a dramatic change of course, or some simple refinements to your desired behavior.

Most likely, it will involve adding supportive activities and perspectives to make it ecologically sound and highly motivating.

Bring your attention to column #3, and draw a line below what you have written so far.

Write down a behavior here that fulfills (or at least does not violate) the criteria of all columns.

You might want to start by brain storming all measures that you can take in order to enhance or add to your desired behavior so that it fulfills the criteria at each level.

This way, you will come up with a main behavior for this column, as well as a collection of supportive behaviors and adjustments that will help to ensure that you succeed.

Remember that brain storming means you open your mind to many possibilities.

You may want to start on a separate sheet and exhaust your ideas, then return for more after letting some time pass.

You might want to call some friends or a mentor to discuss this step.

In making sure that your ideas are in harmony with your criteria, you might ask questions such as, *"What ways are there for me to do a school program that will (from column #1, Capability) improve my income, skill, and prestige, and (from column #2, Belief) allow me to continue the work I am doing now in a meaningful way and keep making a living?"*

Pick out the best idea for column #3.

Step #9. Map and adjust the Override criteria and limiting beliefs.

Review your Override criterion that you noted above the columns.

Notice what submodalities give it power.

b) Also, note what strategies it implies.

c) Observe what meta-programs give this criterion it's shape. (Meta-programs are the higher level programs that affect how we think and perceive. For example, some people focus more on what they are avoiding, while other focus more on what they want.)

b) Now take your revised desired behavior from column #3, and adjust the strategy, meta program, and submodality features of the criteria of the desired behavior to match the strategy, meta program and submodality features of the highest level, Override, criterion.

c) Do the same thing for the column #1 Belief criteria (the values and conditions that give the limiting beliefs a sense of legitimacy).

This may seem like an odd request, but remember that you are harmonizing your desired behavior with criteria from all columns, and this adjustment will actually help to drive your desired behavior now that you are no longer waging an internal battle between conflicting levels of criteria.

Step #10. Test

Over the next few days or weeks, notice if you carry out the desired behavior enough to achieve the positive outcomes you intend it for, such as getting good grades so you can get into a good graduate program.

How well have your interventions worked and how might you improve them?

Are there other logical levels at which you should intervene?

Discover and correct any ecological or other conflicts.

Additional Advice

This pattern can go very far in helping you achieve very useful depth of insight as well as valuable, creative, fresh solutions. It helps you develop capacities that are quite under-realized in most people.

We strongly suggest that you make a project out of this pattern for any really challenging or complicated situations in which you are trying to cultivate or engineer behavior that is more appropriate that what you seem to be automatically drawn into.

By keeping it handy and revisiting it from time to time, you are likely to find that it can go much farther than one time can achieve. Reviewing Dilts' neurological levels can help generate ideas.

What additional support or interventions might help you secure this new behavior?

Use your environment to reinforce what you come up with. Posters, sticky notes, and recordings can all help reinforce and re-mind you.

Remember the behavior mod-ification example above. It takes advantage of context and behav-ior modification principles. It is not an obvious strategy, because it does not directly or obviously address the desired behavior or confront the undesired behavior.

In working with a client, you can keep track of the details by writing them down yourself, while guiding the person to step into areas that represent each of the elements on the paper.

In this approach, the original one suggested by Dilts, the per-son steps into spots on the ground that correspond to each of the col-umns. This assists with anchoring and eliciting states.

A common problem is to find that the criteria preventing your desired behavior occur at the same or higher levels than the criteria that support your desired behavior.

When that happens, people feel mystified as to how to sort things out.

Keep thinking it over and you will find a way.

For example, put criteria that are on the same logical level side-by-side and keep asking what makes them different.

At first it might just appear to be that the desired behavior is more relevant to your long-term status, or it might bring a better version of the same benefits or a larger quan-tity of the same benefits. But if you keep asking why that matters, you will come to values at a higher lev-el, even at the identity level. Get as many as you can, and explore ways to make them more compelling as indicated in this pattern.

35.

Aligning Perceptual Positions

"There is an old saying that, you can't kill a frog by dropping him into hot water. As you drop him into the hot water, he reacts so quickly that he immediately jumps out unharmed. But if you put him in cold water and gradually warm it up until it is scalding hot, you have him cooked before he knows it. The encroachment of bad habits in our lives is very much like this".

— Annonymous

CREDITS FOR THE creation of this NLP pattern belong to various contributors.

Get dramatic improvements in your relationships with others and with yourself by correcting bad habits in perception. This pattern addresses the tendency for people to become stuck in a particular perceptual position. For example, the person who is always stuck in the second position may have difficulty hanging on to their own reality, and be too easily manipulated.

But this pattern goes much farther than that, by correcting poor representations of perceptual positions. When people discover and correct problems such as misalignments or jumping into the wrong position, they may experience great improvements in long-standing interpersonal problems.

What Happens When Perceptual Positions are Not Aligned?

Here's a great example. Let's say someone is a bit self-centered or narcissistic. They have trouble tolerating it when someone else has more expensive clothes than they do, or is more important than they are in some way.

When they work with perceptual positions, they may find that

162

when they try position number two, which is looking at themselves through the other person's eyes, they discover that what they are hearing is not really the other person's voice. Instead, they hear what seems to be their own voice telling them that they are inferior, that someone else is better than they are.

But they go on to another discovery. Those thoughts add an emotional energy to that judgement. Those thought are loaded with the feeling that it is not acceptable, that it is horrible that this other person has a better car or whatever.

This person has been so busy trying to push away those feelings that they have been preoccupied with gaining status in any way they can.

This mean they have not realized how they are being driven by a voice that they have lost in the second perceptual position, and that they are being attacked with feelings lost in the second perceptual position.

It gets a little farther out than even that. They realize, doing this work, that the thoughts are not really exactly their own. Those thoughts about inferiority and superiority were the best thing they could come up with when they were a child with a parent who humiliated them and who was very harsh.

You could say then, that they kind of inherited the voice from the parent; the voice was primarily coming out of second position. That judgmental voice had gotten assigned to random people, but is was not from them, it was from the parent, who was very judgmental.

And the feelings?

Those are first position feelings, and that's good, because we are imagining from first position, from inside our own skin. But these intolerable feelings aren't really a reaction to other people having nicer things. Those feelings are the terror of a child who fears the big harsh parent.

It's just that those thoughts and feelings were a defensive or protective posture. Defenses tend to stick around, because they are there to protect us. Unfortunately for this fellow, though, they went out of date long ago.

However, he didn't know what they were, so he became lost in a struggle with what they had become. For him, they had become a drama of who is best, who has the nicest things, who is superior and inferior.

The fear of the parent became the fear of anyone being superior. This, in turn, became a struggle for prestige; a struggle that seems like an adult struggle, but is actually a holdover from the past.

It's very difficult for someone to untangle himself or herself from a drama that masquerades as a grown-up pursuit. Aligning perceptual positions can rescue people from such suffering, and it can unlock maturation that has been frozen, maybe for decades.

The beauty of aligning your perceptual positions is that it makes it much easier to let go of feelings and thoughts that don't belong to you. When you are aligned, the misaligned aspects feel out of place.

You want to put them where they belong: in the past, or given back to the person who started them in the first place.

Many Neuro Linguistic Programming practitioners work without talking about the past. That can work, because alignment happens in the present, and you can let go of thoughts and feelings without knowing where they came from. Most are practical and work with or assess past experience as necessary. They don't, however, get lost in the past; the focus is on outcomes.

What do Aligned Perceptual Positions Feel Like?

Let me give you a sense of aligned perceptual positions. Imagine your-self listening to these words. As you listen, with your eyes open, notice that you can see out of your own eyes, feel your own body, and hear with your own ears. You know that each of those senses are yours, because of where you sense them. You are the center and they are in the right positions.

So what we have done is use a real experience with your rep systems that you can refer to when you do visualization or a perceptual position alignment exercise.

To sum up, when all your rep systems are in the same perceptual position, you see, hear, and feel your senses in the right physical location. If you are imagining yourself in the first perceptual position, then it is like you are actually in your own body, looking through your own eyes. You feel grounded or connected, even more powerful as an individual.

You will start your alignment by finding where the misalignment is. This means you'll imagine a challenging situation. Then you'll check each primary perceptual position, seeing, hearing, and feeling. Once we know where the misalignment is, we will use that for the alignment.

We'll start by finding whether you have any misalignment

in your first perceptual position. Let's actually imagine something and see if you get the same sense of properly placed senses as you experience real life. Let's see if, in a visualization, *you* are the center of properly placed senses.

Overview: The Aligning Perceptual Positions Pattern

Step #1. Pick a challenging situation.

Step #2a. First Position, Visual

Step #2b. First Position, Auditory

Step #2c. First Position, Kinesthetic

Step #3a. Third Position (Observer), Visual

Step #3b. Third Position, Auditory

Step #3c. Third Position, Kinesthetic

Step #4. Return to First Position (Self)

Step #5. Final Check

Step #1. Pick a challenging situation.

Pick a situation that is challenging for you and involves another person, such as having an argument with someone. Imagine yourself in that challenging situation.

Step #2a. First Position, Visual

Consider how you are seeing; how your imagination is representing the visual sense. *Is your vision 100% exactly where it would be if you were really there, or would you say it is placed a little off from where it should be?*

Step #2b. First Position, Auditory

Let's try this with hearing. In the imaginary and challenging situation, imagine the sounds you might hear in the situation or add some appropriate sounds. *Do they feel that they are coming to you in the same position for real hearing does?*

Imagine what the person might say to you. If they are saying what you are thinking, or saying things that are really how YOU feel about yourself, or what YOU feel insecure about, then you are hearing your own thoughts from a different perceptual position.

That is a significant misalignment. This type of misalignment can make people feel self conscious, or jump to the conclusion that people are judging them too much. Aligning a problem like this is very empowering, because you are owning your own thoughts; feeling much more grounded and confident.

Include your thoughts as well, as though you "hear" your thoughts.

Ask yourself if those thoughts are really yours. Do they feel like they are really from your values and from the core of your mind, or is there anything alien about them, such as a resemblance to someone else's style of speaking. Or are some of your thoughts actually what you think the other person is thinking.

Adjust so that you are hearing your thoughts as your thoughts. If someone else's thoughts or thinking style has intruded, turn this into thinking about what they think, instead.

If you have a judgmental voice, see what it feels like to try to own that voice. See what it feels like to place that voice in your throat and speak those judgments.

Many people find that it seems awkward. They sending those thoughts off to some mean school teacher or bully that isn't even in the scene. That means those thoughts should be gone and no longer even audible.

Step #2c. First Position, Kinesthetic

We will do the same thing with feelings. *Do you have emotions, tension, or any other feelings in this situation?* If you are aligned, your feelings are coming from the part of your body that they should come from.

But if your kinesthetic rep system is not aligned, then your feelings may seem to be coming from elsewhere. They might be a little off, or way off, like when you project feelings onto someone else.

A more common problem, though, is when people mistake other people's feelings as their own. This makes them easy to manipulate. Con artists, addicts, and other destructive people seek out these overly empathic individuals. Codependency involves this problem of being at the mercy of other people's feelings.

Step #3a. Third Position (Observer), Visual

As you look at your challenging situation, move your point of view out and away, so that you are looking at yourself and the other person.

Now you are in third position.

Place your point of view so that you and the other person are both the same distance from your point of view as observer.

Have them be at eye level.

Notice any changes in your experience from this perspective.

See if you find it helpful move closer or farther away, to feel like you have a good sense of perspective. *Is there anything else to adjust, such as any submodalities? For example, is your view dark or fuzzy?*

Step #3b. Third Position, Auditory

Explore your auditory sense. *Are you hearing what is going on from where your point of view is?*

Remember that any thoughts are of you as the observer. So you might think about how you are reacting to observing yourself and this other person, but you are not "hearing" the thoughts of the "you" that you are observing. You might feel emotional about what is going on, but only as an observer who might feel empathy or some other emotion about what they are observing.

Remember, as the observer, any thoughts that belong to the other person, or to yourself in your imagination, should just be in them, not in your mind as observer.

You only know for some degree of assurance what they are thinking when they say it.

It can be very powerful, when you find yourself distracted by what you think the other person is thinking; to get it out of your mind as the observer, and have them speak the words, instead.

This helps secure you in the observer position, and to see if those words are coming from the right person. *Does it really sound like what they would say?*

Remember that, as observer, you would not use words like I and me, but rather, they and them, or him or her.

Step #3c. Third Position, Kinesthetic

As you look at the situation as the observer, with the "you" and the other person at the right distance from you, you are hearing from the observer position. You are also thinking as an observer who has some distance from the emotions in the situation.

Notice what feelings you do have as the observer. If you have strong feelings that belong to someone in the scene, place them back in that person and feel what it is like to really be the observer.

If you need to, adjust your feelings so that they are in the appropriate areas of your body.

Notice what feelings are the most resourceful. *What feelings best support you as an observant, curious, creative person; a person who generates solutions and excellence?*

This process can really liberate your subconscious mind as an empowering and problem-solving force.

Allow yourself to relax in the observer mode for a few moments, creating some space for your subconscious mind to benefit from this objective point of view, and to feed in any of its wisdom as it becomes available to you.

The novelty of this can trigger subconscious resources, because the subconscious is always looking for ways to connect the dots; to help you pursue a meaningful agenda, even when you aren't sure what it is.

And now, the observer perspective is a resource that you can draw upon whenever you like. It is not only a position for a fresh perspective, but also a safe position that can give respite from raw personal feelings, because it is a relatively dissociated state.

Step #4. Return to First Position (Self)

Lastly, we will return to the first position, in order to fine tune its alignment.

Bring your perspective back into yourself in the scenario. After all the work in third position, do you notice anything different about being back in your self-position.

a. First Position, Visual

Check each rep system. Are you looking directly out of your own eyes. If there is any kind of offset, any misalignment, correct that, by shifting directly into your normal vision, seeing directly out of your eyes.

You should now be viewing the other person as you normally would. Adjust any submodalities you care to, such as brightness, clarity, and size.

b. First Position, Auditory

How is your voice? As you speak, make sure it is coming from your throat.

Of course, any internal dialog, thoughts and judgments should really belong to you and be coming from your mind, emanating from you. Make sure your thoughts are in first person, saying, *"I think this,"* and, *"I think that."* Your thought are not talking about you, they are coming from you, they are yours.

And your hearing should be coming directly into your imaginary ears. Adjust the placement as needed, so that it sounds natural and normal.

c. First Position, Kinesthetic

What has changed about your feelings?

Do you have your own feelings, coming from the normal areas of your body that such feelings come from?

Step #5. Final Check

Do a final check and see if you feel aligned in the first position.

Make any final adjustments as you like.

You do not need to spend time trying to make it perfect. You are learning just the same.

Since were finishing, and we know adjustments can spread, spend a few moments back in the third position as the observer, and see if there have been any other improvements.

☙❧

36.

The Allergy Pattern

"A recurrent emotional state always appears together with the attitude of the body and the vegetative state with which it was conditioned earlier. Therefore, when an individual emotional complex has been resolved, a specifically individual body habit is resolved simultaneously."

– Moshe Feldenkrais

CREDITS FOR THE creation of this NLP pattern belong to Robert Dilts.

This pattern has a reputation for reducing or eliminating symptoms of allergies. Please remember that Neuro Linguistic Programming does not claim to *cure* to allergies. The originator of the Allergy Pattern, the NLP master trainer and developer Robert Dilts have worked with numerous people to elicit a strategy that can help reducing the symptoms of allergies.

Overview: The Allergy Pattern

Step #1. Imagine being exposed to the allergen.

Step #2. Anchor a symptom-free state.

Step #3. Enhance the anchor.

Step #4. Anchor several counter-example reference experiences.

Step#5. Fire the dissociated anchor

Step #6. Test

Step #1. Imagine being exposed to the allergen.

Recall being exposed to the allergen. Attempt to elicit some of the symptoms.

Find out what submodality changes change the intensity of the symptoms.

Step #2. Anchor a symptom-free state.

Achieve a state that is dissociated from the allergic state, and anchor it. A good way to do this:

a. Relax a bit, tilting your head and eyes upward.

Imagine that now there is glass between you and the thing you are allergic to.

Imagine being able to float up so that you can observe yourself from above.

b. When you are free of allergic responses, and truly relaxed, create a second, different anchor.

Step #3. Enhance the anchor.

Imagine fully a symptom-free state, and the ideal way you would like to respond to the item that typically caused an allergic response, when you have no allergic response.

Imagine this in some detail, describing it. Imagine this in an associated perspective.

Use the submodalities that you discovered were key to your reaction in building your new response.

Step #4. Anchor several counter-example reference experiences.

a. Associated Memory

Access an actual memory in which you have been near something that is, as much as possible, like the thing you are allergic to, but that does not produce an allergic response.

For example, if you are allergic to cats, you might imagine a clean, processed rabbit pelt or plush toy that causes no response.

b. To help disrupt your frame regarding allergies, do something that will show you that your immune system can tolerate substances that seem as though they should be intolerable.

You can accomplish this by thinking of one or more substances that you think of as being toxic, but which you don't have an allergic response to.

This shows that your immune system can keep your body safe without allergic responses.

For someone allergic to perfumes, the odor of gasoline might be an example. Not that we recommend actually sniffing gasoline fumes outside of your imagination.

It is also useful to identify some substance that is potentially even more "toxic" than the substance which causes the allergy, but to which the explorer's body has learned a more appropriate type of immune response.

Someone may have an allergy to perfume, but not to gasoline, for example. This demonstrates that the immune system can keep the body just as safe, but without the allergic symptoms.

c. Be sure that you observe the appropriate physiology before setting the anchor. It should match the desired state.

d. Are there any problems with ecology or secondary gain in connection with the allergic response?

e. You can enhance this by using re-imprinting, reframing, change personal history or your three anchors to add resources.

Step#5. Fire the dissociated anchor

Fire A1, the dissociated state anchor, and have the person imagine being close to or in contact with the allergen.

Simultaneously fire anchors A2 and A3, for the desired state and the counter example.

Be sure to hold the anchors long enough to see the person's physiology shift fully away from the allergic response.

Step #6. Test

If there is no risk of a medical problem, expose the person to a small amount of the allergen. Increase the amount bit by bit.

Repeat the procedure as needed until a typical exposure produces no allergy symptoms.

Before each increase, simultaneously fire A1, the dissociation anchor, and then A2 and A3, the desired state and counter-example anchors.

You can make this new response stronger by using the critical submodalities from step one.

Let the person be in full control of how the allergen is handled.

If there is any concern, consult an appropriate physician, don't work outside of your scope of practice and create risk.

This pattern can have durable effects. Sometimes, it may need to be repeated to restore its effect.

Exposure to other allergens or sensitigens may restore an allergic response.

❧

37.

Calibration

"This is my simple religion. There is no need for temples; no need for complicated philosophy. Our own brain, our own heart is our temple; the philosophy is kindness".

— Dalai Lama

CREDITS for the creation of this NLP pattern belong to various contributors.

Improve your ability to observe and respond to the physiological and behavioral cues of others. "Calibration" involves linking behavioral cues to internal cognitive and emotional responses.

Overview: The Calibration Method

Step #1. Understanding

Step #2. Observe

Step #3. Confusion

Step #4. Observe

Step #5. Pick

Step #6. Observe

Step #7. Guess

Step #8. More

Step #9. Explain and observe.

Step #1. Understanding

Ask your partner to think of some concept that your partner feels she or he knows and understands.

Step #2. Observe

Observe your partner's physiology closely (as if you were Sherlock Holmes for a moment).

Watch your partner's eye movements, facial expressions, hand movements, etc.

Step #3. Confusion

Then ask your partner to think of something that is confusing and unclear. Once again, watch your partner's eyes and features carefully.

Step #4. Observe

Notice what is different now. Observe changes in appearance and patterns of behavior.

Step #5. Pick

Now ask your partner to pick either concept and think of it again.

Step #6. Observe

Observe your partner's features. Look for changes in appearance or behavior that match the understanding or confusion states that your partner has shown you.

Step #7. Guess

Guess whether your partner chose the understanding or confusion concept. Check with your partner to see if you were correct.

Step #8. More

Have your partner think of other concepts that she or he understands or finds confusing, and see if you can guess which category they fall into.

Confirm your guess by checking with your partner.

Step #9. Explain and observe.

Explain a concept to your partner.

By observing his or her features, determine whether your partner has understood the concept.

See if you can determine the moment they understand your concept.

෯

38.

The Autobiography Pattern

"I think that when we look for love courageously, it reveals itself, and we wind up attracting even more love. If one person really wants us, everyone does. But if we're alone, we become even more alone. Life is strange".

— Paulo Coelho

CREDITS FOR THE creation of this NLP pattern belong to Leslie Cameron Bandler.

Build deep self acceptance with this hypnotic script, by experiencing it through multiple perspectives and sensory channels. Taking the original concept for this script from Leslie Cameron Bandler, I have created a special version for this book.

Read the script below aloud to yourself, giving enough time to complete the steps and allow yourself to fully participate in the exercise.

Recommendation: try to speak out loud the full script and record it. Then, listen to it before you go to bed. If you prefer to hear a voice other than your own, you might ask a trustworthy friend to read it aloud to you.

One of the most common questions about self-hypnosis scripts is "How many times do I need to go through the script?". The answer is very simple – as many times as it takes to see results.

This is a very powerful pattern, however, and I suggest that you would work on it once only, thoroughly, and then let it be for a few weeks. Write in your journal new insights and other life improvements you encounter during that time. The power of self-hypnosis is not in the words you say in the script, but in the images your mind keep on producing after the script has long been forgotten.

NLP Autobiography Pattern – Full Hypnotic Script

(Note: this script is copyrighted. For permission to reprint or to create and sell recordings, please contact the author).

"Let's begin by finding a nice warm position in which you can lie down or sit in a comfortable, yet soothing, way.

While you adjust your posture to make yourself even more comfortable, maybe you can even take a few deep breaths, slowly and tenderly, and allow yourself to become more and more relaxed.

You are doing this exercise to enjoy and feel better about yourself, not to fulfill other people's wishes.

These twelve minutes are for you and only you and only you deserve your next twelve minutes of re-la-x-a-tion.

And some people believe that in doing twelve minutes of Neuro Linguistic Programming, they are not allowed to move, but not you.

You can move, you can stretch, and you can keep adjusting the way your body can REST to make yourself FEEL MORE COMFORTABLE, MORE RELAXED

More thoughts that are coming your way are respectful of your wish to stay calm and relaxed, and they pass by as you guarantee you'll get back to them later. A bit later, after you experience the great appreciation and acceptance your loved ones have for you. Even when you can't really see it or hear it, and it's there.

And while you can imagine or picture to yourself what kind of unconditional love you can create an image of someone who loves you as you are.

It can be a relative, your father or mother, a brother, a sister, your spouse, a friend from the past or the present, someone you know or even someone who died a long time ago.

If you cannot imagine someone close, allow any memory to come to you of someone who helped you in some way in some day which has left you with a feeling of being appreciated and worthy of love.

Take a few minutes, let your mind scan your memories, finding an image. You can continue enjoying the sense that comes from allowing scanning that enhances the relaxation that some parts of your body have begun to experience.

Place aside the image that you found, to let it rest off to the side for a little while, knowing that we'll return to it soon enough.

Now, as you feel some increase in your natural wish to close your eyes, you can also let your shoulders feel their natural weight, feeling your breath as it finds a restfully deep and slower arc, and as you experience a moment, you can almost hear the serenity within your mind.

And as you do, imagine a wide screen, like in the movies, a big white screen spread in front of you, and on that screen you can see an image, a movie, of you sitting at an old wooden desk, writing your autobiography.

And you can choose whether you are using a pen or a pencil, maybe even a feather with blue ink, maybe you're typing your autobiography on a computer or on a typewriter...

...but you see yourself there writing your autobiography with the enthusiasm of telling your life story to the world. The story of your life is being written by you.

And that image of you shows the calm, the relaxing, as you enjoy discovering the hidden treasures in your life, the legacy that you will leave behind, the lessons you have learned, the good and varied experiences that have formed who you are today.

And you can also choose other details in the image of yourself sitting at that desk writing your autobiography.

You can choose the colors of the room, the comfortable temperature, that comfort and ease, as the surface you are on presses up to support you in space.

You may even have a glimpse of the words that you see yourself writing, good words, and as you focus on that image, you might want to imagine yourself really sitting there yourself, moving your fingers writing your autobiography.

And you can begin to get a sense of someone, just like in childhood, when someone who loves you dearly enters the door and you just know for sure who that person is. The same feeling can come to you now as you allow the image of that person to come to you and...

As you are writing your autobiography and you look at the other corner of the room, to notice someone standing there, on the other side of the glass door.

You get that feeling again, that this is the person you thought about moments ago. The person who loves you dearly and who accepts you just as you are.

And you can notice that the person who loves you is looking at you sitting at that desk writing your autobiography, and right then and there you choose to include this person in your book of life.

As you experience this inspiration, you can now describe this person and write about this person, about how wonderful and precious the unconditional love and affection are that you feel around that person, about how you cherish the time you had together.

Taking as much time as you need and want, you are allowed to remain in a deep relaxed state of mind and body and now …

…as you think about you, and give yourself a few moments dissociating yourself from the image, thinking about you sitting at a desk writing your autobiography, seeing yourself in that image.

Seeing from a point on the side of the room, from where the loving person is standing.

Imagining what would it be like standing there next to that person, looking from behind a glass window, looking to you writing there at that desk...as you, standing on the outside, with the person who loves you, unconditionally, as both of you are looking at an image of you writing your autobiography, sitting there in the room...

...while slowly and surely you can experiment further with that feeling, stepping over and entering into the body and mind of the loving person who is standing right next to you, while you are both looking at the person inside who's writing his autobiography, you and your autobiography, at a desk...

In becoming that loving person you can begin to discover the pleasant feeling of that love, and the expanding sense of the world inside that room from their eyes, feeling a special appreciation, a certain respect and that kind of unconditional love that person feels and offers you...

And can you imagine what it would be like, being that person for a little while, to know what it is like thinking lovingly and dearly about you, how it is all about you and your life right now, loving you as you really are, respecting you, appreciating you, enjoying how unique you are. Experiencing life through their eyes, you can have a sense of you through their eyes, through their full acceptance and hope and wishes for you. You can even allow those feelings to be named, as words occur to you to name those loving feelings, taking all the time you need for a good word to emerge, to name those feelings.

As you let it come to you, with the time and space for that, you can simply savor the appreciation and love that you are getting to know so well.

So well that you find yourself carrying them with you as you again stand beside that person, both of you looking at you writing your autobiography at the desk inside the room...

...and you begin to drift back through the glass window, back into your body, into you who is writing, able to write all about this experience, inspired to add it to your book of life, thinking about sharing this with the world, this complete love and appreciation, this joy you increasingly can take in your unique, specialness.

This joy of fully understanding yourself, appreciating yourself, actually loving yourself more and more in this new way.

As you step back into yourself, into the you who is writing your autobiography, you actually

experience holding the pen or pencil or typing, and letting the writing flow through you with complete freedom and ease.

This way, all your experience pours from you into this book, so that you richly describe your new feelings, your memories of knowing complete love through this other person, your glimpse of the future with such full joy in your unique being, writing about imaginary memories of this future as real life experiences, real events with your subconscious mind guiding you through them, guiding you with those rich feelings of respect for yourself, rich feelings of truly accepting yourself, this knowing that you brought along with you, that makes room for your greatness in all senses.

In these moments a year's worth of writing has poured out, so that as you finish, you can enjoy softly, gently closing your eyes, with your breathing deeply and deeper, slowly and slower, and with this satisfaction sending a hint of a smile to your lips.

Now, as you begin counting up toward enjoying feeling fully refreshed and alert, you stretch your arms forward as you count up toward five when you will fully awaken, opening and closing your hands, moving your head and stretching your neck gently upward, and when you reach number five, opening your eyes for fully refreshed, alertness.

As you finish this experience, notice the changes that you feel in your body and mind right now. How great is your appreciation to yourself in this moment?

Take a few moments with to experience just how important that feeling is, how great it is to use it and make it a permanent part of the life you are living, your life, the life you have described in your continuing autobiography..."

Additional Advice

At the end of the session, give the client a few minutes to rest silently, and then discuss the possible future consequences of the mental change. During the post session talk, let the client speak most of the time (use silence to encourage speech), and make notes of possible hidden agendas or mental blocks.

In the next session, address any such issues without exposing your findings to the client. My personal recommendation is to end the session with installing the anticipation of seeing small but meaningful differences in their appreciation of self and of the attitudes other people have toward them.

൭൭

39.

Congruence

*"Are the bones of your sins sharp enough to cut
through your own excuses?"*

— J. O'Barr, The Crow.

ALIGNMENT, AS OCCURS when your parts are aligned, brings much value to NLP, because it empowers our resources. The most basic alignment occurs when our sense modalities are in harmony. If there is a mismatch, then we have internal contradiction.

On a larger scale, we become congruent when our parts harmonize. As you'll recall, parts act like little personalities within us, or clusters of motivations that work together. And ecology refers to parts or other systems supporting each other. So you could say that in congruence, your parts play well together.

On an even grander level, coherence happens when our alignment points in a constructive direction that matches our self in-terest. The highest order of congruence takes place when we align all the way up to and including our higher values and aspirations. This extreme alignment brings perhaps the greatest satisfaction a human being can experience.

When you meet someone who is not congruent, or we could say who is INcongruent, they tend to say things that don't quite match up, or their behavior doesn't match what they say, or their outcomes don't match what they are trying to do. If you explore this with someone who is incongruent, they will reveal deeper and more obvious incongruities; deeper *mis*-matches.

They may show ambivalence about the results they say that they want.

They may get a lot of benefits from the status quo that they say they want to change.

They may reveal insecurities about what they are trying to do.

They may somehow dislike the kind of person they say they are trying to meet, like maybe feeling angry with all members of the opposite sex.

They may have mental health or neurological problems that they have not fully accepted or learned to cope with.

They might deny their serious problems with alcohol or other drugs.

The list goes on. Many things can cause incongruence.

If you are consulting or coaching someone who has some kind of incongruity, you will want to use NLP strategies that help this person resolve these mismatches. We call this ability to get parts to mesh well "reintegration". Alignment provides the foundation of NLP. Alignment makes personal excellence and healing possible.

ভ

40.

The Phobia Cure Pattern

"He who is not everyday conquering some fear has not learned the secret of life".

– Ralph Waldo Emerson

CREDITS FOR THE creation of this NLP pattern belong to Richard Bandler/John Grinder.

Eliminate unrealistic, habitual fears (such as the fear of flying) that can limit people's lives. It can even serve for trauma recovery, reducing or eliminating symptoms of post traumatic stress. This is also known as the **visual-kinesthetic dissociation pattern.** It uses dissociation, moving you to a spectator vantage point, to alter your reaction to the problem stimulus.

Fears, also known as phobias, can be irrational, but bother people for years without letting up. Psychology has various ways of working with these phobias, and medication sometimes resolves them. Trauma to the front of the brain even got rid of a fear of social activity in one documented case.

But we don't recommend hitting anyone in the head; they could end up with a phobia of you. Getting rid of phobias is important, because phobias prevent people from doing things they need to do.

Also, people with anxiety can have slower reaction times when they are supposed to deal with a threatening situation. At first, that sounds strange, because you would think anxious people would react to a threatening situation very fast, as a top priority.

With too much anxiety, however, mental processing can end up being slower than normal. This means they may not handle fearful situations well. That can amplify their fear, creating a vicious circle.

The NLP has come to the rescue for many people with phobias. Researchers have learned that virtual reality can create the same fears as a real situation, but NLP practitioners have been using the imagination therapeutically from the beginning; and your imagination is free, it even comes with it's own software.

In this pattern, you will use the third perceptual position, and some basic steps from something new; time line therapy.

Note: Play it safe. This pattern is designed to be *easy* on people. However, if you suspect that the person has a mental disorder, have them evaluated by an appropriate specialist to determine if this pattern will cause destabilization. It is possible that in extreme cases, it's focus on a negative memory could be re-traumatizing.

Overview: The Phobia Cure Pattern

Step #1. Select the stimulus or situation, and go to the third (dissociated) perceptual position.

Step #2. Run the movie once normal and then backwards

Step #3. Run the movie again in B&W

Step #4. Move into 1st position, run the movie backwards in full color

Step #5. Repeat until the person is desensitized.

Step #6. Optional: Enhance the procedure with strategies such as submodality modification.

Step #7. Re-associate, do an ecology check via future pacing. Consider additional work as needed to support continued success.

Step #1. Select the stimulus or situation, and go to the third (dissociated) perceptual position.

Have the person select a stimulus or situation that they react to with excessive anxiety or fear.

Have the person imagine sitting comfortably in a movie theater, about to watch some video of their life.

Have them imagine that the video is searching backwards for a point just before their first experience of fear pertaining to the situation. The primary purpose of this step is to help them experience what it was like not to have the problem. That is the value of using the third perceptual position (dissociated, watching from the position of an objective observer). This can be used to create a valuable resource state.

Although it is not necessary, this step may also may help them pinpoint how the reaction pattern began.

Step #2. Run the movie once normal and then backwards

Have them watch the situation play out from this dissociated position.

Then have them run the movie backwards to the point where it started.

Step #3. Run the movie again in B&W

Now have them change the movie from color to black and white, and run it again. This time, when it ends, have them freeze the image and fade it to black, the way some movies end.

Step #4. Move into 1st position, run the movie backwards in full color

Now have the person move into first position (seeing through their own eyes).

Tell them to experience the movie first-hand and in full color, but backwards to the beginning of the clip.

Step #5. Repeat until the person is desensitized.

Repeat these movie steps until the client no longer has the fearful reaction. To summarize the steps, get them back into the movie theater, run the movie backwards, switch to black and white, and run the movie forwards.

Finally, switch to first position with full color, and run the movie backwards to it's starting point, where it freeze frames and fades to black.

Step #6. Optional: Enhance the procedure with strategies such as submodality modification.

If this basic version of the method is not successful enough, you can modify it with strategies such as addition additional dissociation. For example, you can have the person move into the projection booth, and watch themselves sitting in the theater, watching the video.

You can also use other submodalities. As you know, people vary as to which submodalities have the greatest impact. Another strategy with this pattern is to trigger a resourceful state and maintain it while watching the video from a dissociated position.

You might trigger the state by thinking of a time when you felt very secure and confident.

If the memory or stimulus is extremely triggering, you can "code" the memory, by turning elements of it into symbols or outlines, so that your body is not imagining the actual stimulus to respond to.

You can also "humorize" the memory, by changing elements to make them ridiculous. For example, you could turn an intimidating person into a little bunny with a party hat, and give it a child's voice.

Consider doing a swish pattern in addition to the phobia cure pattern if necessary.

Step #7. Re-associate, do an ecology check via future pacing. Consider additional work as needed to support continued success.

Once the phobia is not strong when they think of the situation, bring them back to the present, aware of their surroundings, and check the ecology.

How does the client feel that they will be without this reaction, now that they can feel what it's like to be unafraid?

What images of the future do they come up with?

You may need to work with parts if the person does not feel fully aligned with this success. That will help prevent them from sabotaging their success, and it will help them come up with more effective and creative ways to live without this phobia.

☙❧

41.

Pleasure Installation

"Lies are essential to humanity. They are perhaps as important as the pursuit of pleasure and moreover are dictated by that pursuit".

— Marcel Proust

CREDITS FOR THE creation of this NLP pattern belong to various contributors.

Rebuild your happiness. Many of us have lost our connection to happiness. It may be because we need to recover from something that was psychologically overwhelming, or from the frog-in-a-kettle death of happiness that creeps up on us as we become over-invested in superficial things.

Whatever the reason, this pattern can be instrumental in restoring that connection. It also helps you better grasp the values that you hold and that affect how you can expand your life happiness.

Overview: The Pleasure Installation Pattern

Step #1. Make your happiness list.

Step #2. Select one of the items.

Step #3. Mind map your happiness values.

Step #4. Place a second tier on your mind map.

Step #5. Enjoy the enhanced happiness state.

Step #6. Carry your enhanced happiness into other activities.

Step #7. Expand your pleasure activity zone.

Step #8. Test

Step #1. Make your happiness list.

Make a list of many things that bring you happiness.

If you think of happiness as being what hap-pens when you consciously enjoy experiencing pleasure, this opens up a world of pleasurable sensations that you can enjoy.

Anything from a thrilling sport to a meditative environment can go on your list.

Step #2. Select one of the items.

Select an item that is especially good. It must be one that you can clearly tie to sensory experience.

Taking a hot herbal bubble bath with epsom salts and is an example that involves several submodalities.

Step #3. Mind map your happiness values.

You can do this in your mind, but we suggest that you take a piece of paper. In the center, place the happiness experience that you selected.

Ask yourself the question, *"What personal value and meaning turns this pleasure into happiness?"*

Draw a line from the experience, and write the answer at the end of that line.

An example is, *"This is a time for stress management that is good for my health, I know I'll feel relaxed and flexible after this, and a like that it symbolizes class and luxury."*

Keep creating answers like this until you are satisfied with this exploration.

Step #4. Place a second tier on your mind map.

For one of the answers, ask another question: *"What personal value and meaning makes this answer a pleasure for me?"*

Draw a line from the answer and write the new answer at the end of the line. Generate as many answers as you like.

Do this for each of the first tier of answers, so that you have two layers of answers, one around the other.

Step #5. Enjoy the enhanced happiness state.

Take a few moments to relax and take in the meanings that you have noted and that drive your pleasure state.

This is sensory pleasure expanded into happiness through your values.

Step #6. Carry your enhanced happiness into other activities.

Amplify your pleasure state and step into it. Imagine other pleasurable activities and what it can be like to bring this state into those activities.

Step #7. Expand your pleasure activity zone.

Think of other sensory-based experiences to which you could anchor this pleasure state.

Imagine being involved in these activities in this state.

Notice how it can change how you participate and what kind of creativity or other positive traits come from you.

Imagine how it might expand your involvement with learning, work, or interpersonal situations.

Step #8. Test

Over the coming days and weeks, notice any ways that you are able to experience activities, situations, and relationships with constructive pleasure.

Return to this pattern to refine your skill based on the results.

Using this pattern can make it much more obvious where you really need to use it, once you get a feel for it.

☙❧

42.

Exploring Causes & Effects

"When we do the best that we can, we never know what miracle is wrought in our life, or in the life of another".

— Helen Keller

THE "L" IN NLP stands for Language, and we do use a lot of linguistic models and tools in our work. When a client comes in and seems to have a hard time to pinpoint the triggers or causes to unwanted behaviors or thought patterns, we use a linguistic tool called *"Connectives"*.

Connectives in language are words and phrases that connect or link between ideas, making an association one statement and another. Milton Erickson was using connectives a lot, inducing a trance by connecting and associating between vague ideas or facts and hypnotic suggestions.

Here are some examples of connectives in the English language:

"and", "before"/"after", "therefore", "because", "although", "whenever", "while"/"meanwhile", "if", "or else". There are more connectives, of course, but for our purposes in NLP we really don't need a lot.

To help a client define exactly what it is that prevents them from behaving the way they want or forces them to behave the way they do not want, simply ask them to make a statement of the Effect and insert a connective word. For example, if a client comes to see you for smoking cessation but cannot pinpoint the trigger/s for his smoking habit. You can ask him to make a statement and complete the sentences:

"I smoke when…" – revealing location or time related triggers – "I smoke when I drink coffee".

"I smoke if…" – revealing emotional reasons – "I smoke if I am upset/concerned/annoyed/happy".

"I smoke because…", "I smoke after/before…", "I smoke whenever…", etc.

☙❧

43.

Applying Logical Levels

"A man can fail many times, but he isn't a failure until he begins to blame somebody else."

– John Burroughs

THE LOGICAL LEVELS concept in NLP was first introduced to the field by Robert Dilts, one of the most productive NLP master trainers and researcher. Dilts developed his logical levels to guide the process of intervention. Rather than focus on physiology and behavior, or emotional states, Dilts tells us to focus directly on strategies, sub-modalities, beliefs and identities. His levels help to put them in perspective.

Lets apply this to a phobia and see how it works.

The first level is about where, when and with whom the phobia occurs.

That is the environmental level. It is the context of the behavior. You can't really understand a behavior without context. After all, there are times that the phobia does NOT occur; there are people with whom the phobia does not occur. What is special about the times, places, and people connected with this phobia?

The second level is the specific behaviors that occur.

This is the behavior level. This level helps you get specific in defining or identifying the behavior. It helps you escape the trap of vagueness that can help keep people in a neurotic tangle.

The third level is capabilities and strategies.

How does the phobia get expressed as far the person's existing skills go. If they panic in an airplane, what skills do they use to channel that energy constructively. How to the prevent themselves from screaming and running up and down the walkway? Or are their energies expressed in utter chaos?

The more capabilities that a person has that can serve as resources for coping with the phobia, the more complex and functional the person's behavior can become. Chaos looks more complex than organization, but that is because organizations use complex rules and abilities to stay organized.

On the surface, they are usually orderly and appear easier to understand. In reality, they are complex and require exploration and study to understand their complexity.

The fourth level is beliefs and values.

What can the client tell you about their conscious values that guide what they do around this phobia. The phobia itself may seem to the person to be very much counter to their values, but there is more going on that just the phobia. There is how they react to it from this higher level. A good place to start is to simply ask the client why they do what they do. Don't just ask about the phobia itself, but what they do to cope, or how they avoid situations, or how they explain their behavior to themselves and others.

You can clarify their values further once you have this. You can ask them what they are trying to accomplish, or what they feel are their obligations or responsibilities in the situation.

From there, you will see that they have heartfelt values, and other values that seem to have been attached to them by their parents and others. Their values exist along with beliefs. They have beliefs about where their values come from and what would happen if they did not have their values and act on their values.

The fifth level is identity and mission.

How does your client perceive himself? How does having the phobia affect his identity? How does his identity affect the phobia? That one is especially interesting because the phobia doesn't happen in a vacuum. The person's identity is kind of like an environment for the phobia.

The client might say, *"Well, I'm a very private person, and I keep these things to myself. I will never fly on a plane because no one should see me like that. I'll tell my relatives that I'm helping a sick friend and can't come out for the holidays."*

One way to get at the identity level is to ask who the person feels they are when they are dealing with the phobia, or what roles they are acting out; roles like parent, role model, employee, airplane passenger, and so forth.

The sixth and final level is spirituality and purpose. This level addresses the client's connection to a higher reality. What is it that they believe about spirituality or the universe that guides them. This is an expanded version of the two levels that precede this level.

The previous two were of beliefs and values, and of identity and mission. This spirituality and purpose level exists because people tend to have this level of belief.

Even non-religious people usually have values that they feel extend beyond them and define their place in the world.

Those values tend to shape their behavior as strongly as religious beliefs shape a believer's behavior. If nothing else, this level helps to summarize the way that beliefs and identity work together to create another level of meaning.

Does this all sound like too much to think about for a silly phobia?

Well I'll wager that you already think about these levels more than you realize. But these six levels help you to put such thoughts into perspective, and to ask some questions to round out your understanding; understanding that will help you provide a relevant response. You don't have to spend an hour asking all the questions that go with each level. With experience, you'll get better and better at knowing what questions to ask which people. You will develop an efficient approach.

☙❧

195

44.

Pleasure Reduction

*"Addiction is a symptom of not growing up. I know people think
it's a disease... If you have a brain tumor, if you have cancer,
that's a disease. To say that an addiction is a disease is not fair to
the real diseases of the world".*

— C.C. Deville

BREAK OUT OF addictions, compulsions, and obsessions by reducing the pleasure they create. It is for behaviors that are based on real needs, but that have become excessive.

Overview: The Pleasure Reduction Pattern

Step #1. Select an "overused pleasure."

Step #2. Determine the meta-state levels that give this meaning for you.

Step #3. Repeat this to derive higher levels of meaning.

Step #4. Take in the full enjoyment gestalt.

Step #5. Reduce the meaning and enjoyment.

Step #6. Future pace this reduced meaning and enjoyment.

Step #7. Generate other sources for the highest meta-level meaning states that you identified in step two and three.

Step #8. Test.

Step #1. Select an "overused pleasure."

Pick something that you need to reduce or eliminate.

Step #2. Determine the meta-state levels that give this meaning for you.

In the center of a sheet of paper, write down the pleasurable activity. Draw a circle around it.

Think of the pleasure, and ask, *"What positive meaning and values to I give to this pleasure?"*

Write each answer briefly in the space immediately around the circle.

Think of each answer as a kind of state that embodies feeling and meaning pertaining to this pleasure.

Step #3. Repeat this to derive higher levels of meaning.

For each of the answers, ask the same question, and surround it with the answers you get.

Step #4. Take in the full enjoyment gestalt.

Review all the answers, experiencing them as a complete profile for a kind of happiness that drives the behavior in question.

Step #5. Reduce the meaning and enjoyment.

Determine which of the meanings are the most important in driving you to excess.

Do this by placing your hand over one answer cluster at a time.

For each cluster, ask, *"If I could take away this cluster of meta-states, how much would it reduce the pleasure?"*

Continue to do this, until you clearly see which meanings exaggerate the importance of the pleasure, and which are more intrinsic to the pleasure, that is, more essential or basic to it's real meaning.

For example, health is a core value for eating, while having something to do while watching television is not a core value for eating.

Step #6. Future pace this reduced meaning and enjoyment.

Think of something that can reduce the pleasure of the activity. For example, seeing yourself getting fat by eating too much.

Imagine yourself engaging in the activity, and say to yourself, for example, *"This is only food. I can enjoy it nourishing me, but that's all."*

When another kind of pleasure or meaning slips into your mind, imagine the negative factor, such as getting fat.

If the behavior is something that you need to eliminate completely, that you would say something like, *"This meth-amphetamine is only a way to try to feel more joy and vigor. I can allow healthy alternatives to fill my mind."*

Of course, this pattern is not intended to substitute for any treatment that is required for addiction or compulsion. It is intended to help.

Step #7. Generate other sources for the highest meta-level meaning states that you identified in step two and three.

Step into the higher-level meta state, which is a combination of all the highest level meanings you found in steps two and three.

Fully experience the pleasurable nature of this state.

Invite your creative part to show you other ways to experience this pleasure, and to create the meaning that these pleasures come from.

Generate the sense that it is fully possible to live a life filled with this pleasure, but without excess.

Step #8. Test.

See how well this pattern reduces the selected behavior to an appropriate level, and how well it helps you create pleasure and meaning through healthy pursuits.

❧

45.

Developing Sensory Acuity

"No two equals are the same".

— Principia Discordia

WHEN YOU LEARN to observe people well you will notice that they make minute subconscious changes. They are not aware of most of their involuntary movements or minor changes in physiology.

Investigators are well-trained in noticing the most delicate minor changes in people's physiology.

They can tell whether the person is lying simply by noting the changes of skin color (blushing, for example, even for a second, is very noticeable).

Even though you can improve your sensory acuity with eye accessing cues, sometimes they are not enough or are completely inappropriate for the person you're interacting with.

The physiological changes that you can notice in others can be considered to be on a continuum:

Skin color: Light Dark

Muscles tone: S y m m e t r i c a l Asymmetrical

Breathing rate: Slow Fast

Breathing location: Low High

Size of lower lip: With lines No lines

Pupil dilation: Dilated Not dilated

Eyes focus: Focused Not focused

☺☺

46.

The Loving Yourself Pattern

*"Dwell not on the past. Use it to illustrate a point, then leave
it behind. Nothing really matters except what you do now in
this instant of time. From this moment onwards you can be
an entirely different person, filled with love and understanding,
ready with an outstretched hand, uplifted and positive in
every thought and deed".*

— Eileen Caddy

Credits for the creation of this NLP pattern belong to Suzie Smith and Tim Halborn.

Enhance your ego strength and self esteem by improving your ability to love and appreciate yourself.

Overview: The Loving Yourself Pattern

*Step #1. Explore your memories for places where you had pleas-
ant experience*

Step #2. Describe the attributes of this person

*Step #3. Work with the second perceptual position, in the loving
person.*

Step #4. Anchor this appreciation state.

Step #5. Receive the loving perception.

Step #6. Anchor the lovable state.

Step #7. Test and future pace this anchor.

Step #1. Explore your memories for places where you had pleasant experience

Explore your pleasant memories for someone who intensely cared about you, and who had a positive effect on you.

It most not be a person who misused any power or influence affecting you. This person will serve as a model for love.

Step #2. Describe the attributes of this person

To get a full sense of the elements that you feel contribute to being a loving person, describe the attributes or qualities of this person, particularly those that made them a loving person.

Step #3. Work with the second perceptual position, in the loving person.

Imagine floating over to this person, taking their perceptual position. See yourself through their eyes.

Describe yourself from their perspective. *What qualities of yours does this person appreciate about you?*

Notice how this expands your sense of yourself as a loving and lovable person.

Step #4. Anchor this appreciation state.

Use an appropriate image, word, touch, or other stimulus to anchor this state.

Step #5. Receive the loving perception.

Tune in to your sense of the person loving you. Imagine allowing this in as a form of energy.

Fully experience your feelings as the person looks lovingly at you. Also experience your own feelings of self appreciation.

Attend to your self talk and how it reflects these perspectives.

Notice any ways that these experiences change how your perceive the world around you in this memory.

Step #6. Anchor the lovable state.

Filter out any distractions from this lovable state, and amplify the state. Anchor it with an appropriate stimulus.

Now you have anchored a loving and lovable state that are also tied to qualities that you and others can appreciate about you.

Take some time to enjoy any new ideas and perspectives that you have experienced about yourself.

Step #7. Test and future pace this anchor.

Fire the anchor of being lovable.

Future pace by imagining situations in which it would be helpful to be in touch with your own lovability.

Remember that these future situation do not have to be situations in which you are guaranteed to be approved of. In fact, some situations might involve people who are not loving people, or who don't appreciate you.

Imagine being around people like that, but with an unshakable sense of your own lovability.

Think about how much more difficult it is to manipulate or intimidate someone experiencing this high lovability level that you are amplifying.

 glossary

47.

Abandoned Predisposition

"For anything worth having one must pay the price; and the price is always work, patience, love, self-sacrifice. No paper currency, no promises to pay, but the gold of real service".

– John Burroughs

CREDITS FOR THE creation of this NLP pattern belong to various contributors.

A predisposition is a tendency which is not yet a habit. It is when you hold a particular thought pattern and can't let go of it or when you act in a particular way and catch yourself "too late."

This pattern helps you to abandon the predisposition by turning the compulsion into an aversion. In other words, it turns a specific thing or action you "like" into a "dislike."

Review your knowledge on submodalities before you try out this pattern.

Overview: The Abandoned Predisposition Pattern

Step #1. Determine the problematic predisposition.

Step #2. Elicit the current submodalities (Image A).

Step #3. Elicit submodalities from the aversion image (Image B).

Step #4. Change the submodalities of the predisposition image.

Step #5. Lock the new submodalities firmly in place.

Step #6. Test.

Step #7. Future pace.

Step #1. Determine the problematic predisposition.

Think of something that you like doing/thinking but wish you did not like. Can you define it in a statement?

Step #2. Elicit the current submodalities (Image A).

As you think about this predisposition, elicit the submodalities of this mental image.

Specifically check for driver submodalities such as Size, Light, Distance, etc.

Step #3. Elicit submodalities from the aversion image (Image B).

Now think of something you dislike and elicit the submodalities in that image.

Again, specifically check for driver submodalities.

Step #4. Change submodalities of the predisposition image.

Take the submodalities you've elicited from Image B and use them on Image A.

If in Image B, for example, the image was to the left and 3 feet in size, make Image A go to the same location and enhance (or reduce) to the same size as image B. Work through all driver submodalities.

Step #5. Lock the new submodalities firmly in place.

Imagine that you could "stamp" Image A as it is now with the copied submodalities of Image B, making the new submodalities locked in Image A firmly.

Step #6. Test.

Now when you think about the thing you used to like doing / thinking, how is it different?

If there is still a tendency to like doing/thinking X (image A content), go back through the steps and elicit more driver submodalities.

Step #7. Future pace.

Imagine a realistic and specific time in the near future, when you might find yourself tempted to do/think X (image A content), can you feel the aversion?

☙❧

48.

Chaining States

MAKE YOURSELF IMMUNE to negative states. Create an automatic reaction that creates a resourceful and positive state instead.

Overview: The Chaining States Pattern

Step #1. Choose an unresourceful state.

Step #2. Identify a positive direction.

Step #3. Turn this direction into steps to the positive state.

Step #4. Anchor each step.

Step #5. Chain the states.

Step #6. Test.

Step #1. Choose an unresourceful state.

Select an unresourceful state for this pattern.

Unless you are a beginner, select one that poses a challenge when you try to shift into a positive or resourceful state. It should also be one that tends to suck you into an increasingly negative state once you are in that state.

Step #2. Identify a positive direction.

Explore what would constitute a positive direction from this state, based on the ideal state that you would like to go to.

For example, if the experience of failure tends to have too much of an effect on your self esteem, pulling you down into self-recrimination and self-doubt, your ideal state might be one of total self-support and confidence.

The direction that this implies can be something like *"awareness of inner resources such as gifts, skills, talent, and positive self talk"* and *"memories of past successes."*

Step #3. Turn this direction into steps to the positive state.

Based on your ideal state and the direction that you selected, create intermediate steps that bridge from your negative state to your positive one.

Step #4. Anchor each step.

Experience each step as an increasingly positive state.

Fully access each state and anchor each to a different knuckle that will serve as a trigger for the state.

Step #5. Chain the states.

a. Fully access the first state by triggering its anchor.

b. When fully in that state, fire the next anchor to access the next state while continuing to hold on to the first trigger for a few seconds.

c. Release the first anchor.

d. Repeat this process five times.

e. Do steps a through c for each remaining step in sequence from negative to positive. Do not rush this process. Attain a very full experience of each state.

Step #6. Test.

In the coming days and weeks, notice what benefits you experience from this process.

See if you have an easier time shifting out of the negative state you worked on during this pattern, or if you avoid entering it in the first place.

☯

49.

Pragmagraphic Swish Design

"Success is simply a matter of luck. Ask any failure".

— Earl Wilson

Credits for the creation of this NLP pattern belong to Robert Dilts & Todd Epstein.

Resolve compulsive patterns; the acts that a person feels compelled to do, despite knowing better. This can include addiction, blurting out thing you thought only your parents would say, eating comfort food, switching on the television when you have paperwork to do, and many other behaviors.

Since is it much harder to change a compulsive behavior once your drive has reached a high level, this pattern is an opportunity to prevent the behavior before your drive becomes too strong, by helping you become aware of it on a more subtle level, before it is strong. It weakens the connection between the drive and the triggers that activate it, and replacing it with a constructive drive.

> ## *Overview: The Pragmagraphic Swish Design Pattern*
>
> *Step #1. Create a "map" of physical locations the states.*
>
> *Step #2. Step into the "Must" position.*
>
> *Step #3. Step backward to the "Desire" position.*
>
> *Step #4. Step backward into the "?" position (the trigger)*
>
> *Step #5. Get clear on the submodalities involved in "?"*
>
> *Step #6. Step into "Creative Choice."*
>
> *Step #7. Do submodality work in the "?" position.*
>
> *Step #8. Repetitions of step 7.*
>
> *Step #9. Test*

Step #1. Create a "map" of physical locations the states.

Choose physical locations for (A) "Must," (B) "Desire," (C) "?," and (D) "Creative Choice."

Step #2. Step into the "Must" position.

Choose a compulsive behavior. Physically stand in the "Must" location.

Experience the feelings you have when you do the behavior. What does it feel like when you "MUST" do the compulsive behavior.

Step #3. Step backward to the "Desire" position.

Move to the "Desire" position by physically stepping backward.

This spot is the feeling that you have just before "Must" breaks into your awareness.

Step #4. Step backward into the "?" position (the trigger)

Step back again, this time to the "? "position. This is the trigger that comes just before (B), "Desire." You may not have been aware of it before, but it is a feeling that triggers the "Desire."

It may include thoughts, and the feelings or thoughts may be triggered by a situation, such as the smoker who always lights up in their car.

Step #5. Get clear on the submodalities involved in "?"

Notice the submodalities that are most influential in increasing the intensity of (C).

Discover which submodalities decrease the "?" feeling.

Step #6. Step into "Creative Choice."

Step into the "Creative Choice" location.

Attend to the feelings that stem from this state.

You may have experienced this state while exploring the submodalities that decrease the "?" feeling. You can think of other "Creative Choice" experiences as well.

Notice which submodalities have little or no impact.

a. Get clear on the submodalities.

Experience the submodalities that give the most gusto to your "Creative Choice" feeling.

Notice which have no impact.

b. Notice the submodalities shared with "?"

Notice which of the submodalities intensified "?" and "Creative Choice."

Step #7. Do submodality work in the "?" position.

Return to your "?" spot.

Elicit the strengthening submodality for "?" (e.g. bright and big), as well as the one that reduced the intensity of "Creative Choice."

Notice how this creates a sort of pull into your "Desire" location.

Gradually intensify the "Creative Choice" submodality. If it is dim and small, it will become bright and large.

At the same time, slowly reduce the intensity of the submodality for "?"

Keep going until their intensities have completely reversed. "?" is now low intensity, and "Creative Choice" is high intensity.

As you do this, move from your "?" spot into the "Creative Choice" spot.

Step #8. Repetitions of step 7.

Step out of "Creative choice" and repeat step seven as quickly as you can. Do this at least five times.

Step #9. Test

Test your results by stepping back into the "?" spot and discovering which direction you find yourself wanting to move toward.

Notice what occurs when you attempt to return to your prior compulsive feelings and behavior.

☙❧

50.

Collecting Resources

"Good judgment comes from experience. Experience comes from bad judgment".

— Jim Horning

WHEN you're in the process of achieving an outcome or goal, you are "consuming" or using resources. A resource could be anything, really. A resource could be a mental capability, such as knowledge, curiosity, creativity or perseverance.

A resource could be a physiological trait, such as endurance or strength. A resource could be a physical entity, such as money or an office. A resource could be the help of others, such as your teachers, mentors or friends. There is one possible problem which you should be careful not to run into, while you're on your journey to fulfill your outcome.

You see, when you look into the future, while working on your goal, you are usually very subjective about that image. Most likely, you will make "realistic" predictions based on what you know about yourself, your capabilities, your environment and worse of all –your past. You will judge how this outcome will affect you and the people around you.

To stay objective in determining the real resources you already have, and the ones you would need to develop or reach, ask yourself the following questions:

1. *What exactly do I want by having this outcome?*

2. *If this outcome was someone else's, what resources does that person need in order to achieve this outcome elegantly and rapidly?*

3. Using the "As if" frame: *If I look at myself from the point of view of X (someone who likes me), what are my current strengths and most important resources?*

Identify resources to work on – By looking at my answers to #2 and #3, which of these resources do I still need to work on in order to have/be able to use? Who can help me this week to accomplish this need?

☺☻

51.

Advanced Visual Squash

"Success is not measured by what a man accomplishes, but by the opposition he has encountered and the courage with which he has maintained the struggle against overwhelming odds".

— Charles Lindbergh

Build your congruence and success by resolving parts conflicts. Integrate parts that are not aligned.

Overview: The Advanced Visual Squash Pattern

Step #1. Identify the conflict, and separate the parts.

Step #2. Put well-formed sensory representations of each part in each hand.

Step #3. Understand the positive intentions of each part.

Step #4. Share resources between the parts.

Step #5. Develop an image of the integrated, shared resources.

Step #6. Turn the parts to face each other, and observe the changes that result.

Step #7. Integrate the parts by bringing your hands together

Step #8. Enhance the integration by experiencing it fully, and bringing it into your body.

Step #1. Identify the conflict, and separate the parts.

Choose an internal conflict and identify the incongruent parts.

For example, if you have trouble saving money, identify the part that wants to spend liberally, and the part that is frugal.

Step #2. Put well-formed sensory representations of each part in each hand.

What would each part look and sound like?

How might it move or gesture?

Develop a well-formed sense of each part.

Place one part in each hand.

Select which part goes into which hand based on how you feel about them.

Step #3. Understand the positive intentions of each part.

Ask each part to tell you its positive intentions in this conflict.

Relax and let ideas emerge.

Note which seem to be the most important. A good way to phrase the question is, *"What is the good that you desire from this behavior of yours?"*

Step #4. Share resources between the parts.

Notice what is similar between the two parts' positive intentions.

Ask each part what resources it could use from the other part.

Work with the parts until both have a good sense of this.

Create an image of each resource. Imagine energy flowing from one hand to the other, and say, *"Give a complete copy of these resources to the other part (list the resources to be copied)."*

Imagine an image of each resource flowing through that energy into the other part. Do all of this once for each part.

Notice the changes in each part's behavior and appearance. (This is called submodality mapping across.)

Step #5. Develop an image of the integrated, shared resources.

Get an image of the combined resources of the two parts. Place this image in the center between your hands.

Step #6. Turn the parts to face each other, and observe the changes that result.

Have the images in each hand turn to face each other.

Turn the palms of your hands toward each other.

Let your imagination modify these images to express how they are changing.

Step #7. Integrate the parts by bringing your hands together

Allow your hands to come together only as fast as you can allow the integration of these parts into one special part that expresses the good intentions and resources of each.

When working with a person, use this phrase as you place your hands in the same position as theirs.

Then move your hands together slightly faster than they do.

Invite and allow the parts to blend into and enhance the image of integration.

Step #8. Enhance the integration by experiencing it fully, and bringing it into your body.

Once your hands come together, fully experience the feelings involved.

Allow the image to morph as it expresses the changes in your feelings and resources.

Bring the image and energy into your body by bringing your hands to your chest.

☙❧

52.

Digital Vs. Analogue Submodalities

"Well, the secret of happiness is that it's an inside job".

– Stephen Pollen

WHEN a submodality is digital, what we really mean is that it contains information expressed using known symbols. You can take words that you have heard, and write them. Now they are visual. Put them in Braille. Now they are kinesthetic, if you know Braille, anyway.

Put them on a giant billboard in Times Square, and you have added the size submodality. Light them up and you have added the brightness submodality.

All those other submodalities were analogue.

In other words, you can scale them up or down or in some other way, and they are still the same basic sound, sight or feeling. But if you take that billboard and add a bunch of letters to it, the digital message will not be the same. Make a red light brighter, it's still a red light.

Add fifty letters at random to your marketing slogan, and it doesn't mean anything anymore. It's easy to break a digital modality. But you can scale analog modalities a lot before you can no longer perceive them effectively.

For example, you'd have to make a color so bright that it is blinding, or so dark that it is invisible. It is important to choose the right digital submodality. For example, we don't recommend tasting Morse code. It would be very slow to get a message from caramel, strawberry… strawberry, caramel, strawberry, strawberry… Strawberry, caramel, caramel, strawberry.

That was NLP in Morse code, and it was slow just saying the flavors, much less tasting them. I suppose it could be fun, though. Even if you don't know Morse code.

એજ

53.

Submodality Overlapping

"Sometimes you've got to let everything go — purge yourself. If you are unhappy with anything . . . whatever is bringing you down, get rid of it. Because you'll find that when you're free, your true creativity, your true self comes out".

— Tina Turner

CREDITS for the creation of this NLP pattern belong to various contributors.

Build up weaker submodalities to improve creativity and problem solving though as you represent things in a richer way.

The brain relies on representations that it can hold in various aspects of memory that it can move and manipulate as information.

Improved submodalities improve this aspect of intelligence.

Also, you can make your speaking and writing more compelling by using your enriched awareness of submodalities to generate enhanced and varied submodality references.

Overview: The Submodality Overlapping Pattern

Step #1. Select a relatively weak modality that you would like to improve.

Step #2. Describe or imagine something, relying primarily on your favored rep system.

Step #3. Switch over to the rep system you are improving.

Step #1. Select a relatively weak modality that you would like to improve.

Think of which of your rep systems you most favor.

Step #2. Describe or imagine something, relying primarily on your favored rep system.

For example, if you are primarily visual, you might think of a nearby park in as much visual detail as possible.

Also describe it verbally. Refer to several submodalities, such as color.

Step #3. Switch over to the rep system you are improving.

Let's say you want to improve your auditory rep system.

In the example above, you would recall all the sounds that happen there.

In the above example, you would have birds chirping, children playing, and swings squeaking.

As with the visual mode, include submodalities such as loudness, pitch, and sound reflections (echo and reverberation such as that which reflects from walls). Verbally describe all of this as well.

❧

54.

External Stimulus Threshold

"Our generation has an incredible amount of realism, yet at the same time it loves to complain and not really change. Because, if it does change, then it won't have anything to complain about".

— Tori Amos

A THRESHOLD IS A line between two states of mind: bearable and unbearable. Sometimes, in order to change a behavior, you have to induce the triggers and resourceful states at the same time, making sure that the resourceful states win in each "threshold battle".

This is a pattern to do just that. It involves two practitioners and one client. The reason you want another person helping you performing this pattern on a client is that you could concentrate on the client's abreactions while firing the anchors, and your colleague will role-play the undesired behavior's triggers.

Overview: The External Stimulus Threshold Pattern

Step #1. Identify the unresourceful state and its most influential stimuli.

Step #2. Break state.

Step #3. Anchor resourceful states and stack them.

Step #4. Role playing of the unresourceful states.

Step #5. Trigger the stacked anchors.

Step #6. Continue until no abreaction is present.

Step #7. Future pace the resourceful states.

Step #1. Identify the unresourceful state and its most influential stimuli.

You should work with your client ahead of time to recognize exactly the series of events that take place right before they find themselves already engaged in the undesired behaviors or states.

When questioning the client on internal events, make note of their eyes accessing cues. Your colleague will need those to induce the states later on.

In addition, write down verbal communication scripts if they are important for the induction of the undesired states.

For example, if the client has presented a problem of non-proportional or inappropriate anger towards his son, check if it's something that the son is saying verbally and write it down. If hearing the words "dad, are we there yet?!?!" is a trigger, note the tonality but also the syntax of the words themselves, digitally.

Focus on one habitual state or behavior, not more.

Step #2. Break state.

Ask the client some neutral questions to break the state. Ask them to walk around for a bit or do any other physical movement to forget about step #1.

Step #3. Anchor resourceful states and stack them.

Now work with your client and anchor as many resourceful states as possible.

Use the problem state as a guide – what could be a good contradicting state to the negative one?

Include comforting states such as "composure" or "gratitude".

Stack anchors by using one master anchor for each one of the positive states. Stacking anchors simply means that you anchor the same way while inducing different states each time.

What happens eventually is, that when you fire the master anchor, the client gets a rush of all the positive states "stacked" on that trigger.

Be careful when you choose the location and manner of the master anchor. You want to make sure that this is not something that can cause an inner conflict later on in the session.

Do not use popular anchoring locations, such as the back of the hand or the shoulder or knee. These are known in Neuro

Linguistic Programming, but you never know what has happened in your client's life and body until they met you. Anchor the master trigger where you are certain there is no way for disturbance by any other internal process.

Test the stacked anchors a few times by firing a master anchor, breaking state, and repeating.

This is a step you do not want to hurry up. Work slowly and thoroughly, maintain a high level of sensory acuity and take note of every abreaction you get from the client.

Take special care if the abreaction appears when you fire the master anchor. If it does, you were too careless in choosing the master anchor! An abreaction at this stage means that the master anchor is also inducing some conflict in your client.

When that happens, go back to step #2, stay there for awhile, talk with your client about anything other than the subject of the session, and then work on this step again.

Do not worry, even the best NLP practitioners get these challenges, and as a flexibility test you should welcome it and work through them. You'd be a much better change-maker because of such incidents.

Step #4. Role playing of the unresourceful states.

Allow your colleague to step in and work with your client to recreate the scenarios which hold triggers for the unresourceful states and behaviors.

Give your colleague the eye accessing cues worksheet and any other useful information that could be used in the role playing.

Step #5. Trigger the stacked anchors.

As your colleague keeps the role playing going with your client, fire the anchors!

Do exactly what you did at the end of Step #3, when you tested the stacked anchors, and fire them all.

Stay focused and maintain sensory acuity because this is a hard and long process for all of you.

Step #6. Continue until no abreaction is present.

Abreactions are those minute subconscious "hiccups", that signal you, the practitioner, that the client has some emotional reaction to whatever is going on in the session at that time.

When you cease to notice these abreactions, it means that the client has passed the threshold point and his mind is now pretty much set on using the resourceful states as a reaction to the events that used to trigger the undesired behaviors and states.

Step #7. Future pace the resourceful states.

First of all, break state. Let your client rest for a few minutes, and then fire the anchors again and future pace for upcoming opportunities.

55.

Decision Destroyer

"When making a decision of minor importance, I have always found it advantageous to consider all the pros and cons. In vital matters, however, such as the choice of a mate or a profession, the decision should come from the subconscious, from somewhere within ourselves. In the important decisions of personal life, we should be governed, I think, by the deep inner needs of our nature".

— Sigmund Freud

CREDITS for the creation of this NLP pattern belong to various contributors.

Exchange limiting decisions for constructive ones in order to improve success and mood.

We can view our behavior and feelings as expressions of many decisions that we have made during our lives. These decisions may be conscious or subconscious. In other words, you might be aware of the need to make these decisions (equivalent to skill level "conscious incompetence") or unaware of the need (equivalent to skill level "subconscious incompetence").

These decisions may have profound effects on our development and continued functioning because they were made before we could even speak. These decisions can be about the nature of the world, of people, and of ourselves.

Most of us have some habits deprive us of much success and happiness because of the way they affect how we relate to the world, to others, and even to ourselves.

Decisions that have such harmful effects tend to arise when we are psychologically overwhelmed. This can happen in adulthood, but it is especially troublesome when we make them in childhood.

This is because of their effect on our development, and because of how deeply ingrained they are as "pre-verbal" decisions.

When we make decisions before we have the necessary wisdom to make them with, we end up with destructive ways of relating to the world, to people, or even to ourselves.

Patterns of dysfunctional relationships, poor self esteem, and sabotage can often be traced back to these unwise decisions. We can think of the collective nature of our decisions as a "mental map" of our world. We navigate our world and relationships using our mental maps.

Overview: The Decision Destroyer Pattern

Step #1. Select and clarify a limiting decision.

Step #2. Develop and anchor a positive decision.

Step #3. Associate into the limiting decision and anchor it.

Step #4. Float back to earlier experiences, seeking the first one.

Step #5. Go forward, returning to your positive decision.

Step #6. Go earlier to your first limiting decision.

Step #7. Experience that early decision while fully accessing the new resources.

Step #8. Quickly zoom to the present, integrate the experience, and future pace.

Step #1. Select and clarify a limiting decision.

Think of a negative pattern in your life. Based on the introductory comment to this pattern, verbalize an underlying decision that has guided your behavior in a dysfunctional way. If it sounds irrational, that is okay.

Decisions made earlier in life sound especially illogical. Think about the decision to clarify things about it.

For example, when does it seem that you made it? How does it affect your life?

Step #2. Develop and anchor a positive decision.

Develop a constructive decision that would be an excellent improvement over the limiting decision.

Enhance it until it is well formed.

For example, it should be specific. Enhance it further by developing the positive feelings you have about it into a positive decision state.

Enhance the positive state until it is strong.

Anchor the state.

Step #3. Associate into the limiting decision and anchor it.

Float back above your timeline to the point when you first recall acting upon the limiting decision.

Observe it from this dissociated vantage point.

Associate into this point in time and experience the time when you made the decision. Anchor the limiting decision state.

Step #4. Float back to earlier experiences, seeking the first one.

Float to earlier points on your timeline where your behavior has expressed the limiting decision.

Go back to the point where you actually made the decision. If you had already gone to the earliest memory in step three, then skip this step.

Step #5. Go forward, returning to your positive decision.

Go forward in your timeline to your superior decision, and again access its positive state.

Step #6. Go earlier to your first limiting decision.

Float back past your earlier limiting decision, to a point just fifteen minutes prior to that decision.

Bring the positive state with you as you associate into that point in time.

Step #7. Experience that early decision while fully accessing the new resources.

Re-experience the situation and early decision while maintaining full access to your positive resource state.

Notice how your experience of this situation, and of yourself in the situation, are changed.

Step #8. Quickly zoom to the present, integrate the experience, and future pace.

Quickly zoom forward along your timeline to the present moment.

Stop here and take some time to absorb what has happened.

Future pace, seeing how situations similar to the pattern that was negative might play out with your new perspective and state.

☺☺

56.

The Godiva Chocolate Pattern

"I can charge a man's battery and then recharge it again. But it is only when he has his own generator that we can talk about motivation. He then needs no outside stimulation. He wants to do it".

— Frederick Herzberg

CREDITS FOR THE creation of this NLP pattern belong to various contributors.

Increase your motivation by associating intense pleasure with a desired behavior.

This is also the perfect place to introduce a concept of change-work that will make your practice a whole lot easier and much more productive. This is the concept of staying out of your client's way!

Inducing intense pleasure in a person is the most elegant outcome to be proven how this concept works in real life. You see, the more you talk during the initial stages of the trance in this pattern (step #2), the less effective it's going to be eventually.

You have to give your client enough time to be convinced that what they feel is pure pleasure, and that they really do not need the physical object they imagine in order to feel such an intense level of pleasure.

This approach serves two outcomes: first, you can work with that client much easier on unhealthy habits; obviously, if they have experienced the same pleasure without the original inducer (cigarettes, chocolates, cyber-porn, etc.), they can trust you enough to remove these ones completely and replace them with something that they can control.

Secondly, you want them to go as deep in a trance as possible, on their own. People are easily distracted. Unlike the myth, hypnosis does not give you full control over their senses.

You should avoid speaking too much, especially in the early stages of trance, even if you mean well and speak slowly and quietly, you still have to let them go deeper on their terms.

Once they are reminded of a source of pleasure, their subconscious mind will do the hard work for you. It will send them right into trance, because the need to feel again something so good is automatic.

Do not disturb a natural process when you can use it for the successful outcome of the session.

Overview: The Godiva Chocolate Pattern

Step #1. Select a source of intense pleasure.

Step #2. Imagine indulging in this pleasure.

Step #3. Imagine the behavior that you want to increase.

Step #4. Complete an ecology check.

Step #5. Put image one behind image two.

Step #6. Open a hole in picture two so you can see picture one.

Step #7. Shrink the hole back down.

Step #8. Repeat at least three times.

Step #9. Test.

Step #1. Select a source of intense pleasure.

Think of a food or other thing that you have an intense craving for, and that you take immense pleasure in. The creator of this pattern must have chosen Godiva Chocolate.

The more of a compulsion you have to enjoy this indulgence, the better.

Step #2. Imagine indulging in this pleasure.

Use all rep systems to imagine partaking of this indulgence.

Amplify the submodalities that give it its compelling intensity. Refer to this as image one.

Step #3. Imagine the behavior that you want to increase.

Select a behavior that you really want to increase.

Picture yourself doing this, and form a dissociated image of this. We'll call this one image two.

Step #4. Complete an ecology check.

Imagine what it would be like to be highly compelled to engage in this activity. What kind of outcomes might occur?

Can you think of any reasons that you would not like this?

Adjust your image or goal behavior as needed until it makes it through your ecology check.

Step #5. Put image one behind image two.

Use your imagination to place picture one (the compulsion) behind image two (the desired behavior).

Now, picture one is hidden by picture two.

Step #6. Open a hole in picture two so you can see picture one.

Allow yourself to see a little bit of picture one by opening a small hole in picture two.

Expand the hole so that you get a good view of picture one.

Fully enjoy the excitement that comes from this image.

Step #7. Shrink the hole back down.

Cover image one by shrinking the hole, so that you see image two again.

Step #8. Repeat at least three times.

Repeat steps six and seven at least three times or until you feel that you have associated compulsive excitement with the desired behavior.

Step #9. Test.

Over the next few days, see if you feel better about the desired behavior, and see if it increases.

If not, see if repeating this process is helpful.

୧୨

57.

Using Rep Systems

"Sometimes a scream is better than a thesis".

— Ralph Waldo Emerson

A REP SYSTEM IS how we perceive what comes in through our senses. We may see it, hear it, taste it, feel it, or even smell it. Whatever it is, we call it INFORMATION. The reason we call it information, is that your brain interprets it and uses it. If breakfast is burning, your first warning is the smell. The smell is information.

The beauty of rep systems is that they go way beyond how things get into your brain. You can recall and think about your experiences, and create new ones, with the power of your mind. Much of the power of NLP comes from your ability to work with rep systems. Another phrase for rep system is sense modality.

The rep systems include the obvious ones; the five senses. Here are the three main ones. They are what we see (called the visual rep system), what we hear (called the auditory rep system), what we feel (called the kinesthetic rep system).

The other two obvious ones may be needed at times. They are what we taste (the gustatory rep system), and what we smell (the olfactory rep system).

Those are the obvious rep systems; the five senses. But there are two factors that give rep systems great value in understanding and achieving excellence. The first is how we talk to ourselves, or hear what others have said. We call this the auditory digital rep system. Changing the talk inside our minds is a very powerful tool.

The other valuable factor is knowing which rep system a person favors. That is, which rep system do they rely upon most of the time. This is called the preferred rep system.

Once you know what their referred rep system is, you can make a better connection by using that rep system more. You can also make more powerful tools, because that rep system is more powerful for that person.

Rep systems are valuable because they are the way our experiences are coded. They are the DNA of our thoughts and behavior. They are where it all comes from. We encode or absorb our experiences and ideas with rep systems. We call up this information through our rep systems. This is called *accessing* or *retrieving* the information.

It isn't always obvious. Ask someone how they know something or why they did something, and they will give you a pretty limited answer. Most people will tell you that they just "know" something, or "felt" like it. But advertisers don't spend millions of dollars figuring out exactly which sounds and images to put into a television commercial just for the fun of it.

And manufacturers don't spend millions on designing just the right shape, color, and smells of products and logos for their egos. It's all about representational systems, and how they are loaded with meaning and motivation. By decoding the rep systems of successful people, you can get access to secrets that have taken many years or generations to acquire.

By decoding the rep systems of someone who is failing, you can become much more valuable as a success resource.

The way a person sequences and selects rep systems is a strategy. There is a rep system strategy for everything we do. By becoming aware of this, we gain extraordinary flexibility and latitude for creating better strategies. One reason for this is that rep systems are so basic, that they afford us great leverage to influence the resulting behaviors AND the results in our lives.

How do I Know What Rep System is Being Used?

People will tell you what rep system they are using without even knowing it. The secret is in their words. If they talk about how things look, what they saw, colors, and other visual words, they are thinking in pictures quite a bit. They are mostly using their visual rep system. The visual rep system is the one that people use the most.

If they talk about what they hear, how things sound, how loud they are, and other auditory words, they are emphasizing their auditory system.

Same thing for feelings. If they sense that someone is dishonest, and have a gut feeling about what stock to buy, they are mostly accessing feelings. That is, they are in their kinesthetic rep system.

Years ago in the U.S., a conservative politician named Barry Goldwater used a kinesthetic phrase in his advertising:

"In your heart, you know he's right."

That's pretty funny, because by the time he was campaigning, everybody knew that your heart pumps blood, and your brain knows things. But when people have strong feelings about something, they think they know it. This fact has been used by politicians throughout history.

But Goldwater lost his 1964 bid for the presidency of the U.S., because the liberals used even more powerful feelings and images involving fear of nuclear weapons and grief over the Kennedy assassination.

When Hitler was creating his speeches, he spent a good deal of time learning what got the crowds really excited. Of course, we'd like you to use rep systems to do good things, not to invade sovereign nations and sport a bad haircut.

Now, here is something fun and valuable that you can start doing to learn about rep systems. Whenever someone tells you about something, notice which rep system they use the most.

What Do I Do With a Primary Rep System Once I Find It?

Let's say you want to sell me a vacation package. Listen to this, and ask yourself what rep system I'm using. "I just don't SEE how I can afford to take a vacation." You heard the word see, as in visual. I can't SEE how I'll afford it. Most people use the visual rep system more than the other two main ones, hearing and feeling. This tells you that you must create pictures in my head of your wonderful vacation package. You know that pictures will especially help to influence me.

But consider the internal aspect of seeing. I can't see it because my concern about finances won't let me see it. So when you talk financing, that is the most important point for the visual rep system.

Show me how I'm locking in value while the cost will increase for everyone else.

Show me a graph.

Show me big, simple numbers.

Make me see other people missing out and being jealous of me.

Before long, I could be seeing a whole new opportunity.

Now let's say my wife is along, and she has a great influence over my buying decisions, or maybe a total influence. Listen for her rep system.

"Honey, I'm UNCOMFORTABLE with us committing to something when your work is so FEAST or FAMINE."

This wife of mine is all about feelings. No wonder she lights up the room. Uncomfortable, feast, famine... When you're coming up with things to influence her with, you'd better touch her feelings.

She needs to think about how she'll feel finally having some quality time with her feast or famine

husband. On our vacation, she can look forward to sunshine, warm sand, and the plush beds and carpeting of the air conditioned resort.

Did you notice which of those things were not from an external sense?

Warm sand affects your senses through your feet. But where does the feeling of quality alone time come from? Inside! Hey, remember feast or famine. You'd better tell her about the amazing food.

This is a huge lesson for influencing with rep systems. You should appeal to the internal sources as well as external. In fact, the internal sources may be many times more powerful than the external ones. This is because they are often about motivations and values.

NLP uses the term predicate for the clue words that tell you what rep system someone is using. Predicates, as you have seen, are words like see, hear, and feel. Predicates are not always so obvious, though.

If I tell you I'm CERTAIN, I might be in the auditory digital mode. That's the one where my internal talk is very dominant. But what if I not only tell you I'm so CERTAIN, but I also gesture forcefully with my fist.

In that case, I'm telling you I FEEL strongly about it. Instead of knowing I'm right in my head, I know it in my heart; I FEEL it, and I want you to FEEL it, too. Are you with me, or against me?

Feelings make choices very simple. So they can make your job simple.

So there's another important tip. Body language can be very important. If someone cocks their head and looks kind of skeptical, that's a sign that they aren't hearing things that they can agree with. They may be taking apart what you said in their own heads, because you weren't being analytical or logical enough for them.

In that case, you need to build more trust so they can get into the feelings or images, or you need to offer up your most compelling evidence, that is, the facts that show that you are right. And keep working on building that trust. You don't need to drop the other sense modalities, but you need to deliver the facts. And did I mention building trust? We'll teach you a lot about rapport-building soon.

But here is a trust-building technique you can start using right away. It's called matching predicates.

As you talk to people, practice using the same rep system that they are. See how this affect how they act toward you.

Are they more open to your ideas?

Do they show you friendlier body language?

Do they smile more or give you a softer, kinder facial expression?

Since body language is a non-verbal predicate, see what body language you can use that goes along with the rep system you are emphasizing. If they are hearing, cock your head, put your finger to your ear, lean forward a little bit with an ear turned a little toward them.

If they are seeing, tilt you head up just a little and raise your eyebrows a bit, soften your eyes, like you're letting them in.

If they are feeling, use more emotional gestures. Nothing too dramatic for now, just enough to show where your heart is; or at least where it is supposed to be.

Keep in mind that people may change their primary rep system depending on the subject, or even the point of the conversation they are in. So don't think people have only one rep system. Be flexible and follow them into different rep systems.

Also, it's good to appeal to all rep systems during your discussion. In psychology, there is a thing called neurological recruitment. This big phrase means that the more brain cells you can get to think about something, the more powerful it is. If you're in an airplane, you want ALL the engines firing.

Using more rep systems means you are influencing with more power. Emphasize one at a time, but use all of the three primary ones: seeing, feeling, and hearing.

Another valuable method is to watch for eye movements. These are called eye accessing cues. We call them accessing cues, because the eye movements tell you what senses the person is accessing, or tapping into, in order to think and express themselves.

People have claimed that the research does not support NLP's use of eye accessing cues, but the research has some serious flaws. We suggest that you see for yourself. And remember, this is not always true for every person.

☜☞

58.

Auditory Rep. System Development

"Deep listening is miraculous for both listener and speaker. When someone receives us with open-hearted, non-judging, intensely interested listening, our spirits expand".

— Sue Patton

CREDITS FOR THE creation of this NLP pattern belong to Robert Dilts.

Improve your auditory rep system in order to better perceive sound, its meanings, and subtleties. This can enhance your modeling and communication.

You can practice this strategy also with a recording, but be sure to record your own voice as well. To make it even more useful, listen to your recorded voice a few times to get used to it.

Overview: The Auditory Rep. System Development Pattern

Step #1. Listen to a sound.

Step #2. Reproduce the sound.

Step #3. Compare.

Step #4. Internal Representations.

Step #5. Submodality Rating.

Step #6. Reproduce

Step #1. Listen to a sound.

Notice an ongoing or recurring sound in your surroundings. Carefully listen to it for roughly ten seconds.

Step #2. Reproduce the sound.

Using your voice, reproduce that sound as closely as possible. If it is a sound that you can't imitate very well, imitate any aspect of it that you can. For example, rhythm, warble, grittiness, and any other submodality of the sound.

Step #3. Compare

Try this with a partner. Compare how you reproduce the sound.

Step #4. Internal Representations

Ask your partner what internal representations were used and in what ways they feel their voice resembles or does not resemble the sound.

Give the same information to your partner.

Step #5. Submodality Rating

Take a look at the list of submodalities.

Listen to the sound with each of these in mind, but filter for each submodality, one at a time.

Can you add any of the submodalities to your imitation of the sound?

Refer to appendix B for a list of submodalities.

As you do this, compare with your partner where you feel the sound belongs in the range of each submodality, on a scale of zero to ten, with zero being "not at all" and ten being the highest level, or 100%.

Include in your discussion what you used as a reference to rate the submodality. For example, take volume. *Louder or quieter than what?* Consider grittiness. *Grittier than James Brown, or smoother than Enya?*

Step #6. Reproduce

Reproduce the sound again.

Notice any improvements, and how your awareness has improved. *What submodalities had the biggest effect on your discernment?*

Compare with your partner.

☙❧

59.

Visual Rep. System Development

"The man who does not read good books has no advantage over the man who can't read them".

— Mark Twain

MUCH LIKE THE Auditory Rep. System Development pattern, this pattern will help you refine the subtleties and perceptions of your visual representational system. It will improve your abilities to distinguish submodalities, which is a necessary skill when working with NLP patterns. It will also freshen-up your creativity and problem solving capabilities.

The visual rep. system is memory based. Visualization, in essence, is a big word for saying that you remember what a certain item looks like.

Overview: The Visual Rep. System Development Pattern

Step #1. Take an onion and put it in front of you.

Step #2. Close your eyes and imagine exactly the same onion.

Step #3. Open your eyes and take another good look at the onion.

Step #4. Close your eyes again and multiply the onion's size.

Step #5. Return to normal size and change colors.

Step #6. Return to normal color and change structure.

Step #7. Repeat.

Step #1. Take an onion and put it in front of you.

In many traditional and old-fashioned visualization guides you would find the instruction to imagine an orange or a banana. We believe that this is no test to your imagination, and it does not provide any value in imagining something you've seen 10 thousands of times in the past.

Normally, you wouldn't take an onion and observe it intensely. You would do so with an orange just before you're about to peel and eat it.

Concentrate now on the onion and try to grasp the "big picture", how it looks like, the colors, the shades, and so on.

Step #2. Close your eyes and imagine exactly the same onion.

Now, with your eyes closed just keep the image you've seen with your eyes open in your mind's eye. That's all. It's easy, and it takes almost no effort to see something and recalling it the same second you close your eyes.

Step #3. Open your eyes and take another good look at the onion.

What you do now is confirming that the image in your head matches, more or less, the image your eyes are getting from the surrounding.

The reason for this step is that further on in this pattern we will manipulate the mental image the same ways you subconsciously manipulate other images that affect your emotions. This will also convince you how powerful and in-control your imagination can be.

Step #4. Close your eyes again and multiply the onion's size.

Now you're doing some image manipulation. Your brain is better than any version of Adobe Photoshop and much faster than any quadruple Intel processor on the most elegant Mac computer.

Close your eyes and imagine the same onion. As you do so, double its size. You could simply "bump" the image closer to you; when things are closer, they seem bigger.

Here's a more complicated request – double the size again.

Now the onion would probably be much closer and almost "in your face". If it isn't close enough to make your eyes tear, double the size again!

Step #5. Return to normal size and change colors.

Open your eyes and look at the onion again.

Close your eyes and imagine the same picture you've seen with your eyes open. The onion is now back in its normal size.

As you look at the mental image, imagine that the onion is changing colors. Go randomly and fast. Choose any color you wish and for 30 seconds or so, keep changing the color every second.

Go beyond the usual colors like blue, black, yellow, white, green or red. Try purple, army green, beige, cinnamon, coral, lavender blue, orange-peel, pink, yellow-green, smooth violet, tyrian purple, teal, tangerine, spring green, sapphire, salmon, rose, rust, pale blue and so on.

Step #6. Return to normal color and change structure.

Now open your eyes again and take a good look at the onion. Close your eyes and imagine this normal looking image. This time you are going to manipulate the onion's structure or "physics".

Imagine the onion becoming elongated, thin and long.

Now back to normal. Imagine it become fat or chubby.

Now back to normal. Imagine it becoming like the digit 8, fat on the edges and very thin in the middle.

Now back to normal. Imagine it with a huge hole in its middle, big enough so you can look through it.

Now back to normal. Imagine the onion having a chunk been taken off it, much like the Apple logo.

Now back to normal. Imagine the onion becoming flat, completely flat. Now back to normal.

You can keep these mental experimentations going as far as your creativity takes you.

Step #7. Repeat.

One crucial element to any skill development outcome is repetition. If your visualization skills are not as good as you'd like them to be, repeat this pattern every day or every other day.

☙❧

60.

State Of Consciousness Awareness

*"A human being is part of a whole, called by us the Universe, a
part limited in time and space. He experiences himself,
his thoughts and feelings, as something separated from the
rest a kind of optical delusion of his consciousness. This delusion
is a kind of prison for us, restricting us to our personal desires
and to affection for a few persons nearest us. Our task must
be to free ourselves from this prison by widening our circles
of compassion to embrace all living creatures and the whole of
nature in its beauty".*

— Albert Einstein

CREDITS for the creation of this NLP pattern belong to various contributors.

This pattern increases your awareness of your states and how they affect your perspective. This awareness is valuable in nearly every aspect of Neuro Linguistic Programming and life in general. Any effort you make to enhance your states and patterns calls on your awareness of these things in order to make the discriminations called for by the pattern.

Overview: The State Of Consciousness Awareness Pattern

Step #1. Review today's states.

Step #2. Represent the states.

Step #3. Annotate the states.

Step #4. Test.

Step #1. Review today's states.

Note the states you have experienced today.

Review your day, taking note of the major states that you have experienced so far.

Step #2. Represent the states.

Draw a circle to represent each of these states.

Inside the circle, draw a simple face, like a happy face, to represent how you felt. It can be as simple as happy and frown faces.

Step #3. Annotate the states.

Rate the intensity of each state with a number from one to ten.

Underneath, note the main internal representations and changes in physiology that you experience in this state.

Put an asterisk (*) next to the main triggers of the states.

For example, if you were treated rudely this morning, what was it that really triggered your feelings?

Looking at submodalities, it might have mainly been an aspect of the person's tone of voice.

Remember to include meanings, not just sensory experience. Perhaps it was what the person was implying with their tone, rather than the tone itself.

Step #4. Test.

See if doing this exercise enhances your ability to detect the changes and subtleties of your states, and how your thoughts and circumstances can trigger them.

☯

61.

Non-Verbal Cues Recognition

"Somebody must take a chance. The monkeys who became men, and the monkeys who didn't are still jumping around in trees making faces at the monkeys who did.".

— Lincoln Steffens

CREDITS for the creation of this NLP pattern belong to various contributors.

Practice recognizing non-verbal cues and getting to know you're your own face expresses emotions that you experience, even when you are not trying to show them. This skill will help you function almost like you can read minds.

People can observe an extraordinary number of non-verbal cues.

It is estimated that there are over 1,500 cues for interpreting the state of mind that a person is in. You will improve your skill in reading others, by trying it out on yourself, making subtle observations of the interplay of the over 90 muscles of your face. Practice this exercise a good number of times over several days, until you are very good at running yourself through the prescribed emotions.

> ## *Overview: The Non-Verbal Cues Recognition Pattern*
>
> *Step #1. Make initial observations in a mirror.*
>
> *Step #2. Create a very subtle smile.*
>
> *Step #3. Take yourself through emotions.*
>
> *Step #4. Repeat until you are good at it.*
>
> *Step #5. Exercise the expression of polarities.*
>
> *Step #6. Test.*

Step #1. Make initial observations in a mirror.

Step in front of a mirror, or get one for this purpose, and take a good look at your face.

Look carefully, examining your face for even the most subtle and delicate features.

Consider these surfaces:

Facial skin, in general – it's color, thickness and stretch.

Ears – not how big, but in what shape.

Earlobes

Forehead

Eyebrows

Eyes

Eyelids

Eyelashes

Nose

Nostrils

Cheeks

Cheekbones

Lips

Jowls

Hair

Wrinkles

Moles

Step #2. Create a very subtle smile.

As you watch your face, create the most subtle smile you possible can; one that will be almost impossible to see.

Increase the smile until you can see it.

Step #3. Take yourself through emotions.

Without trying to express them in any way in your face, take yourself through the emotions listed below.

Take your self into memories that will e0voke each memory, one at a time. Spend about five seconds entering the state, observe your expression for two or three seconds, and take about one second to break state, then move to the next emotion and do the same thing.

This fast tempo is a key to success for this exercise.

When you break the state, it can help to take a power breath through your nose and look up at the same time, then release the air, and move on to the next emotion.

Except for the last memory (surprise), don't use the auditory modality for these memories, since it takes time to listen to, and it can flood us with other memories. If you are highly emotionally sensitive, you may want to have a friend with you for this exercise.

Here are the emotions:

Fear

Joy

Anger

Acceptance

Sorrow

Anticipation

Disgust

Surprise

Step #4. Repeat until you are good at it.

The next steps require you to be good at the preceding steps, so repeat steps one through three a good number of times over several days before you move on to the remaining steps.

Step #5. Exercise the expression of polarities.

This time through, you will be using a different set of emotions that are on polarities developed by Aristotle. Have a drink of water to prepare. We will be going at a slower pace this time.

Give the first emotion eight to ten seconds, and then five to seven seconds for transition, and then eight to ten seconds for the paired emotion, then five seconds to cool down, breaking the state.

Continue with the next pair in the same way until you are done with all pairs.

You will be going for a more intense emotional experience this time, so use all sensory modalities, including auditory. Going for more intense emotions will teach you a great deal about yourself.

Practice this part of the exercise over a few weeks. This will definitely take you out of the "phantom" reality of what you think your facial expressions convey, and into accurate understanding.

Here are the pairs:

Anger vs. Calmness

Friendship vs. Enmity

Fear vs. Confidence

Shame vs. Shamelessness

Kindness vs. Rudeness

Pity vs. Adoration

Indignation vs. Acceptance

Envy vs. Gratitude

Step #6. Test.

Over the days and weeks after you have fully completed this process, notice how your awareness of your public identity, and your ability to perceive subtleties in others' expressions has expanded.

☙❧

62.

Compulsion Blow-Out

*"Every action must be due to one or other of seven causes:
chance, nature, compulsion, habit, reasoning, anger, or appetite."*

— Aristotle

CREDITS FOR the creation of this NLP pattern belong to various contributors.

A compulsion is an irresistible urge to behave in a specific way, most likely and especially when it's against a person's conscious will. Compulsions are different than habits. Habits can be somewhat consciously controlled, and there are productive habits as well as non productive ones.

Compulsions are not within your conscious control (therefor we say it's against your will), and they are all non productive.

This pattern desensitizes compulsions that range from fingernail chewing to obsessing about being jilted.

Overview: The Compulsion Blow-Out Pattern

Step #1. Select the compulsion.

Step #2. Identify the primary trigger.

Step #3. Identify the two strongest submodalities of the trigger.

Step #4. Intensify the submodalities to an extreme.

Step #5. Repeat until there is significant desensitization.

Step #6. Recommend additional help.

Step #7. Test

Step #1. Select the compulsion.

Choose a compulsion that the person wishes to eliminate.

It should be one that has some kind of external trigger.

Even nail biting has an external trigger. It is the sensation of fingernails extending to a certain length, or just existing.

Step #2. Identify the primary trigger.

Determine what circumstance or factor triggers the compulsive behavior.

Step #3. Identify the two strongest submodalities of the trigger.

Review the various submodalities of the rep systems involved in the trigger.

For example, with nail biting, there are usually very specific sensations that are related to fingernails, but are much more subtle and specific, such as a tingling or pressure felt inside the body in connection with sensing the fingernails or even being conscious of them.

Step #4. Intensify the submodalities to an extreme.

Have the person use their imagination to increase the sub-modalities to the highest possible level.

If there is a sense of the nails sticking out, imagine them protruding very far.

If it is a feeling of pressure in the body, imagine being closer and closer to exploding.

Step #5. Repeat until there is significant desensitization.

Take the submodalities back to normal, and increase them to an extreme.

Do this until the person shows signs of feeling that the process is boring, trivial, or otherwise not triggering.

Step #6. Recommend additional help.

Do not attempt to replace treatment for a psychiatric problem such as drug addiction.

Recommend that a person with potentially harmful behavior get an appropriate assessment for possible treatment.

Step #7. Test

See if the person reduces their compulsive behavior, is more open to additional work, or exhibits other signs of improvement.

Repeat this process as needed.

Additional Advice

You can add other approaches and NLP patterns for compulsive or obsessive behavior. Interruption is another approach. When the person feels like carrying out the behavior, they engage in an incompatible behavior that disrupts the impulsive drive.

An example would be tightening the stomach while pressing the palms together intensely.

Thought-stopping is another method, where the person substitutes another thought that is very "loud" and distracts from a compulsive thought. An energy ther-apy such as emotional freedom technique or a cognitive somatic therapy such as eye movement desensitization and reprocessing may help.

People with obsessive compulsive disorder may benefit from understanding the disorder and experiencing therapy that helps them understand that their compulsion is fueled largely by a brain dysfunction that can be seen graphically in a brain scan. Seeing such a brain scan is part of this treatment.

63.

Creating Positive Expectations

"One must still have chaos in one to give birth to a dancing star".

— Nietzsche

MY FIRST LESSON in the Hypnotherapy College was about expectations. First, we started discussing our own expectations from the course; then, the teacher said what he considered to be most important... the client's expectations.

It doesn't really matter who you are, how tall you are, how much experience you had in doing therapy or Hypnosis or NLP.

It doesn't matter if you're a native, a foreign student or you're naturally stuttering. The client expects something, and you have to make sure it is positive.

It's not only directed to active Hypnotherapists. Even if you're just "playing" with Hypnosis; learning it for your own use, to get better, to communicate more persuasively or whatever – this is one concept that can be expanded to many other areas of life.

To create a positive sense of expectation in another person (a client, a child, a co-worker, etc.), act confidently. Even if you're not really sure what you're doing is right, in Hypnosis it doesn't matter much. You cannot do harm.

The little "trick" of acting as if you know what you're doing, and focus on your client and not on your own thoughts and memories... that's how you create a sense of confidence.

I wouldn't want a nervous insecure person to hypnotize me! Would you?

But if he acts confidently, responding to your hints and seems like he's reading your thoughts? It will be much easier, much more comfortable and hopefully also effective.

If you're not convinced yourself that you OWN the skills, that you're the best option to choose in solving that specific problem, when a client arrives at your door, you'll be too nervous to serve properly. I had the same issue.

That's why I gave plenty of free sessions to people, but without telling them why.

The first few sessions were not effective, since I kept focusing on my own feelings and memories instead of those of the client; later on, I forced myself to focus ON the client instead of thinking what I should do/say next.

Make sure your client knows he's about to get results. Make sure you say it with every fiber of your being. Look at their eyes.

Speak with no "hmmm..." or "well...".

Use the Meta Model to negate speculations or objections. Don't react to any word the client says.

Even if he says "I don't believe in Hypnosis", agree with it.

I would have said, "You're not alone; Me too. I believe it's simply a tool you can use to help yourself, nothing more. By the way, how did you sleep yesterday? Oh, interesting... and right at that moment when you feel drousy and a bit out of this world, what did you think about? Any specific memories that have made you more comfortable as you went more and more relax... ".

You can use whatever the client offers you. If you get uptight, thinking "oh my god! He said this or that...", it won't work.

Use whatever the client says, affirm it, say it's true and that you agree with it.

This way his mind won't have any reason to argue. In other words – stay cool.

If you follow these few advices you'll create a sense of positive expectation in your clients. They will feel comfortable, and will have an easier time trusting you.

That's what you really want – trust. If you act with integrity, confidently and calmly, you'll earn trustworthiness.

From that base, your road to fulfill a great therapeutic session is really short. Without it, you can keep spreading 10,000 hypnotic suggestions but none will work.

Did I just make you expect positive results from your next session? I wonder.

64.

Breaking Limiting Associations

"At the age of 20, we don't care what the world thinks of us; at 30, we worry about what it is thinking of us; at 40, we discover that it wasn't thinking of us at all".

— Anonymous

CREDITS FOR the creation of this NLP pattern belong to various contributors.

One of the most important ways out of stuck thought patterns is to develop a better-articulated sense of how our minds work. That is, to develop a more subtle and detailed recognition of our thoughts and rep systems and how they form interlocking patterns. As you know, much of Neuro Linguistic Programming is about unlocking these patterns to allow for more flexibility.

The Breaking Limiting Associations pattern is a very rapid pattern, once you learn to work with it. If you and your client have identified in advance a well formed outcome and the problem-atic thinking patterns that disturb the achievement of this outcome, you only need to work one by one through them using this pattern.

In addition, this pattern is powerful mostly because of its use of the body. The client has to move around, which involves more senses. The more the client is engaged in the process to be changed, the better and longer lasting results that process would bring.

When you work with patterns that involve the client moving around and being active, it is better if you explain the steps ahead of time. In this pattern, for example, it would serve you well to decide ahead of time where the anchors on the floor should be.

Walk the client through it before using the pattern. It will make everything go smoother.

Also, remember that when you use active patterns, that is patterns that involve physical action by the client, speak slower. Do not rush it, because your client needs to organize and re-organize thoughts and physiological movements, and being in trance they need more time than normal awake states.

This is also not the kind of pattern to use right in the first session you have with a client. Establish some trust first, work on other issues for the first session if this one is the best choice for a specific issue the client has presented.

The reason is that this pattern may cause automatic and random breaks of state for the client. Physical movement requires attention.

That's also the reason you should have trust with the client, and more than so – explain the steps ahead of time. It makes the need to move from one spot to another less of an "unknown" and more comfortable and logical.

Overview: The Breaking Limiting Associations Pattern

Step #1. Select a problem and identify it's typical context.

Step #2. Anchor to the floor.

Step #3. Anchor a resource state.

Step #4. Transfer the resource state to the problem spot.

Step #5. Add stimuli while returning to the resource position.

Step #6. Figure-eight your eyes through the rep system positions while focusing on the problem pattern.

Step #7. Break state. Notice any resourcefulness in your state or ideas. Run an ecology check.

Step #8. Test.

Step #1. Select a problem and identify its typical context.

Select a problem that tends to occur in a particular environment or situation.

Think about what in the context leads to the behavior.

Make note of factors such as time of day and the kind of people or pressures that are involved.

Step #2. Anchor to the floor.

Get into the problem state and anchor it to a spot on the floor.

Take a little time to get to know the state and it's submodalities.

Step #3. Anchor a resource state.

Determine what resource state would make it easy to eliminate the problem.

Pick another spot on the floor, and imagine stepping into the state there. Anchor the resource state to that spot.

Notice the details of that state.

Step #4. Transfer the resource state to the problem spot.

Move back to the problem anchor spot, but access the resource state and amplify it.

Hold the image of the problem pattern while fostering the physiology of the resource state.

Step #5. Add stimuli while returning to the resource position.

Tap your right foot.

Move your left finger to your chin.

Look up right while going, "Hmmmmm," as though you were having a deep thought.

At the same time, step back into the resource anchor spot.

Step #6. Figure-eight your eyes through the rep system positions while focusing on the problem pattern.

As you think about the problem, focus on each rep system as you move your eyes into each corresponding rep system direction in a sideways figure-eight pattern (like the infinity symbol).

Step #7. Break state. Notice any resourcefulness in your state or ideas. Run an ecology check.

Break your state.

Notice any changes in how you experience the problem. Look for fresh ideas or a more resourceful state.

Ask yourself if there are any objections to experiencing the problem from this more resourceful place, or dropping the problem for a more successful behavior.

Step #8. Test.

In the next few days, notice any changes in this problem behavior pattern and how you experience it. See if your behavior is more successful in any way.

∞

65.

Secondary Gain and Personal Ecology

"Exert your talents, and distinguish yourself, and don't think of retiring from the world, until the world will be sorry that you retire".

— Samuel Johnson

Personal ecology means that you consider your personal needs, aspirations, and values in the outcome. Personal ecology gives an important edge to your plans because it brings about inner alignment.

If any part of you feels at all uncomfortable with the outcome, then you should add, remove, or improve whatever aspects of your outcome need you to adjust them.

Once you're totally on board, in other words, once you have your motivations fully aligned, then you have put yourself in a much better position to succeed. Personal alignment provides a powerful force.

You can also take a look at the flip side of this question:

What is there about the status quo that might give you a reason to stay stuck?

Might your subconscious mind have any reasons to jinx your plans?

You should definitely address any problems like that in your outcome.

And everyone, no matter how strong their will or how smart or courageous, everyone has incentives to not move forward with their plans.

Dealing with this now aligns the forces of your personality for success.

☙❧

66.

Whole System Ecology

"Even the mighty and ferocious cannot conquer the small but secure; Thus a man-eating tiger cannot swallow a single porcupine."

— Liu Ji (14th century general)

YOU HAVE ALREADY started thinking about your personal ecology. There are other individuals and systems as well. By systems, we mean families, schools, regulatory government agencies, businesses and so on.

Does your outcome, as defined so far, impair your relationship with any other individuals or systems?

What can you do about it?

Ask the helpful question, *"If I could have it now, would I take it?"*

Maybe the answer is obvious, but this question really gets you thinking about possible downsides or imperfections in your outcome. The question, "If I could have it now, would I take it?" can inspire you to evolve your outcome. Of course, nobody wants paralysis by analysis, but don't under-think your outcome.

Put your mind into that outcome as if you have achieved it, and open your thinking to means of improving that outcome. The time to rework your outcomes comes before you start investing a lot of resources.

The way to align with your highest goals is to stay flexible about your outcome; to rework the outcome as needed; to shape the outcome into something even better. Now you are developing one of the hallmarks of NLP: ecology; where all parts of you agree with the outcome; where your desires, your values, and your needs are all aligned into one powerful direction.

☯

67.

Meta-Model Challenging

*"Language is not an abstract construction of the learned, or
of dictionary makers, but is something arising out of the work,
needs, ties, joys, affections, tastes, of long generations of humanity, and has its bases broad and low, close to the ground".*

— Noah Webster

CREDITS FOR THE creation of this NLP pattern belong to Richard Bandler & John Grinder.

With this pattern, you will practice the fundamental skill that assists with modeling and with ensuring adequate communication. Refer to Appendix C for a full explanation of the meta-model and its violations in language.

Overview: The Meta-Model Challenging Pattern

Step #1. Identify meta-model violations when spoken to you.

Step #2. Whenever you hear a meta-model violation, ask about it.

Step #3. Continue until you have a well-formed understanding of what the other person is saying.

Step #4. Test

Step #1. Identify meta-model violations when spoken to you.

As someone speaks to you, listen for meta-model violations such as excessive generalization or deletion, and inappropriate presuppositions.

Notice whether you can have good sensory representations of what the person is saying.

As you "map over" into sensory representations, you are likely to find that there are missing pieces, that tempt you to "fill in the blanks" by going out of sensory representation or using your imagination.

How well can you tell what the person is referring to and what they mean?

For more of these meta-model distinctions, refer to the appendices.

Step #2. Whenever you hear a meta-model violation, ask about it.

For example, if two ideas that don't belong together are treated as if they do (complex equivalence), then ask. *"How is it that protesting war is dividing the country?"*

Perhaps the person doesn't know that countries are always divided over issues, and this is the nature of politics throughout history. Perhaps they know that, but fear a military coup will result from it this time around.

If the person is irritated or becomes manipulative when you ask meta-model questions (questions that clarify meta-model violations), see if you can find out what the person is attempting to prevent you from knowing or doing. You can start by directly asking why they are getting mad (or whatever their reaction is).

Needless to say, this should be a situation in which you are safe and don't have much to lose by alienating this person. This is just for practice, after all.

Step #3. Continue until you have a well-formed understanding of what the other person is saying.

Step #4. Test

Test by expressing your understanding and seeing if the person agrees, or test by seeing if you have a clear understanding of how to respond effectively.

To use an obvious example, if the person gave you directions, did you arrive at your destination?

☙❧

68.

Meta-Model Intentional Usage

"If language is not correct, then what is said is not what is meant; if what is said is not what is meant, then what must be done remains undone; if this remains undone, morals and art will deteriorate; if justice goes astray, the people will stand about in helpless confusion. Hence there must be no arbitrariness in what is said. This matters above everything".

— Confucius

CREDITS for the creation of this NLP pattern belong to Tad James.

Produce constructive change as efficiently as possible with the very structured questioning of this pattern. It includes presuppositions in the course of asking meta-model questions.

The purpose of this very structured questioning is to help produce constructive change as efficiently as possible.

Discuss a personal problem with someone (questions included).

Ask the following questions in the specified order in the course of the discussion. Phrase the questions as you wish, in order to fit the situation and the person you are speaking with.

a. *"What do you believe is the problem?"*

b. *"What is the cause?"*

c. *"How have your efforts to solve the problem failed so far?"*

d. *"If the problem were solved, what would be different (how would you know)?"*

e. Note: At this point, we flip into a positive frame that moves into a solution state. *"What do you want to change about this problem?"*

f. *"When will you stop it from limiting you?"*

g. *"How many ways do you know that you have solved the problem?"*

h. *"I know that you have already begun to change and see things in new ways."*

Test.

Observe changes in physiology, attitude and behavior.

Note any changes that occur in the person's life in the next days or weeks.

∞

69.

De-Nominalizing

"But behavior in the human being is sometimes a defense, a way of concealing motives and thoughts, as language can be a way of hiding your thoughts and preventing communication".

— Abraham Maslow

CREDITS for the creation of this NLP pattern belong to various contributors.

Get much more control over your mind and your life, by resolving the meta-model violation known as nominalization. This works because nominalizations remove the actor from the scene.

If I say, *"I have to go visit my stupid relatives,"* I'm not saying who is in charge of the "have to." If I decide to be empowered, I can say, "I'm going to make my mom happy by visiting my stupid relatives," or, *"I decided it wasn't worth going through that misery."*

Even better, if you can say it honestly, *"I'm going to create a completely new and mind-expanding experience with my relatives."* We nominalize when we turn verbs into nouns. If you talk about "the relationship," it seems to have a life of its own. Where is your (and the other person's) leadership and vision?

Overview: The Denominalizing Pattern

Step #1. Select a nominalization from your own thinking.

Step #2. De-nominalize by turning at least one noun into a verb.

Step #3. Talk about it without nominalization.

Step #4. Test.

Step #1. Select a nominalization from your own thinking.

Think about situations in which you feel less powerful. You might feel overwhelmed, frustrated, or coerced.

Find a nominalization in the way you talk about the situation.

Step #2. De-nominalize by turning at least one noun into a verb.

Find a way to turn at least one noun into a verb. This change puts someone into the driver's seat. The more challenging or empowering it feels, the better.

If it challenges you to take responsibility in some way, that is a special challenge to embrace.

Step #3. Talk about it without nominalization.

Explore ways to talk about the situation without nominalization, and by including the verb(s) you identified.

Instead of, *"This job is killing my soul,"* you might have, *"I am super motivated to get a different job, and fast. I'm networking and telling everyone I meet to keep an eye out for good opportunities in my field."*

Step #4. Test.

Do you feel that you are in a more meaningful, connected, empowered state?

☙❧

70.

The Forgiveness Pattern

"Don't tell your friends their social faults; they will cure the fault and never forgive you".

— Logan Pearsall

CREDITS for the creation of this NLP pattern belong to various contributors.

Rid yourself of the brooding resentments that can sap your creative energies.

Overview: The Forgiveness Pattern

Step #1. Associate into your higher values and self esteem

Step #2. Sense the difference between the fundamental human essence of the individual as opposed to their behavior.

Step #3. Feel your anger over harmful behaviors that some people engage in.

Step #4. Take permission to sense the humanity of all, including people who engage in hurtful behavior.

Step #5. Expand your state to include a sense of releasing, and associate it with the hurtful behaviors.

Step #6. connect with the aspect of yourself that is capable of responding to these hurtful behaviors.

Step #7. Test.

Step #1. Associate into your higher values and self esteem

Include a sense of sacredness or human dignity to all people in this state.

Step #2. Sense the difference between the fundamental human essence of the individual as opposed to their behavior.

Step #3. Feel your anger over harmful behaviors that some people engage in.

This anger is not at the fundamental humanity that we protect with civil rights. You are sensing anger that arises from certain behaviors, especially behaviors that violate those rights.

Step #4. Take permission to sense the humanity of all, including people who engage in hurtful behavior.

Step #5. Expand your state to include a sense of releasing, and associate it with the hurtful behaviors.

Allow your self to conjure a sense of releasing, and imagine releasing, for now, your attachment to these behaviors. This attachment may consist of ruminating about them, over-focusing on how they must be punished, and other ways of being attached. This step is not intended to reduce your capacity, commitment, or responsibility for addressing such behaviors, of course.

Step #6. Connect with the aspect of yourself that is capable of responding to these hurtful behaviors.

This can include your power of speech and ability to cultivate it over time. It can include your awareness and understanding of the boundaries that these hurtful behaviors cross in order to be hurtful. It can include your preparedness to defend those boundaries under certain circumstances.

Step #7. Test.

Notice if this process has reduced your resentment and expanded your forgiveness.

Notice in the coming days or weeks how any changes in your forgiveness are playing out.

☙❧

267

71.

Aligned Self

"The truest wisdom is a resolute determination"

— Napoleon Bonaparte

CREDITS FOR THE creation of this NLP pattern belong to various contributors.

Aligned self means heading in a strong direction because your values, beliefs, sense of identity and purpose in life are all working together. This pattern helps you achieve or reclaim that state. We say "reclaim" because many people complain of falling out of alignment for various reasons. Self-alignment creates a wonderful snow ball effect, in which the more you are aligned, the better your results in life, and the more you are able to align because of the positive feedback, empowerment, and support that results. This pattern uses Dilts' logical levels, listed in the appendix.

Overview: The Aligned Self Pattern

Step #1. Select a resource.

Step #2. Create visual space anchors for each neurological level.

Step #3. Focus on each space, exploring how it will contribute to your alignment.

Step #4. From the bottom (behavior) step into each space working up. Enhance the state of each space, and carry it into the next space.

Step #5. Take time for integration.

Step #6. Future pace.

Step #7. Test.

Step #1. Select a resource.

What would help you in becoming more aligned in your values, beliefs, sense of identity and purpose in life?

What would make you feel more purposeful or hopeful?

States such as calm resolve, creative joy and appreciation of developing mastery systematically are good candidates.

Step #2. Create visual space anchors for each neurological level.

Select a visual space for each of what will become six anchors: environment, behaviors, beliefs and values, capabilities, identity, and spirituality.

Step #3. Focus on each space, exploring how it will contribute to your alignment.

Start at the highest level (spirituality) and work your way down.

a. Focus on the environmental space. Ask, *"When and where do I wish to express X (the resource you selected)?"*

b. Focus on the behavior space. Ask, *"What behaviors will help me express X in those times and places (from the previous step)?"*

c. Focus on the capabilities space. Ask, *"What capabilities will help me express X in the form of those behaviors in those times and places?"*

d. Focus on the beliefs & values space. Ask, *"What beliefs and values will help me express X through these capabilities, the feed those behaviors at those times and places?"*

You are asking as to what beliefs and values will support you and direct you toward you highest goals, as well as what is meaningful and valuable about the capabilities from the previous step.

e. Focus on the identity space. Ask, *"What kind of person has these beliefs and values? What kind of person expresses X?"*

f. Physically stand in the physical space. Ask, *"What is my overarching purpose in life? What is my life mission?"*

Take some time to verbalize these thoughts, but without becoming mired in creating the perfect mission statement.

Step #4. From the bottom (behavior) step into each space working up. Enhance the state of each space, and carry it into the next space.

a. Enhance this spiritual space by amplifying and enriching the state.

Take that state with you as you step back into the identity space.

b. Enhance the sense of identity.

Notice how the spiritual state helps you do this as you experience your sense of identity and highest values or spirituality at the same time.

Take the identity and spiritual states with you as you step into the capability space.

c. Enhance your sense of capability.

Notice how the spiritual and identity states support this sense of capability. Take that state with you as you step back into the beliefs and values space.

d. Enhance your sense of beliefs and values.

Sense how your spirituality, identity, and capability states contribute to your beliefs and values.

Bring this state to the behavior space.

e. In the behavior space, enhance your potential for taking action.

Notice how your spirituality, identity, capability, and beliefs and values support this kind of action.

Notice how the spiritual state puts you in connection with the universe and humanity.

Discover how your sense of identity puts the behavior in the context of who you are as a person.

See how your capability state puts more power into your action potential. Finally, see how your beliefs and values give meaning and importance to this behavior.

Take all these levels into your environment space.

f. In the environmental space, explore how all the preceding levels support your ability to harmonize with the context of the behavior, as well as to derive resources from the context. Resources can be as airy as inspiration, or as palpable as concern about upsetting the boss.

Step #5. Take time for integration.

Spend some time experiencing all of these levels blending into a superstate.

Notice any new insights, ideas, or scenarios coming to mind.

Keep an open focus so that these thoughts can flow through as you process this new experience.

Step #6. Future pace.

Imagine moving through life with this state engaged.

Notice ways that you are more aligned in these future scenarios.

Step #7. Test.

In the coming days or weeks, notice any ways that you are more direct and empowered in pursuing meaningful goals, or in developing or changing your goals.

☙❧

72.

Circle Of Excellence

"Excellence in any department can be attained only by the labor of a lifetime; it is not to be purchased at a lesser price".

— Samuel Johnson

CREDITS FOR THE creation of this NLP pattern belong to John Grinder and Judith De-Losier.

With this pattern, you can produce high-performance states. It helps you become more aware of the internal sensations and the behaviors that can help you produce a positive state. It also helps you perceive cues from others. The technique includes establishing an internal anchor for a state of excellence.

Overview: The Circle Of Excellence Pattern

Step #1.   *Choose your resourceful state.*

Step #2.   *Choose a time to trigger the state.*

Step #3.   *Create a symbol for an excellent state.*

Step #4.   *Step into this symbol and recall the memory.*

Step #5.   *Observe internal patterns associated with the state.*

Step #6.   *Amplify the state.*

Step #7.   *Step back and break the state.*

Step #8.   *Test*

Step #9.   *Repeat*

Step #10. *Extend this work to appropriate situations.*

Step #1. Choose your resourceful state.

Select a resourceful state that you wish to experience at will, such as creativity.

Step #2. Choose a time to trigger the state.

Think of a time when you experienced a rich version of this state.

Step #3. Create a symbol for an excellent state.

Imagine that you have a circle before you on the ground. If you prefer, you can select a specific color, symbol or other visual or auditory cue to associate with the state.

Step #4. Step into this symbol and recall the memory.

Step into the circle or symbol.

Fully associate into the state and relive the experience, amplifying the state.

Experience the memory from first position.

Step #5. Observe internal patterns associated with the state.

Notice the patterns you produce that are associated with this

273

state. To do this, internally focus your attention, noticing all relevant internal representations, characteristics of submodalities, patterns of breathing and tension, and anything else you can experience.

Step #6. Amplify the state.

Amplify and enrich the state by increasing the submodalities in all rep systems. This includes things such as the clarity and compelling qualities of your own inner voice, as well as brightness and size of images.

Step #7. Step back and break the state.

Step back out of the circle or symbol and break this state.

Step #8. Test

Test this circle of excellence that you have created, by stepping forward into it. How well do you access the state?

Step #9. Repeat

Repeat the first seven steps until you trigger the state easily.

Step #10. Extend this work to appropriate situations.

Think of some situations that you would handle better from this state. Imagine taking your circle of excellence into these situations, using future pacing to prepare for them.

☯

73.

Assertiveness Installation

"The basic difference between being assertive and being aggressive is how our words and behavior affect the rights and well being of others".

— Sharon Anthony Bower

ASSERTIVENESS is a very important trait, yet people often fall into habits of being too passive or aggressive. These habits can be subconscious, and people often fail to realize how much they are losing and how many bad experiences come from poor assertiveness.

Overview: The Assertiveness Installation Pattern

Step #1. Analyze the non-assertive behavior.

Step #2. Assess what stops the assertive behavior.

Step #3. List ways the assertive behaviors can be useful.

Step #4. Expand the assertiveness state.

Step #5. Go through the timeline, generating examples of assertive behavior.

Step #6. Diminish the images of non-assertive behavior.

Step #7. Future pace.

Step #8. Test.

Step #1. Analyze the non-assertive behavior.

Determine what the person does instead of asserting himself/herself in a specific situation.

In addition to the behavior, uncover the chain of thoughts and other internal representations that take place prior to and during the non-assertive behavior.

For verbal thoughts (self talk), get a good sense of their position.

For example, how much are their thoughts acting as a broadcast for someone else's thoughts.

And how much are they trying to preempt what other people might think.

Dynamics such as these show problems with perceptual position misalignment. And this is a clue for you, by the way, to notice issues that you might want to handle with other patterns before continuing a process.

As for the stronger sensory elements, look at submodalities as well.

You are looking at what drives the person toward the non-assertive behavior. Do not just assume that the submodalities have to be from the known driver submodalities (size, location, etc.).

It could be any type in any modality. Be thorough in your investigation of submodalities in this step, because that might determine the success of the whole procedure.

Step #2. Assess what stops the assertive behavior.

Notice any ways that an impulse to be assertive is stopped.

One way to derive this is to simply mention two or three assertive behaviors that might apply to the situation.

Then ask, *"When you think of doing this, what happens?"*

The person is likely to describe a dominant rep system, such as the kinesthetic sense of feeling fear in their stomach, along with some thoughts.

Help the person express these thoughts and develop them into specific beliefs such as, *"If I asked for that, it would mean that I was a needy person. People like that are disgusting."* (Notice the nominalization regarding disgust. Who is disgusted, and why?)

Clarify the ways that stopping assertiveness can be useful.

Step #3. List ways the assertive behaviors can be useful.

Develop with the person a list of ways that one or more of the assertive behaviors can be useful.

Make sure that this list appeals to the broadest possible spectrum of values that the person holds dear.

Make sure that this includes as many selfish motives as possible, as well as any ways that the results of their assertive behavior would benefit any people or groups that the person feels are deserving.

For example, if self care makes them more productive, they will be able to contribute more to the world in the long run.

Also, their medical bills will be lower, so they can contribute more to their favorite cause.

Be sure to include the pleasure of experiencing an assertive state that is free of guilt or other causes of shyness.

As you are doing this step, be sure that you are using each element to foster a state of easy, confident assertiveness in the person.

Another issue to consider is morality and ethics. Your client might have other parts that object such a stream of thoughts, making oneself more important in one's eyes. Allow these parts to speak up and use the Parts Negotiation pattern is needed to make sure they do not interrupt in the rest of this procedure.

Step #4. Expand the assertiveness state.

Bring the person's attention to the ways they are beginning to experience an assertiveness state.

This includes any rep system elements, including thoughts. Ask elicitation questions, such as – what do you see, hear, feel? Elicit submodalities as well, and maintain a high level of sensory acuity.

Note which rep systems are most compelling, and of the thoughts, which values expressed by the thoughts are most compelling.

Begin future pacing by, for example, having the person imagine carrying out assertive behavior buoyed by this state and fully expressing this state.

What kind of posture, gestures and facial expressions would be expressed? Again, if you maintain a high level of sensory acuity, you would notice their posture, gestures and facial expressions and give them verbally as feedback to the client in order to prove that the process is already working.

Include a fantasy of people reacting very normally and favorably to this behavior in order to reduce the fear and create positive expectations on the subconscious level.

Since voice is so important in assertiveness, have the person imagine vocal tone, volume, and pacing that are likely to gain cooperation and make the assertive requests.

Again, bring up the positive feelings that go with the assertive state and behavior.

Be very supportive of these feelings, and help the person amplify them.

Use the submodalities that were most influential on this specific client.

Step #5. Go through the timeline, generating examples of assertive behavior.

Have the person go through their timeline, thinking of many examples of assertive behavior. This includes any times that the person expressed an aspect of the assertive behavior.

For example, they may feel badly about having said something meekly, but if they used the right words, have them focus on this very intently. The purpose of this is to modify the person's self concept into that of an assertive person.

This way they will have a greater expectation of being assertive, more permission to be assertive, and better competence at being assertive. They will also express assertive cues such as body language that set expectations in others. This will cause people to respond in ways that elicit more assertiveness in the person.

Step #6. Diminish the images of non-assertive behavior.

Bring the person's awareness to their images of not being assertive. These images may include memories and fears.

Ask them to send those images behind the assertive images.

Have them imbue the nonassertive images with the qualities of the assertive images. For example, if the assertive images have a more lively, colorful quality, have the person modify the nonassertive images to have that quality.

Have them do the same with other modalities and submodalities, such as vocal tone and accompanying thoughts.

Move unassertive feelings to the same location as the assertive feelings, and modify the unassertive feelings to match key aspects of the assertive feelings.

Continue making these adjustments until the person feels very congruent with assertiveness, even though these unassertive elements were being processed.

Step #7. Future pace.

Go back to future pacing, having the person imagine carrying out assertive behavior in various situations.

Be sure that they bring the assertive state into the situation, and that their future images have the qualities of the assertive images that have been developed.

Step #8. Test.

Have the person give you feedback over the coming days or weeks about any changes in their behavior that have to do with assertiveness or anything else that they think is important.

◎

74.

Self Esteem Quick Fix

"Self esteem is the reputation we acquire with ourselves".

— Nathaniel Branden

CREDITS FOR THE creation of this NLP pattern belong to various contributors.

This pattern can help you rapidly recover from an attack of bad self esteem. It is excellent for recovering from a failure, or from someone who had a toxic effect on your self esteem.

Overview: The Self Esteem Quick Fix Pattern

Step #1. Select a negative self-esteem image.

Step #2. Dissociate from the experience.

Step #3. Create powerful self-esteem imagery.

Step #4. Practice shrinking and restoring the self-esteem image.

Step #5. Set up the swish.

Step #6. Swish ten times.

Step #7. Challenge yourself to handle extreme pleasure.

Step #8. Future pace.

Step #9. Finish the pattern.

Step #10. Test

Step #1. Select a negative self-esteem image.

Think of a time in your life when you felt bad about yourself, when your faults and weaknesses were totally in the foreground of your mind. This first step is the only one that is unpleasant. The most powerful memory may be one in which other people were trashing you, and this negativity infected your self esteem. Step into the experience.

Notice where in your body these negative feelings are located. Intensify them and notice anything else about them, such as their size and shape.

Notice the images that come up for you as you do this. Whatever image most symbolizes this experience will be your "cue image." We will use this for a swish.

Notice any sounds associated with this image.

Step #2. Dissociate from the experience.

Now, we'll step out of this experience.

Stand up, move around, and open your eyes. Do other things to break state.

Blink faster, move your facial muscles, wave your right hand,

stretch your left, think about what a UPS truck looks like.

Continue with state-breaking activities until you are full extracted from the negative self esteem state.

Step #3. Create powerful self-esteem imagery.

Now you're going to create an image that represents the strong resourceful and positive self esteem you're about to own.

Imagine seeing yourself with profound self esteem.

Use all major rep systems.

How would you appear in terms of your expression, gait, gestures, and posture?

How would you sound?

How would people react as they are enjoying your pure self esteem?

When this has some momentum for you, imagine yourself in a new situation, propelled by this self esteem.

Notice how it is stimulating and motivating to be in a new situation.

Add to this the sense that this reality is in the very near future. It crowds out any previous caring that you had about past attacks upon your self esteem or well being. This state is very much in the moment and involved in creating a bright future.

Now amplify the submodalities of this state. Enlarge and brighten it. Saturate the colors in your mind.

Include the submodality of attitude and thoughts by becoming aware of your resources such as you sense of choice, support, and creativity.

Notice how this image and state are attractive. Connect with this attraction, becoming more drawn to it.

Build the attitude that you need this and must have it. Build your sense of the possibility of it, and the ways that is already real, whatever they may be.

Put a mysterious smile on that image of yourself.

Imagine you can her him think, *"I feel good to be me."*

If you find any negative feelings about anyone saying that, set them aside for now, and tune into the ways that you can appreciate someone enjoying being themselves, and the ways that we all can benefit from and enjoy such a feeling. Punch up the submodali-

ties of this voice, making it resonate all around you.

Step #4. Practice shrinking and restoring the self-esteem image.

Make a mental frame around that image of you with the high self-esteem.

Shrink it so it becomes a tiny little picture in the open space in front of you.

Make it sparkle at you.

Very quickly, take that sparkling little dot in the distant space in front of you and jump it right back to its previous size and aliveness.

Include the, "It feels good to be me," attitude and actual voice in all it's richness.

Open your eyes for a moment, then close them and think of a black screen. Now see that high self esteem image again.

Shrink it again, into that sparkling dot. Now take it back to full size. Alternate this shrinking and expanding with a lot of intensity.

Step #5. Set up the swish.

Shrink the high self esteem image and place it right in the middle of the horrible disturbing image you discovered in the beginning of this pattern.

Shrink the negative image quickly into a tiny gray dot in front of you, and at the same time quickly, blow up the tiny dot into your full-size self esteem image, so that it completely covers the negative image. Amplify the submodalities of this positive image.

Repeat this swish pattern, beginning with the negative image and the dot-size self esteem image.

Say SWISH as you do this. When you bring back the negative image, don't say swish. When you swish back the positive image, include the verbal, "It feels good to be me," coming from that image.

Do it again, snapping your fingers at the same time.

When you swish in the positive image, let the good feelings wash over you and flow through you.

Step #6. Swish ten times.

Open your eyes and move around a bit.

Close your eyes, imagine a blank screen, and we'll start the real change. Do the swish ten times, as fast as you can. Do it with as much emotion, enthusiasm, and determination as you can muster.

Remember: The negative image is a black blinking dot. When you swish, say swish and snap your finger.

When the bright, colorful self esteem image is full size, have it blast out the, *"I feel good to be me,"* sound and see your mysterious smile. Each time, before repeating the swish, open your eyes, close your eyes, and see the blank black screen.

As you do the ten repetitions, see how fast you can make the swish happen.

Step #7. Challenge yourself to handle extreme pleasure.

Positive self-esteem can dramatically enhance every part of your life and make it much more pleasurable. This step attaches your compelling image of high self-esteem to all aspects of your life. Self-esteem affects every single detail in your life.

Since memories are such triggers, we'll start by attaching this positive state and image to the past. Then we will do new situations, since they are your opportunities to trigger effective states. Finally, we'll do the future in order to make your goals and plans more attainable.

Reach out with your hands and grab the strong image of high self esteem, just like you would grab a big mirror. Grab it, lift it and notice something new: there are thousands of thousands of high self esteem images behind it! These images are of you being successful in everything you do in life. In these images, you are strong, committed, powerful, happy, thrilled, excited, and pleasurable.

As you lift the image, all the other images are lifted with it. Smile to yourself and throw it up high above you. Everything spreads out in the open air above your head. A split of a second later, they all fall down, spreading all around you. In front of you are thousands of future images covering the ground. To your sides are thousands of opportunities that you seize. Behind you are thousands more showing you valuable energies of the past. That leads to the sparkling points along your past timeline.

Imagine them, each framed with a blinking, shiny frame, yelling for your attention.

Get in touch with the growing internal state of confidence in facing challenges. This state is supported by the memories of your power.

Send any remaining images of you that are negative back behind the positive images.

Have the positive images so intense in their submodalities and added elements of blinking and brightness and yelling for attention, that they fully command your attention away from any negativity. These images continue to interrupt any negative or wandering thoughts with, *"Look at me. I feel GOOD being me!"*

Step #8. Future pace.

Imagine yourself waking up tomorrow and finding that these images are still all around you, blinking and yelling for attention.

See yourself with that mysterious smile. Imagine people enjoying this quality of yours, and how you affect them in positive ways.

Step #9. Finish the pattern.

Do whatever you'd like to complete the pattern, and open your eyes, cultivating a fresh, eager readiness for the rest of your day or evening.

Step #10. Test

Bring up one of the negative images and see if it still has any power over you. If it does, you can repeat this exercise from time to time. If you have trouble getting the image, that's even better.

Also, see if you notice any effects of improved self esteem over the coming days or weeks. This may include opportunities coming your way, people reacting to you in better ways, and feeling more motivation and optimism. It can even mean being more comfortable or at peace with being realistic about negative situations or challenges, and more creative about finding solutions.

৩৩

75.

The Smart Eating Pattern

"Now, good digestion wait on appetite, and health on both!"

— William Shakespeare

CREDITS FOR THE creation of this NLP pattern belong to various contributors.

One of the key causes of excessive eating is poor awareness of when one is one is actually hungry as opposed to simply being tempted or using food as an antidote to stress.

Another problem is that, although it can be appropriate to eat a number of smaller meals rather than three large meals per day, those small meals have excessive carbohydrates. Students and knowledge workers use a great deal of blood sugar because the brain consumes it for thinking in surprising amounts. Thus, they must be careful to avoid snacking beyond their actual needs, and to avoid a blood sugar roller coaster that is caused by consuming refined sugars and starchy food. The current **"diabesity"** *(diabetes and obesity)* epidemic (also known as syndrome X) is directly related to over-consumption of refined carbohydrates through products such as soft drinks.

Overview: The Smart Eating Pattern

Step #1. How do you know it is time to eat?

Step #2. What would be best to eat?

Step #3. Compare the before and after.

Step #4. Contrast with an unhealthy item.

Step #5. Future pace.

Step #6. Test.

Step #1. How do you know it is time to eat?

Determine how you know that it is time to eat.

Carefully look for the rep systems and submodalities involved.

Include your internal feelings, such as tension, mental fog, and irritability.

Be sure to include the feelings of your stomach. What does *"empty"* really feel like?

Step #2. What would be best to eat?

Ask your inner wisdom what would feel best to have eaten. That is, what would make me feel good after I ate it, in the short-term?

Consider various foods that are available to you right now, and imagine that you are finishing eating them.

Notice your most subtle feelings.

You can find a range of feelings such as healthy and balanced, bogged down and sleepy, and very satisfied, but in a gluttonous way.

Keep trying different foods until you find at least one that makes you feel very balanced and healthy.

Inspect the rep systems and submodalities that tell you it is an idea food. How do you "know" that you feel balanced and healthy.

If none do this for you, then consider additional foods that are not available right now.

Step #3. Compare the before and after.

Compare this "ideal food" feeling with the feeling you had before you ate it, that is, the feeling that tells you it's time to eat.

Which one feels better?

If the "before" feeling seems better, perhaps you should try out more imaginary foods to find something better. Or does it mean that you should simply wait longer before eating your ideal food?

Step #4. Contrast with an unhealthy item.

Try comparing the "after" feeling with a not-so-healthy item, such as a candy bar.

Carefully inspect the difference between these feelings.

Go forward in time a few hours to see how the unhealthy item "after" feeling is. Go forward a few days and feel that result.

How do these sensations compare to the feelings of step three?

Step #5. Future pace.

Once you have found food choices that make you feel balanced and healthy, see how many more food items you can think of that provide healthy, balanced feelings.

Imagine making those food choices into the future.

Amplify the healthy, balanced feelings and imagine them growing over time as you make these food choices.

Imagine yourself as a very spry, active, bright elderly person with those healthy, balanced feelings surrounded by young people who are eager to gain wisdom from you.

Step #6. Test.

Over the coming days and weeks, notice how this pattern influences your food choices. Sense how those choices make you feel.

See how you can enhance this patter so that it works best for you as an individual, getting the best effect upon your food choices and resulting energy and mental clarity.

Additional Advice

Making it less comfortable to reach the type of food you want to avoid craving for is one very easy task. Simply stop buying it! Skip it when you get to the candies section in the supermarket.

Another well-known nutrition trick for sweet craving is fruit juices and smoothies. I don't have enough space in this book to explain it thoroughly, so just give it a try and see how it works for you. Do not buy concentrated juices and always read the labels. Even when it says "100% juice", it might say "from concentrated" in small print.

Another tip that helps me a lot in the morning – for an energetic wake up drink one glass of fresh orange juice, the squeezed type of course. It's a rush, I guarantee it.

One last advice – do not give up or avoid the foods you really love. If Pizza is your favorite food, go for it once a week. If your mind knows that you're not going to become a health freak (which is, on its own, a health risk as well), it will become more and more patient through the week and let you lose the weight, knowing that once a week you're giving in and enjoying your most favorites. Of course, don't go overboard here! But don't make it a stressful change.

☙❧

76.

Boundaries Installation

"People are always blaming their circumstances for what they are. Never esteem anything as of advantage to you that will make you break your word or lose your self-respect"

— Marcus Aurelius

CREDITS FOR THE creation of this NLP pattern belong to various contributors.

Personal boundaries are the borders that we maintain between what is acceptable and what it not in how we are treated.

Boundaries that affirm us, but that are flexible enough to allow meaningful interaction with others are considered healthy boundaries.

Boundary crossings occur when someone does not respect our dignity, power, and well being. A comment or joke that is sexist but not directly insulting can be considered a subtle boundary crossing.

People who have weak boundaries may take on others' problems.

It happens when a person thinks he or she is a good friend, while in reality they let themselves to get overwhelmed and absorbed with another person's emotions and problems. A good friend should be there to stay strong for you, stay sensitive yet unaffected, so that they can pull you up and support you.

This does not happen if that "good" friend is taking a part in feeling the pain or assuming responsibility for alleviating it. People with weak boundaries become victims of themselves, and by becoming miserable for other people's problems, they actually push them away. When those others are dependent or destructive, the person with poor boundaries is called *codependent*.

These people lose themselves in harmful patterns. Some of them are even consciously aware of that habitual self sabotage. They may not be able to act in their own interest until they get their partner to agree with them or stop having bad (manipulative) feelings about it. They tend to have perceptual position distortions in which they have other people's attitudes and thoughts mixed in with their own. They wonder why their relationship is not getting better when they are working so hard, without fully considering that they are the only one working on the relationship. People with overly rigid or extended boundaries may place unreasonable demands on others to comply with excessive expectations.

This pattern helps people define and strengthen boundaries that are too weak or unclear.

Overview: The Boundaries Installation Pattern

Step #1. Select a pattern reflecting weak boundaries.

Step #2. Create a boundary-affirming imaginary space.

Step #3. Imagine the force field.

Step #4. See yourself in second position from a highly supportive perspective.

Step #5. Amplify your uniqueness in first position, and future pace this state.

Step #6. Elicit creative expressions of your uniqueness and boundaries by testing them with a boundary violating fantasy person.

Step #7. Future pace.

Step #8. Test.

Step #1. Select a pattern reflecting weak boundaries.

Think about the information on poor boundaries and codependency.

Find a patter in your life that bears some resemblance to at least one of the elements or something else that shows a weak boundaries.

Step #2. Create a boundary-affirming imaginary space.

Imagine a physical space around your body that extends out about two feet.

Fill that space with your boundary-affirming and boundary-enforcing qualities such as attitudes and personality characteristics.

Consider qualities such as assertiveness, perceptiveness, commitment, honesty, ability to read others, and so forth.

Be sure that these are not generic, they must be qualities that are unique to you.

What is the quality of assertiveness that comes from you?

What is positive about it?

Include only the positive aspects in your imaginary space. If any of those qualities seem week, don't allow that to be relevant in

placing them in your imaginary space.

Take the collective sense of these qualities and anchor it.

Step #3. Imagine the force field.

Imagine that your boundary space is surrounded by a force field that is getting so strong that nothing can penetrate unless you allow it. It defines you as being a unique entity, separate from others in the sense of being an individual capable of interacting and benefiting from interaction.

Be sure to sense this from the first perceptual position (first person).

Anchor this strong, "boundaried" sensation.

Step #4. See yourself in second position from a highly supportive perspective.

Move to second perceptual position.

Imagine that you are seeing yourself through the eyes of a person who is very supportive of your boundaries and thinks the world of you, even if you need to invent that person for this pattern.

Discover what it's like, as this understanding person, to express strong approval for you as a unique individual and for your boundaries.

Take a little time to clearly express this in a way that is fully connected and full of feelings.

Do whatever you need to do in order to make this a powerful, valid resource.

Step #5. Amplify your uniqueness in first position, and future pace this state.

From first position, amplify and experience the validity and power of all that makes you a unique, "boundaried" individual.

Future pace this state as a way of being in the world and a way of navigating life.

Step #6. Elicit creative expressions of your uniqueness and boundaries by testing them with a boundary violating fantasy person.

Imagine experiencing someone who is not respectful of your boundaries in some way.

Allow your state of unique self and good boundaries to elicit creative responses from you. You can stop the fantasy to adjust your response, or loop it and try various responses each time through.

Be sure not to be caught in the trap of trying to change the other person or convince them of anything. If they are manipulative, they will not respond to that in a constructive manner.

Step #7. Future pace.

Imagine moving into the future with your healthy boundaries and unique identity.

Allow imaginary scenarios to come up as you enjoy projecting this state into the future.

Step #8. Test.

In the coming days and weeks, notice any ways that you express your uniqueness despite demands or manipulation from others that would turn you away from your unique self expression or meeting your needs in your own self-affirming way that connects you with supportive people and valuable resources.

Notice any ways that you defend and enhance your boundaries, including maintaining your own thoughts independently from others' thoughts and attitudes.

಄಄

77.

Criticism Analyzer

"Be who you are and say what you feel, because those who mind don't matter, and those who matter don't mind."

— Dr. Seuss

CREDITS FOR THE creation of this NLP pattern belong to various contributors.

This pattern let's you experience criticism without taking it too personally. It uses the concept that words are not real.

If criticism sets of a chain reaction inside you that results in anger, shame, or defensiveness, you need to remember that such suffering is optional.

This pattern gives you control over these reactions.

Fear of criticism is one of the most disabling fears of all. The importance of learning how to accept criticism well can be seen in our most primitive need – to be liked. Social status and relationships with other people are very important to us. Human beings are social creatures; we need these connections for two main reasons – survival and pleasure.

There is no real joy if you just have fun alone, is there? The greatest joy is when you share the happiness, when you win as a team and not just as an individual. Did you ever wonder how come men hug each other and cry on the football field? Did you see a player crying and hugging himself on his own?

The survival aspect of social life is also obvious – we need the service and escort of other people to run our lives. You need the shopkeeper, the mechanic, the physician, the bus driver, the electric company technicians and so on. But you also need your family, to be supported and nourished; you need your spouse to feel intimacy and love, which is also a basic survival need.

You need other people in your life, nobody is an island. But with the gift of relationship comes also a catch 22 – you cannot be social without knowing how to handle criticism well. Yes, some people will want to criticize you for their own good, not yours. But many will not.

Many will be careful and perhaps brave enough to let you know what you're doing wrong (in their opinion) or how your inaction or actions, behaviors, choices and emotional expressions are affecting them.

Learning to accept criticism well and knowing how to handle it maturely is one of life's greatest skills and one that will boost your self esteem and self respect.

Overview: The Criticism Analyzer Pattern

Step #1. *Select a situation in which you responded badly to criticism.*

Step #2. *Generate a state of safety.*

Step #3. *Respond to the person with validation.*

Step #4. *Ask for more information.*

Step #5. *Imagine the response in an effective way that is not disturbing.*

Step #6. *Reflect what you have received.*

Step #7. *Get to an "agreement frame."*

Step #8. *Generate your own representation in a top left position.*

Step #9. *Compare the representations of you and your critic.*

Step #10. Respond from your understanding, and do it in a classy way.

Step #11. Seek closure.

Step #12. Take this to the relationship level.

Step #13. Test

Step #1. Select a situation in which you responded badly to criticism.

The first time, do this exercise in your imagination. In the future, this can become like a reflex that you do rapidly.

Then you will get to the point that you do it unconsciously, with your mind freed to be even more of a master.

Imagine a situation in which you were criticized and it was either painful, or you do not care for how you reacted, or you did not like the results that came from your reaction.

Step #2. Generate a state of safety.

Create safety by sending the other person farther away until it feels comfortable. This might be an extra foot, or it could be so far you can't see them (like on the moon).

Add a force field or tough Plexiglas shield between you and the other person. Once you feel safe, anchor this sensation.

Step #3. Respond to the person with validation.

Imagine saying something to them, such as, "(Name), thanks for telling me this."

Change the words to fit the situation. If it's a formal business relationship, you might want to sound like this, *"(Name), thanks for taking the time to discuss this issue with me. Your observations and ideas are very important to me, so I'll take this feedback very seriously."*

Or if it is a romantic relationship, try something like, *"Honey, I'm really glad you trust me so much that you can share something like this with me. My vision for our relationship is that we can be this open and create even more support for each other and have really good times together while we're at it. It might take me some time and effort to really get what you need one hundred percent, but I will keep trying and listening. To me that's a sacred promise."*

Step #4. Ask for more information.

The person will know that you care and that you can handle criticism if you ask them to offer more details. Also, the more you know, the better you can respond, whether you need to disagree, negotiate, or offer up a major mea culpa. You can use a phrase such as, *"Tell me* more about this," or ask about something that you don't fully understand.

Step #5. Imagine the response in an effective way that is not disturbing.

Imagine the person filling in some details.

Practice the perceiving of what they say as though you are watching a movie that plays out the details as they see them.

Make the image small enough that it is not at all overwhelming or troubling. This gets you some distance or objectivity, but keeps you in a state of receptivity.

Step #6. Reflect what you have received.

Reflecting is very important in communication.

Practice it here by restating what the other person has told you. It's best to summarize what you feel are the most important parts. This shows the person what stands out to you, and helps them know what to emphasize when they clarify their ideas and concerns.

You can begin with a phrase such as, *"I want to make sure I*

understand you, so let me tell you what I stands out to me so far." You can end with something like, *"How am I doing?"* or *"Are those the main things?"*

Step #7. Get to an "agreement frame."

You may not be able to do this justice in your imagination, but be prepared to have some back and forth in the real world. The person will probably want to add or repeat some things.

People who do not feel validated will repeat points a lot of times, so the more you can help them feel valid, the more time you'll save.

When they add points, summarize them as in step six. This is a good point at which to elicit exactly what they want from you or from the situation. Some people jump into criticism before they have figured this out, especially if they are assuming that they can't get what they want.

Eliciting their wants can calm them down and get them into a more creative and even a more cooperative mindset. Once the person is comfortable with your level of understanding, you have achieved the agreement frame.

Step #8. Generate your own representation in a top left position.

Your understanding is probably different from that of the other person. At the minimum, you will have some different priorities, that is, you will feel some different things should receive the most emphasis.

Create a representation in the top left of your mental and visual space.

This representation shows your understanding of the situation. It should include sights, sounds, words, and feelings.

Have it show not only details, but your priorities, needs, beliefs and values. It is powerful to visualize at least one ideal outcome. Emphasize the rep system that helps you gain the most clarity.

For example, if it is self talk, the images may not be so important.

Step #9. Compare the representations of you and your critic.

How do the movie you made of your critic's understanding contrast with the representation you made of your understanding and priorities?

Step #10. Respond from your understanding, and do it in a classy way.

Respond to your critic with some areas of agreement, starting with a phrase such as, *"I do agree with you on some important points..."*

This time, emphasize what the other person wants that you can agree with, and that you intend to cooperate with.

Then convey the ways that you disagree, starting with a phrase such as, *"I can't completely agree an a few point, though. Where (issue) is concerned, I think..."*

This is a good time to indicate what you aren't willing to cooperate with, along with what you need to see happen.

Use language that fits the situation. How hard or soft you sound is a strategic decision.

Step #11. Seek closure.

Bring the discussion to a focus on decisions.

This can range from them being satisfied that you have acknowledged them, to a need to negotiate commitments, or agreeing to disagree and take the issue to a higher authority.

Step #12. Take this to the relationship level.

Ask the other part what would help them feel better about your relationship, whether it is a working relationship, a romantic relationship, or some other kind of relationship.

Offer your own needs in this regard, as well.

Discuss it in a way that generates hope and optimism about your future together.

Close by emphasizing your appreciation for their coming to you openly, rather than for the specific details.

Step #13. Test

As the situation unfolds, see if this has enhanced the relationship and your ability to respond in a way that fills the other persons needs, including their need to feel that you care and see their needs as valid and serious.

See how well they are able to do the same for you. If there are problems, assess them.

If you feel the person is strictly being manipulative and wants an unfair advantage, then you will need to shift to a different strategic frame that involves gamesmanship of some kind, limit-setting, and ways of gaining more power to protect your interests.

⊗⊘

78.

The Excuse Blow-Out Pattern

"Nothing is impossible; there are ways that lead to everything, and if we had sufficient will we should always have sufficient means. It is often merely for an excuse that we say things are impossible".

— Francois De La Rochefoucauld

CREDITS FOR the creation of this NLP pattern belong to Michael L. Hall.

This pattern helps you get things done by turning subconscious excuses into alignment. This stops procrastination.

Overview: The Excuse Blow-Out Pattern

Step #1. What's your excuse?

Step #2. Assess the excuse pattern

Step #3. Preserve the Values of the Excuse

Step #4. Reject the old excuse.

Step #5. Test your anti-excuse response.

Step #6. Future pace.

Step #1. What's your excuse?

Choose something important that you want to accomplish, but have been procrastinating on. Think about what happens when you get close to doing the actions that are necessary for this accomplishment.

What do you do instead?

What feelings and thoughts come up just before you get detoured?

Can you identify any conscious excuses?

Perhaps instead of excuses, you have thoughts that redirect you.

For this exercise, we'll call them excuses.

If the pattern is not conscious, run through the sequence in your mind and listen for subtle thoughts, pictures, and feelings that you hadn't exactly noticed before.

Look for vague, irrational ideas or feelings that sound silly when you put them into words. Those can be the ones that slip away from awareness unless you are actively looking for them. Old, habitual, irrational thought patterns tend to be the least conscious, yet they can pack a lot of power.

Get to know these excuses not just as something that you under-stand, but also as a state that you can feel. Explore the submodalities that give this state the power to divert you from your aim.

Step #2. Assess the excuse pattern

Answer the following questions:

Is it really just an excuse?

Do you want to keep this excuse?

Do you need to have this excuse in your life?

Does it serve your life at all?

Does it enhance your quality of life or empower you to be a better person?

If there is some part or facet of the excuse that you might need or want to preserve, what is it?

What facets of the excuse may serve a positive purpose for you? (Find the hidden agenda.)

Step #3. Preserve the Values of the Excuse

The previous questions helped you connect with value in the excuse pattern. You can preserve the benefits, yet change the pattern so that you can get accomplish your goal.

Start by identifying any aspect of the excuse that is valuable. for example, are you trying to juggle too many things, and fear that you will lose other important priorities?

Imagine that you can remove all of this value and set it on a spot that is separate from the excuse pattern. Now the excuse pattern is a useless, empty shell.

Step #4. Reject the old excuse.

Access a strong "NO!" state. Muster up an intense, inner "Hell No!"

Remember a time when you felt absolutely against something that was completely, intensely unacceptable to you.

The more disgusted you were, the better.

Amplify this into a Hell No state.

Expand the state so that you feel it throughout your body, even into your hands and feet. Anchor this state.

Imagine the empty excuse immediately in front of you and step into that excuse with the NO! state.

Stomp on the excuse with the power of your "Hell, No!"

Hold it in your hands and smash it into the ground.

Stomp it into pieces.

Step #5. Test your anti-excuse response.

Imagine the desired activity.

Notice what happens as you think about moving toward it.

Notice what you feel, see, and think.

Notice any excuses that remain in the shadows of your mind.

See how they may interfere with your life, love, or success.

Work on any remaining excuse patterns, beginning with step two.

Step #6. Future pace.

Remind yourself of your intense Hell No state and how you applied it vigorously to your excuses.

Imagine the earliest upcoming time when you will want to work on this goal in some way that you would have typically ended up avoiding.

Imagine yourself (in a dissociated image, as if you are looking at yourself from the corner), at the moment you would choose to start the activity. At that moment, start smashing the excuse. Say, "Hell no!"

Access the most open, eager state that you can, and imagine starting the activity. If you feel like you what to actually do the activity now, go right ahead!

Additional Advice

Go slowly at first and then repeat the pattern while speeding up the process.

Go for weaker excuses first, just for training with the pattern. Don't take the heavy challenges up front.

Make sure your whole body and mind are involved in the process of change. If you feel a twist in your stomach when you remind yourself of the excuse, it's working!

If you feel any discomfort or hesitation when you think of starting the activity, it means there is still an excuse lingering. Dig deep and get to know this feeling. Turn it into words so you can understand it better. Work on it with this exercise.

☙❧

79.

The Basic Motivation Pattern

"Don't wait until everything is just right. It will never be perfect. There will always be challenges, obstacles and less than perfect conditions. So what?! Get started now. With each step you take, you will grow stronger and stronger, more and more skilled, more and more self-confident and more and more successful."

— Mark Victor Hansen, author of The One Minute Millionaire

CREDITS for the creation of this NLP pattern belong to various contributors.

The following strategy demonstrates how the various elements of imagination, expectation, criteria, submodalities and association can be combined into a simple strategy to help people better inspire and motivate themselves to take actions which will lead them to desired outcomes.

Overview: The Basic Motivation Pattern

Step #1. Imagine enjoying a key achievement.

Step #2. Enhance and anchor the state as a pleasure motivation state.

Step #3. Future pace with this state.

Step #4. Test

Step #1. Imagine enjoying a key achievement.

Imagine that you have achieved one of your greatest dreams in life. Imagine yourself fully enjoying it.

Experience the sights, sounds, and feelings of this enjoyment.

Step #2. Enhance and anchor the state as a pleasure motivation state.

Amplify the compelling and motivational aspects of this experience.

Do this by adjusting submodalities such as brightness and size. This is a pleasure motivation state. Anchor it.

Step #3. Future pace with this state.

Carry these feelings into imagining yourself taking steps that will actually move you toward your dream outcome.

Trigger your anchor for the pleasure motivation state to enhance this state.

Step #4. Test

In the coming days and weeks, notice if you find it easier to take steps toward this or other dreams or desired outcomes.

☯

80.

The Winning Over Internal War Zone Pattern

*"The inner speech, your thoughts, can cause you to be
rich or poor, loved or unloved, happy or unhappy, attractive or
unattractive, powerful or weak".*

— Ralph Charell

CREDITS for the creation of this NLP pattern belong to various contributors.

Resolve a problem that nearly everyone suffers from; inner wars. These are wars of internal self talk that turn your mind into a battle field. Often, this self talk explodes into vivid imaginings of worst-case scenarios. This kind of visualization all to often churns out self-fulfilling prophecies.

A common Internal War Zone consists of your imaginary arguments or fights with others. Such imaginings have a seductive power that engages your inner resources while forming a habitual inner pattern that takes over all too easily. Worse, this pattern can harm your relationships and success by souring your attitude.

Overview: The Winning Over Internal War Zone Pattern

Step #1. Let it come to you.

Step #2. Dissociate.

Step #3. Soften.

Step #4. Go beyond yourself.

Step #5. Make the picture go away.

Step #6. Experience gratitude.

Step #1. Let it come to you.

You need to catch yourself in action.

This method can only assist you if you can catch yourself right when this internal dialogue begins.

You suddenly find yourself arguing with another person within your own mind, most likely while doing some everyday activity like driving or doing the laundry.

Define it. Who's that person?

What has initiated that internal argument and conflict?

Give them a face, a name, a place, a situation and define your own outcome.

Step #2. Dissociate.

At this point, it is very important for you to dissociate yourself from the charged emotions.

You need to "get outside" of that conflict in order to control it. If you stay associated, that is, within your own emotions, then you cannot really direct the whole situation.

Now, as you dissociate yourself, taking a third person position, see yourself and hear yourself as if you're standing a few feet away from that battle zone. You're still in that Internal War Zone, but you're now in a mediator position, in between.

Step #3. Soften.

Make that image softer. Make the voices sound softer.

Do whatever works for you, whether it means going a bit slower, using softer words, a softer tone of voice, or any other modification that softens the effect.

You might try making the image more pleasant and colorful, emphasizing browns and greens.

You can even put soft music in the background. You're in charge.

Step #4. Go Beyond Yourself

Move to a position just behind the other party, so that you can see the back of his head and see yourself more or less from his point of view.

Hear the arguments you're saying from this vantage point.

Do your words really reflect reality, or do you find yourself exaggerating?

How would that other person feel if you actually said these words?

Would it help you get what you really want?

Step #5. Make The Picture Go Away

Internal War Zones are almost never useful, regardless of the outcome.

Except for times that you are truly practicing a valuable skill or doing an effective desensitization process, you can dispense with this wasteful mental pattern. There's no point in practicing feeling bad.

Make the picture go away. You did what you had to do. You understood your position, you saw the situation through an objective point of view and you know how the other person sees you as you put up your verbal fists and fight. It's over. Let it go.

You can let go simply by dimming the picture, returning to the associated image of yourself, and dimming again the picture until you can't really recognize what the argument is about or who is there.

If you can't see it, it isn't real; that's the key point here.

Step #6. Gratitude

The feeling of gratitude is the antidote to making yourself feel bad.

Think of at least ten things that you can feel gratitude for.

Count through them in order to keep track.

The first might be your eyes and sight, the second, your sharp mind, the third having friends, the fourth, your skill to appreciate others as well as yourself.

What else will you think of?

If ten comes easily, keep going!

One person told me he got to a 100 and he got stuck there.

How much of a good feeling could it be starting within an Internal War Zone and getting stuck eventually in the Gratitude and Self Appreciation Zone?

☙❧

81.

Inducing Amnesia

"Too many parents make life hard for their children by trying, too zealously, to make it easy for them".

– Johann Wolfgang von Goethe

AMNESIA IS A very useful tool when you work with clients. Milton Erickson used to induce amnesia from the very first contact with the client. The idea is that if the client "forgets" (the client's mind actually pushes the given time period into the subconscious) a certain part of the change work, they will be less likely to interfere with the results consciously.

For example, if in the session you and the client have covered that he is binge-drinking alcohol because he wants to be more socially accepted, it would be more useful to use amnesia after you establish new and healthy resources for the client to be socially accepted.

This way, when the client goes on with his life, the mind "forgot" why was it that he feels like binge-drinking at a moment, and once there is no good reason, the alternatives become more prominent.

If the client would remember "why I binge drink", the emotional roller-coaster can lead him into binge-drinking again, regardless of your session's success. You can initiate amnesia with a simple confusion method – "and I wonder if you would remember that when you came in this door, you took your right leg in and if you could forget to forget that when you leave this door you will put again, your right leg out". This is a very simple suggestion to tie the entrance to the room with the exit, and by that "pushing down" the time period in between into the subconsciousness.

☙❧

82.

Thought Virus Inoculation

"When negative feelings are suppressed positive feelings become suppressed as well, and love dies".

— John Gray

THIS NLP patterns was originated by Robert Dilts.

This pattern creates a defense against destructive (toxic) thought patterns, conceived by Dilts as "thought viruses".

Overview: The Thought Virus Inoculation Pattern

Step #1. Establish the following spaces on the floor. Step into each one and elicit the corresponding state.

Step #2. Test the spaces.

Step #3. Process a toxic thought by taking it through this sequence.

Step #4. Step through each space with the new belief.

Step #5. Future pace, checking the ecology of the new belief.

Step #6. Test

Step #1. Establish the following spaces on the floor.

Step into each one and elicit the corresponding state.

a. Neutral Space

An objective state from which you can review the process.

b. Prior Limiting Beliefs Space

Experience a belief that you no longer have, and that was limiting or childish, such as believing in Santa Claus.

c. Early Doubting Space

Experience the time at which you begin to doubt a limiting or childish belief that you no longer have.

d. Old Beliefs Museum Space

Get in touch with all of your prior limiting or childish beliefs.

e. Empowering Belief Space

Think of a belief that is functional and ecologically appropriate.

Experience the sense of empowerment that comes from this kind of belief.

f. Open to Belief Space

Connect with something that you previously were not open to believing, but are now open to believing. Get the sense of openness to belief.

g. Sacred Space

Elicit the congruent and committed feeling of being fully connected to your mission in life.

Step #2. Test the spaces.

Have the person step into each space from the meta-position space.

Amplify and re-anchor the state for any spaces that do not trigger the corresponding state.

Step #3. Process a toxic thought by taking it through this sequence.

a. Come up with a toxic belief to take through the process.

b. Have the person take this belief through each state in the sequence above.

c. Continue cycling through this sequence until the person is ready to deposit the toxic belief in the Old Beliefs Museum Space (part d).

d. Step into the meta-position and develop an empowering belief that can fill the void left by the old, toxic belief. The new belief must be functional and ecologically sound.

Step #4. Step through each space with the new belief.

Follow the sequence of steps as before, but this time with the new belief.

If the person begins to experience any confusion, have them step into the meta-position and clarify the belief so that it can function in the state where the confusion developed.

Step #5. Future pace, checking the ecology of the new belief.

Take this belief into imaginary future situations and look for any ecological problems to address.

Refine the thought in any ways that are necessary.

Step #6. Test

In the coming days or weeks, notice any ways that this new belief influences your attitude and results in life.

Notice any limitations or problems, and refine the belief as needed.

❧

83.

The Inner Peace Questionnaire

PROCRASTINATION – List the outcomes (big & small) that you have already started working on, but didn't continue...

In Action – List the outcomes that you're currently working on, but haven't completed yet...

Day Dreaming – List the outcomes you would like to achieve, but you weren't able to start working on yet...

Self Sabotage – List the personal-change outcomes which you have not been able to achieve.... (ex. Stop smoking, exercising more, etc.)

Communication Crisis – List the poisonous relationships you're still engaging in. It could be with a colleague, a family member / relative, a friend, a flight attendant...

☙❧

84.

The Relationship Clarifying Pattern

"A relationship is like a rose, How long it lasts, no one knows.
Love can erase an awful past, love can be yours, you'll see at last.
To feel that love, it makes you sigh, To have it leave, you'd rather
die. You hope you've found that special rose, 'cause you love and
care for the one you chose".

— Rob Cella

CREDITS for the creation of this NLP pattern belong to Robert Dilts *(under the name "Characterological Adjective").*

This pattern helps you identity characterological adjectives (CA's).

CA's encode basic characteristics of relationships. Each CA implies a counterpart. For example, the CA of "victim" implies the counterpart of "victimizer."

Getting to the essence of a dyadic relationship opens the gateway to understanding the dynamics of the relationship and how the two parties contribute to enduring patterns, including patterns that are dysfunctional.

Overview: The Relationship Clarifying Pattern

Step #1. Select a difficult person or situation.
Step #2. Get a typifying word from third position.
Step #3. Place yourself onto the screen and into this situation.
Step #4. Isolate the CA's

Step #1. Select a difficult person or situation.

Come up with a person that you have trouble communicating with, or a situation that gets in the way of you being creative and productive in getting desirable results. In such a situation, you would feel stuck.

Step #2. Get a typifying word from third position.

Imagine that you are observing the situation from a seat in a movie theater. Allow your mind to come up with a word that captures the essence of the situation, such as "obstructive" or "narcissistic."

Step #3. Place yourself onto the screen and into this situation.

Observe your own behavior and come up with a word that captures the essence of your reactions and involvement with this situation or person.

For example, "reactive" or "gullible."

Step #4. Isolate the CA's

Think of the two words or phrases that you came up with, such as "obstructive" and "reactive" or "narcissistic" and "gullible."

Notice how these two words or phrases are counterparts to one another.

You have gotten to the essence of the dyad by isolating the characterological adjectives.

☙❧

85.

Building & Maintaining Rapport

"They asked Gandhi 'what do you think about western civilization', he said 'I think it would be a wonderful idea'...".

— Robin Williams

RAPPORT IS A POSITIVE connection between you and another person, or you and a group.

You have seen lecturers, comedians and others build rapport with an entire audience. Perhaps you have experienced a good connection with a sales person, and by relaxing into that connection, found it easier to make a buying decision. You've probably met people who had a strong, instant effect on you, either good or bad.

What is it about the politicians and actors, the sales people, and the charismatic people you meet, that give them the ability to create rapport? Is it just natural chemistry? Sometimes. But professionals such as politicians learn to build rapport.

Rapport is one of the first areas that NLP became fascinated with as it developed. The therapists that NLP studied early on had rapport-building abilities, but they had very different styles, at least they had very different approaches and personalities. But, as you have learned, NLP is not content to just look at the surface. It models, it analyses, and it finds the active ingredients that make things like rapport take place.

This is what you will learn next; the active ingredients of rapport; the ingredients used by professionals in many areas of life to sell, to lead, and even to heal others.

This Doesn't Sound Ethical. Is NLP Just Manipulation?

Although this is not a course in ethics or philosophy, we do want to share a couple ideas on this with you. NLP wants to see people develop meaningful values so that they can lead more fulfilling and meaningful lives. This does not happen at random. Except for the hero who is surprised by the heroic act that comes out of them in a crisis, most great people of history have done a great deal of sometimes painful soul searching. They have drawn from various sources of inspiration. They talk about the feeling of standing on the shoulders of giants, even though history regards them as giants. Except for a few with very large egos, most of the great people in history confess to feeling like anything but giants.

But the things that they are proud of, are that they aspired to higher values, and that they worked to build the skills they needed to have a meaningful impact on the world.

We see the same thing is people today; people who don't expect to be in history books, but who are fascinated by excellence; people who want to know how their role models do what they do. These people use rapport-building skills to achieve excellence in their chosen pursuits.

The first lesson in rapport, much like other NLP skills is flexibility. If you think showing interest in people helps build rapport, consider the person who is too shy to handle you showing interest.

If you think a dynamic, outgoing personality creates rapport, consider the person who would feel overwhelmed or pushed by that. If you think speaking from your heart and your vision generates rapport, consider the person to defends themselves with sarcasm and cynicism.

What NLP has discovered about rapport transcends earlier efforts to build rapport with a list of personality traits. That is not flexible; that is a cook book approach. The master chef isn't glued to a cook book.

The second lesson in rapport is conscious application. It is not simply a gift or a coincidence, it is a skill.

Since most people prefer to think that rapport is only a natural thing, they may be uncomfortable with purposely creating rapport. We say that if you care about your mission in life, and if you care about your values, then you have a responsibility to learn to build rapport.

Rapport is part of your mission. You may be surprised to find that being pretty technical about it at first is very important. It's a little like a musician who practices scales for hours on end but emerges from this and other training with a great ability to play jazz. Rapport-building is the jazz of NLP.

What Skills Should I Start With?

Start your rapport-building skills with what we call sensory acuity. You have already started building this skill. We taught you to recognize what rep system people were using by listening to their predicates and watching their eyes and body language. Those are sensory acuity skills. Everything a person does is a message to you on how to build rapport with them. All you need is to know the code and the guidelines.

Have you ever been in the same room with someone and felt uncomfortable, or known that something was wrong, but didn't know why? With sensory acuity, you can describe everything about the person that was telegraphing signals to you.

For example, changes in posture can signal tension, extra skin moisture can signal anxiety or alarm, same thing with changes in heart rate that you can see from the carotid artery in the neck.

The face creates brief flashes of facial expression that are not con-trolled by the conscious mind. This has been shown in research using high speed video. And those are just a few body language elements.

Consider speech. On the physical level, you can hear stress in the voice. A dry mouth is a sign of anxiety or alarm. But also consider the hidden messages in what people say.

Their accent not only tells you where they are from, but their accent and vocabulary tell you their educational level. They drop hints on things like their feelings about personal responsibility and what kind of people they trust and don't trust.

As you connect with people during the week, pay attention to these signals, in fact, to all the different signals that people send off. A good cardiologist will tell you that when they started medical school, they only heard two things when they listened to a heart. Lub and dub. Lub dub, lub dub. But with experience, they came to hear all sorts of other things, like prolapsed valves, heart murmurs, and much more. So it is with sensory acuity. The more you pay attention, the more you will come to see, hear and feel. When you aren't building rapport, you can use this skill at parties reading people's palms as a diversion.

How Should I Practice This?

A great way to start is with people that you already know something bout.

Notice how the various signals they put out go with the things you know about them. Then think of as many people as you can who share one of those traits, and what they had in common.

The next step is to rate in your mind the stress level of every one you see for a week.

Notice how their stress level can change up and down in an instant. Watch for paleness, facial expression changes, tension, rigid body language, slight withdrawing in apprehension, how hard they are trying to act natural, and so forth.

Here is something that will help you with this part. When people feel fear or excitement, they are activating a part of their nervous system called the sympathetic nervous system.

This does a lot of things, and you can observe many of them. Here are the most obvious ones: pupil dilation, that is, pupils getting larger; thinning of the lips, more muscle tension, paler skin, more skin moisture, more aggressive or withdrawn body language (yes, it can go either way), a tighter voice, the face

stretched somewhat more, and faster foot motions, perhaps even being more on their toes. These are all the things that the body does when it thinks it may have to fight or run away. Perhaps you've heard of the fight or flight reaction. Well, this is it, this is the action of the sympathetic nervous system.

When you do rapport building, you will see a very different set of signals from people. They are similar to what you will see in practicing hypnosis.

Then How Will I Actually Create Rapport?

The key to rapport is to adopt an overall state that is similar to the other person. You start by using your sensory acuity to size up the various subconscious signals that they are putting out, and telling you what state they are in. This is called calibration. Calibration is basically using the persons subconscious signals to know about their inner state.

Once you have done that, you can cultivate that state in yourself.

After all, people tend to like people that are similar to themselves. They can relate and they feel that they will be understood. They also feel some security because that makes you seem more predictable.

It may be a little easier, though, to simply start gently imitating certain key behaviors. This is called mirroring, or matching. This helps build your sensory acuity, because you have to pay attention to the aspect that you are imitating. It also teaches you a lot about calibration, because, as you imitate their key signals, that will tend to produce a state in you that is similar to theirs.

This is kind of subtle, but if you wanted to, you could go pretty far before anyone would think that you were imitating them. You will probably be surprised at how far you can go.

The only reason you do not go too far is usually that you don't want to have completely different personalities and then be in the same room with two very different people that you have done this with. You would be wondering who to act like, or maybe you'd suddenly need to leave because of a family emergency just to get out of there.

Let's go through each of the behavior-mirroring skills that are especially powerful ways to develop rapport.

Posture

Posture is pretty easy. Without mirroring every single thing about other people's posture, practice adopting the basic stance or sitting position. Resting on the same arm (except as a mirror image, your right to their left) gives you a similar alignment. A more leaning forward, straight up, or leaning back posture match is good. This leaves out the more obvious things like crossing arms or legs. But you can try this as well, especially if it is not a person who would be looking for this kind of thing.

Movement

Movement is another. What is their general style of movement? How fast, how much gesturing, how open or closed. This sort of thing. Make your movement kind of similar to that.

Breathing

Breathing is very interesting. If you match the person's breathing, it can have a powerful effect. It's a little harder than the other things, because it is an ongoing concern about timing, but as you get more comfortable with mirroring, start developing this match up as well. This is used in hypnosis, and affects the timing of your verbal statements, speaking during the exhale.

❦

86.

The Falling In-Love Pattern

"Some of the biggest challenges in relationships come from the fact that most people enter a relationship in order to get something: they're trying to find someone who's going to make them feel good. In reality, the only way a relationship will last is if you see your relationship as a place that you go to give, and not a place that you go to take".

— Anthony Robbins, author of Awaken The Giant Within

CREDITS FOR THE creation of this NLP pattern belong to various contributors.

This pattern shows how surprisingly easy it is to enhance your feelings of love and affection toward your loved one, to extend infinitely a familiar and endearing intimacy. These exciting results are produced with nothing more than anchoring.

Overview: The Falling In-Love Pattern

Step #1. Clarify what you want to feel toward a special person.

Step #2. Elicit and focus on this loving state

Step #3. Enhance the state with future experiences.

Step #4. Anchor

Step #5. Test the anchor.

Step #6. Test for results.

Step #1. Clarify what you want to feel toward a special person.

Select a special person for this exercise, such as your significant other.

List in your mind or on paper the feelings you would like to feel toward this person.

Even though dynamics in the relationship may have caused some alienation, regaining these dear feelings can help you enhance the relationship.

The usual way is to work on the relationship so that the feelings will return.

This is a "bottom up" approach" because it emphasizes the somatic (physiology).

Step #2. Elicit and focus on this loving state

Bring the feelings that you identified together into a loving state.

Enhance that state by working with the submodalities that are most powerful in inducing this state.

If the state is developing well, you will find it easier to forgive the other person's faults and transgressions, if appropriate.

Step #3. Enhance the state with future experiences.

Enhance the state further by imagining future experiences that you both enjoy together with a strong bond.

Keep adding images, sounds, and feelings to these experiences until you get a sense of being in love throughout your body.

Step #4. Anchor

Once you have a strong state, anchor it.

Step #5. Test the anchor.

After repeating step three and step four a few times (usually 10 or 12 times is plenty), test the anchor.

Do this by breaking the state, then firing the anchor.

If the anchor works, then you should feel a loving connection with this person.

If you are not satisfied with the results, a likely reason is that you did not associate yourself fully in step three, or there was a problem with the anchor you chose.

Step #6. Test for results.

Discover ways to use this process to enhance your relationship.

For example, fire the anchor before working on communication with your partner.

Notice how these explorations affect your relationship.

Additional Advice

Use good judgement in choosing who to work with.

Relationships with a person who is typically manipulative, demeaning, or destructive is not appropriate.

If you find that the state quickly evaporates as you interact with the person, this is most likely because aspects of the interaction trigger even more powerful negative states.

You will need to change those anchors in order to elicit "antidote" states. For example, if you suddenly become defensive, then you will want to have that interaction generate an open, articulate state in which you are good at understanding, but also good at staying connected with your own reality.

See The Boundaries Installation Pattern and the The Assertiveness Installation Pattern for help with this.

෨෨

87.

Avoiding Counter-Productive Suggestions

"Insecurity is the negative expected".

— Merle Shain

"YOU WILL NOT SMOKE anymore",

"you are a smoke free person now",

"you are a non smoker", etc. – all of these suggestions will encourage a person to do just the thing you want them to stop doing – they will want to smoke! The reason is, that our mind cannot negate negations.

You know this one for sure – do not think about pink elephants.

Now, what are you thinking about? PINK ELEPHANTS!

Whatever it is you want the client to not think about, do not mention it at all in a suggestion, and definitely not in its negative form.

Instead of "smoke free" or "non smoker" use something more appealing that confirms a better reality – "clean lungs person" or "clean breathing" or "easy breath" or whatever inspiring metaphor you come up with. There were more than a few cases in court, in which age-regression "specialists" have installed a false trauma in their clients! Look here – "and do you remember if you were raped when you were 6 years old and kept this secret in the dark?"… this is a suggestion for the brain to invent a rape story at age 6 and become convinced that it really happened!

Be careful of using such statements, especially with somnambulistic clients.

☜☞

325

88.

The Cyber-Porn Addiction Removal Pattern

"I'm such a good lover because I practise a lot on my own".

— Woody Allen

THIS IS ANOTHER VERSION of the swish pattern, formulated to eliminate cyber-porn addiction, a widespread problem that has a tremendous impact on productivity and peace of mind. It is not intended as a judgement about pornography, but rather as help for those who are experiencing a loss of control.

This pattern is not offered as a substitute for professional help. If this may be necessary, we encourage you to seek it.

Overview: The Cyber-Porn Addiction Removal Pattern

Step #1. Create the unwanted associated compulsion image.
Step #2. Break the state.
Step #3. Create a healthier self image
Step #4. Secure the new self image.
Step #5. Begin the change.
Step #6. Swish the images.
Step #7. Do the change!
Step #8. Generate pleasure.
Step #9: Test or Toast

Step #1. Create the unwanted associated compulsion image.

Think of the last time you masturbated to online porn.

Step into the experience, experiencing it from the first perceptual position. That means seeing what you saw back then.

Hear what you heard, and feel what you felt.

Imagine it as if it is happening right now. If this step is unpleasant, please understand that this is the only unpleasant step in the pattern.

Notice where exactly in your body the compulsive feeling begins

Intensify this sensation so that it tells you exactly where it is located in your body.

Notice what images you see while you're feeling this.

One image might be more repeatable than the rest.

What sounds are associated with this image?

Make sure that the pornographic media are included in this image.

Make a mental note of this image and the associated sounds and feelings.

Step #2. Break the state.

Step out of feeling compelled to masturbate with online porn.

To break state, stand up, move around, open your eyes, blink faster, move your facial muscles, wave with your right hand, stretch your left, lift your right knee upward, say your birthday date out loud, think of green, think how a UPS truck looks, and think about what you ate for breakfast today.

Step #3. Create a healthier self-image

Now you're going to create a strong, resourceful, and positive self-image. This resourceful image will restore your self control.

Imagine how you would look if you had a better hobby, that is, a positive compulsion.

The best way to destroy a negative compulsion is to replace it with a positive one so that you feel complete.

You can choose any positive habit on your mind, preferably something you love doing but have neglected because of the online porn compulsion.

How would you talk?

What would your voice sound?

How would you dress, walk, run, and drive?

How would you feel in new situations, when you own that positive compulsion?

That image is the near future image of you; the person who has solved that big issue of changing a negative compulsion to a positive one.

He or she doesn't care about who or what caused the porn compulsion.

He or she can't tell why their past porn compulsion is gone, as they now have a favorite positive compulsion.

We call this image the "near future you" to imply that you are already beginning to experience this new sense of self.

Build that image right in front of yourself.

Make it a life-sized, bright, colorful image of you as a person with so many resources and abilities and self esteem, that you can face the hardest challenges and conquer them all.

Experience yourself as a person who has plenty of choices in life, and who has an amazing ability to create more choices.

See yourself as a person who owns a positive compulsion; the one you selected during this pattern.

Look at that image, letting yourself feel its attractive power.

Connect with how intensely you really need to be that way. This is important.

If you cannot feel it at the moment, go back and make the image stronger.

Make it larger, brighter, and more powerful.

If you were to see that image of yourself in the same way that you view people that you admire, how would you appear?

Imagine all the porn addicted people in the world looking at you with true admiration because of your self-respect, self-control, and resulting success.

Imagine your positive interests leading you to increased health, better sexual relationships, and greater self-respect.

Put a mysterious smile on that image of yourself.

Imagine you can hear yourself think, *"I feel good being me."*

Imagine the tone of your voice.

Experience the attractiveness of this person you have become.

Experience the attractiveness of this way of feeling.

Imagine those words, *"I feel good being me,"* happening all around you, bathing you in these good feelings as though you could soak them up.

Step #4. Secure the new self-image.

Make a mental frame around that image of you with your new positive compulsion.

Shrink it down to a tiny little picture in the open space in front of you.

Don't let it stand there quietly!

Make it sparkle and flash at you.

Take that sparkling little dot in the distant space in front of you and jump it quickly back to its previous size. Big, life-sized, and colorful.

Enjoy experiencing the image (including your mysterious smile), and the words, *"I feel good to be me,"* surrounding you.

Open your eyes for a moment, then close them, thinking of a black screen.

Now see that dissociated positive image again.

Shrink it again so it become a tiny black dot blinking in the distance in front of you.

Now bring it back quickly to its normal size.

Continue shrinking and expanding it, really putting your heart into it.

Step #5. Begin the change.

Shrink back the dissociated positive compulsion image and place it right in the middle of the disturbing image that you discovered in the beginning of this process.

Step #6. Swish the images.

Shrink the negative image quickly into a tiny gray dot in front of you, and at the same time, quickly blow up the tiny dot into the full life-size image of your dissociated positive compulsion image, so that it covers all the negative image of the compulsion you are leaving behind).

Make it larger and brighter, with the stereoscopic "I feel good about me" and your mysterious smile as before.

Practice doing the two movements simultaneously.

Put the negative image in front of you, with the black, blinking dot (the dissociated positive compulsion image) in the middle.

Now quickly SWISH them: shrink the first one quickly, and as you do this, enlarge the tiny dot into the full-size confident new positive compulsion image, along with its sounds and feelings.

It helps you do this with speed and gusto when you say "SWISH!" and snap your fingers when you do it.

IMPORTANT: Do not swish the images back!

Open your eyes right after you've done the swish, and experience the positive image in full color and loudness, including the sound of, "I feel good to be me".

Open your eyes, blink for a second, and close them again.

See the negative image with the blinking dot on it – say swish while you snap your fingers – swish the images again, bringing the positive image to life. Let the good feelings of the positive image move all over your body. We're half way through.

Step #7. Do the change!

Open your eyes, move around a bit. Close your eyes.

Imagine a blank screen. Do the swish ten times, as fast as you can.

Do this powerfully, with as much emotion, enthusiasm, and determination that you can muster.

Use your desire to put an end to the negative image in your life as you source of intensity.

Realizing how much this compulsion has taken from you can generate intensity. Remember:

Negative Image – Black Blinking Dot – SWISH & Finger snap – Big colorful positive image, stereo, "I feel good to be me", mysterious smile.

Open eyes, close eyes – blank black screen – back to the beginning. Good!

Step #8. Generate pleasure.

Now, we will attach that new, pleasurable, compelling, dissociated, positive compulsion image to everything in your life.

Reach out with your hands and grab the strong, dissociated, positive compulsion image like you would grab a big mirror.

Grab it, lift it, and notice something new: there are thousands of thousands of high self esteem, dissociated, positive compulsion images behind it!

They were hiding there all that time to surprise you!

Experience images that show you successful in everything you do in life as a strong, committed, powerful, happy, thrilled, popular, excited, person filled with pleasure.

As you lift the image, all the other images are lifted with it.

Smile to yourself, get some momentum, and throw it up high above you. Everything spreads out in the open air above your head.

A split-second later they all fall down, spreading all around you.

In front of you, representing your future, there are thousands of them covering the ground. Just around you there are a couple thousand more.

Around you, as you look back on your past time line hiding behind your back, are thousands more.

Imagine each one framed with a blinking shiny frame, yelling for attention!

Know that it will be amazing, facing challenges in your future where all that your mind can remember is how powerful and how strong your are.

It's almost more pleasure than you can contain.

Images behind you rule the earth and cover and hide the small weak negative images, they rule them, they control the past now, they blink for attention, anywhere you look.

Because, as you try to find a negative memory, all the blinking positive images interrupt the search, they yell for you, "Look at me! I feel GOOOOOOOD being me!"

Play around, pick one up, see the mysterious smile, hear the stereo effect voice around you, see the image as it grows and gets brighter.

Now imagine yourself waking up in the morning, eating breakfast, and seeing your positive images all over the place, blinking and yelling for your attention.

You can open your eyes now and look around.

Step #9: Test or Toast

Take a moment (not too long) and think about your computer.

If you can, sit in front of your computer.

Do you feel compelled to masturbate or to do something else?

In the coming days and weeks, see if you experience your computer life differently.

If you can't remember the negative image clearly, or you did but didn't feel off balance, then these are signs of success.

If you still feel compelled to cyber-porn consider consulting a specialist.

☯

89.

The Spelling Strategy

"Everybody who is incapable of learning has taken to teaching".

— Oscar Wilde

CREDITS FOR THE creation of this NLP pattern belong to various contributors.

This pattern improves your spelling.

We use a lot of the internal visual modality in this pattern. Even if you consider yourself to be more of an "auditory" or "kinesthetic" person, try this method and see how well it is working for you.

There's a lot to be said about people who stubbornly cling to their most favorite modality and almost refuse to be flexible about it, but we'll leave it to online arguments and discussions. Do not fall in this trap – even if your most frequently used modality is auditory, you can still use well successful strategies that depend mostly on the visual modality, such as this spelling strategy.

Overview: The Spelling Strategy

Step #1. View the word.
Step #2. Relax.
Step #3. Picture the word.
Step #4. Clear your mind.
Step #5. Picture the word and write it down. Check it.
Step #6. Picture the word and write it backwards. Check it.

Step #1. View the word.

Look at the word on paper or on screen, spelled correctly.

Step #2. Relax.

With your eyes closed, recall a familiar, relaxing experience. Once you have a strong sense of the feeling, open your eyes, and look at the word.

Step #3. Picture the word.

Look up and left, mentally picturing the correct spelling.

Step #4. Clear your mind.

Open and close your eyes rapidly, get up, move around if you have to.

Step #5. Picture the word and write it down. Check it.

Look back up and left at your mental picture of the word.

Write it down, as if you were transcribing from that image.

Check the spelling against the correct spelling. If it is wrong, go to step one.

Step #6. Picture the word and write it backwards. Check it.

Return your gaze up and left to your mental picture of the word.

This time, write it backwards, from right to left.

Check the spelling and return to step three if it is incorrect.

Additional Advice

Imagine the word in the color that most fits the word. Maybe ludicrous should be purple.

When you form the word in your mind, form each letter one at a time, in a font that is very different from a typical font. If there is a letter or letter combination that you tend to get wrong when you spell the word, make those letter big and bright compared to the rest of the word when you picture it.

As you picture the word, build it one syllable at a time.

Make sure that as you imagine the word, it fits in you mental view. You can experiment with seeing the letters forming a circle and filling your view.

Use your finger to trace the letters in front of you, picturing your finger actually painting the letters as if on a canvas.

♋

90.

Elicitation Of Learning Strategies

"Learning is the beginning of wealth. Learning is the beginning of health. Learning is the beginning of spirituality. Searching and learning is where the miracle process all begins".

— Jim Rohn

CREDITS FOR THE CREATION of this NLP pattern belong to various contributors.

Learning is the process of acquiring new thinking patterns and behavioral capabilities. In NLP, a learning strategy is the syntax of steps one takes in order to learn. There are many learning strategies, of course, and some of them are not very effective.

Effective learning works within a feedback loop, or the T.O.T.E. model in NLP. In order to define a learning strategy, we would need to identify and organize the usage of representational systems (rep. systems) a person is using in order to learn effectively. More importantly, we should identify which

representational system gets the most use during the learning session. This is modeling in essence, but on a much smaller scale than other skills.

The reason that people differ as to what learning strategies are most useful to them is that people are different! I am not surprised that I could do so well in literature in high school but almost failed in math. My literature teacher spoke in a language that made sense to me. She spoke using visual predicates mostly and she used every metaphor she could in order to explain a theme. My math teacher, however, was a very stubborn kinesthetic oriented person. She spoke of numbers in the dullest way, and the only explanation she had as to why an arithmetic rule works as it is was, "that's the way it is." However, it was my responsibility to develop a learning strategy that would help me with math. Apparently I didn't, because I almost failed in that exam.

My best friend in high school, though, had exactly the opposite experience. She was thrilled about math classes, couldn't wait to solve those complex trigonometric problems, and her aversion to literature classes was well known. She had a very different learning strategy than myself. The problem with both us was that we used the SAME strategy (each one respectively) on two different subjects. I used my successful literature learning strategy on math, which proved to be ineffective, and she used her successful math learning strategy on literature, and again

that has proven to be the wrong approach.

The purpose of NLP is to elicit as many successful learning strategies as possible, so that you will always have the freedom and flexibility to move from one to another according to whatever is more effective for your outcome. The development of the awareness and ability to elicit your own successful learning strategies is called "Learning II" in NLP. It means, "learning to learn." The more you know about your own successful learning strategies, the more effective you will be in using, modifying and improving your capabilities.

The Elicitation Of Learning Strategies pattern will help you uncover the syntax you're using to successfully learn something. You can also use it, of course, to model another person's learning strategy and try it out for yourself.

Overview: The Elicitation Of Learning Strategies Pattern

Step #1. Select the learning subject you were successful in.
Step #2. List your outcomes.
Step #3. Evidence procedure.
Step #4. List the actions you took.
Step #5. Problem solving activities.
Step #6. Consider which Rep system you used the most.
Step #7. Elicit your Rep systems syntax.

Step #1. Select the learning subject you were successful in.

Any subject you're good at will do just fine. If you find it much easier to learn literature, as I did in high-school, for whatever reason, write that one down. If it's math, history, general knowledge, logic, languages, or whatever else, make sure you have only one subject in mind. If you can't find a specific subject that you're good at, chunk down to micro-skills.

Search your past for times in which you learned anything fast and effortlessly.

Step #2. List your goals and outcomes.

What were your outcomes in regards to this subject?

What were your goals when you approached the learning of this subject?

Step #3. Evidence procedure.

What was your evidence procedure to know that you have completed successfully the outcome in this subject? For example, if your strongest subject was math, how did you know you were successful in achieving an outcome?

Was it the passing of an exam or simply the solution of a math problem within a given time?

Step #4. List the actions you took.

What were the actual steps you took when you started working on achieving this outcome?

Did you do anything unique for this subject, that you did not do for other learning outcomes?

Step #5. Problem solving activities.

As with any learning opportunity, problems and challenges are always present and might disturb our learning.

What did you do in order to solve minute-to-minute problems that interfered with your excellent learning mode?

Step #6. Consider which rep system you used the most.

Look back at your answers to the steps above and see if you can notice which representational system you used the most.

Step #7. Elicit your rep system's syntax.

Use the following questions to elicit the actual strategy you have used. Refer to your answers to the previous steps, of course, since you've already done most of the groundwork there already:

What has stimulated you to learn effectively?

Did you see, hear, feel, or otherwise sense a cause?

Perhaps you digitally said something to yourself (inner voice), and if so, what is the content of that message?

How did you represent your outcome for learning this subject in your mind?

Did you visualize an image of yourself "knowing" or "excelling an exam"?

Did you visualize an image of yourself associated or dissociated (i.e. Did you see your notebook or did you see yourself looking at the notebook)?

Did you remember the outcome as an image from past successful events?

Did you say the outcome to yourself, and if so how did it sound?

Did you feel the outcome or sense the assurance that this outcome is about to be reality? If so, how did it manifest itself in your body?

How did you know that you're making progress (evidence procedure)?

Did you perceive external visual information (physically) or internal visual information (imagination)? And what was it exactly?

Did you need to hear that you've been making progress (perhaps a teacher congratulating you for accomplishing a task, or your parents being proud that you got an "A")? Was it something you said to yourself or something that another person told you?

Which actions did you take for reaching this outcome?

Did you analyze, organize, re-organize, talk to yourself, have intuition, visualize, touch, sense, discuss, listen, move, draw, watch, take notes, or feel certain emotions? Was it in any combination of the above?

What was the syntax or order of these actions in respect to the actual process of achieving the outcome?

How did you respond to minute problems? You can use the long list above (analyze, organize, re-organize, etc.)

What other questions could you ask yourself to complete this strategy and make it as accurate and close to reality as possible?

Step #8. Test.

Notice any improvements to your ability to learn the subject you chose.

☯

91.

New Language Rapid Learning

"Charles V said that a man who knew four languages was worth four men; and Alexander the Great so valued learning, that he used to say he was more indebted to Aristotle for giving him knowledge that, than his father Philip for giving him life".

— Thomas Babington Macaulay

CREDITS FOR THE CREATION of this NLP pattern belong to various contributors.

This pattern will help you memorize words in a foreign language very quickly. It uses the power of submodalities.

Overview: The New Language Rapid Learning Strategy

Step #1. Select 5 new words.
Step #2. Substitute
Step #3. Use Sub-Modalities
Step #4. Move mentally faster
Step #5. Compress in groups of 5's
Step #6. Test

Step #1. Select 5 new words.

Select five words that you wish to learn from the language you are learning. Establish the intention to learn all five within the next five to ten minutes.

Read through them slowly, pronounce each one and read its translation. Make sure you understand the translation (the meaning of the translated word).

Step #2. Substitute

Take the first word and make it something familiar. Here's how:

As the example below shows, take the syllables of the word apart in your mind.

Use them to build a mental image that is memorable because it is wild and strange in some way. Draw from your own experiences to find imagery and meaning that are significant to you because they come from your personal likes and fantasies.

Here is an example.

For the Italian word "Vuoto" ("empty in English),

a) I deconstructed the word to "Vu" and "Oto."

b) In Hebrew (my native language) the sound "Oto" means "car," so I imagined a huge Volvo.

c) In this imaginary scene, I open the passenger door of that huge Volvo, and on the other side I see a Mexican clown (love them) who yells at me, "Your Vu-olvo is empty!"

In this image I have used personal images and meanings to link "vuoto" and "empty."

Coming up with these can be a challenge at first, but people find that it gets easy with practice.

Keep practicing and you will build this skill while learning a language at the same time.

Step #3. Use Sub-Modalities

Submodalities are great for memory techniques. For those who are not familiar with the term, sub-modalities mean the "modes" of the experience.

For example, let's take my strange Volvo image. Can the Volvo get any bigger? Of course, in my imagination, it can be as big as I wish it to be. Its size is a submodality of the visual sense mode, just as loudness is a submodality of the auditory sense mode (or rep system). The clown can honk the horn loudly to get my attention, breaking the car's windows showing that it is empty (the meaning of *vuoto*).

Sub-modalities for my made up scene can include the brightness of the image, the nearness of the car, its size, whether the imagery is in color or black and white, whether the Mexican clown has a high or low voice, and so forth. If you are not comfortable working with sub-modalities yet, you can still do this pattern without them.

Step #4. Move mentally faster

Run the image as fast as you can over and over again.

Use your body.

Move your arms.

Move your eyes up and to the left when you say the foreign word. Say the foreign word out loud. Put your hand on your chest when you say the foreign word out loud and imagine as wild and as big and as strange as you can the image you came up with. Now do it again, faster.

You can run the pattern faster than you think, because the brain can learn surprisingly quickly.

Use repetition to improve your results. Repetition is very important for getting things into long term memory. By repeating it, imagining a wild associative image, and doing it faster each time, you are embedding each word in your nerve system.

Step #5. Compress in groups of 5's

Once you feel comfortable with imagining wild stuff, do it with the rest of the words, in group of five. That is, go through the group, build a wild image for each one of them, and then repeat them in a row, one through five, repeatedly, faster and faster.

This saves time, and makes it more interesting. Make sure you make up a UNIQUE image for each word. Variety will help your mind distinguish between the words.

Step #6. Test

After the first 20 words, rest for a minute; stretch or do something else. Then take only the foreign words and imagine the wild picture and then the meaning for each one. See if you can feel the meaning without translating.

Do not be alarmed if you can't remember the meaning of all the words. All it means is that you should come up with better, more personal and wilder and stranger images for these words. The rest, which you did remember, you will remember for a lifetime.

❦

92.

Rhythmic Learning

"Rhythm is the basis of life, not steady forward progress. The forces of creation, destruction, and preservation have a whirling, dynamic interaction".

— from the Kabbalah

CREDITS FOR THE CREATION of this NLP pattern belong to various contributors.

Here is a strategy that you can explore and adapt to your own learning adventures. It uses the power of rhythm to create attention and involvement.

Rhythm exists in every cell of your body.

There must be a deeper reason for our fascination and excitement when music grabs our attention intensely. If a song does not have a capturing rhythm, we lose interest.

This strategy uses that natural tendency to seek a continuous cycle, i.e. Rhythm, in our absorption of knowledge. There is more to it, however, than just tapping your foot or hand.

Overview: The Rhythmic Learning Strategy

Step #1. While learning rote material, establish a rhythm that you will keep with your thumb, head, or foot, depending on your preference.

Step #2. Chunk down

Step #3. Test

Step #1. While learning rote material, establish a rhythm that you will keep with your thumb, head, or foot, depending on your preference.

Use a typical rock rhythm that is a little faster than one beat per second. If the material is difficult to absorb, use a slower rhythm.

Keep a rhythm that uses four beats, just like most songs, ONE, two, three, four, ONE...

Run the item you are learning through your mind, keeping rhythm. If it is long, use several rounds of four beats (measures).

Leave room for silence so that it soaks in and conforms to the measures. Silence is a very powerful part of music and the dramatic arts. It is literally part of the communication, and essential to making it compelling.

Here is a rhythm learning example. If you were learning cow anatomy, you might want to learn all the structures around the ear, the regio temporalis. That could be three beats with one left over to complete the four beat measure: RE-gio TEM-por AL-is (beat).

A long word or phrase can take up more than one measure. For example processus zygomaticus osis temporalis could be PRO-CES-sus-ZY-GO-MAT-i-CUS (beat, beat).

The lower case syllables are on the "upbeat" that is in between the main beats. That means there are six beats for this one, plus two silent beats to finish the second four beat measure. That gives us eight beats, or two measures.

Step #2. Chunk down

Once you have done the category, such as the region we just mentioned, you can chunk down to the specific structures or items in that category, maintaining the rhythm and including silences that make it complete.

Step #3. Test

Stick with this for a specific set of words or concepts, and keep at it long enough to cover a definite area or topic of study, such as an anatomical region. See what effect this pattern has on your memorization ability.

Additional Advice

If you have music on that doesn't go too fast, you can experiment with keeping to the rhythm of the music, for variety. It might even give you rhythm ideas, especially rhythm and blues.

If you are a musical person, you can add a unique melody to each item, or even string the items into a song or improvised melody.

93.

Commitment

"Do just once what others say you can't do, and you will never pay attention to their limitations again".

— James Cook

MAKING A STATEMENT OF intention (i.e. Making a commitment) is extremely important when you want your client to see immediate progress and improvement.

The commitment should be made by your client with your instructions.

After inducing a light trance, try for example –

"and now you need to make a firm decision – are you really willing to drop the smoking habit and look forward seeing yourself as a clean breathing person?

Are you fed enough from this poison to let it go right here in this room?

If you agree for this commitment, I will too, and to know if you are, lift your right pinky for saying YES…".

This will inevitably install a new direction in their mind to follow – pay attention that I did not say anything related to "smoke" or "smoking" when I future paced the client – "clean breathing person", not "smoke free" or "non smoker".

Refer to "Avoiding Counter-ProductiveSuggestions"mentioned earlier in this book.

☯

94.

The (Accelerated) Learning Chain

"Other people may be there to help us, teach us, guide us along our path, but the lesson to be learned is always ours".

— Anonymous

CREDITS FOR THE CREATION of this NLP pattern belong to Robert Dilts.

This pattern installs strategies for efficient learning. It uses chaining, a way to link experiences into a sequence that leads to a useful state. These experiences serve as transitional states that move you from a problem state to a resourceful one. There are many ways that you can assemble patterns like the one below, which serves as an example.

Overview: The (Accelerated) Learning Chain Pattern

Step #1. Choose a challenging learning situation.

Step #2. Choose a positive learning experience.

Step #3. Access the states of the positive experience.

Step #4. Sequence these states in time.

Step #5. Turn the states into stepping stones, placed in order.

Step #6. Anchor these steps by stepping through them.

Step #7. Hold the challenging learning situation while stepping through.

Step #8. Test.

Step #1. Choose a challenging learning situation.

Think of something that you would like to learn, but are having trouble with.

Step #2. Choose a positive learning experience.

Think of a good learning experience that has as much in common as possible with the problem you just identified.

For example, if you are learning rote material to memorize, see if you can think of a very successful learning experience that involved rote learning. Be sure that the learning experience you choose is one that led to you learning something well.

Step #3. Access the states of the positive experience.

Access the states that were part of this positive learning.

Explore the elements involved.

List them.

Here are some examples of submodalities that might be involved: feeling supported, feeling things "click" internally, experiencing "the zone" internally, experiencing internal visually constructed images of what you are learning, or internally visually manipulating what

you were learning, feeling excited, interested, and motivated, seeing and hearing your involvement in the learning experience, etc.

Step #4. Sequence these states in time.

Now think of the earliest states and the later states as a sequence, starting with inklings such as awareness and curiosity, and ending with more complicated collections of sense modalities such as deep involvement and mastery. List them as a sequence that begins with your exposure to the material and ends with your successful use of the learned material.

Step #5. Turn the states into stepping stones, placed in order.

Imagine a series of stepping stones in front of you, and mentally place each of these sequenced steps along these stepping stones.

Place a note for each one and marked with a bold marker if this will help you keep the sequence in mind.

Step #6. Anchor these steps by stepping through them.

Spend some time on each of these steps in order to anchor them as representing each of these transitional states.

Step #7. Hold the challenging learning situation while stepping through.

Bring the challenging learning issue to mind.

Move through each step while holding this in mind.

Go through these steps a few times, if possible, before you are back in the challenging learning situation.

Step #8. Test.

Next time you are involved in the challenging learning situation, see how this pattern has changed your experience of this learning.

೧೧

95.

Apposition (Of Opposites)

"Obstacles don't have to stop you. If you run into a wall, don't turn around and give up. Figure out how to climb it, go through it, or work around it".

— Michael Jordan

APPOSITION OF OPPOSITES is a hypnotic suggestion used to enhance the quality of trance or deepen the client into hypnosis.

The way it works is very simple – you address one known physical condition the client is engaged in and instruct the rest of his body at once to fall deeper into hypnosis.

For example, if you started using the hand levitation induction, you could use apposition of opposites by saying: "and perhaps you notice how your hand feels lighter and lighter and your body relaxes even deeper".

With a client you've been working on for more than the first session, you can also push his hand down at once (but gently) as you say "deeper".

☯

96.

Identifying Self Sabotage Elements

"If we did all the things we are capable of doing, we would literally astonish ourselves".

— Thomas A. Edison

THIS IS A LIST THAT I usually give to every client I accept. It will guide you to answer the most disturbing question: "Why does it always happen to me?".

If you ever wondered why it is so hard for you to make a progress in your life or your business, go through this list.

Mark the items that fit you best. Take this list with you for a week or two and notice thought patterns that keep repeating. Sometimes, just by being aware of a limiting thought pattern, it breaks down.

Then, construct an action plan to overcome these blocks, one block at a time.

Again, you really don't have to use a full NLP pattern on a small is-

sue, such as occasional arrogance, for example... you could merely use dissociation and future pacing to solve a relatively small disturbance in your behavior.

Keep the "big guns" for the really big issues.

1. *Addictions*
2. *Aggression*
3. *Anger*
4. *Anxiety*
5. *Arrogance*
6. *Attachment*
7. *Judgmental Attitude*
8. *Over obsessive about own opinions*
9. *Reaction instead of Action*
10. *Scattered thoughts*
11. *Being Too emotional*
12. *Being Too intellectual*

13. Not being grounded
14. Following blindly after another
15. Boredom
16. Carelessness
17. Complaining
18. Compromising
19. Compulsion
20. Envy
21. Fears
22. Feeling needy
23. Frustration
24. Futility
25. Future thinking
26. Delusions
27. Greed
28. Guilt
29. Hate
30. Hopelessness
31. Humorlessness
32. Ignorance
33. Illusion
34. Impatience
35. Impulsiveness
36. Indecision
37. Indifference
38. Inertia
39. Insecurity
40. Manipulation
41. Materialism
42. Mediocrity
43. Moodiness
44. Needing to please others
45. Negativity
46. No fun
47. Obsessions
48. Pain

49. Perfectionism
50. Poor health
51. Low self esteem
52. Possessiveness
53. Poverty attitude
54. Prejudice
55. Pride
56. Procrastination
57. Rationalization
58. Inner conflict
59. Confusion
60. Cowardice
61. Criticism
62. Cruelty
63. Defensiveness
64. Denial
65. Dependence
66. Depression
67. Dishonesty
68. Disorder
69. Dominance
70. Doubt
71. Egotism
72. Insensitivity
73. Intolerance
74. Isolation
75. Jealousy
76. Lack of confidence
77. Lack of creativity
78. Lack of discipline
79. Lack of purpose
80. Lack of trust
81. Laziness
82. Living in the past
83. Low energy
84. Repression
85. Malnutrition

86. Resentment
87. Resistance
88. Ridicule
89. Self pity
90. Self sabotage
91. Selfishness
92. Shame
93. Shyness
94. Stress

95. Stubbornness
96. Suffering
97. Timidity
98. Unexpressed emotions
99. Vanity
100. Withdrawal
101. Revenge

❦

97.

Problem Definition

"I am an old man and have known many troubles, but most of them have never happened"

— Mark Twain

CREDITS FOR THE CREATION of this NLP pattern belong to various contributors.

This pattern helps you find your way out of a problem that you are stuck in. It addresses our tendency to define a problem in a way that makes it seem impossible to solve.

When you approach any technique of problem solving, be sure to experience a resourceful state of mind. The best techniques for problem solving will not do much good if you're not "in the mood" to find solutions, or if you're operating out of stress.

Physical distance, when appropriate, can also help to quiet the mind and put you in a state of creative flow.

Overview: The Problem Definition Pattern

Step #1. Use meta-model distinctions to analyze the problem.

Step #2. Examine the ecology of the problem.

Step #3. Determine the presuppositions hidden in the problem definition.

Step #4. Use the as-if frame to brainstorm alternative problem formulations.

Step #5. Test

Step #1. Use meta-model distinctions to analyze the problem.

Think about how you have defined your problem.

How would you succinctly state the nature of your problem?

Look for *well-formedness* violations in this definition. These include vagueness, over-generalization, and distortions of meaning, causation, and presupposition.

Look for ways that you define the problem as being outside of your control or like a thing instead of a process.

What happens when you take the problem and treat it like a verb.

For example, *"How do you social anxiety yourself?"*

Step #2. Examine the ecology of the problem.

Look at the ways the problem can serve you.

You are looking for things that may sustain the problem because they act as incentives.

For example, social anxiety can cause you to reduce demands on yourself.

Seeing how this happens can help you turn your attention to the problems that would make it difficult for you to tolerate those demands.

With this expanded awareness, you can brainstorm solutions and get help.

Step #3. Determine the presuppositions hidden in the problem definition.

Look for dysfunctional presuppositions that you have unconsciously embedded in the problem as you have defined it.

Do your presuppositions make the problem somehow impossible to solve?

Do they set up a condition for solving the problem that requires an uncooperative person to cooperate with you?

Notice how these presuppositions are arbitrary and unnecessary.

Challenge them.

Step #4. Use the as-if frame to brainstorm alternative problem formulations.

Generate "what if" scenarios in order to come up with new problem formulations.

Since this is brainstorming, go for quantity rather than quality.

Use this as an opportunity to "massage" the boundaries that your mind has created.

For example:

"How would I think of this problem if I had amazingly high self esteem?"

"What if I was a highly aggressive person?"

"What if I had all the compassion, wisdom, and universal connectedness of a saint or the Buddha?"

Look at the problem in these scenarios, and see how it seems different.

Step #5. Test

In the coming days, see what new resources and solutions come to mind regarding this problem.

Watch for new behaviors and feelings.

Has this exercise led to you being more flexible in your thinking and behavior in any ways?

☙❧

98.

Problem Solving Strategy (I)

"Most people spend more time and energy going around problems than in trying to solve them".

— Henry Ford

CREDITS FOR THE CREATION of this NLP pattern belong to Robert Dilts.

This pattern is the first of a series of innovative problem-solving strategies. This one uses the power of metaphor. You will need to have a good handle on metaphor in order to do this pattern.

Overview: The Problem Solving Strategy (I)

Step #1. Select the problem, step into the problem position, associating into the problem.

Step #2. Step into a meta-position.

Step #3. Experience a rich resource from a resource position.

Step #4. Create metaphor for the problem, but that is based on the resource position.

Step #5. Imagine solving the metaphoric problem. Observe the resulting changes in your experience.

Step #6. From your meta-position, apply the metaphoric solution to the original problem.

Step #7. Step into the problem location and check for results.

Step #8. Repeat, using other resource states.

Step #1. Select the problem, step into the problem position, associating into the problem.

Consider a problem that you feel you need to approach in a fresh way.

Choose a location in front of you to step into, that you will anchor to this problem situation.

Step into that position and associate into this problem, experiencing how it happens in first position (through your own eyes).

Step #2. Step into a meta-position.

Select another position that will serve as your meta-position, where you will view the problem from a transcendent or distant position. Step into this position.

Step #3. Experience a rich resource from a resource position.

Think of a resource situation that is unrelated to the problem.

The situation should help you access a very rich and compelling resource state.

For example, it could be an activity that gives you a strong sense of self, mission, creativity, or passion.

Step into a new position that will now serve as your resource position.

Fully associate into the resource experience.

Step #4. Create metaphor for the problem, but that is based on the resource position.

Come up with a metaphor for your problem situation.

In other words, create a new, fantasy problem that is a symbol for your real problem.

Your new, fantasy problem should be inspired by the resource activity, its context, and your resource state.

For example, if skiing was your resource activity, then a real problem such as difficulty concentrating could be symbolized by getting your skis crossed up. The ski problem is now a metaphor (symbol) for the concentration problem.

Step #5. Imagine solving the metaphoric problem. Observe the resulting changes in your experience.

Maintain your distance from the problem situation, and imagine solving the metaphoric problem.

For example, you would come up with a solution to crossing

up your skis by developing good coordination for parallel skis by focusing on controlling one of the skis so that the other naturally follows.

Notice how this solution calls forth any changes in your physical state, internal strategies, TOTE's and so forth.

Step #6. From your meta-position, apply the metaphoric solution to the original problem.

Now step back into your meta-position. Explore how you would take the solution that you just created (for that metaphoric problem) and think metaphorically in order to translate it into a solution in the actual problem situation.

For example, focusing on body language and controlling one of your skis to get parallel skiing is like clarifying you goals and reasons for focusing your mind on your studies.

Step #7.

Step into the problem location and check for results.

Step into the problem situation location, and see if you have dissolved your impasse.

Step #8. Repeat, using other resource states.

Repeat this process, using other resource states applied to the same problem. This brings in a variety of your resources so you approach the problem from very different angles.

☯

99.

Problem Solving Strategy (II)

"No problem can stand the assault of sustained thinking".

— Voltaire

CREDITS FOR THE CREATION of this NLP pattern belong to various contributors.

This pattern helps a team of 2 or more people resolve a problem by creating a shared experience of an appropriate resource. The idea here is that if all involved persons are aligned with each other, any conflicts they may have had between themselves are no longer a factor in their effort to solve a given problem.

This pattern is not only for business teams; you can use it by working with members of the same family or even couples. When there's a problem to be solved by more than one person, their shared interest and alignment alone might give all of them a stream of creative ideas for solving the issue. Using such a strategy might also deepen a bond between people or help to mediate conflicts between them.

> ## Overview: The Problem Solving Strategy (II)
>
> *Step #1. Identify a resourceful experience.*
> *Step #2. Pre-mirror a shared resource.*
> *Step #3. Post mirror a shared resource.*
> *Step #4. Move to 2nd position.*
> *Step #5. Move to 3rd position.*
> *Step #6. Return to 1st position, facing the same direction.*
> *Step #7. For teams, repeat with pairs.*
> *Step #8. Test.*

Step #1. Identify a resourceful experience.

Think back to a recent time in which you've had an experience you could define as resourceful.

It should be an event in which you were fully congruent and competent, you've been acting like a master and you have achieved your outcome.

Associate into this memory. See what you saw, hear what you heard, feel what you felt and notice how this acquired resourceful feeling actually feels like.

Feelings can be expressed in terms of movement, so where and from where does this feeling go/come from?

Step #2. Pre-mirroring a shared resource.

Stand up facing your partner.

Demonstrate the movement of your resourceful feeling to your partner.

Show him or her how it feels.

Do not speak, just move your body to illustrate the feeling.

Stay associated to the memory.

Step #3. Post mirroring a shared resource.

Remain in the 1st position (associated) and mirror your partner's response to your movements. That is, mimic your partner's movements.

Step #4. Move to 2nd position.

Exchange places with your partner.

Move to 2nd position and act as if you are him or her.

Be sure to notice the movement you've elicited from yourself in step two, it will change.

Step #5. Move to 3rd position.

Move to the observer position (third position), and carefully observe the both of you. What is similar? What seems different?

Note the similarities and differences in the expression of the resourceful feeling's movement that you and your partner show to each other.

Step #6. Back to 1st position, facing same direction.

Move back to the first position, fully associated in the resourceful memory.

You and your partner should now face the same direction, standing side by side. Now both of you begin again the resourceful feeling's movement (each his own), and continue until you find a similar move. It can be anything, long or short, rapid or slow. This is the "we" zone.

Step #7. For teams: repeat with pairs.

If you're doing this pattern with multiple teams, work in pairs and then combine them.

Repeat in the same manner so that all four, six, or eight, and so on, are eventually aligned in a shared movement that gives each his own subjective resourceful experience, but at the same time it is a shared one.

Step #8. Test.

Testing is easy. It involves the solution of the problem at hand!

Team up and work on the problem; every time you face a conflict, re-group the same direction format and use the shared movement maneuver.

If you feel a sense of "we are going to solve this one together", you have accomplished this exercise successfully. If not, it needs to be repeated, perhaps with a stronger subjective resourceful experience of each team member.

Additional Advice

When working with teams of people that you don't know personally, work hard first on establishing group rapport with them and establishing your position as a leader. Even if the team's current leader (a boss, a manager, a supervisor) is present, make sure that he or she knows in advance that you're taking this approach in order to help the group come together and not to take over his or her responsibilities or authority.

The best way to initially establish leadership is to use the one-up-man-ship concept. That's a concept that is in use by churches for years.

Notice how the priest is standing always higher than the public, always in fancier and special clothing, always looking calm and in control, always moving with intention, and always speaking with confidence.

You can do the same in any setting. In business situations, dress as if you own the place and you're the richest guy around. Walk in a consistent rhythm, not too fast and not too slow, look around and speak to mere strangers with confidence and never ever apologize. Even if you're late, do not say "I'm sorry I'm late, but I had this or that...". Say something like, "I know I'm late so we'd better start now."

❀

100.

The Walt Disney Strategy

"Disneyland will never be completed. It will continue to grow as long as there is imagination left in the world".

— Walt Disney

CREDITS FOR THE CREATION of this NLP pattern belong to Robert Dilts.

This pattern helps you use the creative idea-generating talent of the famous animator, Walt Disney.

Overview: The Walt Disney Strategy

Step #1. Create four locations for states.

Step #2. Step into location #1, Dreamer.

Step #3. Step into location #2, Realist.

Step #4. Step into position #3, Critic.

Step #5. Select an outcome that you really want to achieve.

Step #6. Step into position #2, Realist. Associate into your scenario of realizing the important goal.

Step #7. Step into position #3, Critic. Is anything missing or off track?

Step #8. Step back into position #1.

Step #8. Repeat this cycle a few times.

Step #9. Continue repetitions

Step #1. Create four locations for states.

Start with your meta-position and step into it.

The main three will be
1) Dreamer,
2) Realist, and
3) Critic.

Step #2. Step into location #1, Dreamer.

Think of a time when you freely and creatively dreamed up some great new ideas. Relive the experience. Relive this experience.

Step #3. Step into location #2, Realist.

Think of a time when you were in a very realistic frame of mind, and devised a clear, realistic plan that you were able to put into action.

Relive this experience.

Step #4. Step into position #3, Critic.

Think of a time when you criticized a plan, but in a constructive way.

You had criticism that would be put into use and in a positive or even an inspired state. Relive that experience.

It helps to have position #3 far enough from the other positions so as not to interfere with their anchored states.

Step #5. Select an outcome that you really want to achieve.

Step into position #1, Dreamer. Imagine from third position (watching, dissociated) that you are achieving this goal.

Experience and think about it in a free-wheeling way.

Step #6. Step into position #2, Realist. Associate into your scenario of realizing the important goal.

Experience, one at a time, the perspective of each person in your scenario of success.

Now experience the events leading to your success as a storyboard (a series of images that are in order of occurrence, as in the pictures used to prepare for a movie).

Step #7. Step into position #3, Critic. Is anything missing or off track?

Turn any criticisms into questions for the dreamer (the you that you are observing).

Step #8. Step back into position #1.

Brainstorm answers for the questions from your critic.

Step #8. Repeat this cycle a few times.

Once you are satisfied, finish by thinking of something completely different, and that you enjoy and are good at.

While you do this, walk again through the three positions.

Step #9. Continue repetitions

Continue cycling through steps five, six and seven and eight until your plan feels fitting at each of the locations.

Additional Advice

It is somewhat useful to use the perspectives of the realist, the dreamer and the critic in other NLP patterns. However, make sure not to identify yourself with any of them.

Keep all perspectives as resources, not as belief systems.

The reason is that you do not want to be a dreamer most of the time or a realist most of the time, or worse – a critic most of the time. You want the freedom and flexibility to use any of these perspectives according to whatever is suitable for the outcome you're pursuing.

Walt Disney was known to be non judgmental when it comes to crazy ideas. The strangest stories and strangest most outrageous ideas can bring to life a new idea that will be successful. So do not put an X on any of your thoughts.

You can use Edward De Bono's "Po!" strategy to come up with outrageous ideas. Simply step into the Dreamer perspective, think about the problem or challenge you're facing, and say, "Po!" + the strangest visualization you can come up with.

Po! What if every person on earth could learn all of the NLP ideas and methods for the price of a book instead of 5 certification seminars… ooh, wait a minute, that gives me an idea!!!

What if there was an NLP sourcebook of all the successful Neuro Linguistic-Programming methods?! There you have it, in your hands!

Here's a glimpse to Mr. Disney's mind: "I love Mickey Mouse more than any woman I have ever known".

☜☞

101.

The Binary Code Of Forgetfulness

"Seven to eleven is a huge chunk of life, full of dulling and forgetting. It is fabled that we slowly lose the gift of speech with animals, that birds no longer visit our windowsills to converse. As our eyes grow accustomed to sight they armor themselves against wonder".

— Leonard Cohen

CREDITS FOR THE CREATION of this NLP pattern belong to various contributors.

If you can forget, and you can cause other people to forget (no matter what), you are in a very powerful position to change yourself to any degree. Your complete list of non-useful behaviors and destructive subconscious thought pattern issues can all be solved with the simplest skill of all: forgetting.

We usually attach negative meanings to the skill of forgetting. When we forget, we are conditioned to perceive it as meaning that either you didn't care enough, your brain is not functioning properly, or you did not remember it in the first place.

Most people believe that forgetting something is beyond their control, as if it is a matter of luck or coincidence or simply lack of neurological resources regarding specific areas of memory. While that can be true at times, it is not usually the real cause.

You can forget on cue. You can remember anything you want to remember, for how long you want to remember it and then forget it again when you choose to. You can refer to our free memory improvement course and to our Accelerated

Learning section to learn more about how to remember.

Forgetting, however, is probably a new conscious skill for you if you are not a very skillful hypnotist by now.

How many times have you heard the phrase, "oh, just forget about it..."? People have instructed you to forget something you were planning to remember. Sometimes you complied if it was not important, and sometimes you didn't if you thought that this person is thinking you're not serious enough for the job.

In fact, you can come to this conclusion on your own; you can remember ABOUT forgetting. If you can forget little things like your keys or where you put your latest IRS return, one more little thing won't be that hard to forget either, right?

How about if you could forget that your spouse were very annoying yesterday evening? Completely forget all about that event.

Could it be useful for your relationship?

Could it save some of the aftermath grudge?

What if you could forget you had a headache?

Do you really think you are not able not to do so on cue?

Can you remember a time when you had a headache and then suddenly you had to be very focused or occupied about something, and you simply forgot your headache?

In fact, that headache didn't bother you anymore; it seems like it has dissolved into darkness – or forgetfulness.

Key point to remember: there is NO pain if you can't remember it. The nervous system is so sensitive that it sends a very nasty message to the brain when something isn't functioning right or when an organ is hurt. The pain is the response to make sure that you, as a whole, know something is wrong with your body and you're going to find the remedy for it.

If you didn't have a pain associated with stomachaches, how would you even know that your body is trying to deal with substances that hurt it? How much damage does you body need to absorb before you notice it, has it not produced the pain?

Pain is useful. Pain is not your friend but it is a trusted messenger. Once you have done all the actions needed to help your body get on the road to healing, you can plan to forget the pain. And when you do, if you can't remember it, it is not a problem anymore.

There are many war stories about soldiers that lose an arm or get hurt by flying bullets – and they do not feel the pain until hours later, until the battle is over. That is the power of being able to forget, whether for a few moments or for a lifetime, it is useful. Obviously you should use it with care.

Some people make it a point to remember every single detail of their lives. I believe, sincerely, that this is a very bad mistake. First, since you already distort reality as you experience it (basic NLP if you haven't read it yet), *how can you make sure you remember your life as it truly is?*

You cannot.

Therefore, by making it a point to remember every single detail, good or bad, you're actually making choices as of which version of the event you would keep. Since that's true, isn't it obvious that who you are today is based on choices and distortions you have made all of your life, often subconsciously? In hypnotherapy, we call this "living a lie." We are all living some kind of a lie. But some of us are simply living a better functioning lie/life.

Being able to forget those things that are not extremely important but in their current version do disturb and ruin your present chances to succeed, that is a skill worth learning and perfecting.

Now you may know within your heart that sometimes, when you are really trying very hard to forget something, you actually remember it even better. Forget the number "365." Forget it now.

Last year I did that trick with my niece. She's 8 years old now, but even at that age she could not forget how many days are in one year, what is it then?

You see? You can't forget. If you live in the U.S, try to forget the combination of these 3 numbers: 911. forget it now. That number actually has 2 distinctive but very powerful and permanent anchors: 911 (police) and 9/11.

Is it going to be useful to forget how many days are in a year? (What was that number again?) No. Is it useful to forget that if you're in the U.S and need to dial the police emergency number that is 911 and if you're hearing the term "nine eleven" you should you forget what happened at that date? NO. It is not useful, and that is why people are not forgetting it.

If it is important enough it will stay, usually on its own. If it doesn't stay on its own (like thick biochemistry books you need to learn for your next exam), you should make a point to remember it.

You can plan to forget.

You can make a point to yourself that you want to forget something. It is so easy, that you don't have any idea how within the next hour you are going to posses an almost perfect that skill.

In fact, at first I wanted to show you how you can forget you even read this article – but then, you wouldn't know how to do it later... and it would be some kind of a vicious loop – teaching you how to forget and by that making you forget what you learned... So I won't do that to you. Just yet.

Helping Others To Remember

Before we move on to the practical side of this lesson, let's talk just a little bit about helping other people to remember, and how useful that is.

First of all, before you start daydreaming of your all-mighty hypnotist-powers, throwing suggestions around and making people forget

stuff, bear in mind that, unless they approved it, you are not able to vdo so.

"Approve it" means – they have approved the communication between you two (or more). That means that you have taken a position of "one-upmanship" in the relationship.

You can certainly persuade people, change their minds and influence many aspects of their thought patterns, but to establish that authority, there must be a position of one-upmanship. That's the ultimate trusting state a client is putting himself "under" when he's allowing the hypnotherapist to work with him.

Helping others to forget can be useful when:

In some cases, therapists feel that it is in the client's best interest to forget the content of some work, so that they will not sabotage the work with their conscious minds.

You are a salesman, and you want the client to ignore your competitors.

You are a father or a mother and you want your kid to forget a traumatic episode or some unfortunate argument in the family, so he won't be influenced to collect the non-useful beliefs in the future. "I am bad and that's why my parents yelled at me," is not the right frame of mind for a six-year-old to grow with. Making him forget it and implementing a new useful frame can mean a lifetime difference, literally.

You were training a misguided, zealous NLP student, and you want to forget all the crap they taught that person that he or she has accepted as the ultimate truth.

You are a stage hypnotist and you want to demonstrate the power of hypnosis to hundreds of people... by making them forget they paid you $150 for an one hour show.

The useful examples are endless.

Now let's go directly to the juicy stuff. How could you make yourself or others forget whatever you wish?

The Binary Code of Forgetfulness

Instead of the usual steps, this is a transcript of an actual hypnotic session. You can try it out as is, as well as learn from it and integrate it into your hypnotic work.

It works like the binary code of computers, 1's and 0's, just that when we use the 0's we actually

use minus 1. Confusing? I've just started to confuse, it gets stronger soon.

You see, because it does make all the difference in the world when you discover, that even when suddenly all kind of things that you simply could remember simply to remember instead of forget to remember when you wanted to remember to forget what those things were not!

It's easy to understand when you learn the Binary Code of Forgetfulness.

Think for a moment of a situation in your past that would be useful for you to forget, maybe an event that left you with a bad stream of feelings and nasty thought patterns.

There's a neurological process that holds the key, I am certain, and we call it the Forget Key. You can use that key when you know that just because, if you're trying to remember something right now, or even better, if you just stop and you start to think about that specific situation (whichever that is) in which you had that feeling, then, you must know, just before that specific situations started, you didn't even have that feeling, yet!

So how come you could remember to remember that feeling long after the event has dissolved into the past, into that place on your timeline that is almost always hidden? At least, you can hope because otherwise you'd be confused whether it is your past or your future lying there in front of who you are, if you are that person.

Now, while all of the above sounds, or being read, very confusing, it is not confusing that much when you consider all these terms, forgetting, remembering and things that are not yet what you need them in order to remember them as you do remember. Confusion, however, and this confusion is included obviously, is the golden root to a more deeper and long lasting understanding of that very useful skill,

Now, I don't know if you are already aware of it or just about to be aware of it, but if you think of WHERE you WERE in that situation, but instead, if you were (decided maybe) to forget to remember what it actually was and instead of that think, how would you do like to feel in that situation?

Maybe all of a sudden, you can now remember what is that you wanted to remember instead of what it was that you couldn't forget! In fact, I believe it is the other way not-around.

If you want to get more confused and blame me for that confusion, go ahead, because we're going to clear it all up for you. Very clean, even cleaner than what it wasn't just before.

Think! If you do not remember what it IS that you don't want to remember, then isn't it clear that you're remembering to forget what it is that you shouldn't, or on the other end, it is very clear, that, what was left is for you to remember what it is that you want to feel exactly when you want to feel it. Isn't it not what I'm not saying?

It gets better, just now:

Because now, with that terrible feeling that you didn't have, well, you know, that you WON'T have but you didn't want to have, that you used to have until you simply couldn't remember of what it was, now, because if you did remember, it couldn't be logical, because if you remember what it is that you want to feel, then you will! How could you remember what it is that you couldn't remember not to forget to remember anyhow?

Now, before we move on, what would you rather feel in that situation, yet not again?

Because if you think about it, can you remember what it is you feel about any thing, any time or any way, if you know you'd rather feel good or better, because you see there are times when you remember to feel bad, then you could forget to remember not to forget to remember any more about this idea. And you do need to do just that, because you already remember far too much so just forget about it!

Listen, if instead of doing what it is that you weren't doing anymore because you remembered to forget about it, haven't you had to do something else? Instead of?

And instead of what it is not, if you for example looked right at what is left, then it would not matter to you, because what is right (point to his right arm) and that is my right (point towards your right arm) but my right is on YOUR left.

You see, it means that you would have to take the whole thing and turn it around from the inside out all the way through the middle, pull it up and throw it back down, and once you choose to do something new, it will grow into a new pattern.

And it can sound confusing, but isn't it right? What's left for you is to be able to take the right thing and put it under the right perspective, because if you already have an idea that you don't want, then there's no reason to not remember to forget it! And in the future, when it is time to remember, then just remember to feel GOOD! How easier could we even make it?

This one will be hard to test, because we'd have to remind you of what you forgot. But you could put the memory in an envelope and mail it to yourself if you really want to test this! Just don't try to bring up the memory right after the session.

Now here's a step by step guide:

Let's go over the code and then demonstrate how to make it work for you:

Plus 1 – to remember
Minus 1 – to forget
Plus 1 – not to forget (= *remember*)
Minus 1 – not to remember (= *forget*)
Plus 1 – remember to remember (= *remember*)
Minus 1 – remember to forget (= *forget*)

Plus 1 – forget to forget (= *remember*)

Minus 1 – forget not to forget (= *forget*)

Plus 1 – you know (= *remember or the following is true*)

Minus 1 – But instead (= *forget or cancel the previous*)

And so on. It's very easy to understand. If you want them to hold the piece of information or the conclusion or the suggestion you're giving them, you're ending your code as a sum of Plus 1. If you'd like their minds to forget a behavior, pattern of thought or other useful-to-forget things, you conclude at Minus 1 (or more).

Step #1. Follow this example.

Observe how we to the math. First we'll provide the text, then we'll break it down.

"You see, because it does make all the difference in the world when you discover, that even when suddenly all kind of things that you simply could remember simply to remember instead of forget to remember when you wanted to remember to forget what those things were not! It's easy to understand when you learn the Binary Code of Forgetfulness."

you simply could remember – Plus 1

simply to remember – Plus 1
forget to remember – Minus 1
remember to forget – Minus 1
what those things were not! – Minus 1
Sum = Minus 1

It's very easy after you practice for a while. I used to use my thumbs as indications – right thumb for the Plus 1 and left thumb for the Minus 1. When one of them is up I would know that the equation is not balanced and towards which end it influences the listener – if my right thumb was the only thumb up, it meant "remember", when the left was it meant "forget" and when both it meant balance.

You end your Binary Code hypnotic suggestion with a balance when you just want to send the person into a very deep TDS.

Step #2. Try computing it yourself.

Now, you can try it yourself. Here's another passage from the first part of the lesson, to see if you can mark down the binary code from it:

"Now, before we move on, what would you rather feel in that situation, yet not again? Because if you think about it, can you remember what it is you feel about any thing, any time or any way – if you know you'd rather feel good or better, because you see there are times when you remember to feel bad, then you could forget to remember not to forget to remember any more about this idea. And you do need to do just that, because you already remember far too much so just forget about it!"

Plus 1, Minus 1 = 0 (*balance*)
Plus 1, Minus 1, Plus 1 = Plus 1 (= *remember*)
Minus 1, Minus 1, Minus 1 = nonsense, unless you want them to remember you're annoying

There are almost no rules for the Binary Code of Forgetfulness. The only thing to keep in mind is that you should have a balanced set of Plus 1 and Minus 1 statements, and eventually be either Plus 1 or Minus 1 in the end of it, or at least balanced. That means, that going for 10 times of Minus 1 will not create the effect you would like. You have to create the illusion of balance so their minds won't be over protective and cancel everything you said. Once there are almost the same number of Plus 1 statements and Minus 1 statements, it would be extremely hard and complex for anyone to keep track of it. Say Minus 1 ten times and only once Plus 1 and it's obvious what you're trying to do.

That's the ultimate power of this method. We use it in therapy for so many things from pain relief to trauma resolution and much more.

Step #3. Practice this in the field.

Try this with clients or friends, getting good at keeping score. It does not require a complicated approach to be effective.

Step #4. Test.

See how well the method works in managing the material that your clients are dealing with. Practice inducing both forgetting and remembering.

❧

102.

Conflict Resolution

"So there are five ways of knowing who will win. Those who know when to fight and when not to fight are victorious. Those who discern when to use many or few troops are victorious. Those whose upper and lower ranks have the same desire are victorious."

— Sun Tzu

CREDITS FOR THE CREATION of this NLP pattern belong to Richard Bandler and John Grinder. Robert Dilts further developed this pattern.

This pattern helps resolve conflict while generating commitments to fulfilling higher-order goals and values.

Overview: The Conflict Resolution Strategy

Step #1. Clarify the issues in terms of their polarity and logical level.

Step #2. Elicit a meta-position.

Step #3. Determine the positive intentions underlying the polarity and get them in touch with them.

Step #5. Get agreement on a higher-level intention.

Step #6. Generate alternatives to fulfill the higher intention.

Step #7. Get commitment to a plan.

Step #8. Test

Step #1. Clarify the issues in terms of their polarity and logical level.

Think about the key issues of the conflict.

Think of them as polarities in which there are two sides in opposition.

At what logical level does the conflict primarily occur?

For example, money is a common topic of conflict in relationships.

This is usually argued at the behavioral level, because what to do or not to do is the question.

Step #2. Elicit a meta-position.

Get into a meta-position that transcends the conflicting positions.

Step #3. Determine the positive intentions underlying the polarity and get them in touch with them.

a. Determine the positive intentions driving each party in this conflict.

You should find that it is at a higher logical level that the more obvious issues of the conflict.

Often, the underlying intentions turn out not to be in opposition,

particularly when viewed in terms of their benefit on a systems level.

Systems-level concerns would be about things like managing everyone's stress and having a happy family.

Longer-term thinking also tends to refocus onto a higher logical level. The child's college education is, in part, an appeal to the parent's identities as good parents.

b. Have each party recognize and acknowledge the other party's positive intentions. Help them understand that this does not mean that they endorse the other party's logic or conclusions, or compromise on anything that they are uncomfortable with.

Step #5. Get agreement on a higher-level intention.

Continuing from your meta-position perspective, chunk up until you uncover an intention that both parties can agree to.

Meta-position is easily achieved by moving to the 3rd or the 4th perceptual positions.

Step #6. Generate alternatives to fulfill the higher intention.

Explore with them what alternatives to the conflicting positions might exist that would fulfill their higher intention.

Generally, the breakthrough ideas are better than a mere compromise or middle ground. The idea may or may not be highly innovative, but was usually obscured by the conflict.

Once couple realized that they had the same long-term vision, but that they lack structure for realizing it.

They saw that they would be able to agree on even the most painful spending restrictions if they were less vague about what had to happen. They decided to set more specific goals and determine a monthly savings goal that would be necessary to achieve their long-term goals.

In order to meet the savings goal, they would make whatever short-term sacrifices were necessary.

Step #7. Get commitment to a plan.

As in the example above, help them commit to specific choices that are aligned with their higher-order values and plans.

Help them specify the means for making these choices and plans happen.

Mitigate for any ecological concerns. You can certainly use the Ecology Check pattern to get out of the way any possible disturbance to agreement.

Step #8. Test

Follow up with them to see how well their new commitments and agreements are working out. As always, attend to ecological concerns.

See what additional higher values and roles might help to inform their decisions and follow through.

☙❧

103.

Co-Dependency Resolution

"We control fifty percent of a relationship. We influence one hundred percent of it".

— Anonymous

CREDITS FOR THE CREATION of this NLP pattern belong to various contributors.

This pattern helps people think and act more independently by eliminating codependent behavior.

> # *Overview: The Co-Dependency Resolution Pattern*
>
> *Step #1. Think of a person that you feel you are over-involved with.*
>
> *Step #2. Experience from a metaphorical point of view the connections between you and the other person.*
>
> *Step #3. Imagine not being tied to the relationship. Clarify the ecology of these ties, and any underlying positive intentions.*
>
> *Step #4. State the desired outcomes and the commitments you experience in the relationship.*
>
> *Step #5. Create your ideal self that experiences high-quality relationships.*
>
> *Step #6. Connect the ties to your ideal self, and imagine experiencing the benefits of this self.*
>
> *Step #7. Enhance your boundaries with the other person in a detailed way that affirms your realism about them and your adult integrity.*
>
> *Step #8. Test*

Step #1. Think of a person that you feel you are over-involved with.

For this pattern, the ideal person is either failing to engage in some important self-care such as managing an addiction, or is not adequately controlling a harmful behavior, such as abusiveness.

Step #2. Experience from a metaphorical point of view the connections between you and the other person.

Explore the submodalities with which you represent these ties.

You might want to start with the feelings in your body and see how images can emerge from these feelings.

People often see things like ropes or apron strings.

Step #3. Imagine not being tied to the relationship. Clarify the ecology of these ties, and any underlying positive intentions.

a. Imagine that these ties fall away or dissolve in a way that frees you completely from the relationship.

Notice all objections or ecological concerns that arise.

Notice any secondary gain that the seemingly negative aspects of the relationship offer. This may require some digging and humility.

b. Explore the positive intentions of any part of you that is uncomfortable with eliminating the ties.

Step #4. State the desired outcomes and the commitments you experience in the relationship.

a. Consolidate this information into clear statements of desirable outcomes and meta-outcomes of the ties in this relationship, and the relationship in general.

b. Clearly state what you give to the relationship, and what you sacrifice in order to maintain the ties.

Step #5. Create your ideal self that experiences high-quality relationships.

a. Generate an image and sense of an ideal self, in which you experience your constructive desired outcomes and make your most meaningful commitments, while receiving profound benefits in the form of constructive, meaningful relationships that include a rich, positive, harmless primary relationship.

Notice any negative reaction you have to the words used: rich, positive and harmless.

Imagine this ideal self being completely at ease with and motivated by these words. Imagine any negative assumptions about them becoming dry and crisp, and falling away.

For example, an association between "harmless" and "boring" would develop clear boundaries as a concept that is tagged to the ideal person, and flake off, dropping away like a dead leaf. Draw upon what you gained from step four in doing this step.

b. Place an image of this ideal self in the appropriate position in your mental space or visual field.

Step #6. Connect the ties to your ideal self, and imagine experiencing the benefits of this self.

a. Connect the ties to your ideal self. Observe yourself experiencing the benefits. Desensitize the related discomforts.

Return to your sense and image of your ties to the other person that you selected for this pattern.

Imagine disconnecting each tie and reconnecting it to your ideal self.

See all the benefits that you have identified in these steps as being created by this ideal self through proactive, assertive, persistent behavior.

Notice any negative associations with these words: *proactive, assertive, and persistent.*

Have them flake away as before.

b. From first position, experience the benefits.

Focus on the support for your integrity.

Associate into this ideal self, and imagine experiencing all the benefits of constructive, harmless relationships that inspire you and create a rich world for you.

Notice things like others' approval and support.

Notice how it comes from the relationship, not from you allowing violations of your boundaries.

Notice how comfortable other people are with you having clear boundaries, being assertive, being proactive, and being persistent in pursuing your dreams.

c. Savor the positive feelings of these benefits.

Give yourself the gift of some time to soak in the best feelings that come from imagining all this. Savor these feelings like savoring a hot bath.

Step #7. Enhance your boundaries with the other person in a detailed way that affirms your realism about them and your adult integrity.

a. Have your constructive experiences nudge the other person towards their ideal self.

Imagine that each of your assertive, proactive, and persistent dream-fulfilling acts, and that each positive, supportive experience that you have with other people sends out a wave of gentle force.

These waves move the other person that you identified for this pattern.

Each wave moves the person toward their own ideal self; an ideal self with consistently constructive behavior and clear boundaries.

b. Desensitize your attachment to whether the other person makes constructive choices.

Notice the attachment that you experience to the idea that this person MUST choose to associate into this ideal self.

Allow that attachment to become clearly defined and crisp, and to flake away. This allows the other person to make their choice, free of your past denial and magical thinking.

c. Imagine inner strength while fully connecting with your deeper codependent attachments and fantasy.

Imagine having the inner strength as your ideal self to allow this other person to be who they really are instead of your fantasy version.

Allow yourself to experience not knowing what choice they will make.

Notice how deep the attachment to the fantasy version of this person goes into you.

Fully connect with your discomfort about not knowing what choice they will make, and with your attachment to your prior fantasy version of this person.

d. Desensitize your deeper codependent attachments.

Allow your discomfort with not knowing, and your attachment to your prior fantasy version of this person to gently clarify and become crisp, protrude, and flake away.

Allow your ideal self to fill the remaining hole with healing energy that closes and returns you to your normal shape.

Step #8. Test

a. In the upcoming interactions with this person, notice any changes in how you manage your boundaries and how well you remain connected with your reality.

b. Notice whether your positive attitude and behavior bring out a different side of this person.

c. Notice how giving up on your fantasy of this person helps you make more realistic decisions about how to relate to them.

d. Notice any ways that you elicit and enjoy benefits from other relationships.

☙❧

104.

Meta-Programs Identification

"As a leader... I have always endeavored to listen to what each and every person in a discussion had to say before venturing my own opinion. Oftentimes, my own opinion will simply represent a consensus of what I heard in the discussion. I always remember the axiom: a leader is like a shepherd. He stays behind the flock, letting the most nimble go out ahead, whereupon the others follow, not realizing that all along they are being directed from behind".

— Nelson Mandela

CREDITS FOR THE CREATION of this NLP pattern belong to various contributors.

This pattern makes you into a more effective communicator by helping your pace the meta-programs of another person.

This is very important in sales, leadership, and coaching, as a rapport-building skill that improves your perception and understanding.

Overview: The Meta-Programs Identification Pattern

Step #1. Assess the person's meta-program use.

Step #2. Communicate with their style of meta-program use.

Step #3. Transcend the limitations of your own meta-program style.

Step #4. Test.

Step #1. Assess the person's meta-program use.

Analyze the other person's communication in terms of the meta-programs that they are using. See the appendix on meta-programs as needed.

Step #2. Communicate with their style of meta-program use.

Use the same meta-programs as your person as you communicate with them.

Step #3. Transcend the limitations of your own meta-program style.

Take note of any ways that your own driver meta-programs may be causing you to miss anything about your person's use of meta-programs.

Expand your communications with them as insights emerge.

Step #4. Test.

Notice any ways that using their meta-programs improves your rapport with them, including your ability to empathize with them or understand their perspective, motives and thinking.

❀

105.

Limiting Meta-Programs Challenging

"The skillful leader subdues the enemy's troops without any fighting; he captures their cities without laying siege to them; he overthrows their kingdom without lengthy operations in the field. With his forces intact he disputes the mastery of the emp".

— Sun Tzu

CREDITS FOR THE creation of this NLP pattern belong to various contributors.

This pattern will help solve communication patterns by reveal- ing the meta-program mismatch or meta-program violations (see appendix) involved.

Overview: The Limiting Meta-Programs Challenging Pattern

Step #1. Identify the meta-programs and any violations or inappropriate use.

Step #2. Evaluate the effectiveness.

Step #3. Challenge the person to use a better meta-program approach.

Step #4. Test.

Step #1. Identify the meta-programs and any violations or inappropriate use.

Identify the meta-programs another person is using.

Notice any meta-model violations or inappropriate use of meta-models.

Notice any ways that your own preferred meta-model style could conflict with the other person's. Take care not to be distracted by the content of the discussion, because that interferes with "going meta."

Step #2. Evaluate the effectiveness.

Assess the effectiveness of the person in using their meta-programs under the current circumstances. Is their meta-program use appropriate for the content and objectives of the communication.

Step #3. Challenge the person to use a better meta-program approach.

Invite the person to consider the situation using what you believe to be a more effective meta-program, or to use a meta-program more effectively. If the person knows the language of NLP, you can work on a more technical level.

Step #4. Test.

Have the discussion with the improved meta-model use. Does this help you come to better conclusions or have other benefits?

☙❧

106.

The Meta-Programs Change Pattern

"The real persuaders are our appetites, our fears and above all our vanity. The skillful propagandist stirs and coaches these internal persuaders".

— Eric Hoffer

THIS PATTERN HELPS US improve the scope and flexibility of our meta-program use by directing our attention in a way that is somehow opposed to or expanded beyond the current meta-model. For example, if the model is an "away from" then you would use a "towards."

Overview: The Meta-Programs Change Pattern

Step #1. Identify your typical meta-programs. Determine any ways that they contribute to poor outcomes.

Step #2. Explore alternate meta-program strategies.

Step #3. Future pace potential strategies, and select a new meta-program approach.

Step #4. Do an ecology check.

Step #5. Install your new strategy. Plan to re-evaluate it.

Step #6. Test

Step #1. Identify your typical meta-programs. Determine any ways that they contribute to poor outcomes.

Review the meta-programs in the appendix.

Determine which ones you most typically use.

Of those, which do you use with the least flexibility.

Review the kinds of situations in which you tend to have the least favorable outcomes.

This will tell you a lot about any patterns of misuse, overuse, or erroneous use of meta-programs that you have been experiencing.

Take notes on all of this.

Remember that meta-programs are merely observable tendencies and none of them is fixed or permanent.

When you notice a meta-program distinction, note the 'continuum' it has. Most meta-programs move from one extreme to the other, and you will notice that most, if not all, people you meet are almost never in the extreme.

More important to remember is, that a specific tendency can, should, and does change over different contexts and different states of mind. To illustrate with a metaphor, you might tend to stay 'away' from snakes on a regular day, but if the other option is to meet an alligator, you'd be keen to move 'towards' the snakes instead… this is an extreme metaphor to get you to stay 'away' from tagging people according to a random meta-program you notice in their communication.

Step #2. Explore alternate meta-program strategies.

For each meta-program you have identified, make some notes about how the pattern of use can be improved.

An overused meta-program can lead you to think about expanding your use into more or different meta-programs.

A meta-program being used inappropriately might work well in some contexts, while in other contexts, another meta-program would be more effective.

When thinking about alternative meta-programs to use, consider ones that are the most different.

Also consider using the opposite one, as in the "toward" and "away" example.

Step #3. Future pace potential strategies, and select a new meta-program approach.

Give your imagination a good workout as you imagine various situations in which you can apply these alternative strategies.

In particular, imagine situations that resulted in poor outcomes.

Run through the situation with different meta-program strategies until you apply one that results in the most effective ways of experiencing or responding.

Meta-program change is such a high-order change that it may take some exploring in order to transcend your current style.

The end result is that you have chosen a different meta-program to emphasize at this point in your life, or you have chosen a different meta-program strategy for a specific type of situation in which you now intend to produce better results, or both.

Step #4. Do an ecology check.

Once you have chosen your different meta-program approach, evaluate it for ecology.

Run through each of the logical levels (see appendix).

Give yourself permission to install it and see if any part objects.

Refine your plan until you are satisfied with the ecology.

Step #5. Install your new strategy. Plan to re-evaluate it.

Give your permission to "install" this new strategy for the time being, understanding that you can uninstall it or refine your plan at any time.

You can even mark your calendar to remind you to reconsider or refine your new approach.

Step #6. Test

By the planned review date, assess your results with this new strategy.

Refine it as needed.

Commit to a new re-evaluation date.

❦

107.

The Analogical Marking Method

*"Few are open to conviction, but the majority of men
are open to persuasion".*

– Johann Wolfgang von Goethe

CREDITS FOR THE CREATION of this NLP pattern belong to Richard Bandler and John Grinder, modeled from Milton Erickson.

Best known as a way to imbed commands into communication, analogical marking means that a portion of the communication is "marked" for greater attention by the subconscious. This marking is typically done through a change in inflection, tempo, body language, or volume. Bandler and Grinder observed this in the hypnotic work of Milton Erickson.

Another use is priming. **Priming** is similar to embedded messages, but it is more general and vague in the sense that it helps to elicit a state or establish familiarity with something in order to increase the odds that the person will choose it or make choices in a particular direction. For example, secure base priming improves a person's ability to react in a less defensive or aggressive manner.

Overview: The Analogical Marking Method

Step #1. Select a situation for using analogical marking.

Step #2. Choose what you will communicate with this approach.

Step #3. Prepare the communications.

Step #4. Practice the approach.

Step #5. Apply the approach.

Step #6. Assess the results.

Step #7. Continue to refine and practice this method.

Step #1. Select a situation for using analogical marking.

Select a typical situation in which you want to communicate more effectively, and in which imbedded messages or priming could be helpful.

Step #2. Choose what you will communicate with this approach.

Write down a number of things that you would like to communicate, but that might arouse inappropriate defenses.

Continue accumulating these until you have a several that you feel can be converted into imbedded messages.

Make sure that your approach is ethical. You must not attempt to manipulate a person in a manner that is not in their best interest.

Step #3. Prepare the communications.

Create sentences that could be normal-sounding parts of your communication with this person, and that include your imbedded commands or priming words or phrases. If necessary, review material on Milton Erickson's use of analogical marking.

Step #4. Practice the approach.

Before using this approach, practice delivering these communications.

Try them with several different types of analogical marking, including changing your inflection, tempo, body language, and volume.

Step #5. Apply the approach.

Once you feel that this can be done in a way that is very natural, use this approach in the actual situation.

Step #6. Assess the results.

Notice how the person responds. Were there any awkward moments or looks?

Did the person respond in any way that suggests your approach was helpful?

Step #7. Continue to refine and practice this method.

Continue to refine and practice your use of analogical marking until you are able to do it without preparing in advance. Many people discover that they do it without even realizing it.

☙

108.

Persuasion By Chunking Up/Down

"It's not the mountain that lies ahead of you that stops you... it's the pebble in your shoe"

— Muhammad Ali

CHUNK **Up – or Chunking Up** – means that you move from specifics to generalities.

Chunk Down – or Chunking Down – means that you move from generalities to specifics.

Chunk Up is answering questions such as, "what is this for?", "does it mean that you/I/we/this...", "what is the intention?", "what could be the purpose?", etc.

Chunking up doesn't necessarily mean that you move all the way to the most general statement you can make about the subject. It means that you only move to a MORE general statement, not necessarily the highest/most general.

Chunk Down is about answering questions such as, "how could we use it?", "is it...", "does that mean that we could do...", etc.

Chunking Down doesn't' necessarily mean that you move all the way to the least general or most specific statement. But, you only move towards a more specific set of ideas.

The Chunk Up -> Chunk Down pattern of persuasion can be described as a range:

Whatever you say or hear can be marked as a point on that Chunk Up -> Chunk Down range. From that point, you can either chunk up and generalize or chunk down and be more specific.

To enhance rapport and get a sense of agreement and unity between you and another person, chunk up! Rarely do people refuse to agree to nominalizations. When you say, "love is wonderful", how many people will disagree? That's a huge chunk. If you say, "your love is wonderful", there's an opening for a debate and not necessarily an immediate agreement.

You chunk up to get agreement. You chunk down to solve problems.

How do you eat an elephant? Remember that joke, right... one piece at a time. That's chunking down – a person presents a problem to you and asks for your help to solve it. If you chunk down long enough, they will find their own solutions on their own, making their own decisions and thanking you for opening up their eyes. You don't have to know EVERYTHING, you just need to chunk down further.

You chunk up to hypnotize. You chunk down to de-hypnotize.

You don't need to be a hypnotist in order to hypnotize others. You see, just by using words and talking to people, you're already generate trance states in others. They don't have to close their eyes and quack like a duck. Hypnosis is everything between a day dream and moon walking. We move in and out of hypnosis numerous times during the day.

When you're in any state of hypnosis, you're more suggestible to be influenced by your surrounding and obviously by your own inner world. When you chunk up, you get people to think about intentions, purposes, philosophy and meaning – by using a

nominalization (a word that describes something you cannot physically point at, like love, influence, subconscious, etc.) you cause the other person to go inside and think about the meaning of what you said. He must make sense of it – and that inner search after the meaning, that's a trance!

Sometimes you would want to de-hypnotize, take a person out of hypnosis. If your chat mate is spacing out too often, have a hard time listening and concentrating or is in pain (another form of self hypnosis – concentrating obsessively on the physical feeling of pain) – you can de-hypnotize that person by chunking down. When you dig into details, the present reality kicks in and the world of philosophy is faded.

If you remember, in one of our articles about Milton Erickson's method to relieve pain, we spoke about chunking down. By analyzing the physical pain, wherever on the body it is, you make it smaller and less important. The brain goes from "oh, it is painful in my teeth" to "oh, there's that rough sensation in the 3rd tooth from the right, on its front side right above that small white dot".

In hypnotherapy we use chunking down a lot when dealing with phantom pains – pains that are felt as if they are real, even though there is no physical reason or indication.

එ⊘

109.

The Classic Confusion Method

"Communication works for those who work at it."

– John Powell

CREDITS FOR THE CREATION of this NLP pattern belong to Milton H. Erickson.

Confusion is useful for breaking state and producing "downtime," a very internal state that promotes hypnosis, reprocessing, patience, and introspection. The classic method, as demonstrated originally by Milton Erickson, is to use vague or otherwise confusing language. This language most typically calls on the conscious mind to become occupied with interpreting it.

An example given by Erickson involved telling a patient, "One can only write right from right to left, one cannot write right from left to right and write is not right nor is right write while left, though left can write though not be right, yet left can write right from right to left if not from left to right." Another example of the confusion technique would be to suddenly stop in the middle of a sentence, reach over and touch the subject in a number of places on the arm and then ask, "Which arm were you touched for more time than the time before you were last touched?"

Overview: The Classic Confusion Method

Step #1. Select a situation for using confusion.

Step #2. Construct communications that will use confusion.

Step #3. Practice the approach.

Step #4. Apply the approach.

Step #5. Assess the results.

Step #6. Continue to refine and practice this method.

Step #1. Select a situation for using confusion.

Select at least one communication situation in which you could make good use of confusion. Determine at which points confusion would be useful. Remember that it can promote hypnosis, reprocessing, patience, and introspection.

Step #2. Construct communications that will use confusion.

Construct actual communications that use one or more confusion strategies.

Review material on Erickson's use of confusion as needed.

Step #3. Practice the approach.

Before applying these strategies, practice them.

Step #4. Apply the approach.

Try them out as planned.

Step #5. Assess the results.

Assess the person's reaction. Did it go as planned?

Step #6. Continue to refine and practice this method.

Refine and practice this method on an ongoing basis.

☙❧

110.

Applying The Law of Reversed Effect

"Life does not cease to be funny when people die any more than it ceases to be serious when people laugh".

— George Bernard Shaw

THE HUMAN MIND HAS rules, natural laws that govern its ways of functioning. One of the most important rules we all should get to know is The Hypnotic Law of Reversed Effect.

This law simply states, that the harder you focus on something to do, the harder it becomes or even worst. For example, the harder you'll try consciously to encourage and keep an erection (considering you're a man of course), the harder it becomes... not your penis, but the result you're trying to achieve.

The harder you'd try to force yourself consciously (with reason, persuasion, etc.) to sleep, you'll just be more and more awake.

Reversed effect... you give more effort but get the reversed result.

Why is it hypnotic?

Because it works under the surface. You try to force a logic conclusion, like "I need an erection now" or "I have to sleep now because otherwise I'd be late tomorrow morning", and you force it on the part of your mind that understands it in reversed. The subconscious doesn't obey straight orders; it's not the army. You say "I want an erection because there's none", and your subconscious is focusing on that fact.. There's none. Here's the direction – no erection. Confusing? I bet.

It also works the other way around. You can formulate a suggestion according to the Hypnotic Law of Reversed Effect. However, you must use indirect suggestions to work the magic and not direct orders.

Here are some examples:

"and it seems to me you can concentrate on other aspects of the sexual experience while your body gathers the blood towards your penis. In fact, the more you concentrate on pleasing your partners, the HARDER IT BECOMES..."

That's a bullet proof suggestion made to a client who suffered... guess from what.

"Now you may have the idea of being able to open your eyes while in Hypnosis, but it may seem strange and how so that the harder you try the harder it becomes, because there's a sense of no urgency to take care of all the things you've left BEHIND you and above you can still imagine that crystal view... and I dare you to make that poor attempt with your eyes, since the harder you try the tougher it becomes while you're keeping this sensation of coolness, freshness, relaxation... No need to rush... make the attempt, and let it rest..."

"so you told me that the anger just builds up within you and in a split of a second it bursts out with rage and you have no control over what seems to be so trivial, your emotions, your body, your sense of wholeness and calmness... and I wonder if you can force that anger right now, if you can create it with your own command, since the harder you try the harder it becomes and seems much easier to stay calm and quiet and absorb the world instead of reacting to it... nothing much left in life if not fulfillment and happiness and that anger that you have tried to build within you and seems like it's the hardest job in the world.. Can't even remember where it was the first time, however you can try and try and try and once you're tired of trying let it go... there's are easier choices... "

Study the Hypnotic Law of Reversed Effect well, since it can be applied to many things. Think where. The harder you think...

☙❧

111.

The Nested Loops Method

"We're all made of stories. When they finally put us underground, the stories are what will go on. Not forever, perhaps, but for a time. It's a kind of immortality, I suppose, bounded by limits, it's true, but then so's everything".

— Charles de Lint

CREDITS FOR THE CREATION of this NLP pattern belong to Milton H. Erickson.

Influence and persuade others merely by telling them stories.

This is one of the best, if not THE best, method of conversational hypnosis. It involves no inductions, no snapping fingers, no need to get an approval for a hypnotic session.

It's also very easy to learn and practice.

It can be used for almost any situation where you would want to implant hypnotic suggestions without being obvious (which also means almost certain failure), and without the need to induce a person into hypnosis.

- You can use this method to talk with your kids before bedtime, and install some positive suggestions that will benefit them and the family.

- You can use it to talk with your boss about a raise (or to be precise, tell your boss when he'll give you a raise).

- You can use it to talk with your employees to motivate them and to inspire creativity.

- You can use it in training (just like Bandler has been doing for years and years with his stories).

- You can use it in writing, like I do from time to time.

- There is no end to the ways you can use The Nested Loops method.

The Nested Loops method is another classic method that Milton Erickson has created and used successfully for many years.

By using this method, you're building tension, just like they do in regular storytelling.

You create five stories, that are interesting to your audience (which you should know, of course).

You open one story after the other, and on a cue point you switch to the next story (the graphic below demonstrates it).

Once you open the fifth story, you include your hypnotic suggestions in it and then you close story number five, and continue to complete and close the stories in reverse order.

That's the classic application of this method, and it is thoroughly explained below.

There are number of reason why this method works so well to influence people:

1. Our mind doesn't like loose ends, so your mind begins a TDS (Trance-Derivational Search) in order to close the open loop.

Your mind looks for the completion of it, and while it waits for it, more stories are opened, overloading the mind's attempts to keep track. It is all done subconsciously, of course.

2. Concentration on the content and entertaining details of the stories will confuse the listener, and will cause his mind to drift from the structure to the details; chunking down, in other words.

By the time you get to the fifth story, your listener's mind has less tendency to resist suggestions and these will most likely be accepted immediately.

3. There is no "watch out" sign. When you induce hypnosis, some people will go into a defensive position, guarding their subconscious mind as though it were a precious fortress.

Hypnotherapists work long and hard at bringing down these defenses, and it takes a lot of energy and time.

By telling a story in a casual conversational style, without even mentioning the word "hypnosis" or snapping your fingers, the defenses are down (unless that person has a good reason not to trust you).

4. The loop is habitual. Our mind picks up patterns quite fast. Once one loop has been closed (story number five), the listener's mind expects that the rest will be closed too, and it is much more alerted to pick it up.

Once another one is closed (number four or five), it forgets all about the suggestions and lets them sink into the subconscious with the stories.

It is much more important to the mind to close the loops than to deal with the suggestion that has been "slipped" in between them.

Overview: The Nested Loops Method

Step #1. Create a well-formed outcome.

Step #2. Come up with an indirect suggestion.

Step #3. Build the five stories and cue points.

Step #4. Introduce the beginning of story #1

Step #5. Tell the stories, open the loops.

Step #6. embed the suggestions within story #5.

Step #7. Close the rest of the loops.

Step #1. Create a well-formed outcome.

You must firmly decide what you want to accomplish and with whom. You need to know your outcome as well as your audience's needs, wants and desires. By knowing this information, it will be easier for you to construct your stories and suggestions in the most effective manner.

Ask yourself questions such as:

Who do I want to influence?

What do I want to suggest to them? (Don't write the suggestions yet, just your outcome.)

Who are they exactly? Is it better if I work with only one at a time?

What are their needs? What do I know about their needs, wants and desires? If I could sum it up in one word, how would I name what they want themselves?

What type of stories would be most appealing to them? (You'll know the answer once you answer the previous questions.)

When would be the best time to sit down and talk to them without interruption?

Do they already trust me, or do I need to establish trust (and rapport, of course)?

Step #2. Come up with an indirect suggestion.

Since we're talking about a conversational hypnotic method, it would be much more effective to use indirect suggestions. Saying something like, *"and you would find yourself passionate about cleaning your room,"* is a very direct suggestion. Saying instead, *"and you know, I felt great after cleaning my room, just like you do with yours…"* provides an indirect suggestion.

Since it takes time to master this method (as with every good thing), start with only one suggestion. Later on, once you learn to go through these steps without planning too much, you can use more suggestions.

Step #3. Build the five stories and cue points.

There are very few rules for these stories:

1. They must be entertaining, since we're using five of them. If they are boring, you'll have a sleeping audience.

2. The method will work better if you use real-life stories from your own past. Do not use stories that involve the person you're trying to persuade; they have their own version of this memory. Don't even include their role, as that is too obvious. If you must, you can make up your story.

3. Learn to tell those stories in an interesting way. Record yourself before you try it out on someone else. Fine tune your story telling until there is nothing in the content or in the delivery that is likely to annoy. Craft it into an engaging, thrilling tale.

4. The length of your story shouldn't be an issue, but don't say 100 words where five would be enough. Say it short but say it all, and in an interesting manner. You can repeat some key points if needed.

Once you've chosen your five stories, break each into a Cue

Point; a place where it would be appropriate to cut the story, but that does not give away the end of the story.

Step #4. Introduce the beginning of story #1.

Now comes the tricky part; how to get them to listen to you. It's hard to advise you exactly what to do, since every situation is different.

The easiest situation is when you're have control over the environment as you do when you're a presenter in a training or a father putting his kids to bed.

In a business meeting, where there would be normally several interactions between you and the listener, you can still use this method, but keep in mind that you will have to let the other party speak from time to time.

I always introduce the beginning of story number one by saying, "You know what, I must tell you something that just popped up in my mind and reflects almost exactly what you said…"

Another option would be, "Let me tell you a story…", or even better, "Did I ever tell you about the time I jumped from a bridge…"

The first sentence is crucial because it is used to initiate the momentum of listening to your story. The the more completely you occupy their conscious mind with interesting stories, the better you will maintain the momentum.

Step #5. Tell the stories, open the loops.

A good idea (actually, a very good idea) is to remember the order of the stories you tell them. I do so by using my right hand fingers, and tie each story to a finger. I start with the thumb, and in my own imagination I picture a keyword from the story tied into my thumb.

So for example, if story number one involves a monkey, I see that monkey biting my right thumb. If the second story involves a diaper, I can see my index finger covered with a diaper, hitting the monkey who's biting my thumb. That idiotic image will definitely remind me of the order of my stories.

You tell story number one up to the cue point, and then you use some linking phrase to break it and go to the beginning of story number two.

You can use almost anything here. *"And the police man asked me about my uncle, who you know is a carpenter. By the way, I never told you, but I did work for him for a couple of months when I was 17. In fact, in that summer, just after my birthday, he felt so sick that I had to do all of his work. In one client's house..."*, and they have the policeman story unfinished while hearing about your sick carpenter uncle.

When you get to story number five, that's the time for the next step.

Step #6. Embed the suggestions within story #5.

That's where the juice is. You tell story number five from beginning to end, while in the middle of it, right after the Cue Point, you slip in a few suggestions. It is so easy you won't believe me unless you try it.

"And you see, at that exact moment, what would you have done? I bet you get a feeling, a good feeling about doing it, and just like you would do your homework as fast as possible to get it done the same day you get them, just like when I went through that mission of...".

They won't even realize what is going on. Your previous stories have already overloaded their minds, now the suggestions are not being analyzed.

Tie the loop of story number five (complete the story) smoothly, as though you had never interrupted it.

Step #7. Close the rest of the loops.

Don't leave their minds hanging there, searching for the end of the loops. Close each remaining loop in reverse order. After closing story number five, you have a way to go back to close story number four, becuase the Cue Point of story number four is what initiated story number five.

Continue closing these loops until you finish story number one.

If you like, you can drop in a couple of questions to encourage time distortion. After finishing story number one, ask questions like: "By the way, you told me before that you're interested in XYZ, tell me about it." Of course, XYZ has to be something that the person told you before you initiated the Nested Loops method.

❧

112.

A Sample Nested Loops Story

ERE IS AN EXAMPLE for a Nested Loops story. As you read, please remember that this method is most effective when used out loud. Therefor, try to imagine me speaking to you with these words:

"You know, this is amazing because for the last few days I didn't really get any question about this method, although it is quite an impressive and effective one.

Everybody uses stories, you know, some are doing it well and some are doing it well but not in an effective or influence or both ways down... and see, right as I write to you, I am reminded of that first time I ever read a story that have truly influenced me. I am not sure if you are familiar and know this one – the catcher in the rye. it is truly a lovely story that does influence you in many ways. Two of the ways that it has impressed upon me were

exactly what I thought they would be, but much more – first, I started seeing people around me that acted exactly like that kid in the story... now who wrote that one... hold on, let me use my neurons well – wrote it, I believe, JD Salinger. what is that JD anyway? Is it a shortcut or is it his name? anyway, what I was saying, I read a lot of stories in my life and some were good and some were not. and you would think that all a good story needs is a good plot, but it isn't so, at least so I believe, because you see, I believe a story should challenge your own beliefs. doesn't really matter which beliefs, and if you do believe in them or only caught them for awhile, but it is for me an essential thing that you will be challenged. Otherwise, what's the point of paying 20 bucks for 300 or 400 (how many are those today anyway?) pages of a fiction. It's not real you know... just like the subconscious ain't real. it's a fiction, you probably know this by now but let me tell you how I thought of it: I think the subconscious is a fairy tail, because you see, no one can point out exactly where in our brain or even in the whole nervous system which lies all over your body, you know, where is it then? can you touch your nose with your right finger and tell me whether it's there? how about your eyebrows? neck? back? stomach? pancreas? little piggie? "and that little piggy went to the market...", my grandma' did this gig to me even when I was well grown up (in fact, I was 22 years old). She kept telling me I don't eat enough, though she only saw me like maybe once a week. A great woman she was, even as a nana (grandma') she kept telling jokes, even dirty jokes! you'd be surprised how funny it is that your grandma' is telling jokes like these... and isn't that just not only amusing but gives a sense of youth-full-ness, gratitude and relaxation... now double that because she did tell extensively funny jokes. anyway, I miss her.

I was saying about the subconscious is not real. you know it isn't. can't point to it, can't put it in a barrell (old meta-model conspiracy)... it's a nominalization. It's actually a process, or more so –

a group of processes that is just it – subconscious.

In other words – all the processes of your nervous system that you are not aware of at this specific moment, because you don't pay attention to many different things at once as you read this. because you know, as you read this you have to first let your eyes catch the letters and form them to the words that I have written previously, and then let your inner voice form it to auditory conversation that is way inside your mind. that's consciousness. now add noticing you're blinking and your ever deeper breath, and friend – you don't have many conscious options... all the rest is 'sub' of the consciousness. and because you don't pay much attention to whatever happens outside of this scope of reading these words and making sense of whatever I'm saying, it is surely important to us, I believe, to screen our reading list.

Read the stories that worth reading, read things that challenge our beliefs – there, I said it again, didn't I? a challenge.. A story that will make you think if the way that you interpret reality is the reality itself. Harry Potter did it for many children.

And Jerome David Salinger did that exactly in his Catcher In The

Rye story... oh, yes, that's it. JD is Jerome David... ahhh, I remember. Right. Now... he wrote many books, but that was the book that got my attention.

The Catcher In The Rye is marvelous, truly, go read it if you can. I can still remember its main character, Holden Caulfield, a 17 years old boy, who's also telling the story... that boy is troubled with that transition from boyhood to adulthood. And he got me thinking so much you know...

Amazingly enough, not everybody are reading stories, and not everybody who are reading, are reading the right stories. And even those who are writing stories wonder why their stories are being read less than others who write even less-seemingly-interesting stories... and that's because the language these writers use is more effective and influence better. And my goal in the article you commented on was to expose one of many methods to influence others by doing a series of stories with Nested Loops.

I can only assume you can see the effectiveness and power of this easy to learn easy to do method. Can you not?"

☙❧

113.

Subliminal Persuasion

*"Do not anticipate trouble, or worry about what may
never happen. Keep in the sunlight."*

– Benjamin Franklin

SUBLIMINAL REFERS TO things that you do not consciously perceive. Although you don't perceive subliminals, they may have an effect on you.

People have various ways to make something subliminal. For example, they can make it appear too briefly or too dim for anyone to perceive it consciously. People can produce sound so quiet that no one can consciously hear it. For example, psychological researchers can flash words so quickly, that no one consciously sees the words, yet those unseen words or images can affect people.

Another kind of subliminal, the kind commonly used in Neuro Linguistic Programming, uses words or body language in a way that the person does not perceive, because they do not pay attention to it. This kind of subliminal is not invisible because you could consciously perceive it, if you paid attention to it. This kind of subliminal evades your conscious awareness. The speaker makes this possible by keeping your conscious mind busy paying attention to something else, or by getting you into trance, where you have little, if any, conscious mind to perceive anything with.

The famous hypnotherapist Milton Erickson has given us many ways to use subliminal communication. For example, he used something called embedded commands, where words that form part of a sentence provide their own secret message.

You can also create subliminal messages with ambiguity. If you say something with two possible meanings, the person may not perceive the meaning that provokes their defenses.

However, they will perceive the other message that does not provoke their defenses.

Nevertheless, that message, the one that they aren't consciously aware of, can have a real impact. As we said, subliminals can't exert their influence with the strength of full commands or complicated messages. Subliminal recordings don't work in the way they are typically advertised. However, you can use subliminals as part of an approach that uses state management to get its results. Subliminals create more subtle effects than the old – fashioned subliminal recordings that people started creating back in the 1950's.

In advertising, they have discovered that if something feels familiar to you, then you will prefer it over something you don't feel so familiar with.

This happens even though you only got the feeling because you were exposed to the thing through a subliminal source, such as a brief image, or something you didn't notice that appeared in a movie.

We want to make this point clear; a subliminal image or idea gets into the brain, but not into conscious awareness. This is like the difference between hardness and pitch or color. A coin has a certain hardness, whether you perceive the hardness or not. But light only appears to have the property of color because of three different light-sensing organs in the eyes that the brain uses to construct color. The same thing applies to the pitch of a musical note.

The difference in wave lengths of two low pitches and two high pitches may sound like the same difference, but the actual difference, if you count the waves, turns out to be much larger between the higher notes. We are pointing out that perception, and effect are two different things. You don't need to be aware of something in order for it to affect your state of mind.

Lets return to the idea of things that have a subliminal effect simply because the person does not notice them. Consider product placements in the media. Even though people don't usually consciously notice product placements in movies and TV shows, advertisers spend enormous amounts of money to get product placements.

This provides an example of something that COULD be consciously perceived, but acts as a subliminal by going unnoticed. Similarly, you'll notice that TV commercials don't usually give you a lot of information about a product. Instead, they give you impressions, feelings, and exposure.

Subliminals can also do something called priming. You can use subliminals to amplify a person's emotional needs or other states. This doesn't control them like a robot, but it does increase the odds that they will do something that EXPRESSES that state. For example, psychological researchers have shown that people are more likely to act secure and well adjusted when the researchers prime them with positive, secure messages such as "mommy and I are one." It may seem unbelievable that "mommy and I are one" could have an effect on people, but researchers have built up a good body of research using this very phrase.

Notice the primitive nature of the phrase "mommy and I are one". Subliminals exert their influence with a few words, a very simple idea, or just an image. This happens because subliminals don't appeal directly to the more complex areas of the mind; they appeal to the primitive areas. Even when, as with words, the subliminal message requires processing by higher brain areas for initial interpretation, they still exert their influence through the more primitive parts of the brain. When a message or experience primes people to feel more secure in some way, psychology calls this "secure base priming".

Unfortunately, people who know how to control the masses use priming, but they attack the secure base. This causes people to act out of fear. This can get a population to go along with starting wars or discriminating against minorities. It can make people hyper-vigilant, that is, overly alert to possible danger, so they are more likely to watch news that covers alarming things. Viewers are so important to TV stations that the news broadcasts will go to great lengths, even creating false impressions.

A news organization in Denver, Colorado broadcast a series of stories about violence Denver called "the summer of violence". However, Denver actually had less violence that summer. The station had used a cynical, manipulative way to get people to watch. In contrast, NLP serves to produce excellence wherever it can, not to steal peoples' time with dishonesty.

❧

114.

Intonation

"Next in importance to having a good aim is to recognize when to pull the trigger".

– David Letterman

HERE IS THE biggest secret of persuasion: intonation. This is one technique that nobody can detect, because it is a covert persuasion technique disguised as normal conversation.

In NLP we recognize 3 patterns of intonation:

Question

When you form a question the end of the sentence is usually expressed in a rising pitch. Express out loud any question and you'll notice how the whole sentence might sound in your normal pitch, but the end of it, right near the questions mark, is always higher in pitch, isn't it?

Statement

When you form a statement, however, the whole sentence is usually expressed in the same pitch. You might have "ups" and "downs," but whatever you say can be easily distinguished from a question or a command. In persuasion, you might want to begin using only statements before moving on to questions and commands.

Command

The biggest mistake people make when they want to get another person to do something is to form a command in an authoritative voice. That's the wrong approach simply because nobody likes to be told what to do! When you form a command, the end of the sentence usually drops in pitch. To make it effective, use the "polite" hypnotic command forms, such as "could you please..." (regular pitch) + "sign here" (lower voice).

☯

115.

The Embedded Command (I) Method

"Plan the sale when you plan the ad".

— Leo Burnett

CREDITS FOR THE creation of this NLP pattern belong to Milton Erickson, modeled by Richard Bandler and John Grinder.

As in the analogical marking pattern above, embedded commands are communications that are inserted into a larger communication. They are typically marked out with analogical marking. This pattern and the next give more opportunity to practice this aspect of communication.

One way to insert an embedded command is as a quote or a question. Here are some examples, with the embedded command marked of in single quotes.

"Somebody once said to me, 'your hand is beginning to lift without you noticing'"

"I knew a man once who really understood that 'you can really be happy' if you 'put your mind to it'"

"I told the last person who was sitting in that chair to 'take a deep breath and fall asleep.'"

With analogical marking, you can highlight an embedded command that appears in a sentence that appears to say the opposite of the command. For example, *"There's really no need to 'close your eyes and take a deep breath.'"*

Overview: The Embedded Command (I) Method

Step #1. Select a situation for using embedded commands.

Step #2. Choose what you will communicate with this approach.

Step #3. Prepare the communications.

Step #4. Practice the approach.

Step #5. Apply the approach.

Step #6. Assess the results.

Step #7. Continue to refine and practice this method.

Step #1. Select a situation for using embedded commands.

Select a typical situation in which you want to communicate more effectively, and in which embedded messages or priming could be helpful.

Step #2. Choose what you will communicate with this approach.

Write down a number of things that you would like to communicate, but that might arouse inappropriate defenses.

Continue accumulating these until you have a several that you feel can be converted into embedded messages.

Make sure that your approach is ethical. You must not attempt to manipulate a person in a manner that is not in their best interest.

Step #3. Prepare the communications.

Create sentences that could be normal-sounding parts of your communication with this person, and that include your embedded commands.

Remember, embedded commands are usually very short sentences or sentence fragments with the meaning that you want. If it's necessary, review material on Milton Erickson's use of embedded commands.

Step #4. Practice the approach.

Before using this approach, practice delivering these communications. Try them with several different embedded commands.

Add analogical marking (see the pattern above) such as including changing your inflection, tempo, body language, and volume.

Step #5. Apply the approach.

Once you feel that this can be done in a way that is very natural, use this approach in the actual situation.

Step #6. Assess the results.

Notice how the person responds. Were there any awkward moments or looks? Did the person respond in any way that suggests your approach was helpful?

Step #7. Continue to refine and practice this method.

Continue to refine and practice your use of analogical marking until you are able to do it without preparing in advance. Many people discover that they do it without even realizing it.

❧

116.

The Embedded Command (II) – Advanced Method

"There are no two people alike...no two people who understand the same sentence the same way...So in dealing with people try not to fit them to your concept of what they should be".

— Milton H. Erickson

CREDITS FOR THE CREATION of this NLP pattern belong to Milton Erickson, modeled by Richard Bandler and John Grinder.

This is a more advanced embedded command pattern that extends the previous Embedded Command (I) and Analogical Marking. This one involves embedding the command in sections, spaced over a larger communication. This pattern depends more on analogical marking as a subliminal cue than the simpler form of embedded command. The subconscious mind strings together the fragments of the embedded command and gets the message, especially when the person is in a suggestible state.

Here is an example of this pattern:

"You can 'trust your subconscious mind' to know that it will never have to 'reveal to your conscious mind' anything that you don't want me to know, 'right now'. This uncomfortable incident that you think is ruining your life is part of your past. You can 'come back next week' and 'talk about anything you want, in a direct and comfortable way'."

Notice that you can string together the more impactful and state-related words to see what kind of priming is going on. As in the above example, you have trust, know, reveal, anything, right, now, past, anything, want, direct, and comfortable."

Similarly, there is a focus on self in this string: *You, can, you're, know, your, you, want, know.*

In service of causing downtime, there is a double negative plus immediacy to parse: never have to reveal, don't want to, right now.

There is also manipulation of time and personal power through conjugation and implying an alternative to replace what is in the past, next week. It also casts doubt on their understanding of their problem: "that you think is ruining your life...is...past...next week... anything...direct and comfortable way."

You can use meta-models as filters to help you brainstorm as you create the more subtle embedded commands such as the ones we just covered, as well as to analyze and learn from the work of masters such as Erickson. (You can, use, help you, you create, analyze, learn from, masters.)

Except when you are purposely using negatives, just shifting language into an exclusively positive frame is an excellent way to get into the embedded message creation mindset, because of how it forces you to see components of your text that you took for granted. (Purposely, shifting, positive, excellent, creation, see.) The subtle embedding falls more into the area of priming than actual commands.

Overview: The Embedded Command (II) – Advanced Method

Step #1. Select a situation for using embedded commands.

Step #2. Choose what you will communicate with this approach.

Step #3. Prepare the communications.

Step #4. Practice the approach.

Step #5. Apply the approach.

Step #6. Assess the results.

Step #7. Continue to refine and practice this method.

Step #1. Select a situation for using embedded commands.

(If you like, use the same material from the previous embedded command pattern to get through steps one, two and maybe three quickly.)

Select a typical situation in which you want to communicate more effectively, and in which embedded messages could be helpful.

Step #2. Choose what you will communicate with this approach.

Write down a number of things that you would like to communicate, but that might arouse inappropriate defenses.

Continue accumulating these until you have a several that you feel can be converted into embedded messages.

Make sure that your approach is ethical. You must not attempt to manipulate a person in a manner that is not in their best interest.

Step #3. Prepare the communications.

Create sentences that could be normal-sounding parts of your communication with this person, and that include your embedded commands.

Remember that you are to break up your command into fragments that you will place in several parts of the communication.

You must include analogical marking, such as including changing your inflection, tempo, body language, and volume, to ensure that the subconscious mind strings them together.

Step #4. Practice the approach.

Before using this approach, practice delivering this communications.

Step #5. Apply the approach.

Once you feel that you can do this smoothly, use this approach in the actual situation.

Step #6. Assess the results.

Notice how the person responds.

Were there any awkward moments or looks? Did the person respond in any way that suggests your approach was helpful?

Step #7. Continue to refine and practice this method.

Continue to refine and practice your use of embedded commands until you are able to do it without preparing in advance.

Many people discover that they do it without even realizing it.

117.

Erickson's 55 Hypnotic Phrases

"It requires less character to discover the faults of others than is does to tolerate them".

— J. Petit Senn

MILTON H. ERICKSON, perhaps the most known, successful and sought-after hypnotherapist of all times (besides Mesmer which had the honor of hypnotizing kings), had a way to form hypnotic suggestions that didn't even seem hypnotic at all.

Erickson used to combine numerous hypnotic suggestions while he spoke to his patients (and later on, after Bandler & Grinder did their research, it was known that he used hypnotic suggestions with almost anyone!).

The best way to use and practice these hypnotic phrases is the simple way: say one and complete it with whatever suggestion you want to apply.

Now, please remember: these are not magic tricks. You can-

not simply go to strangers on the street and say something like "and wonder if you can wonder what it would be like having me as your boyfriend…". You'll get slapped, kicked, scratched or worst. Be careful.

Hypnotic phrases won't work if the listener didn't agree in advance to either receive therapeutic intervention or to be hypnotized by you. The only other option is that the listener is someone very close to you who have a lot of trust and dependency feelings towards you. It can be your daughter or son, your husband or wife or parents. But that's also depends on the situation and the manner in which you use these hypnotic phrases.

Let's begin.

Hypnotic Phrase #1:

"And you can wonder, if you would, that..." – you can complete this one in many ways. For example, you could work with a client on smoking cessation, and apply this line near the end of the session – "and you can wonder, if you would, that you have left the old smoke-inhalation habit behind you. If you would, you may also wonder how far it may seem as if it happened in a different life". Quick tip – when I worked with people on smoking cessation, I never said "you don't smoke anymore"; because this line is like saying "smoke! Smoke! Smoke some more!". I used to rephrase the habit 'smoking' to smoke-inhalation... which almost never heard of in real life. This way, it becomes an un-known, something to be alarmed about.

Hypnotic Phrase #2:

"Can you pay attention to..." – get creative here. This is a great induction phrase. "Can you pay attention to the sound of the air conditioning zooming, to the air breeze, to the smell of the fresh flowers on my desk, to the fabric of the recliner you're sitting in, to the depth of your breathing? And did you notice how little by little it may get deeper, as with each breath that you take even more

air comes in slower than before as a sense of...". Got the idea? While their mind is waiting for the question mark in order to respond, their subconscious mind has taken the suggestions and acted upon them.

Hypnotic Phrase #3:

"And you can allow yourself to be pleased about" – ah, what a great way to end a trance work. That was one of my favorite suggestions. "and you can allow yourself to be pleased about all the things you've accomplished today. It has been hectic, isn't it? Getting INTO trance, doing all this important work devoted JUST for you, making all the changes, taking care of yourself and improving yourself so you can be more for yourself and for your family and for your country and for the community you live in, but mainly – yes, mainly – to serve your own sense of mission. It's ok, you can smile a little smile, some people choose to smile after I start to count, 1 2 3 4 5, but you can start now as you find yourself wide awake at the count of 5 (say 5 with a smile).. And counting (with excitement) 1 2 3 4 annnnnd 5! Wide awake! Wide awake! You did a great job. Well done".

Ok, I gave you a few examples, now it's your turn to free your mind and come up with your own suggestions to complete these 55 hypnotic phrases:

Hypnotic Phrase #4: "… it might be a way that meets your needs, when…"

Hypnotic Phrase #5: "and I wonder if you can enjoy the following experience, starting with…"

Hypnotic Phrase #6: "and don't be surprised when you get into…"

Hypnotic Phrase #7: "And you may begin to wonder when…"

Hypnotic Phrase #8: "certainly I have no idea what's going on inside of your mind right now, but may I guess that you ask yourself how powerful would it be to imagine that…"

Hypnotic Phrase #9: "and you may be amazed to find out how much pleasure you can squeeze from…"

Hypnotic Phrase #10: "Now I would like you to have a new experience…"

Hypnotic Phrase #11: "With your permission…"

Hypnotic Phrase #12: "and you most probably discover how it's like when…"

Hypnotic Phrase #13: "so sooner or later, I just don't know exactly when, you…"

Hypnotic Phrase #14: "and I was just wondering if you will be surprised as…"

Hypnotic Phrase #15: "how much curious could you be if you'd know that…"

Hypnotic Phrase #16: "Perhaps it's time to take a little bit of joy on your way to…"

Hypnotic Phrase #17: "now, you already know how to…"

Hypnotic Phrase #18: "and maybe you wouldn't (spelled out – would ENT) mind noticing how…"

Hypnotic Phrase #19: "and I wonder if I can ask you to, DISCOVER something…"

Hypnotic Phrase #20: "and I would like you to take note of the physical sensations that are taking place right now in your body, from the tip of…"

Hypnotic Phrase #21: "first, XYZ, but then later ZYX…"

Hypnotic Phrase #22: "now, have you begun to notice that…"

Hypnotic Phrase #23: "I wonder if you'd allow yourself to enjoy how naturally and easily…"

Hypnotic Phrase #24: "I just wonder if you'd find joy in…"

Hypnotic Phrase #25: "and that thing that makes you curious right when…"

Hypnotic Phrase #26: "will you be surprised to find out that…"

Hypnotic Phrase #27: "and while you notice…"

Hypnotic Phrase #28: "and perhaps you begin to notice that…"

Hypnotic Phrase #29: "I wonder if you have ever noticed…"

Hypnotic Phrase #30: "will you be surprised to find out that your arm is not even near your face anymore? because…"

Hypnotic Phrase #31: "and I wonder if you can begin allowing your…"

Hypnotic Phrase #32: "that only a decision you're about to make just when…"

Hypnotic Phrase #33: "most likely, you'd notice a few changes in the way you…"

Hypnotic Phrase #34: "now it's very likely, no actually, most likely…"

Hypnotic Phrase #35: "would you be willing to experience how…"

Hypnotic Phrase #36: "now don't be concerned if you don't go as fast as others into trance, because you see, some people take their time to ENJOY their time and we have as much time as you'd ask for, even if before you know it…"

Hypnotic Phrase #37: "it's so nice to notice…"

Hypnotic Phrase #38: "and you shall know as you knew before, that…"

Hypnotic Phrase #39: "it may be the time you felt that joy with…"

Hypnotic Phrase #40: "and it appears to me that you are already in that place where…"

Hypnotic Phrase #41: "give yourself that opportunity to…"

Hypnotic Phrase #42: "perhaps sooner than you would expect…"

Hypnotic Phrase #43: "and if you wish you would…"

Hypnotic Phrase #44: "and I wonder how soon you can wonder..."

Hypnotic Phrase #45: "there's a famous children song that I have forgotten about, and you may be able to record it, with the spider on the wall that..."

Hypnotic Phrase #46: "it's most amazing when you find out how..."

Hypnotic Phrase #47: "now you know better than anyone that..."

Hypnotic Phrase #48: "and it's comforting to know... isn't it?..."

Hypnotic Phrase #49: "you might have a strong compulsion to act more..."

Hypnotic Phrase #50: "I would like you to appreciate howonderful the..."

Hypnotic Phrase #51: "can you remember a time when..."

Hypnotic Phrase #52: "and while you remember I want you to hold another sweet memory of..."

Hypnotic Phrase #53: "so it's almost like knowing, really knowing..."

Hypnotic Phrase #54: "and you know you're going to learn, really learn, how it's like when..."

And the last one for now, which is also one of my favorites:

Hypnotic Phrase #55: "and isn't it just amusing..."

◑◐

118.

The Frame Of Agreement

*"I start with the premise that the function of leadership is
to produce more leaders, not more followers".*

— Ralph Nader

CREDITS FOR THE CREATION of this NLP pattern belong to various contributors.

An ongoing disagreement, or a long lasting conflict between two people can often be resolved be taking the discussion to a higher logical level (see appendix). This pattern uses *logical levels* to facilitate agreements. It can be useful in mediation and with groups.

Overview: The Frame Of Agreement Pattern

Step #1. Elicit meta-model information.

Step #2. Identify higher logical level elements to the arguments, and reflect this. Attempt to get a solution from this.

Step #3. If this is not yet possible, elicit a more productive state and move to higher-level motivations.

Step #4. Get clear expressions of these higher outcomes from the parties.

Step #5. Confirm agreements that exist at higher levels, establishing a yes set. Again, seek to resolve the conflict.

Step #6. Follow up as needed.

Step #1. Elicit meta-model information.

The following elements of questioning will help you create a meta-model of each party's position, as well as to get the information you need in order to pace them and develop the rapport that you will need as a credible change agent.

a. Ask each person to boil down their argument to the outcomes that the desire.

b. Have them specify the values and beliefs underlying the outcome.

c. Ask what is most important and valuable about those values and beliefs.

d. Ask any additional questions that will help create a well-formed meta-model.

Step #2. Identify higher logical level elements to the arguments, and reflect this. Attempt to get a solution from this.

a. Notice the elements that their arguments have in common, and identify which of those occur at higher logical levels (see the appendix).

b. State their positions in terms of their higher level agreements.

c. See if you or the other parties can propose a solution that everyone can agree on.

Step #3. If this is not yet possible, elicit a more productive state and move to higher-level motivations.

If it is too soon for such an agreement, consider the following:

The more high-level agreements that you have bring to their attention, the smaller their disagreements will appear to them.

The more you emphasize their most mature, intelligent agreements, the more you will be priming a mature, intelligent state for them to draw upon in resolving the problem.

Help them come up with potential solutions by drawing upon these resources.

Appeal to commonalities at a higher level than the one you previously appealed to in step two.

Step #4. Get clear expressions of these higher outcomes from the parties.

Have the parties express their meta-outcomes, that is, outcomes at a higher level than the ones specified.

This process was started in step one, but was not made into detailed outcomes.

Step #5. Confirm agreements that exist at higher levels, establishing a yes set. Again, seek to resolve the conflict.

Get everyone into a yes set, continuously confirming agreements at these higher levels.

When possible, seek specific agreements that will resolve the conflict.

Step #6. Follow up as needed.

Once you have achieved an agreement, follow up to see that it is working out. You can establish a timeline for follow up with the parties involved.

119.

TDS Manipulation

*"...I mean... in this day and age... when the link between
sex and pregnancy has been proven...".*

— Homer Simpson

TDS STANDS FOR "Trance-Derivational Search". This is a natural phenomenon, that is obvious in children when they play or learn. It is also very obvious in adults while they meditate or day dream.

The concept of manipulating the TDS phenomenon is relatively simple, but a bit more complicated in action. In terms of persuasion and influence, you expand the Trance-Derivational Search of another person by asking questions, that must be answered by "searching" the mind from within.

"What is the color of your eyes, I can't really tell..." – Brown, no TDS here since it's a very common knowledge for any person.

"When she said she loves you, in which direction her eye went to?" – that's a TDS question, since normally the other person wouldn't notice the direction of the eyes (unless he studies NLP of course).

"Think about the most exciting experience in your life, that happened at least 5 years ago" – that's a deeper TDS request, since our short term memory still keeps significant experiences from the last few years, in order of priority. However, if you in advance ask for an expansion of the time frame, there are numerous experiences to be considered, hence – a deep search must be performed in order to give you the answer.

How would you know if someone is going for a TDS?

The signs of hypnosis are the same signs of a trance derivational search. To hypnotize anyone you would encourage a trance deriva-

425

tional search, that goes in the direction of From Outside To Inside. To wake a person from hypnosis, you would still use TDS but in the opposite direction, From Inside To Outside, while at the end of the outside statements you just use directions for physical perceptions.

The signs of Hypnosis/TDS are generally:

A change in the breathing pattern – usually they'll breath deeper and slower.

A change in the skin color – the general rule (since we are people of different colors) is from darker to brighter or shinier.

A change of the size of the lips – the lower lip would probably be more swollen. The upper lip may move upward and seem dryer.

A change in the eye movements – the eyes would either close naturally or glazed or even fixed on a certain point with very slow movements.

A slower movement pace of the body, something that resembles a slow-motion scene.

A slower pace of responding to direct orders – in one case, when I said "move your right finger" it took 4 minutes before it happened really.

Less sensitivity to pain – don't test it unless you're hypnotizing, though, you never know how strong the other person's brother is.

In order to use that phenomenon in persuasion, you first need to recognize whether or not the other person is in a TDS. If he is, then your job is easy, just use Truth/False statements:

"Isn't it true that..."

"Wouldn't you agree that..."

"How often do you really see..."

If you get caught as being aggressively persuasive, use the Remember to Forget technique. Even resisting individuals within a TDS, those that protect their mind as if it was a precious castle, even they cannot keep up with the Binary Code of Forgetfulness or even some simpler TDS questions.

The practical uses of manipulating TDS are endless. You can manipulate a trance derivational search in anybody, with anyone, in any situations and anywhere.

Kids are less influenced by that effort, by the way. The reason is that their TDS is so fast, that it's you that have to keep up with their thoughts and might end up being influenced yourself...

☟☟

120.

Values Hierarchy Identification

"Strength and wisdom are not opposing values".

— Bill Clinton

VALUES ARE THE HONEST answer to the question, "what is most important to me?". Values define and refine your "intuition", feeling of what is right and what is wrong. Values provide the higher-level direction for your decisions making. Not knowing your values, and their relative hierarchy, can get you into a lot of troubles. Frustration and destructive behavior, self-sabotage and even crime are only a few symptoms of a simple, yet subconscious, problem – dis-alignment with your highest values.

Not knowing and not conforming to your highest values does not have to lead you to prison. Consider the times of making hard decisions, or hardly making decisions at all! If you knew your highest values, and what is most important to you – and in which order it is important to you – the decisions would make themselves. You would only have to choose the actions and strategies that align with your values. That would make you, naturally, feel aligned, satisfied and confident.

Identify the values you're holding currently and the hierarchy in which they are organized.

Overview: The Values Hierarchy Identification Pattern

Step #1. Get into a relaxed state.

Step #2. Complete a list of values by answering the 3 questions.

Step #3. Determine the hierarchy by evaluating each value versus another.

Step #4. Perform an ecology check.

Step #1. Get into a relaxed state.

Whenever working with a higher level structures, such as beliefs or values, it is always advisable to do so in a state of relaxation and having positive expectations. You do not work here with strong negative emotions, and having any random emotional storm might cause a conflict and hinder your exploration of your true values in life.

First things first – do anything you have to do to become relaxed and comfortable. If you work with a client, induce a light trance, use some relaxation script (progressive relaxation is good, but remember to wake the client up before proceeding). The client should be wide awake and not in hypnosis while working with this pattern.

Step #2. Complete a list of values by answering the 3 questions.

The 3 questions for eliciting existing values are:

1) What is most important to you?

2) If you had your 80th birthday tonight, celebrating with relatives and friends, what kind of words would you most appreciate them saying about your life?

3) If you had to give up on everything you have, but get to keep one characteristic of your 'old life', what would it be?

Refer to the Additional Advice section below for a (huge) list of common values to get some ideas.

Step #3. Determine the hierarchy by evaluating each value versus another.

At this stage you take each of the values you chose in the previous step, and determine their importance hierarchy. You do so by taking each value, in order, and comparing it to each other value. Is 'Health' more important to you than 'Affluence' (most likely)? So now 'Health' is bumped up the list, before 'Affluence'. Now is 'Health' more important to you than 'Faith'? If yes, it goes up the hierarchy again.

And so on, you take each value and compare it to each other value in the list. It takes time and patience. But when you're done you will feel a very unique emotion – decisive composure.

Step #4. Perform an ecology check.

In many NLP patterns we have a 'Test' step as a last one. In this pattern we prefer to do an ecology check, since you cannot really test your values. Either you feel right about a value or you don't.

But your current values and the hierarchy in which they are organized, might not be very useful for your current outcomes. Values and their hierarchy are changeable. Perform an ecology check by asking: *"Does any of the challenges in my life seem logical now that I look at this list?", "Is there a better way of organizing my values so that they would fit to my current needs?"*

Additional Advice

Here's a list of common life values:

Health, Love, Freedom, Contribution, Fun, Creativity, Family, Growth, Passion, Carefulness, Affection, Accomplishment, Decisiveness, Wisdom, Service, Talent, Simplicity, Virtue, Reliability, Friendship, Respect, Resolve, Originality, Openness, Mindfulness, Longevity, Leadership, Intimacy, Generosity, Gentility, Faith, Grace, Enthusiasm, Experience, Uniqueness, Endurance, Dominancy, Direction, Commitment, Security, Balance, Beauty, Care, Courage, Encouragement, Fitness, Agility, Helpfulness, Hospitality, Mastery, Impact, Modesty, Organization, Peace, Power, Privacy, Reason, Realism, Serenity, Sympathy, Toughness, Trust, Youthfulness, Wonder, Punctuality, Productivity, Perseverance, Intuition, Independence, Flow, Discipline, Self-actualization, Charm, Certainty, Awareness.

☙❧

121.

New Behavior Generator

"If you want a quality, act as if you already had it".

— William James

CREDITS FOR THE CREATION of this NLP pattern belong to various contributors.

Develop a new and more adaptive behavior; a cohesive, outcome-based strategy. The power of parts makes this pattern effective.

Overview: The New Behavior Generator Pattern

Step #1. Identify an issue and the needs for a part that will handle that issue effectively.

Step #2. Elicit a part for this role, eliciting an appropriate state and set of resources.

Step #3. Have them create third position scenes in which they express the part.

Step #4. Do an ecology check.

Step #5. Edit the scenarios to address all objections. Improve motivation.

Step #6. Run through the scenarios in first position and anchor the state.

Step #7. Instruct the subconscious to create a highly effective part from this.

Step #8. Test and refine the part.

Step #1. Identify an issue and the needs for a part that will handle that issue effectively.

Based on a key issue, come up with a part that the person needs.

By part, we mean a functional, cohesive collection of strategies such as assertiveness.

You can call the part by its function, for example, an *assertive* part.

Step #2. Elicit a part for this role, eliciting an appropriate state and set of resources.

Elicit an appropriate state that will support this part, and build up the person's connection to the specific resources needed for the part to fulfill it's role.

An excellent strategy to include is having the person recall all situations in which they expressed this part in some way, even if it was incomplete.

Be sure to expand this re-experiencing into all rep systems.

Step #3. Have them create third position scenes in which they express the part.

Have the person create detailed mental scenes of expressing this part.

Have them experience the scenes from the third perceptual (dissociated) position.

Step #4. Do an ecology check.

See if any part of the person objects to anything about these scenes.

Be sure to check in all rep systems for parts that object.

This can be a good point at which to use finger signals in trance.

Step #5. Edit the scenarios to address all objections. Improve motivation.

Have them edit the movie (dissociated mental images from step three) to adapt for any objections raised until all are satisfied.

As this is accomplished, repeatedly direct the person's attention to their growing senses of alignment and motivation.

Step #6. Run through the scenarios in first position and anchor the state.

Now have the person experience these new scenarios in first (associated) position.

Have them anchor the state.

Step #7. Instruct the subconscious to create a highly effective part from this.

Instruct their subconscious to extract the rules and motives from these scenes and construct a part that will be available as needed.

The subconscious is instructed to build a very effective, efficient, savvy, and elegant part for this purpose, and to give it the tools and authority to do the job with ease.

Step #8. Test and refine the part.

In the coming situations that need this part, notice any improvements. In particular, notice any ways that this part is being expressed.

Take note of any ways you can enhance this part, and refine it through this process or other appropriate patterns as you go.

Additional Advice

When working on generating "new" behavior, you want to work with parts that are natural to the person you're working with. If the person is very shy and has social anxiety, you wouldn't want to begin your change-work with him/her by generating a "socially popular" part. This will cause unnecessary anxiety and internal conflicts.

Given the last example, you would first work with behavioral change patterns, such as the Swish or Anchoring, and then when the person's feelings are neutral in regards to social settings, you can work on generating a socially popular part.

In addition, do not confuse learning skills with behavior generation techniques. Here we try to emphasize natural human skills, not creating a whole new one from scratch. You are not going to teach a person how to excel in tennis through this specific technique, but you can certainly help them become more assertive and self-confident when they go on the tennis court (or anywhere else for that matter). For learning skills, you would need the full Neuro Linguistic Programming modeling process.

ᘒᘔ

122.

Active Dreaming

*"Sometimes you've got to let everything go — purge yourself.
If you are unhappy with anything . . . whatever is bringing you
down, get rid of it. Because you'll find that when you're free, your
true creativity, your true self comes out."*

— Tina Turner

CREDITS FOR THE CREATION of this NLP pattern belong to various contributors.

Get ideas, answers, solutions, and information through active dreaming.

The power of sleep and daydreaming to enhance our creativity drive this pattern. It starts with stating a general intention and moves on to induce a specific state that keeps you in control of the process.

Overview: The Active Dreaming Pattern

Step #1. Select an intention and place it in a passive mental space.

Step #2. Access an up time state of "not knowing" while taking a walk.

Step #3. Note what comes into the foreground for you.

Step #4. Take second position with each one, one at a time.

Step #5. Explore the results from a meta-position.

Step #6. Test.

Step #1. Select an intention.

Come up with an intention to get an idea, answer, decision, or problem solution. Choose a very general intention. For example, if you want to solve a problem, don't specify conditions for what qualifies as a solution.

Step #2. Access an up time state while taking a walk.

Take a ten minute walk, and focus on your peripheral vision.

Focus on external sounds in order to reduce internal dialog.

Foster a relaxed state, letting go of your worries for now.

Step #3. Note what comes into the foreground for you.

As you take your walk, notice what you spontaneously focus on; what your attention is automatically drawn to, in any rep system.

Step #4. Take second position with each one, one at a time.

For each thing that jumps into your attention, take second position with it. That is, experience it by identifying with it.

What might it be like to be that thing? Whether it's a tree, the wind, or a rock, notice its attributes as though you could do this first hand.

Explore things such as the sensation of time passing, your perspective and height, the effect of the elements on you, and so forth.

Step #5. Explore the results from a meta-position.

Adopt a meta-position, in which you can observe all the information that you explored from second position with various objects you encountered.

Recall your original intention for this pattern.

Experience your new information, understanding, and experiences in connection with this intention.

Give your subconscious mind trust and time to process this experience and generate novel insights.

Step #6. Test.

In a few days, ask yourself if anything has changed about the topic of your intention for this pattern. Try this pattern on a variety of topics once successful.

☙❧

123.

Emotional Pain Management

"Many of us spend our whole lives running from feeling with the mistaken belief that you cannot bear the pain. But you have already borne the pain. What you have not done is feel all you are beyond the pain".

— Saint Bartholomew

CREDITS FOR THE CREATION of this NLP pattern belong to various contributors.

Resolve excessive emotional reactions to gain control, objectivity, and poise. This is also known as the *"emo"* pattern. This pattern is especially helpful for highly emotional people, whose reactions can be out of proportion, or not appropriate to the context. "Contrastive analysis" and submodalities give this pattern its magic.

Overview: The Emotional Pain Management Pattern

Step #1. Pick a situation in which you over-react with emotion. Identify the key kinesthetic submodalities.

Step #2. Find key differences in submodalities between this state and a similar one that is positive.

Step #3. Identify the driver submodality that links to two states.

Step #4. Do the same process for the visual and auditory rep systems.

Step #1. Pick a situation in which you over-react with emotion. Identify the key kinesthetic submodalities.

Pick a situation in which you have an emotional reaction that causes you to over- or under-react, to lose your objectivity, to experience emotional suffering such as high anxiety, or to lose your poise.

Associate into that experience.

Notice what kinesthetic submodalities are involved in that reaction. You may find submodalities such as pressure or pulsing, heat or cold, tension or depression.

Step #2. Find key differences in submodalities between this state and a similar one that is positive.

Think of an emotional state that has some similarity to the emotional reaction you are working with. However, the emotional experience must be positive. For example, excitement is similar to anxiety, but can be positive. Constructive motivation and passion for good outcomes can be similar in some ways to jealousy, but be positive.

Experience the kinesthetic submodalities of this positive state. **Hint**: You don't have to come up with a positive situation in order to come up with this positive state. The important thing is how the positive state is similar to the troublesome one.

However, once you think of the positive state, it may help you to think of one or more situations in which you experience it in order to associate into it and review the kinesthetic submodalities that it contains.

Step #3. Identify the driver submodality that links to two states.

Review all the submodalities that you have experienced in each of these two states.

Notice what submodality is most shared between the two; which is most similar. This is called the *driver submodality*. It remains the most stable when you move between these two different states.

Step #4. Do the same process for the visual and auditory rep systems.

Do this pattern for your visual and auditory rep systems, one at a time.

Use the same two reactions as you used for the earlier steps.

☯☯

124.

The Inner Hero Pattern

"All great masters are chiefly distinguished by the power of adding a second, a third, and perhaps a fourth step in a continuous line. Many a man had taken the first step. With every additional step you enhance immensely the value of you first".

— Ralph Waldo Emerson

CREDITS FOR THE CREATION of this NLP pattern belong to Robert A. Yourell.

Bring out the best in people who are not aligned with their higher values. This pattern is very important for working with people who act in ways that can get them into trouble, such as through violence or problems with authority or with social systems.

One of Robert's most persistent gambits is to build rapport by recognizing the struggles of the other person in a way that highlights their highest values and their stamina and strength in pushing ahead, despite the obstacles, whatever they are. This helps to anchor a state of alignment with higher values, and prime the person for a state of effort in service of their higher values in a non-defensive manner.

I call this, "finding the inner hero." Everyone wants to be a hero, and they feel you have connected to a deep place in them when you acknowledge (in a natural way) their heroism and struggle. You have to do it without "blowing smoke" or otherwise coming off as artificial.

That means you really have to connect with the reality of these things, not invent them. This way, you are not too distracted by their inappropriate behavior, their personality quirks, or the ways they bait you before they start to trust you. This makes you into an "entrainment effect" bringing out more of the positive aspects of the client. With this approach, you can make non-aligned (with higher values) behavior more alien and easier to let go of for many people.

Failing to do this is the root of much of the conflict or alienation that can happen between coaches and their clients. It happens all the time social service providers and people who work with domestic violence and DUI programs. A similar problem occurs when teachers make children's learning disabilities worse by approaching them the wrong way.

Overview: The Inner Hero Pattern

Step #1. Pick a person for the pattern.

Step #2. Begin a discussion that is related to the issues at hand.

Step #3. Use reframing in the style of motivational interviewing.

Step #4. Reinterpret what they say to amplify their alignment and ability to pursue their goals with vigor.

Step #5. Prepare to lead.

Step #6. Lead the person to constructive ways to act on their higher values.

Step #7. Reinforce the best responses.

Step #8. Seal the deal.

Step #9. Test.

Step #1. Pick a person for the pattern.

Try this with someone who tends to "act out." That is, they get themselves into trouble or conflicts because they have problems with authority, managing their impulses, or getting into struggles with other people.

It must be a person that you are in a position to influence in some way.

For example, a child of yours, an employee you supervise, or someone you are coaching.

Step #2. Begin a discussion that is related to the issues at hand.

Talk with them about an issue that you need to discuss, but do it in a roundabout way.

Start by eliciting from them their efforts to manage the situation, or just to manage life in general so they can keep going.

Focus on some struggle that they have.

Step #3. Use reframing in the style of motivational interviewing.

As they talk with you, notice what higher values are motivating them, even if they are acting on those higher values in foolish or destructive ways.

When you comment or respond to them, highlight the ways that they have strength and stamina in carrying on and not giving up.

Also highlight all ways that their struggle is aligned with their higher values.

Especially go for the highest logical level, identity. You can highlight these things by briefly acknowledging them, making facial expressions and sounds that show that you were struck by something they said, and any other method you like to use.

Step #4. Reinterpret what they say to amplify their alignment and ability to pursue their goals with vigor.

As you do step three, also "interpret" by saying things that emphasize or bring out these aspects.

For example, *"You have really chosen life, taking these steps to bring you out of feeling so low,"* and, *"Even though the person you have this conflict with is distracted by the conflict, on some level, they have to realize that you are advocating for people having meaningful lives,"* and *"as a person who can fight for what you believe in, it's obvious that you are being a champion for people's rights."*

Step #5. Prepare to lead.

If you have much experience with NLP, you can see that so far we have been doing an advanced form of pacing with priming mixed in.

This is, of course, a set up for leading, as in "pacing and leading."

Think of the kinds of behaviors and outcomes that would be constructive for this situation.

Bear in mind that your "client" may come up with something even better, at least in the sense that they would be more motivated to do it in their own style.

Make sure that the outcomes and behaviors you are thinking of are fully aligned with the higher values that you found your client acting on in step three.

Step #6. Lead the person to constructive ways to act on their higher values.

As you comment and interact, point out how their efforts are aligned with their values, and get them thinking about the outcomes that they ultimately want.

They may come up with less constructive ideas for controlling people, getting revenge, or putting themselves in harms way just to make a statement about how bad the situation is (this is typical of people who are stuck in an adolescent level of development).

Respond to these by getting them brainstorming on ways to be even more fully aligned with their higher values.

For example, *"That might even get you in the papers for a day, at least on page seven, anyway. But what is the long term thing that you'd like to see come out of this?"* or, *"I wonder how a person might approach someone that causes this kind of trouble so that they would lighten up a little and be more fair to people?"*

Step #7. Reinforce the best responses.

Any time the person says something that is closer to a constructive or resourceful strategy or attitude, reinforce it with a very positive response.

Don't be artificial about it.

For example, *"That could really get things moving!"* or, *"Ha! They'd never expect that. They wouldn't know what to say,"* or *"They would have start realizing that you've been right about this, because the proof would be right in their face!"*

Notice that you can help to maintain rapport and keep your reinforcement on a somewhat subliminal level by injecting some of their negativity and authority issues into your response.

The responses here have a twinge of resentment in them.

That's okay, because the thrust of the responses is in the right direction, while staying on the client's wavelength.

You can customize the tone of your responses to match the client's attitude, whatever it may be.

Step #8. Seal the deal.

Get some agreements about what you and the person will do about the issue.

If the person is only ready for a baby step, don't be judgmental; treat it with appreciation and respect.

Then they will trust you on an emotional level, and make more steps with you as they test the water.

Remember that you are introducing them to a very different "reality" than the one they are used to.

Patterns like theirs take a lifetime to develop.

Step #9. Test.

Observe them and talk with them as things unfold, and see how well your "hero" style conversations are working.

See if you can find new ways to gain rapport.

Modify your style as they progress so that you are always helping them to push the envelope.

❧

125.

The Wholeness Pattern

"For everything there is a season,And a time for every matter under heaven:A time to be born, and a time to die;A time to plant, and a time to pluck up what is planted;A time to kill, and a time to heal;A time to break down, and a time to build up;A time to weep, and a time to laugh;A time to mourn, and a time to dance;A time to throw away stones, and a time to gather stones together;A time to embrace, And a time to refrain from embracing;A time to seek, and a time to lose;A time to keep, and a time to throw away;A time to tear, and a time to sew;A time to keep silence, and a time to speak;A time to love, and a time to hate,A time for war, and a time for peace."

— Ecclesiastes 3:1–8

CREDITS FOR THE CREATION of this NLP pattern belong to Robert Dilts.

Experience symptoms in a profoundly new way.

Move into a new state of wellness through the healing powers of your body-mind.

This is an advanced pattern. I would suggest, that if you'd like to try it on yourself, have a close trusted friend or a competent NLP practitioner guiding you through the procedure.

Overview: The Wholeness Pattern

Step #1. Access a contemplative or spiritual state.

Step #2. Imagine, from third person, experiencing an ideal state of health.

Step #3. Observe your symptoms and their associated feelings and judgments.

Step #4. Fully access this awareness, and flow the feelings and representations into your left hand and become an image.

Step #5. Thank the symptoms and elicit its positive intentions.

Step #6. Thank your symptoms and recognize them for communicating.

Step #7. Focus on your inner healer and its associate body area and feelings.

Step #8. Flow the inner healer feelings into you right hand, and allow an image to emerge. Thank the aspect.

Step #9. Learn of your inner healer's positive intentions.

Step #10. Appreciate your symptom's communications and positive intentions.

Step #11. Merge the two parts, encouraging their mutual acceptance.

Step #12. Encourage the states to form a cooperative relationship in service of a larger vision and their own initial higher intentions.

Step #13. Get the parts to agree to this.

Step #14. Visualize healing energy as you integrate the two parts.

Step #15. Affirm for yourself the significance of this new wholeness.

Step #16. Take in these new energies, timeline to the beginning of your destiny with this energy, and move forward.

Step #17. Share this experience and a metaphor for it with trusted others, and ask them to share a healing experience and metaphor for their healing.

Step #1. Access a contemplative or spiritual state.

Step #2. Imagine, from third person, experiencing an ideal state of health.

Imagine being completely physically healthy, with a clear mind, emotional balance, and grounded physical strength.

See yourself in this state from third position.

Step #3. Observe your symptoms and their associated feelings and judgments.

Switch your focus to your symptoms, noticing exactly where in your body you feel their presence.

Notice that emotional feelings accompany that awareness.

Identify what those emotions or judgments are.

Step #4. Fully access this awareness, and flow the feelings and representations into your left hand and become an image.

Raise your awareness of the symptoms to a full or intense level, along with their emotional or judgment aspects.

Allow these feelings and representations to flow into your left hand as you your palm open.

Notice this flow with all rep systems.

Allow an image of the symptom and it's feelings to form an image in your left hand.

Step #5. Thank the symptoms and elicit its positive intentions.

Offer thanks to your symptom for revealing and offering itself.

Ask your symptom what it is trying to communicate to you.

Inquire as to its positive intention and its purpose.

Open your mind into a quiet, passive, listening state, and notice what inner messages come through for you.

Hint: If no positive intentions come through, you may be experiencing a "thought virus" expressed as symptoms.

To test this, get in touch with an aspect of yourself that harbors this symptomatic state.

One way to get in touch with this aspect of yourself, is to kindly tell the symptoms that you are no longer a home for them, and that it is time for them to move into pure and useful energy.

If any part of you is attached to the symptoms, then you may find that it becomes present and you can inquire as to the positive intentions that have led to this aspect harboring or encouraging the symptoms. If this is the case, do not be alarmed. We are going to work through it.

Step #6. Thank your symptoms and recognize them for communicating.

Once you have discovered these positive intentions, thank your symptoms for communicating with you.

Recognize that they have been committed to the positive intentions that your harboring aspect has revealed to you.

Step #7. Focus on your inner healer and its associate body area and feelings.

Shift your focus to the aspect of you that want health and wellness.

We'll refer to this as your inner healer.

Notice exactly where in your body this aspect most obviously resides.

Notice how this area feels to have this aspect present.

Step #8. Flow the inner healer feelings into you right hand, and allow an image to emerge. Thank the aspect.

Increase your sensing of your inner healer to a higher or intense level. Allow these feelings to flow into your right hand. Allow an image of this healing aspect to emerge.

Thank this aspect for being present and connecting with you.

Step #9. Learn of your inner healer's positive intentions.

Ask your inner healer what it's positive intentions are for you now.

Access an open, receptive state of mind and receive whatever messages are available now.

Step #10. Appreciate your symptom's communications and positive intentions.

Turning your attention to your symptom, thank it as well for communicating with you.

Offer appreciation for its commitment to its positive intentions.

Step #11. Merge the two parts, encouraging their mutual acceptance.

Imagine now that your symptom image and inner healer image are turning to face each other.

Ask them to access states of understanding and appreciation, and to experience the other parts value, but from their own perspective.

Encourage this until you feel that each part accepts the other state's positive intentions.

Step #12. Encourage the states to form a cooperative relationship in service of a larger vision and their own initial higher intentions.

Now explain to these states that they need to work together in new, meaningful ways in order to produce value that expresses their higher intentions.

Help them to discover their common mission, in a spiritual sense. Convey how wonderful it feels to be part of a team, to build trust, and to begin to realize a great vision.

Step #13. Get the parts to agree to this.

Recognize the abilities and resources of each part and how they can contribute to this vision, and to realizing the higher positive vision of each part.

Gain an ecological and congruent agreement from both parts to form a teamwork relationship that supports them in pursuing their individual and collective aims.

Step #14. Visualize healing energy as you integrate the two parts.

Return to your contemplative or spiritual state, and experience energy flowing into you that is the perfect color and quality for harmonizing and balancing you. Adjust the energy so that it is the perfect intensity, vibration, and quality for your healing experience.

Imagine your unbalanced energies being brought into this flow and converted into pure and useful energy.

Turn your palms to face each other, and then slowly begin to bring them together.

Encourage a positive integration of your inner healer and your symptom aspect.

Watch them merge, bathed in your healing and balancing energies.

See what new image emerges from this.

Step #15. Affirm for yourself the significance of this new wholeness.

Tell yourself that you are creating personal wholeness, as

you join important aspects of yourself.

Tune in to your motives that are aligned with this; that tell you this is what you truly desire.

Take time to notice how this is congruent for you, as it creates a new level of true alignment.

Tip: If you find anything incongruent or non-ecological about this, you can work forward from step three to process any remaining issues.

Put the issues together as a symptom for the purpose of the pattern.

Step #16. Take in these new energies, timeline to the beginning of your destiny with this energy, and move forward with this new alignment into a vision of your wellness and into the future.

Now bring the image of these integrated aspects into your heart, as you notice the quality of energy or aura emanating from this new part.

See it being emitted as another quality of healing energy that you can breath in with the rest of the healing energies that you are experiencing.

Allow these energies to carry you back through time, prior to your birth, experiencing your being in the womb, and experiencing the dynamics through your lineage that led to your birth, back to the beginning of time that contained your destiny from the beginning.

From that point, allow the forces of the universe to roll forward, bringing your healing and balancing energies through life, through your lineage, and into your present moment.

Notice these forces bringing energy into the power of your mind, projecting a fully healed, physically able, mentally clear, calm, state from which you can savor life.

Observe as this wave of energy flows out into your future.

Step #17. Share this experience and a metaphor for it with trusted others, and ask them to share a healing experience and metaphor for their healing.

Take some time to share these experience with others who you know to be able to talk about experiences of healing from a fairly aligned place.

Ask them to share with you a brief metaphor that they feel represents a healing experience of theirs, and do the same for them.

☙❧

126.

The SCORE Pattern

"The whole problem with the world is that fools and fanatics are always so certain of themselves, but wiser people so full of doubts".

— Bertrand Russell

Overview: The SCORE Pattern

Step #1. Gather the information
Step #2. Generate new insights
Step #3. Test

CREDITS for the creation of this NLP pattern belong to various contributors.

Solve problems more effectively by organizing information in a more useful way. The SCORE model drives this pattern with a flexible, multifaceted style of thinking.

This style resolves problems and gathers the information that you need. It is called multifaceted thinking. This style of thinking allows you to think in more than one mode at the same time.

This allows you to benefit from multiple perspectives and styles of thinking as needed. Flexibility in thinking is a great asset. The SCORE model is based on the idea that we need, as a minimum for effective decision making, a grasp of the symptoms, causes, outcomes, resources and effects in play in a given situation.

This model supports the fundamental NLP skill of conceptualizing the current state, the desired state, and the bridge from one to the other by using appropriate resources.

Step #1. Gather the information

Begin by gathering the information you need according to the SCORE model. These are as follows:

a. Symptoms:

Symptoms are the more obvious aspects of a situation that cause us to define it as a problem.

Once you have these, go farther, asking yourself what symptoms you have not noticed.

Clarify for yourself how you conceptualize or symbolize these symptoms, and how you judge them.

b. Causes:

Causes are the dynamics that gave rise and maintain the problem situation.

The causes may not be obvious, so you may need to investigate, hypothesize, and test your conclusions.

Knowing that there may be multiple causes and that not all causes are acting at any given time, and that the cause may form a domino effect or sequence can be helpful.

Looking for ecological aspects of causes can be important as well.

Use a brief ecological check here.

c. Outcomes:

These are the goals and objectives that you desire.

These can range from terminating a negative situation to a highly sophisticated new ecology and vision.

d. Resources:

Resources are whatever will assist you in realizing your outcomes.

This includes information, good will, inner subconscious resources, capital, insight, and anything else that will further your efforts, even if you consider the effort itself.

e. Effects:

This means the results of whatever you have done, whether you got the outcome you desired or not. It includes the direct effects of your actions, and the indirect effects, that you might refer to as side effects or unintended consequences.

Effects become resources when you perceive them as feedback, and create a loop from effects into feedback resources and into new strategies and outcomes.

Strategies can be perceived as symptoms when they are destructive or ineffective, as causes when they give rise to the situation, as outcomes when they result from new information and ideas, and as resources when they are assets for achieving the desired outcomes.

Strategies are intermediary outcomes that people seek in developing mastery, so that they can achieve larger outcomes and long-term goals.

Step #2. Generate new insights

Take all that you learn from applying the above SCORE analysis in order to generate new insights and strategies as described above.

Note any ways that it can help you better visualize or define your desired outcomes, how it can help you get a better sense of where you are in the progress, dynamics, and ecology of the situation in relation to potential or known resources, and what new strategies you are developing with your new insights gained.

Step #3. Test

Apply your new insights and strategies.

Observe the results.

Use the results as additional feedback in further refining your strategies.

Always keep an eye out for solutions and resources that are outside of your current frame.

This is often where the greatest breakthroughs come, since most people and organizations have been approaching problems from within their current frames for some time.

They have either been getting limited results, or the situation has changed without them updating their frame.

Since your frame is, in a sense, a critical part of your strategy, it must be accounted for.

☙❧

127.

Life Transitions Tracking

"A mind not to be changed by place or time, the mind is its own place, and in itself can make a Heaven of Hell, a Hell of Heaven".

— John Milton

CREDITS FOR THE CREATION of this NLP pattern belong to various contributors.

This pattern uses archetypes to help us come to terms with a major change or perceived threat, and to leverage that new relationship in service of our well being.

It applies NLP processes known as spatial sorting, somatic syntax, and characterological adjectives. It uses them in relation to archetypes associated with mystery and danger.

Overview: The Life Transitions Tracking Pattern

Step #1. Identify your current major transition issue.

Step #2. Spatially anchor the Dragon (transition issue), and place a series of archetypes around it as specified in this step.

Step #3. Determine from which archetype you are experiencing the Dragon

Step #4. Step into that archetype and explore its somatic syntax.

Step #5. Move through each archetype and then step into the most appropriate one.

Step #6. From the meta-position, process your experiences.

Step #7. Test

Step #1. Identify your current major transition issue.

Identify the transition issues that you are facing that this time.

We will call them the "dragon."

Think about the aspects of the dragon.

This can include changes in your status, relationships, environment, and so forth.

Step #2. Spatially anchor the Dragon (transition issue), and place a series of archetypes around it as specified in this step.

Choose a spatial anchor for the Dragon archetype.

Place the following archetypes to form a circle around the Dragon.

a. The Innocent:

Does not yet consciously experience the Dragon

b. The Orphan:

Experiences the Dragon as an overwhelming threat

c. The Martyr:

Experiences the Dragon as persecution

d. The Wanderer:

Is adverse to the Dragon, and avoids it

e. The Warrior:

Experiences the Dragon as an adversary to engage in battle

f. The Sorcerer:

Experiences the Dragon as powerful, but as having it's own meaning and destiny, and even as a potential resource.

Step #3. Determine from which archetype you are experiencing the Dragon

Access an objective state (a meta state) and discover from which archetype you are experiencing your dragon.

If you find it hard to accomplish, go through perceptual positions #1 to #2 and then to #3, which in essence is an objective, yet close enough to notice everything, position.

Step #4. Step into that archetype and explore its somatic syntax.

Step into the spatial location occupied by that archetype.

Explore the somatic syntax (the associated body movements and posture, gesture and voice tones, expressions and stance) of that archetype.

Take your time here, it is important to work slowly.

Step #5. Move through each archetype and then step into the most appropriate one.

Work your way through each of the archetypes in this way, discovering their experience vis a vis the dragon.

Once you have completed this circuit, step into the space that felt most appropriate for your relationship with your dragon.

Note that this tells you what steps in transition are coming up, based on the sequence of the archetypes provided.

Step #6. From the meta-position, process your experiences.

Return to your meta-position and think about your discoveries and lessons from this experience.

Step #7. Test

Over the coming days and weeks, notice any changes that you are experiencing in regard to this major transition.

Post the archetypes where you can see them, with the current one marked.

This will inspire your thinking about how to develop the most resourceful relationship and strategies for this chapter and your next chapter.

∞

128.

Transformation Archetype Identification

"In a time of drastic change it is the learners who inherit the future. The learned usually find themselves equipped to live in a world that no longer exists".

— Eric Hoffer

CREDITS FOR THE creation of this NLP pattern belong to various contributors.

Continue the Life Transitions Tracking Pattern (above) by determining which process archetype is most important in your development at this time. Before doing this exercise, do The Life Transitions Tracking Pattern.

Overview: The Transformation Archetype Identification Pattern

Step #1. Pick three items representing your core.

Step #2. Share in a small group.

Step #3. Select your hero archetype.

Step #4. Select your archetype of transformation.

Step #5. Create a metaphor in which, through your archetype of transformation, you become your hero archetype.

Step #1. Pick three items representing your core.

Pick three items, one from each of the three categories.

It must represent something that you want to be and will always be.

We'll call this your core.

a. Animals

b. Historical Figures

c. Mythical Figure

d. Plants

e. Natural phenomena

f. Automobiles

g. Part of the body

h. Other

Step #2. Share in a small group.

In a small group, have each member share their three symbols with the other members.

Use this format: "I am like the (item) because (reason)."

Step #3. Select your hero archetype.

Select from the following the hero archetype that represents the person you are becoming during this step in your personal development.

a. Wise old man/woman

b. Mother/father

c. Wizard

d. Queen/king

e. Healer, teacher, storyteller, etc.

In your group, have each member share their hero symbol in the format, *"I want to be more like (symbol) because (reason)."*

Step #4. Select your archetype of transformation.

Your hero archetype presupposes an archetype of transformation.

Select a symbol that represents that process archetype from the following:

a. Enlightenment

b. Rebirth

c. Resurrection

d. Metamorphosis

e. Transformation

f. Incremental evolution

g. Transcendence

h. Quantum leap

i. Other symbol

In your group, have the members share their symbol using this format:

"The process of my next step in my evolution will be like (symbol) because (reason)."

Step #5. Create a metaphor in which, through your archetype of transformation, you become your hero archetype.

Review the three archetypes that you have chosen.

Create a metaphor that is strong on imagery, like a storyboard for a movie or a comic strip.

In this metaphor, your core must transform into your chosen hero archetype through your archetype of transformation.

Additional Advice

Have your group members share their metaphoric stories.

❧

129.

The Grief Pattern

"The only cure to grief is action".

— G. H. Lewes

CREDITS FOR THE CREATION of this NLP pattern belong to Robert Dilts.

Resolve grief in a comforting, healing way.

Overview: The Grief Pattern

Step #1. Connect with your loss of a person.

Step #2. Access a resourceful, objective state.

Step #3. Think of two entities to serve as your guardian angels.

Step #4. Create a hologram of the person you have lost.

Step #5. Enliven this lost person's image.

Step #6. Experience this person as a mentor, and visualize a gift from them.

Step #7. Visualize a gift for this person, from your own perspective.

Step #8. Create a heart connection with this person.

Step #9. Share this experience with someone.

Step #10. Join your mentor with your other mentors.

Step #11. Bring these mentors and your gift into the loss situation to further your healing.

Step #1. Connect with your loss of a person.

Pay attention to your feelings of separation, sadness, or grief.

If this would be appropriate (depends on the situation and the people involved), start by thinking of the person you have lost.

Step #2. Access a resourceful, objective state.

Mentally move out of this, into a meta-state.

Create a resourceful state of wisdom and balance. Take your time here and really associate into this resourceful state.

Step #3. Think of two entities to serve as your guardian angels.

Think of two persons or entities that you would like to serve as your guardian angels.

They must be two mentors that, in some sense, will always be part of you as a person.

Step #4. Create a hologram of the person you have lost.

Use your hands and your imagination to "sculpt" a life-size hologram of the person you are missing.

Imagine creating them in their ideal state.

Notice any painful or negative ideas or recollections in connection with this person.

Now put the negativity into balloons with baskets to carry them away as you let them go.

Step #5. Enliven this lost person's image.

Imagine that you can invite spiritual energy to bring the person to you in this form, with the ability to speak in their own voice.

Step #6. Experience this person as a mentor, and visualize a gift from them.

Experience it from their perspective.

Notice how this person can be a new mentor for you.

Ask this being, *"What is the gift that you have wished to give me?"*

Go to the second perceptual position, perceiving yourself through their eyes, and allow the answer to come through.

Visualize a symbol for the gift.

Step #7. Visualize a gift for this person, from your own perspective.

Move back into your first position (seeing through your own eyes).

Answer the same question, *"What is the gift that you have wished to give me?"*

Imagine a symbol for your gift to this person.

Step #8. Create a heart connection with this person.

Exchange these gifts, and imagine that your hearts are becoming gently connected by an eternal silver beam of energy.

Step #9. Share this experience with someone.

Honor this gift and it's place in your life by sharing this experience with someone you trust.

For now, imagine how you might share this gift, keeping it alive.

Request insight from your new mentor, who can act as a resource in helping you share this gift and all of its meaning.

Step #10. Join your mentor with your other mentors.

Experience your new mentor connecting with your other mentors, and being welcomed.

Step #11. Bring these mentors and your gift into the loss situation to further your healing.

Bring your gift, and your mentors, including your guardian angels, into the loss situation.

Give yourself time to experience their healing and insightful energies as they transform your sense of balance, knowing, and expanding as a person.

☙

459

130.

The Pre-Grieving Pattern

"If you wish me to weep, you must first show grief yourself".

— Horace

CREDITS FOR THE creation of this NLP pattern belong to various contributors.

Resolve fears of future losses, eliminating many worries.

Become more resilient by better tolerating and recovering from losses that will occur in the future, even extreme losses, such as disability.

Overview: The Pre-Grieving Pattern

Step #1. Focus on a potential loss that is difficult to face and pre-occupies your mind at times.

Step #2. Explore your experience of things that you readily accept as temporary. Include your beliefs and values, and your memories of creatively moving on after these acceptable losses.

Step #3. Map the balancing representations onto the anticipated loss. See yourself creatively moving forward in life after having resolved the loss.

Step #4. Future pace experiencing and expressing these gifts.

Step #5. Refine as needed for ecological integrity.

Step #6. Install via your timeline.

Step #7. Test.

Step #1. Focus on a potential loss that is difficult to face and preoccupies your mind at times.

Focus on a future loss or potential future loss that you sometimes become preoccupied with.

It may be a person, thing, or situation.

Step #2. Explore your experience of things that you readily accept as temporary. Include your beliefs and values, and your memories of creatively moving on after these acceptable losses.

Think of some things that you appreciate despite knowing that they are temporary.

Focus on the ones for which you are most accepting that they are temporary.

Notice the ways you have a balanced or positive experience of these things, and how to manage their passing.

You may even look forward to replacing some things, as is the case when technology is improving.

Notice how your beliefs and values support your balanced relationship to these things and their nature.

Notice how you represent the temporary nature of these things through submodalities.

Add to this the actual experiences you have had of creatively moving on with your life after the losses that you were accepting of or at peace with.

Notice how you carry with you an appreciation for what the person, situation, or thing meant to you.

Step #3. Map the balancing representations onto the anticipated loss. See yourself creatively moving forward in life after having resolved the loss.

Map the balancing representations that you explored in the previous step onto an anticipated loss (from step one) that can be more difficult to accept.

You can do this, for example, by adjusting the submodalities involved in that difficult loss so that they match the most potently balancing submodalities that you experienced in the prior step.

Now imagine yourself after adjusting to the loss from step one.

Picture and sense yourself from the third position (dissociated) as you creatively move forward in life after having adjusted to the loss.

Notice how you carrying with you an appreciation for the person, situation, or thing that you have lost, thus honoring the memories and gifts.

Step #4. Future pace experiencing and expressing these gifts.

Generate an even more resourceful future.

Spend some time imagining future situations where you experience and express the gifts from the person, thing, or situation that you have lost.

This might take the form of sharing life lessons with another person, or creating a valuable skill from a gift that the person, thing, or experience brought forth in you.

Step #5. Refine as needed for ecological integrity.

See if any parts of you object to creating this resourceful future.

Use these objections to enhance the future that you are creating.

Step #6. Install via your timeline.

From a meta-state, view your timeline.

Install your future representation in the appropriate time.

Step #7. Test.

Short of actually waiting for the projected loss to take place in order to test this pattern, you can apply it to losses that are in your immediate future, even though they may not be as serious as the one you chose this time around.

Additional Advice

You can repeat this exercise to better cope with the same thing, and for additional future losses.

You can anchor the resourceful loss state in step two, and then do the exercise beginning from step three after triggering the resourceful state and recalling the most effective submodalities for mapping onto the new loss.

You can use this exercise to have a more balanced state when you deal with a potential loss, so that you will remain objective when there is risk of loss.

This kind of objectivity can sometimes prevent a loss, such as when one saves a relationship or a job because of the maturity, caring, and poise that they express. Others may experience you as less self-absorbed and more expansive as a person.

❀

131.

Self-Nurturing

"Never esteem anything as of advantage to you that will make you break your word or lose your self-respect".

— Marcus Aurelius

CREDITS FOR THE CREATION of this NLP pattern belong to various contributors.

Accelerate your maturation and emotional strength by drawing upon your adult resources to resolve unfinished emotional development. The value of good parenting resources as conceptualized by NLP drives this pattern.

Overview: The Self-Nurturing Pattern

Step #1. Create a chart of your unfulfilled childhood emotional needs and the corresponding characteristics your parents or caretakers needed in order to fulfill them appropriately.

Step #2. Build an ideal parent model and enhance it with any additional ideas.

Step #3. Visualize these parents expressing their parenting gifts.

Step #4. Timeline back to the day you were born. Transfer your powerful good parenting resources into your parents or caretakers.

Step #5. Watch your life move forward with magically perfect parents who fulfill your needs appropriately.

Step #6. Re-calibrate your prior negative experiences.

Step #7. Follow your timeline into your present, in the state of receiving unconditional love.

Step #8. Integrate and future pace.

Step #9. Test

Step #1. Create a chart of your unfulfilled childhood emotional needs and the corresponding characteristics your parents or caretakers needed in order to fulfill them appropriately.

On an imaginary blackboard or on paper, draw a line down the middle.

On the left, list the emotional needs that were not fulfilled for you as a child.

On the other, list the characteristics that your parents or caretakers needed in order to fulfill those needs.

Step #2. Build an ideal parent model and enhance it with any additional ideas.

Use these characteristics to build a mental model of ideal parents.

Use all representational systems to experience these parents.

Add anything else that you know about good parents or what you were missing.

As you think of these perfect parents, any number of ideas may come to you.

What would it be like to get help with homework in a really supportive way, or to be guided toward constructive behavior in a constructive way, or simply to get plenty of attention and desirable activity?

Step #3. Visualize these parents expressing their parenting gifts.

Visualize these parents in action, handling situations that some parents would find challenging.

See them being very successful and resourceful as parents.

If you are working with a study group, or have friends or colleagues interested in this, discuss it with them to further enhance your model either during this pattern, or at another time for future use.

Step #4. Timeline back to the day you were born. Transfer your powerful good parenting resources into your parents or caretakers.

Access your timeline and float back to the day you were born.

Observe that experience as your adult self, bringing with you all the resources you have developed, including your ever-increasing understanding of good parenting.

Allow the momentum and magic of all the resources you have brought back to imbue your parents with perfect parenting abilities.

See all this resource energy flood into this time from your future, swirling as it suddenly stops at this moment, drawn to your parents as vortices for their power.

Even if you are not now connected with your parents, even if one or both of them were not present, create parents or caretakers for this scene.

Step #5. Watch your life move forward with magically perfect parents who fulfill your needs appropriately.

Watch your life unfold forward into your timeline, but with these magically perfect parents. Observe how they fulfill you needs as an expression of their magical, yet human gifts.

Step #6. Re-calibrate your prior negative experiences.

Pay special attention to experiences that had been negative, and see how resourcefully your parents now deal with the situation. Let the positive outcomes build your positive abilities and personality characteristics as you develop through them.

Step #7. Follow your timeline into your present, in the state of receiving unconditional love.

Trigger your state of experiencing your parent's new unconditional love, and tell your subconscious mind that these experiences can generalize, bringing your forward more and more rapidly, to your present time.

Step #8. Integrate and future pace.

Continue to hold the anchor to your state of receiving unconditional love. Allow yourself to integrate these experiences and sensations, as your momentum carries you into future experiences.

These future experiences show you how your expanded development will allow you to express wonderful resources for far better outcomes.

Step #9. Test

In the coming days or weeks, notice any ways that your relationships or care-taking behavior improve, or ways that your personal boundaries become more effective.

ꕥ

132.

Awakening To Freedom

"The end of wisdom is to dream high enough to lose the dream in the seeking of it".

— William Faulkner

CREDITS FOR THE CREATION of this NLP pattern belong to Richard Clarke.

Give and receive support for awakening through personal growth in this dyadic (pair) exercise. Enhance your vision, mission and spirit through this support for awakening. With your partner in this pattern, you will bring out the best in each other by taking turns in the role of Awakener. Express your integrity and congruence to enhance the Awakener role. Align and connect with your own vision and mission as a catalyst for others to experience their vision and mission.

Transcend the old-fashioned style of morality and judgment that neutralizes personal expansion. Instead, maintain your perception of the other person's limitless possibilities and their innocence in doing the best that they knew in their past. This way, you keep the channel of communication open, inspiring the toward fresh insight, resourcefulness, and constructive personal power.

Overview: The Awakening To Freedom Pattern

Step #1. Get into Awakener and Explorer roles, give your partner instructions.

Step #2. Set up and ask the Why question.

Step #3. Get the Explorer's reaction to the question.

Step #4. Repeat step two.

Step #5. Continue repeating step two.

Step #6. Switch roles.

Step #6. Test.

Step #1. Get into Awakener and Explorer roles, and give your partner instructions.

Start out in the role of Awakener, with a partner who is in the role of Explorer.

Give your Explorer partner the following instructions:

Think about an unproductive "self pattern." What is its basic structure?

Notice any unproductive beliefs that are attached to this pattern, such as, *"Oh, I have to put on a happy face and pretend I'm confident until the next big disappointment. This kind of success is for other people, not me."*

Think of as many examples of this self pattern as you can. There are probably many throughout your life. Some of them may be subtle, or comprise a string of many little iterations that turned into a bigger pattern of loss, missed opportunities, or failure.

Make sure you understand the consequences of this pattern. *How has it affected your life?*

Continue with these instructions to your partner:

What would it be like to be free of this pattern?

What kind of results might you expect to see in the future?

On the other hand, what does this pattern do for you?

Is it helping you in any way?

Be sure to consider any "sneaky" ways that it is helping you, that is, dysfunctional ways.

For example, see if it is helping you avoid any challenges, fear, or responsibility.

Even consider any way that it might be helping you to manipulate other people or avoid criticism.

Does it simply give you a feeling of having a familiar self that you really don't need to be?

Now have your Explorer partner share with you, the Awakener, what he or she is discovering.

As Awakener, listen from a state of respectful openness, fully accepting the Explorer.

Step #2. Set up and ask the Why question.

As the Awakener say to the Explorer (still from a respectful, validating place), *"You have the full support of my being to freely explore, because this expands and strengthens you and your meaning in the world. You are completely free to do what you will with this pattern. You are free to continue it, but, as the explorer, you also ask why you would continue such a pattern."*

Step #3. Get the Explorer's reaction to the question.

Have the Explorer notice its inner reaction to the question of

why. Have the Explorer share any reaction with the Awakener.

Step #4. Repeat step two.

Repeat the statement and question of the Awakener to the Explorer as in step two.

See what response the explorer has this time.

Do this from an open-minded space that allows the Explorer to have a fresh response each time.

Different aspects of your experience are likely to emerge from this, expanding your knowledge of yourself and of your potential.

Step #5. Continue repeating step two.

Do step four several more times, at least three times.

Step #6. Switch roles.

Switch roles, becoming the Explorer with your partner taking the Awakener role.

Step #6. Test.

In the coming days or weeks, notice any new ways that you experience this pattern, including any ways that you let go of it or innovate.

See if you get any better results in life from this new perspective and resourcefulness that comes from these parts being more harmonious and able to exchange knowledge.

Have a time set aside to discuss this with your partner in this exercise.

◈

133.

The Longevity Pattern

*"Nobody can go back and start a new beginning, but
anyone can start today and make a new ending".*

— Maria Robinson

CREDITS FOR THE CREATION of this NLP pattern belong to Robert Dilts.

Develop positive beliefs and resources for almost any kind of issue. Directly install the beliefs and strategies of the vital elderly models.

While this is not an advanced NLP pattern, I would still recommend that you would wait until gain confidence and skill in other Neuro Linguistic Programming tools, such as anchoring and moving through perceptual positions.

Overview: The Longevity Pattern

Step #1. Imagine your timeline.

Step #2. Start from your meta-position.

Step #3. Step into your positive future.

Step #4. Access past resources.

Step #5. Reframe and potentiate negative memories as appropriate.

Step #6. Create a resource vortex.

Step #7. Connect your resources with your future goal as you experience it.

Step #1. Imagine your timeline.

Imagine that your past, present and future are represented by a line that goes from left to right in front of you.

Select a physical location in front of you, that you can step onto during this pattern.

Step #2. Start from your meta-position.

Look at your timeline from a meta-position (your objective or transcendent perspective).

Be sure to have a physical spot for this position.

Step #3. Step into your positive future.

Start by stepping onto your timeline where the present time is located.

Face toward your future. See how your future timeline extends into the infinite future.

Elicit a relaxed physical and mental state, and walk slowly into the future.

Imagine that you are moving in a positive direction, in a positive state.

Focus your mind, in positive terms (what you are going toward, rather than avoiding), on your health as something that you enhance over time in many ways.

Add elements to this sense of your future health.

Include a sense of your influence and what you can actually control; the feeling of deserving excellent health; a positive representation in every sense modality; ideas and images of how you are of value to others and society, and how your age and experience are assets; a sense of the larger reality that led to your existence and that supports your continued existence; the visual representation of your physical posture and body language as being uplifting, balanced, and expressive.

Step #4. Access past resources.

Turn to face toward your past.

Focus your mind on all feelings and experiences of vitality and well being that you have generated in this pattern, and slowly walk toward your past.

Connect with many of the resources of your past, especially experiences that can remind you of your abilities and beliefs that support you in achieving your goals and in generating new positive beliefs and action.

Notice any special people that helped you generate those resources, including your ability to appropriately trust and believe in others.

Take the time to savor each point in your timeline where resource experiences and generation are especially noteworthy.

Fully connect with these experiences and savor and relive them.

You may not always remember details, but follow the good feelings that are part of this kind of experience, and they will help you access a positive state and maybe even connect you with more of the resource memories that we are focusing on.

Step #5. Reframe and potentiate negative memories as appropriate.

Here's what to do when you encounter negative memories during your walk into the past.

If the memory holds no value in supporting your resources (but bear in mind that negative memories often do hold great value), then it's find to simply step around it and continue on. However, if you feel that there may be some value in the memory, then take the following steps:

a. Step off your timeline and onto your meta-position. Now you are not in a position to re-experience the memory.

b. Determine what resource would have helped you derive resources from this experience. This can be as simple as getting perspective by thinking of worse experiences that people have survived and grown from. It can be as sophisticated as giving that moment your adult perspective to determine what resources are in that situation and taking them with you. In other words, you are deriving positive meaning from the negative experience.

Even if it is a memory of something negative that you did, your awareness of it as a negative shows you your values and motivation to become fully aligned with them.

c. See how the negative experience has contributed to positive experiences.

This may have happened because it served as some kind of warning, or make you tougher or more sensitive and aware.

Remember to analyze this in terms of logical levels (see appendix) to uncover dynamics that you might otherwise miss.

d. Think about the positive underlying motivations that have been a part of the negative event.

Even if a person behaved badly, notice positive intentions or drives that you can draw upon and redirect positively in future situations.

e. Find the humor in the situation. Humor tends to come from getting an unexpected shift in perspective.

Surprise and variety are human needs. This will help you cultivate your sense of humor and ability to innovate.

f. Once you have found one or more effective reframes, step back into the timeline and negative experience.

Now imagine re-experiencing it from your expanded perspective.

g. At the beginning of this step, you thought of at least one resource from your life that would have helped with this experience.

Recall the time in your life in which you were most connected with this kind of resource.

Find that spot on your timeline, and step into that spot. Associate into that resource experience.

As you fully experience the associated resource state, experience it as an energy and see what color it manifests as.

How does it vibrate?

What other submodalities do you notice in any sense mode?

How does it feel to run through your body as a healing energy?

h. Beam that energy down your timeline into the negative experience, and maintain that beam of energy until you notice a positive change in that experience. See what resources are liberated by this energy.

Continue until you reach the earliest supportive memory.

Step #6. Create a resource vortex.

Turn to face your future again.

Slowly walk toward the future, and relive your supportive and resourceful memories.

Collect them, taking them with you into your future.

Cultivate the sense of all these supportive people and resourceful situations being with you now.

Amplify the state of resourcefulness.

Step around any negative memories as you go.

They do not detract in any way from your positive memories.

Step #7. Connect your resources with your future goal as you experience it.

Listen for a song that captures the sense of your resourceful state and supportive memories, as well as your health and vitality.

Get into the spirit of that song as you proceed into your future.

Continue until you arrive at your future goal on your timeline.

Experience all of the resources that you have brought with you as well as your goal and the optimal state for attaining your goal.

Integrate these sensory representations into a single, positive experience.

Notice and fully feel the connection between this future and all the people and resources of your past that are connected to it in some way.

Experience the congruent connection between all of your life events and your vital, healthy future.

֍

134.

Change Personal History

"History is fables agreed upon".

— Voltaire

CREDITS for the creation of this NLP pattern belong to various contributors.

Modify negatively coded memories so that you can realize your potential unfettered by such memories. It works especially well for a person or situation that pushes your buttons, that is, that you have an unresourceful reaction to. Before you use the pattern, remember that it might need some modification to fit your unique needs and abilities. We cannot stress enough how important it is that you approach this pattern flexibly.

Overview: The Change Personal History Pattern

Step #1. Access the negatively coded memory after establishing an exit cue.

Step #2. Ugly TDS

Step #3. Go to your earliest related memory, then break state.

Step #4. List your present resources.

Step #5. Anchor these resources.

Step #6. Create your "emotritional" anchors salad.

Step #7. Take a break.

Step #8. Savor some inner peace.

Step #9. Future pace.

Step #10. Test.

Step #1. Access the negatively coded memory after establishing an exit cue.

Create an exit cue that will allow you to stop the pattern if you do not feel it is going in a good direction for some reason.

Put a special object in front of you, where it does not belong.

If you suddenly need to stop the process, grab the object to trigger the "return to previous state" cue. Anchor a more or less neutral state to this object.

Access the negatively coded past experience using all rep systems, and from the first (associated) position.

Anchor the state associated with this experience by using a unique gesture.

Step #2. Ugly TDS

As you'll recall, TDS (trance-derivational search) occurs every time you go inside your mind and search for meaning or for memories.

This can lead to a trance.

An "Ugly TDS" occurs when you perform a TDS inside a TDS.

For example, while you're searching for meaning for that negatively-coded experience, you anchor that feeling and do another TDS for another memory that provides similar emotional reaction.

Then you do it again, collecting more and more related negatively-coded experiences.

That's why it is called "ugly" TDS.

To make it easier you can write them down and mark each with the approximate age you were in during that experience.

While you're doing the Ugly TDS, keep adding those to your anchor.

Continue until the ugly TDS becomes slow and it is difficult to find more related memories.

Step #3. Go to your earliest related memory, then break state.

Stop the search and, in your mind, go directly to the earliest memory.

Since you have your age written for each one, it's easy. Stay there.

Now break your ugly TDS state.

Since it involves TDS, it is best to do it actively, by getting up and shaking it off, among other things.

Step #4. List your present resources.

Now we will group some good things together from the currently identity you chose to hold on to.

Ask yourself, *"What kind of resources do I have today, that I wish I had back then, so that the whole experience would have been different and to my advantage?"*

As an adult, or "older you," you have plenty of resources available.

How about Forgiveness, Patience, Resilience, Self Defense, Sarcasm, Devotion, Procrastination, Inner Strength, or whatever else you have there inside of you.

Small or big, it does not matter, any resource that can help you should be listed.

Step #5. Anchor these resources.

Anchor each of these resource states.

Fully feel them, and then establish a new anchor for all of them together.

Choose a gesture that is very different from the one you used for the negatively-coded experience anchor.

Step #6. Create your "emotritional" anchors salad.

Emotritional is a nick name we gave to emotional resources that nourish you.

Take the negatively-coded experiences anchor and the new anchor (the collection of current resources), and collapse them at the same time.

While you do that, let the first negatively-coded experience float into your mind, and take all of the resources that you've anchored (the second anchor) and drop them on that memory.

With all of those resources available, how would the experience have looked back then?

Change the content in whatever way is useful to you.

Once you're done with the first memory, go faster.

Move on to other memories. It doesn't matter in which order you proceed. It may help you to avoid doing them in chronological order, however.

If you find the pattern confusing, bear in mind that confusion can actually enhance its effectiveness.

Step #7. Take a break.

Break the state completely in whatever way you find appropriate.

You may feel tired at this point, but maintain your alertness for a while to make sure that the pattern takes effect.

This would be a good time to eat something or drink some cold water. Distract yourself with what's going on around you.

Step #8. Savor some inner peace.

Inner peace is completed when you forgive and forget.

Now that you have completed this pattern, check to see if there is any "hidden treasure" that you might find disturbing if it is not processed properly now.

Calmly think about that previously negatively-coded memory.

From an objective frame of mind, ask yourself if it means more than a learning experience to you when you look at it?

If not, then you have most likely completed the pattern effectively. If you find that there is still a negative charge, you can make that the target of this pattern or another appropriate pattern in the future.

Step #9. Future pace.

What's good in the past if you can't take it into your future?

Future pace an event that is likely to happen.

Trigger your resources anchor, and mentally rehearse the event several times.

For each mental rehearsal, have a different turn of events take place, so that you have future paced the situation from several angles. This will prepare you to respond effectively and flexibly.

For each version, handle it in your imagination so that it is to your advantage. Being able to spontaneously respond to the ghosts of your past is a liberating and empowering feeling.

Most people find that, having done this pattern, their new responses are quite spontaneous, yet effective.

Step #10. Test.

In the coming days and weeks, notice if you have more peace of mind regarding issues related to this memory, or if you experience more freedom to think about the things that really matter to you, and less about negative things of the past.

Additional Advice

You can add a piece to this pattern when it concerns a person that pushes the client's buttons. Help the client understand the intent of the other party. This helps the client feel a sharper distinction between their reality and that of the other person.

Many of the people who come to an NLP practitioner have difficulty with this particular skill; the skill of being very clear on where they leave off and other people begin.

This leads to many of the problems that people use NLP for. One of them is certainly the negative reactions they experience because they cannot tolerate other people thinking or saying negative things about them.

When working with a client, you can provide some instructions that help them do the pattern. Remember to say words like those I used when firing off the two anchors. "Take the resource state (as you fire the positive anchor) into the negative state (as you fire the negative anchor)… and notice… how it has changed… now…

And when you test the anchors, notice any changes in the client's physiology that can alert you to changes in their state.

135.

The End-Of-Day Pattern

*"If you create an act, you create a habit. If you create a habit,
you create a character. If you create a character, you create
a destiny".*

— Andre Maurois

CREDITS FOR THE CREATION of this NLP pattern belong to Alexander Van Buren.

Make a daily habit of generating behavior and attitudes that are ever more effective and fulfilling with the power of the new behavior generator.

Overview: The End-Of-Day Pattern

Step #1. Review the day from a loving state.

Step #2. Find a rough spot and freeze frame.

Step #3. Identify resources from your day.

Step #4. Use logical levels and your resources to create preferred outcomes and processes.

Step #5. Play the scene through with your preferred outcomes and processes. Modify it until you are satisfied.

Step #6. Continue to the next rough spot.

Step #7. Watch the most positive highlights of the day.

Step #8. Test.

Step #1. Review the day from a loving state.

Create a state of self acceptance and love.

Begin reviewing your day from the beginning, as if you were watching a movie about your day.

Step #2. Find a rough spot and freeze frame.

When you hit a rough spot, especially one where you didn't like you own or others' behavior, freeze the image.

Step #3. Identify resources from your day.

Identify resources from other parts of the day.

Take elements that worked well for you during the day, and briefly think about how they might be useful as resources for the trouble spot where you have frozen the image.

Step #4. Use logical levels and your resources to create preferred outcomes and processes.

Determine what didn't work about this spot.

Compare your actual experience to one that would have been more resourceful.

Keep the resources that you noted in step three in mind.

Using the Logical Levels, ask questions such as the following:

a. Spirit:

What effect did I have on the people involved?

How would I prefer to have affected them?

In other words, how do I wish I had, how should I have?

b. Identity:

Who was I in this situation?

What sort of person would I prefer to have been?

c. Values:

What was important to me in this situation?

What would I prefer to have valued, instead?

d. Beliefs:

What was I certain of?

What clarity or certainty would I prefer to have had? (This can be intellectual, or a feeling or intuition. It can be a level of probability, such as, thinking something had high odds of happening.)

e. Capabilities:

What abilities did I use in this situation?

What capabilities would I pre-fer to have used?

f. Behavior:

What specific actions did I take?

What actions would I prefer to have taken?

Step #5. Play the scene through with your preferred outcomes and processes. Modify it until you are satisfied.

Now play this scene with all of these preferred modes of being and resources in place.

Loop through this scene.

Modify the scene each time through until you are satisfied with it.

The scene should make you feel good as you see yourself get-ting positive results with behavior and an attitude that you can take pride in.

When the scene passes a basic ecology check, you are ready for the next step.

Step #6. Continue to the next rough spot.

Now continue with your movie until you find another spot to freeze, and repeat steps two through five.

Step #7. Watch the most posi-tive highlights of the day.

Once you have made it to the end of the day, you can ask your mind to run the movie briefly, showing you highlights of the best parts, and including the improved scenes in place of the original versions.

Step #8. Test.

In the coming days and weeks, see if you find yourself handling new situations with the resource-fulness that you have been gen-erating in these daily (or nightly) sessions.

Additional Advice

You can briefly review your day and select just one or a few scenes in advance to work on, in order to manage your time effectively.

Do the pattern sitting up is a spot where you won't fall asleep if you are doing it before bed time.

⚭

136.

Negative Associated Emotions Dissolving

"Virtue, dear friend, needs no defense, The surest guard is innocence: None knew, till guilt created fear, What darts or poisoned arrows were".

— Horace

CREDITS FOR THE CREATION of this NLP pattern belong to various contributors.

Transform any mistakes you make from sources of shame and recrimination to sources of learning and empowerment.

Overview: The Negative Associated Emotions Dissolving Pattern

Step #1. Select your mistake.

Step #2. Clarify what why it a mistake.

Step #3. Access its negative feelings and intensify them.

Step #4. Learn from this mistake.

Step #5. Reduce the negative emotions and apply resources to the mistake, including what you can learn from it.

Step #6. Test.

Step #7. Test again.

Step #1. Select your mistake.

Select a mistake which you are highly motivated not to repeat.

Step #2. Clarify what why it a mistake.

Think over the criteria you used to decide that it was a mistake.

For example, what values did this mistake fall short of? Think back on the mistake and notice if you have violated a higher hierarchy value.

Step #3. Access its negative feelings and intensify them.

Access the negative feelings that you have associated with this mistake.

Amplify them until they are fairly intense, adding to your motivation not to repeat the mistake.

Use all driver submodalities you have worked with successfully until now.

Especially focus on the kinesthetic submodalities, since we want to amplify the feelings directly and not just indirectly by intensifying the event that triggers them.

Step #4. Learn from this mistake.

Shift your awareness to all that you can learn from the mistake.

Shift your discomfort into intensity and a drive for learning.

Modulate the intensity so that you can learn without panicking.

It is very valuable to learn to manage intensity such as this, especially negative intensity, so that you can transform it into positive passion and drive.

Use different lenses to derive these learnings.

a. The history of the mistake:

What lead to it?

How did the sequence take place from it's earliest roots?

b. Psychodynamics:

What parts were involved and what where their positive motives?

c. Behavior Mod:

What secondary benefits came from the patterns that contributed to this mistake? For example, is there a pattern of needing to be rescued, vindicated, avenged, or given attention?

Finally, think about how learning from this will benefit you.

Step #5. Reduce the negative emotions and apply resources to the mistake, including what you can learn from it.

Shift your focus to the emotions coming from all of this.

Bring the negative emotions into the foreground.

Imagine a big box with a heavy lid.

Move the negative emotions into that box.

Now bring the positive lessons into the foreground and take them with you as you float back over your timeline to the point at which this mistake occurred.

Saturate that experience with these lessons and reconfigure the lessons so that they become active resource in this scenario.

When you are satisfied, make all similar mistakes stand out along your timeline.

Cruise your entire timeline, beaming these lessons into each of those points in time, as you did with the main mistake.

Step #6. Test.

Bring your attention back to the original mistake.

As you review it, notice whether you still have any negative feelings about it.

If so, see what learning and resources that you can apply to resolve those feelings.

They may even be an ecological problem of some kind to work out.

As you apply your resources, run the scene as a movie from third position (dissociated) until you are satisfied that it is a fully positive experience.

Step #7. Test again.

Over the coming days and weeks, see how your work on this mistake opens new perspectives and resourceful behavior for you.

What new results are you getting?

Do you feel better about any of your circumstances, or do you feel new hope for any pattern in your life?

∾

137.

Core Transformation

"The purpose of life is not to be happy – but to matter, to be productive, to be useful, to have it make some difference that you have lived at all".

— Leo Rosten

CREDITS FOR THE CREATION of this NLP pattern belong to Connirae Andreas.

Live from a new center that comes from a practical, yet spiritual or expanded experience of life. By discovering the core state at the center of each part, overcome serious limitations.

This pattern is more fully addressed in the book Core Transformation by Connirae Andreas. The "core state" gives you a valuable compass that helps you know whether you are on your path, and whether you are coming from a spiritual or expanded place.

When you are dealing with a conflict, it is much easier to envision a positive outcome and approach when you are connected with your core state. It can be a simple as checking in, and seeing whether your strategy for handling the conflict resonates well with your core, or if it feels more like a distraction from your path, that is, like drama or unnecessary harm.

This is just one example of an understanding that can create a very meaningful foundation for your life and contribute greatly to your personal philosophy.

Note: This pattern has many steps and involves some fairly abstract or advanced ideas. It's a good idea to read it through and make sure that you grasp it before actually trying it out.

However, you don't need to understand what the core state experience is up front. That is something that is best understood through experience.

Overview: The Core Transformation Pattern

Step #1. Determine what part you will be working with.

Step #2. Begin the Outcome Deepening pattern: Find out what your part desires, and thank it.

Step #3. Continue the Outcome Deepening pattern by deriving deeper outcomes until you experience your core state.

Step #4. Complete the Outcome Deepening pattern: Enjoy and meditate upon your core state. Name your core state outcome.

Step #5. Begin the Core Emergence pattern: Understand the core state as a source rather than result. Transform each of the outcomes in reverse order in connection with your core state outcome.

Step #6. Continue the Core Emergence Pattern: Move your part up to your current age.

Step #7. Complete the Core Emergence Pattern: Bring your part into your body, if it is located outside of it.

Step #8. Core Emergence pattern II: Repeat step five, but with your part in a grown up state. You can do it briefly this time around.

Step #9. Additional Core Deepening and Emergence patterns: Elicit any parts that object to your core state as a way of being. Take them through the core patterns.

Step #10. Optional progress – for additional core state outcomes

Step #11. Savor your core state, think about the value you have created, and take a break.

Step #1. Determine what part you will be working with.

a. Select an issue that you can experience as a part of yourself, with specific motives that drives behavior that is limited in some way; behavior that is not doing enough to get you through the issue.

You can start simply with a behavior, feeling, or response, if you wish.

Give this behavior, feeling or response pattern a name for the purpose of this exercise. Jot down this name. We'll refer to it here as your *part*.

b. Get to know the part better as a collection of behaviors, feelings, or reactions.

Think about what tends to trigger this pattern. Ask yourself what places, times, and people tend to help trigger this pattern. Make some basic notes about this.

c. Experience the pattern in terms of how you are triggered to react.

Select a specific point in time when this pattern took place.

Mentally step into this scene and re-experience it.

Pay careful attention to what submodalities comprise the mind-set that drives your reaction to the situation.

d. Access this part.

Remember that the behavior, feelings, and responses that come from you in connection with the issue or issues in question are an old pattern that you did not consciously orchestrate or develop.

Instead, experience them as coming from your part, and having a collective life as this part.

Discover how this part "lives" inside of you as a body experience. Where in your body do you mostly feel it?

Describe those feelings. What inner voice expresses it?

Hear or come up with the words that express its message, fears, or motivations.

What mental images are part of this? They may be symbols or scenes that are fearful or motivating.

Carry this out with an inviting state of mind, and invite this part to emerge into your awareness more completely.

e. Thank the part.

Thank this part for coming into awareness and being part of your path.

Tell it that you are looking forward to understanding its purposes and having it as part of the more aligned and fulfilling existence that you and it will create.

Step #2. Begin the Outcome Deepening pattern: Find out what your part desires, and thank it.

a. Ask your part what it desires in connection with this issue.

Be gently direct and open, asking, *"What do you want? What is the highest purpose of having this issue? How does it serve you and I?"*

Note the answer as an intended outcome.

b. Thank the part.

Express thanks for providing this answer.

If you like the outcome stated or implied by the answer, say so.

If not, then express your appreciation for joining on a path of discovery for greater fulfillment and alignment.

You can say this because you are committed to this kind of outcome, and because you have vast, untapped resources to realize such an outcome. You can have the

kind of certainty that comes from commitment.

This is not the certainty of a guarantee that comes from the outside, it is an inner certainty that you cultivate in order to be more resourceful, creative, motivated, and vibrantly happy.

Note: The term *"Outcome Deepening pattern"* was created for this book. Andreas refers to this phase (steps two through four) with a separate name for each step.

Step #3. Continue the Outcome Deepening pattern by deriving deeper outcomes until you experience your core state.

a. Ask your part for a deeper outcome.

Ask the part, *"When you fully experience and have this outcome, what, beyond that, becomes important to have?"*

Note the answer and thank the part as you did before.

b. Keep repeating step **"a,"** deriving deeper outcomes, until you reach your core state.

Name it based on the deep outcome that produced it. We will refer to this outcome-state combination as your "core state outcome."

Although Andreas refers to it as your core state, we use the term core state outcome to disambiguate the core state from the outcome, since this pattern can involve more than one outcome that triggers the core state.

Keep repeating step three, getting a new outcome each time.

It may not be obvious at first, but each new outcome brings you closer to your core state.

You could say that you are moving through to deeper outcomes. Write down each answer in order.

When you reach your core state, you will experience a centered, yet expanded sense of peace.

You might describe it as coming home to yourself.

When people get there, they tend to be very sure that they know they are there, even though it is hard to describe with words.

Step #4. Complete the Outcome Deepening pattern: Enjoy and meditate upon your core state. Name your core state outcome.

Once you experience the core state, take some time to enjoy it. It is a healing experience in itself.

Notice that your core state came when your most recent outcome came up. From this point, we will be using the combination of your core state and this outcome. We will refer to it as your core state outcome.

Give it a brief name based on the outcome that you noted.

Whenever the text says core state outcome, use the brief name or phrase for your outcome in its place.

Step #5. Begin the Core Emergence pattern: Understand the core state as a source rather than result. Transform each of the outcomes in reverse order in connection with your core state outcome.

a. Set up your Core Emergence pattern by thinking of your core state not as an end result of striving, but rather, as a beginning or source.

Your parts may think you have to jump through a lot of hoops before you can get to your core state.

Imagine that this is backwards. Imagine turning it so that your core state is your beginning; the wellspring of your actions.

b. Begin the Core Evolution pattern, by noticing how your

490

core state outcome expands your experience.

From this point, where you see (core state outcome), remember to say the name or phrase for the outcome that connected you to your core state this time around.

Ask your part, *"As you experience your (core state outcome) and know (core state outcome) as a way of being, knowing that (core state outcome) is a beginning, how does already having (core state outcome) expand your experience right now?"* Just notice.

c. Have the core state outcome transform each of the outcomes that you noted, one at a time, from the most recent backwards.

Ask your part, *"Can you notice how your experience of (core state outcome) as a way of being expands (outcome)?"*

Outcome refers to the most recent outcome from 3a. Do this step for each outcome backwards until you complete this for the first of the outcomes.

d. Expand your experience of the original context with your core state outcome.

Now that you have gone through each outcome, ask the part, *"How does already having (core state outcome) as a way of being expand your experience of (briefly state the situation you selected in step one)?"*

Note: Core Emergence is a term originated for this reference. Andreas actually calls this, "reversing the outcome chain," but this conflicts with the metaphor of "core" since getting to a core means deepening.

Also, this work involves several levels of consciousness, implying gaining depth.

Step #6. Continue the Core Emergence Pattern: Move your part up to your current age.

a. Get your part's age.

Ask your part, "How old are you?" Note the age. Since if formed some time ago, it should be younger than you. Usually, it is an age from childhood.

b. Get agreement from your part to move up to your current age.

Ask your part, "Would you like to experience the wonderful things that come from moving forward to (your current age), as you experience (core state outcome)? If the answer is no, work with the state to resolve any issues. There may be an ecological problem to handle.

c. Move your part up to your current age, while fully accessing the core state outcome.

Maintaining your connection with your core state outcome, imagine your part moving forward in time, infused with the core state outcome experience, until it reaches the present.

Step #7. Complete the Core Emergence Pattern: Bring your part into your body, if it is located outside of it.

a. With your part in the present, observe how you represent it.

Now that your part is in the present, infused with your core state outcome, notice how you are experiencing your part.

Where is it located, in or outside of your body, (perhaps in your visual field or primarily as a kinesthetic experience)?

b. Bring the part into your body, if it is outside it.

If your part is outside of your body, invite it to move into the area of your body in which it feels most at home.

Welcome it and notice how this allows you to experience your core state outcome more fully.

c. Expand the resulting sensation.

Invite the part and this sensation to expand throughout your body, so that every cell resonates to this quality of energy.

Does the original area in your body feel this sensation in a way that is richer?

As you experience this expansion, know that you are making this an experience that you can access, and one that will serve as an emotional compass to which you can refer in choosing new directions.

Step #8. Core Emergence pattern II: Repeat step five, but with your part in a grown up state. You can do it briefly this time around.

a. Set up your Core Evolution pattern by thinking of your core state not an end result of striving, but rather, as a beginning or source.

Ask your part, *"As you experience your (core state) and know (core state) as a way of being, knowing that (core state) is a beginning, how does already having (core state) expand your experience right now?"* Just notice.

b. Have the core state transform each of the outcomes that you noted, one at a time, from the most recent backwards.

Ask your part, *"Notice how your experience of (core state) as a way of being expands (outcome)"*.

Outcome refers to the most recent outcome from 3a.

Do this step for each outcome backwards until you complete this step all the way to the first of your outcomes.

c. Expand your experience of the original context with your core state.

Now that you have gone through each outcome, ask the part, *"How does already having (core state) as a way of being expand your experience of (briefly state the situation you selected in step one)?"*

Step #9. Additional Core Deepening and Emergence patterns: Elicit any parts that object to your core state as a way of being. Take them through the core patterns.

a. Take an objecting part through the Core patterns, steps two through seven.

Ask yourself if there is any part that objects to your core state as a way of being now.

If you get a "no" answer, then experience the part that is saying, "no," and remember that it is a valuable part of you.

Take that part through the Core patterns as you did in steps two through seven.

b. Repeat "a" for any additional parts.

Do this for any additional parts involved in the issue.

If any of these parts get to a different core state outcome, write it down.

Do this step if you have the time to expand this exercise.

Think of any additional parts that are involved in this issue.

Take each of them through step five, the Core Emergence part of the pattern, as you did with the main part.

Note: Since the Core Transformation pattern may be time consuming the first time through, you may wish to leave out step nine until you are efficient with this pattern.

Step #10. Optional progress – for additional core state outcomes

Note: Do this step if you have gotten additional core state outcomes (that is, outcomes that connected you with your core state) from step nine.

This can happen when you identify additional parts and take them through the Core Deepening pattern, as you did for the first part during step two.

a. Experience your timeline.

Access your awareness of your timeline.

Experience how it is a flow of all of your experiences leading up to the person you are now.

b. Take your core state outcomes with you as you float back to the moment before you were conceived.

Look at your notes, and bring into your awareness the additional core state outcomes that you got from step nine.

Take each of them with you as you float back to the moment before you were conceived.

c. Flow your core state outcomes into this point in time.

Attract your core state outcomes into this point in time, as though its limitless energy flows into this time and builds, being swept into the momentum of time, beginning to move forward with time.

Your core state transcends all outcomes.

It doesn't depend on them. It is a wellspring for insight, harmonious action, and creativity.

Notice how your core state is a universal experience flowing into your timeline.

d. Move forward in your timeline with your core state outcomes.

Descend into that moment, catching the wave of you core state, riding it forward, and continuing to take your core state outcomes with you in your awareness.

Have these core state outcomes flow through your life experiences.

e. Experience the benefit to your timeline.

As you move forward through time, notice how your core state outcomes enrich your life.

f. Experience the benefit to your future.

Have this wave of core state energy move through your present and into the future.

Notice how this energizes and enriches your future.

g. Repeat several times, going faster each time.

Repeat this timeline flow from "b" through "e" several times, allowing it to go faster each time.

Each time you finish, become associated into the present before proceeding with another round.

This pattern of repeated and accelerated timeline travel builds the durability and accessibility of the core state, brings your positive life memories into the foreground to enhance your self esteem and resourcefulness, and improves your motivation and mood in facing the future. Needless to say, the results will be seen as you experience the growth that comes from using such a set of actions on your philosophy and life strategies.

It is a combination of aspects of the swish pattern, the anchoring pattern, and the Timeline pattern.

There are many other processes involved, but it is not for us here to be dealing with theories. We will leave the academic discussions to someone else or to another book.

Step #11. Savor your core state, think about the value you have created, and take a break.

You have created access to your core state.

This is of profound value. Take some time to meditate upon your core state.

We recommend that you take a break and contemplate this process and outcome by taking a walk or enjoying some other physical activity.

❦

138.

Mapping Anyone's Brain

"To effectively communicate, we must realize that we are all different in the way we perceive the world and use this understanding as a guide to our communication with others".

— Anthony Robbins, author of Awaken The Giant Within

CREDITS FOR THE CREATION of this NLP pattern belong to various contributors.

Build your modeling skill with this form of analysis.

This skill will dramatically improve your ability to understand the world of another person, as well as your own, so that you can influence with excellence.

In this skill, you will be finding and structuring the keys to people subjective experience. It can be done in less than three minutes, non-verbally, using eye accessing cues.

Overview: The Mapping Anyone's Brain Strategy

Step #1. Arrange things with your partner.

Step #2. Get Visual Remembered cues.

Step #3. Get Visual Constructed cues.

Step #4. Get Auditory Remembered cues.

Step #5. Get Auditory Constructed cues.

Step #6. Get Kinesthetic Constructed cues.

Step #7. Test.

Step #1. Arrange things with your partner.

Select a partner for the exercise.

Establish that you will be creating the mind map, and that the person can best cooperate by following your instructions and without answering verbally.

As you proceed with the following steps, not the person's eye movements.

You may want to take notes to review.

When I elicit the accessing cues, I use my 5 fingers:

1 for Vr (Visual Remembered),
2 for Vc (Visual Constructed),
3 for Ar (Auditory Remembered),
4 for Ac (Auditory Constructed) and
5 for K (Kinesthetic).

I then imagine key points around their head as they speak.

For example, if their eyes went up and to the left for Vr, I imagine a floating point there.

Then I make an arrow between that point and the position of their Vc, and so on. This way I can even guess the movements they'll make ahead of time.

Step #2. Get Visual Remembered cues.

Have your partner recall a pleasant memory, and then ask them focus on the visual aspect.

Prompt them to access visual cues with questions such as:

Can you see yourself yesterday? What did you wear?

Step #3. Get Visual Constructed cues.

Have your partner construct a visual impression that they do not already remember, with a question such as:

Now imagine yourself with blue eyebrows. What if the room lost gravity and everything started floating around?

Step #4. Get Auditory Remembered cues.

Have your partner recall the audio aspect of a memory. *"Listen for a bit to your favorite song. How does it sound in your mind?"*

Step #5. Get Auditory Constructed cues.

Have your partner create an internal auditory experience, by imagining something they have not heard before.

"Imagine that BMW is testing their motorcycles by having one hundred riders drive their motorbikes into a four foot deep reservoir of water all at once. How does that sound?"

Step #6. Get Kinesthetic Constructed cues.

We skipped Kinesthetic Remembered, because people generally do not *recall* kinesthetic memories, rather they re-construct the feeling according to visual or auditory cues in the memory.

Try a cue such as, *"Imagine that you are rolling around on an ice berg in light clothing".*

Step #7. Test.

As you develop skill in this area, see how well you can observe and predict eye movements, and how well you can remember which eye movements are associated with each strategy.

Additional Advice

When you work with a partner, practicing any NLP pattern or tool, it is better if you go through the process completely as a client, a few times, and then give it a few days before you change places and work on it as the practitioner. The reason is that we tend to get caught with the need to complete steps or to work methodically through a pattern, that we miss on the non-verbal cues of our "client", and that is crucial sometimes for the success of the session.

Another advise on the same subject would be, that if you work with another practitioner, practicing a pattern that is destined to create a change, work on real problems. Do not invent a scenario or a problem just for reciting a pattern; do it for real. Then, the testing step is also real and you would see results and get really convinced that this "stuff" is really working.

❧

139.

Undetermined State Integration

"If you don't go after what you want, you'll never have it. If you don't ask, the answer is always no. If you don't step forward, you're always in the same place".

— Nora Roberts

CREDITS FOR THE creation of this NLP pattern belong to various contributors.

Help your subject describe his or her state.

Sometimes people simply can't connect with their state to describe it. They will say things like, "I'm not sure what I'm feeling", "It seems vague" or "I feel dull" (indicating that they are also becoming fatigued, physically or mentally).

This pattern comes to get a clearer statement that will enable you, their practitioner, to set a well defined outcome for the session.

Overview: The Undetermined State Integration Pattern

Step #1. Put your finger about one foot from the subject's eyes.

Step #2. Guide the eye movement and blinking pattern.

Step #3. Alter the movements as indicated, and break state.

Step #4. Ask the questions in the manner indicated.

Step #5. Continuous fatigue state.

Step #1. Put your finger about one foot from the subject's eyes.

Position yourself in front of the person and on eye level.

Put your right hand about one foot in front of his eyes with your finger pointed laterally (not toward either of you).

Step #2. Guide the eye movement and blinking pattern.

Ask him to take a few deep breaths and then to close and open his eyes according to your finger's movement rhythm.

Start very slow, moving your finger from 90 degrees to about 45 degrees (downward motion), and then back up again.

Step #3. Alter the movements as indicated, and break state.

Repeat 5 to 6 times with increased rhythm until normal blinking rhythm is reached again.

Then keep the finger motion but move the hand to accessing cues Visual Constructed (up left) and later to Visual Remembered (up right).

The purpose here is to activate the person's brain through controlled eye movements.

Now let him stretch and move freely, blinking fast several times and breathing normally.

Step #4. Ask the questions in the manner indicated.

Ask the following questions and wait only two seconds for the reply.

If he or she doesn't respond immediately, offer the possible answers provided in the parentheses.

Speak in the same rhythm as his blinking.

Questions:

1. What would be the best feeling you'd like to have right now? (curiosity, passion, calmness, excitement, decisiveness, relaxation, security, etc.)

2. How would you know if you felt it? What would be an evidence for you, on the inside, that you're really feeling X (the state they chose)?

3. What would happen once you feel X?

4. If you felt X, in which situations would it be most useful for you? (At work? With your kids? With your spouse? While you're waking up?)

5. In which situations wouldn't it be useful for you to feel X? And with which feeling would you replace it?

Step #5. Continuous fatigue state

If your subject is still feeling fatigue and dull-minded, ask the following elicitation questions:

Was there a time in your past in which you recall feeling X?

How did you know back then that you felt X?

Could you show me how you would look like if you were feeling X right now?

What was it like to have that feeling? Can you feel it now?

Additional Advice

Make sure your hand is not so close that it makes the person uncomfortable. Different people will have different comfort zones.

If there is a possibility of epilepsy, such as when there is a family history, then refrain from using eye movement exercises.

Have the person discuss with their physician whether such exercises are appropriate for them.

The first set of questions should be asked and answered fairly quickly.

If you give the person time to think, their own self criticism is likely to inhibit them.

If the person is agitated, this is not the right pattern to use. Consider using the "State Chaining" technique or "Collapsing Anchors".

140.

Choice Expansion

"We cannot truly face life until we face the fact that it will be taken away from us".

— Billy Graham

CREDITS FOR THE creation of this NLP pattern belong to Robert Dilts.

Generate motivation by harnessing the power of choice points. You could say that choice points occur when you consciously or unconsciously make a commitment of some kind.

A defining characteristic of a choice point is that it, symbolically or literally, makes it difficult to turn back.

For example, when you sign an agreement, take marriage vows, or shake on a bet, you have passed a choice point. This pattern will also help you identify and use the many smaller choice points that, collectively, have a big impact on our lives.

Overview: The Choice Expansion Pattern

Step #1. Scan through your day.

Step #2. Float back to that choice point, viewing it from the third (dissociated) perceptual position.

Step #3. Select choice points

Step #4. Imagine the likely outcomes of each of these imaginary choices.

Step #5. For each outcome, imagine experiencing it in first person.

Step #6. Test

Step #1. Scan through your day.

What choice points did you go through and what choices did you make? What outcome did you intend to produce at those points? For the choices that produced results of some kind today, how effective were your choices?

Step #2. Float back to that choice point, viewing it from the third (dissociated) perceptual position.

Step #3. Select choice points

Select the two or three most important choice points (or more if you have time).

For each, think of three different choices that you could have made. Imagine actually making those choice and taking actions based on those choices, one choice at a time.

Step #4. Imagine the likely outcomes of each of these imaginary choices.

Step #5. For each outcome, imagine experiencing it in first person.

Step #6. Test

As you experience the next few days, notice if your acuity for sizing up choices has improved, and whether your results are any better.

Note any ways that you could enhance this pattern, and use it on key choices that have caused problems.

Also, be sure to use it on upcoming choices, to develop your ability to predict outcomes, and to simply become more conscious of the outcomes you project, since many of our choice points (and choices) slip by us unnoticed until it is too late.

❦

141.

The F/B Pattern

"Finish each day and be done with it. You have done what you could; some blunders and absurdities have crept in; forget them as soon as you can. Tomorrow is a new day; you shall begin it serenely and with too high a spirit to be encumbered with your old nonsense".

— Ralph Waldo Emerson

CREDITS FOR THE creation of this NLP pattern belong to Robert Dilts.

Create resource states in people who tend to focus on the negative or disabling aspect of a situation.

This technique utilizes the tendency of negative and resource experiences to have a great deal in common. They seem quite different because their differences are in the foreground of our awareness. This pattern is a good example of creating resourceful states by linking there from unresourceful states. This pattern is good for people who are too caught up in a negative reality because it works with sensory representations that are shared between the problem state and the ideal state.

This pattern is unique in that it does not focus on the foreground, or "driver" submodalities, as you would with the swish pattern and others. It also for this reason that you should work slowly and methodically through the steps and note your client's abreaction to the process.

With the approach of the F/B pattern, you do not have a fight for dominance between the two foreground experiences. Many users find this pattern to be a gentle and almost magical experience. In my own private practice, the clients who have experienced this process reported it has been one of the most self-comforting experiences they've ever had.

When their focus changes from a limiting or limited frame to a resourceful perception, you can tell it in their eyes and their posture. Relaxation is one of the immediate benefits of this pattern, but it is also just the beginning of the wonderful results it brings about.

Overview: The Foreground/Background Pattern

Step #1. Chose a limiting response.

Step #2. Notice your foreground and background awareness.

> *2A. Notice your foreground awareness.*

> *2B. Notice your background awareness.*

Step #3. Select a counter-example.

Step #4. Explore the foreground and background of the counter-example.

> *4A. Explore the foreground of the counter-example.*

> *4B. Explore the background of the counter-example.*

Step #5. Associate the background and the foreground feature of the counter-example, and connect this state with the foreground of the original situation.

Step #6. Focus on the common ground experience of the original experience.

Step #7. Test.

Step #1. Chose a limiting response.

Choose a clearly definable situation in which you have an automatic limiting response.

An example of this is flying in an aircraft when this causes panic attacks.

Step #2. Notice your foreground and background awareness.

2A. Notice your foreground awareness.

As you imagine this experience, notice what is in the foreground of your awareness.

What aspects are you most aware of at the time that you experience your limiting response?

The panicking air passenger may be aware of the sound of the engines revving up in preparation for take off.

Check all rep systems and sub-modalities for what is standing out.

2B. Notice your background awareness.

Notice what is in the background of your awareness.

What are you not typically very aware of during your unresourceful automatic response?

These must be things that are not limited to the situation, or that you might experience in a situation in which you have a very resourceful response.

Typically, you focus on the most pleasant body sensations that you can find, such as the aliveness of the soles of your feet, or the color of the walls.

Step #3. Select a counter-example.

Find a good counter-example to your unresourceful response.

This will be a time when you could well have had the unre-sourceful or limiting response, but you did not.

For example, memories of flying without panicking would provide counter-examples.

If there is no counter-example, you want to find the closest situation that you can.

For example, if you have been in a bus or tram without anxiety, then you have a good counter-example because of the similarities between the interior of a plane and that of a bus (seating, other people, length, engine sounds, jostling).

Associate into the experience.

Step #4. Explore the foreground and background of the counter-example.

4A. Explore the foreground of the counter-example.

Discover the aspects of this experience of which you are most aware, that is, that are in the foreground.

Intensify the positive experience and anchor it. (We'll call this anchor A1.)

Foreground experiences may be things like a curious internal voice, or a dissociated image of the environment, or a sense of desire for the engine to wind up because it means that you are going to move forward.

4B. Explore the background of the counter-example.

Get in touch with the features that are in the background of both situations (this is the common ground experience).

This may range from body sensations such as the soles of the feet to similarities between the external perceptions.

Step #5. Associate the background and the foreground feature of the counter-example, and connect this state with the foreground of the original situation.

Weld a strong association between the background and foreground feature in your counter-example situation.

You can do this be focusing on the background feature and firing the A1 resource anchor.

Now connect this with the foreground of the original situation.

You can use suggestions to accomplish this.

For example, *"The more you attend to the feeling of the soles of your feet, the more you can experience how your curious internal voice becomes louder and clearer. And as your awareness shifts to the environment of the bus and its engine increasing in speed, you more easily maintain an image of the inside of the airplane."*

As you can see, we are linking the common background and the positive state with the foreground of the situation in which you had experienced a limiting response.

THE BIG BOOK OF NLP TECHNIQUES

Step #6. Focus on the common ground experience of the original experience.

Return to the original experience, and focus on the common ground experience that you found in 4B.

For example, you could place yourself back into the airplane as the engines are beginning to rev, and focus your awareness on the soles of your feet and the color of the walls there.

If this does not improve the limiting response, then try one of these strategies:

Option 1. Find a more powerful fitting counter-example, and repeat the pattern from step 2A. Or...

Option 2. Return to step 2B, and strengthen the association between the common ground elements and the background features of the counter-example.

Step #7. Test.

Focus on the foreground features of the original situation from step 1A.

You should experience the positive state from your counter-example experience.

You can use instructions such as: "Now you can place yourself into the seat in the airline, actually focusing your full attention on the sound of the engine and the sense of acceleration of the plane.

⊙⊙

508

142.

Memory De-Energizing

*"One should guard against preaching to young people success
in the customary form as the main aim in life. The most
important motive for work in school and in life is pleasure
in work, pleasure in its result, and the knowledge of the value
of the result to the community".*

— Albert Einstein

CREDITS FOR THE CREATION of this NLP pattern belong to Dr. Maralee Platt.

Free yourself from troubling memories. Turn them into sources of wisdom.

Overview: The Memory De-Energizing Pattern

Step #1. Choose a memory that troubles you sometimes.

Step #2. Explore the submodalities you notice in the memory.

Step #3. Use a frame as a symbol of the memory and modify it.

Step #4. Bring the image to your left, and extract the learning.

Step #5. Put the image behind you.

Step #6. Have this process generalize.

Step #7. Enjoy happy memories and put them behind you.

Step #8. Test.

Step #1. Choose a memory that troubles you sometimes.

Step #2. Explonre the submodalities you notice in the memory.

Step #3. Use a frame as a symbol of the memory and modify.

Select a single frame from your mental movie of the memory, and use it as a symbol for the entire memory. Push that frame back to the farthest periphery of your awareness and change it to black and white.

Notice that there is a younger you in the image. Shrink it down to a small size and surround it with a frame.

Step #4. Bring the image to your left, and extract the learning.

Reach out and grasp the small image with your left hand, and bring it to your left side.

Use the opposite hand and side if you tend to store your memories on the right. Extract all the learnings available from this memory as represented by the small image. You may not know what these learnings consist of, but that is okay for

this pattern. Just know that you are taking wisdom from this image. Imagine this knowledge flowing into your personal mental library.

Step #5. Put the image behind you.

Now push the image back behind you, symbolically telling your body mind that the experience is behind you, that is, in the past.

Step #6. Have this process generalize.

Instruct your mind to do this with all aspects of the troubling memory.

Step #7. Enjoy happy memories and put them behind you.

Spend some time with happy memories in big, bright, full color. Place them to the right. Enjoy them, then push them back behind you as well.

Step #8. Test.

In the coming days, notice if this memory has been de-energized.

Notice any ways that this frees your creativity and ability to enjoy life and create a more meaningful future.

☯

143.

Somatic Fractal

"Take advantage of every opportunity to practice your communication skills so that when important occasions arise, you will have the gift, the style, the sharpness, the clarity, and the emotions to affect other people".

— Jim Rohn

CREDITS FOR THE creation of this NLP pattern belong to Robert Dilts. Practice intuiting deep structure, and explore how this is a useful skill and understanding. This pattern draws upon Somatic Syntax.

Overview: The Somatic Fractal Pattern

Step #1. Select a shape.

Step #2. Make the pattern with your finger.

Step #3. Add body parts to create a more complex movement pattern.

Step #4. Have your partner guess the original pattern.

Step #5. Switch roles.

Step #6. Test

Step #1. Select a shape.

Do this pattern with a partner. Select a simple shape, such as a triangle or figure eight, but keep it a secret for now.

Step #2. Make the pattern with your finger.

As your partner keeps their eyes closed, make the pattern with your finger.

Step #3. Add body parts to create a more complex movement pattern.

Keep this up, and begin adding body parts. Start small, perhaps with your wrist, and expand out until your entire body is involved as much as possible. Explore this as though you were creating some kind of new dance.

Don't try to make your body express the original pattern as an imitation. Instead, you are allowing it to act as a seed move that inspires new movements,

Step #4. Have your partner guess the original pattern.

Have your partner open their eyes and try to guess the deep structure pattern (the original shape you started with) that led to your somatic fractal (the end result of your movement expansion into a more complex move).

This is called a fractal because, metaphorically, it is a complex expression or result of an underlying formula (the original shape).

Instruct your partner to, *"Notice how you must call upon a kind of intuition in order to seek the deep structure that leads to the more complex movement. Get a sense of how this intuition lives in you and how to access it."*

Step #5. Switch roles.

Switch roles and do the exercise again.

Step #6. Test

In the coming days and weeks, notice any ways that accessing this intuition becomes easier and useful.

Notice any ways that this metaphoric way of seeking deep structure can play out in life situations and be valuable.

ഐ

144.

Resource Fractal

"What man actually needs is not a tensionless state but rather the striving and struggling for some goal worthy of him. What he needs is not the discharge of tension at any cost, but the call of a potential meaning waiting to be fulfilled by him".

— Viktor Frankl, Man's Search For Meaning

CREDITS FOR THE CREATION of this NLP pattern belong to Robert Dilts.

Enhance your problem solving, creativity, or simply your enjoyment of life by creating a synesthetic (multi representational system) expression of an optimal state.

Overview: The Resource Fractal Pattern

Step #1. Access the resource state.

Step #2. Initiate a related movement pattern.

Step #3. Vary the movements.

Step #4. Transfer the movements.

Step #5. Extend the movements to more areas.

Step #6. Use another rep system.

Step #7. Test

Step #1. Access the resource state.

Select and access a resourceful state.

Step #2. Initiate a related movement pattern.

Find within yourself a pattern or kind of body movement that seems to somehow express this state.

You may find a pattern, or the movement may evolve more like a free-form dance.

Give yourself permission to do it your own way, without the burden of judgement or preconceptions.

Step #3. Vary the movements.

With care and mindfulness, make gentle and subtle variations of this pattern. notice how this affects how you experience your resourceful state.

Explore how this connects you to its deeper structure.

Step #4. Transfer the movements.

Transfer this movement pattern and quality to another part of your body.

For example, if you started with your hand, shift it up into your shoulders and neck.

Be gentle if you are not much of a dancer.

Step #5. Extend the movements to more areas.

Extend this movement quality out to many parts of your body, perhaps the totality of your body.

Even invite it to come out in your facial expression.

Step #6. Use another rep system.

Repeat this using another rep system.

This time, you used the kinesthetic in four dimensions (by adding time expression through movement).

You could swap that for visual, by drifting through memories and created images that express the state.

You could create an auditory expression by singing and tapping, or by remembering and inventing sound environments in your mind.

You can add words to it, impressionistically and poetically, or by describing the sound scapes. There are plenty of possibilities for your creativity.

Step #7. Test

In the coming days and weeks, notice any ways that you are using your intelligence and creativity across rep systems (synesthetically) to solve problems, be creative, or simply experience a richer world.

☯

145.

Changing Beliefs – The Logic Approach

"Reality leaves a lot to the imagination".

— John Lennon

I F YOU'RE A good listener, you might notice you have friends who dump their sorrows on you in every possible chance. It's not because they're looking for pity or abuse your friendship, it's because they know you listen and talking gives them some temporary relief from the emotional pain they cause to themselves.

They are also very logical. They can firmly convince you how stuck they are. They can prove that their range of choices is limited. They refuse to listen to anything that contradicts their twisted logic, and the worst part is – they are depressively optimistic about the near future.

To make it softer, they express themselves as if their values and integrity are on the line, and their suffering is a result of them trying to stay moral and honest and generous. They tend to believe that the world is doing THIS or THAT to them, and surely they cannot see their responsibility in the stream of events.

From day to day, the more you listen to them, you get the feeling that they're not really trying to change their situation. At first, you may think they are just stuck for a moment or two and then they'd come back turned over 180 degrees, all well and better. But they do not. They stay stuck in the third and fourth moment and continuously. They may develop some unknown and unexplained physical weakness and tendency to sickness. Their doctors will say they're still doing tests, but have no clue what the reasons for the sickness is. They would hide an extra information from you, one that the doctor says for sure – there is nothing wrong with your body; you are healthy".

They seek attention. They seek the caring look. They seek the emotional punching bag. They want to unload their emotional burden, but within a day or two, they have it all back.

But they are your friends. If you only have one of those, great. If you have more, it is surely a time for a different strategy to handle them, because eventually they may get better while you get worst.

The solution is simpler than you may think. Aristotle thought about it ages ago, but in a different context.

Aristotle came up with the concept of Deduction. It's opposite, Abduction, was added to this thought model as well.

Deduction is the common logic which depressed optimists use to confine themselves in their problems. The logic is obvious but absurd if you dissect it objectively.

"I am a foreigner".

"Foreigners can't get a good job in this country"

"I will never get a good job here".

The equation of deduction is simple:

$$A = B ;$$
$$B = C ; \text{therefore -}$$
$$A = C$$

And it is logical, because the minute you accept the $B = C$ statement, the belief is set in motion. The challenging part here is to handle the fact that they are convinced already before they made this statement. So even if you try to negate $B = C$ and claim that $B = D$ and not C, it is not accepted and even ridiculed by the depressed optimist.

The "cure" for this is using the other process which is called Abduction.

"You are an educated and experienced person"

"Foreigners in this country are not equal one to another in education and experience"

"As long as you are superior to other foreigners, it gives you a higher chance to get a better job in this country"

$$A = B ;$$
$$C = D < B ; \text{therefore -}$$
$$(B > C) = A$$

If you run this formula thoughtfully and design it to fit the depressed optimist you're dealing with, it will get them thinking. If they come up with another excuse, make a decision if it's a valid excuse or a miserable try to get you to think they're hopeless. If it's the second case, give them that non-believer doubting look and they suddenly change a tune.

Friends are there for each other, in better and most importantly in worst. When someone behaves in a destructive way, it is also your responsibility to shake them off and kick them back into normal and healthy way of living. If it restricts your life and limits your own possibilities, push them away. Sometimes the fear of losing a good friend drives people into a major positive change. But use that as a last resort. Besides, it's always more fun to twist and distort a friend's mind and see them curl in discomfort all the way to the "Aha!" and wanton motivation.

൭൭

146.

Logical Levels Co-Alignment

"Vision is the art of seeing what is invisible to others".

— Jonathan Swift

CREDITS FOR THE creation of this NLP pattern belong to Robert Dilts.

Discover and align with your vision and values through the power of metaphor and logical levels.

Help your team succeed when you form a common identity together through this kind of alignment. If you refer to the appendix on Logical Levels, you'll see how this pattern uses the levels.

Overview: The Logical Levels Co-Alignment Pattern

Step #1. Select the location.

Step #2. Answer the "doing" question.

Step #3. Answer the "skills and abilities" question.

Step #4. Answer the "values and beliefs" question.

Step #5. Answer the "identity" question.

Step #6. Answer the "vision" question.

Step #7. Explore the vision overlap.

Step #8. Bring the related state to the identity level.

Step #9. Move to the identity level.

Step #10. Move to the behavior level. Explore the significance at that level.

Step #11. Explore the full results at the location level.

Step #12. Test

Step #1. Select the location.

Select for this pattern an environment that you and your team share with a common purpose.

When you just begin using this pattern, select a place that is neutral and not knowingly holding negative anchors for members of the team.

Step #2. Answer the "doing" question.

Have each team member answer the question, *"What do I desire to do or accomplish in that place?"*

Ask them to go into some detail in their answers.

Step #3. Answer the "skills and abilities" question.

Have each member describe the tools, skills, authority, and abilities that they feel will best empower them to accomplish their aims in this place.

It does not have to be public at first; they can each work on their own list without sharing with the rest of the group until they feel comfortable enough to do so.

Step #4. Answer the "values and beliefs" question.

Have each member describe the values, attitudes and beliefs that drive their desire to exercise these resources to accomplish their aims in this place.

Step #5. Answer the "identity" question.

Have them explain who they are as individuals with these motivations and beliefs driving their use of skills and other resources to create the desired actions in this place.

Step #6. Answer the "vision" question.

Have them describe the vision that they wish to manifest, and that gives dimension to their identity as a person with beliefs and attitudes that drive their use of skills and abilities toward specific actions and results in this place.

Step #7. Explore the vision overlap.

Discuss the ways that your individual vision statements are similar. What do they share? Be sure to explore them for overlaps that are not obvious.

Step #8. Bring the related state to the identity level.

Access the positive state associated with this vision and sharing.

In that state, return to your identity level, experiencing the vision and sense of identity and mission simultaneously.

Step #9. Move to the identity level.

With this sense of vision, identity, beliefs and values, return to your capability space.

Explore what capabilities you have as a team that go beyond your individual identities.

Step #10. Move to the behavior level. Explore the significance at that level.

Take your sense of vision, identity, beliefs, values and capabilities back to the behavior level.

Explore how all of your behaviors, even seemingly trivial ones, affect and reflect upon all the higher levels you have explored, right up to the level of vision.

Now ask, *"What collective actions shall we take together?"*

Step #11. Explore the full results at the location level.

Place all the levels you have explored into the location.

Experience how these insights, understandings, and feelings transform and enrich this space and mission.

Step #12. Test

Over the coming days and months, observe any ways that this pattern has influenced or expanded the team and your individual contribution to it's work.

☙❧

147.

The Embedded Command In A Question Method

*"The right to be heard does not automatically include the
right to be taken seriously".*

— Hubert H. Humphrey

CREDITS FOR THE CREATION of this NLP pattern belong to Milton Erickson, modeled by Richard Bandler and John Grinder.

When embedded commands appear in questions, they have the added benefit of priming a more open, curious state.

The question helps to conceal the embedded command as well. Here are examples: "I'm wondering whether you can feel completely comfortable speaking with me?" "Do you know if you can quietly allow your subconscious mind to come out and talk to me?"

Overview: The Embedded Command in a Question Method

Step #1. Select a situation for using embedded commands.

Step #2. Choose what you will communicate with this approach.

Step #3. Prepare the communications.

Step #4. Practice the approach.

Step #5. Apply the approach.

Step #6. Assess the results.

Step #7. Continue to refine and practice this strategy.

Step #1. Select a situation for using embedded commands.

Step #2. Choose what you will communicate with this approach.

Write down a number of things that you would like to communicate, but that might arouse inappropriate defenses.

Continue accumulating these until you have a several that you feel can be converted into embedded messages. Make sure that your approach is ethical. You must not attempt to manipulate a person in a manner that is not in their best interest.

Step #3. Prepare the communications.

Create questions that could be normal-sounding parts of your communication with this person, and that include your embedded commands. Remember, embedded commands are usually very short sentences or sentence fragments with the meaning that you want. If necessary, review material on Milton Erickson's use of embedded commands.

Step #4. Practice the approach.

Before using this approach, practice delivering these communications. Try them with several different embedded commands. Add analogical marking (see the pattern above) such as including changing your inflection, tempo, body language, and volume.

Step #5. Apply the approach.

Once you feel that this can be done in a way that is very natural, use this approach in the actual situation.

Step #6. Assess the results.

Notice how the person responds. Were there any awkward moments or looks? Did the person respond in any way that suggests your approach was helpful?

Continue to refine and practice your use of analogical marking until you are able to do it without preparing in advance.

෴

148.

The Double Bind Method

"English is the perfect language for preachers because it allows you to talk until you think of what to say".

— Garrison Keillor

CREDITS for the creation of this NLP pattern belong to Milton Erickson, modeled by Richard Bandler and John Grinder.

Improve cooperation in many situations. The double bind is a basic communication pattern that requires that the person you are communicating with accepts a presupposition. This is followed with choices. For example, the most classic and simple version, "Would you like to pay cash or credit?"

Overview: The Double Bind Method

Step #1. Define the context for your communication.

Step #2. Identify the presupposition.

Step #3. Align the situation to the presupposition.

Step #4. Construct a 22 catch choice.

Step #5. Test

Step #1. Define the context for your communication.

Think of a situation in which you would like to increase others' cooperation.

Sales and coaching are great situations for this. However, even a simple persuasion situation, such as convincing your 10 years old son to go to bed at 10pm instead of watching another movie, would do.

Get a clear idea of how you would know the person was being cooperative, which in essence means that you need to establish a quick, well-defined outcome to your communication with that person in that context.

Step #2. Identify the presupposition.

Identify a basic presupposition upon which this cooperation would be predicated. Now, this is not an embedded command, but this should be the conclusion the other person will come to after you apply the double bind in your conversation with them.

Here are some examples:

You are going to buy this, you need this, you are definitely going to base this decision upon your higher values, you can prove yourself by getting a constructive outcome here.

Step #3. Align the situation to the presupposition.

Imagine communicating with people in this kind of situation.

Think of ways you can get them aligned with your basic presuppositions, the ones you've established in Step #2.

The most elegant ways are largely or completely subconscious.

If you are talking to a street kid who is used to proving himself by being touch, you might use numerous anchoring and hypnotic methods to get him primed to prove his manhood by being a constructive leader in a situation that could turn violent without his help.

Notice that this last phrase already distances him from the violence.

Instead of saying, "Don't do it," the presupposition is that he is separate from the situation and has a choice whether or not to help.

It also implies that he is needed, by appealing to his heroic fantasies.

Step #4. Construct a 22-catch choice.

Once the presupposition is firmly in place, construct a choice that is predicated upon this presupposition.

For example, you could keep the circle of revenge going around and around, killing more people on various sides of various conflicts, as if there isn't a bigger world out there for everybody, or you could run and hide, but I'm wondering what you're going to do to turn them around and save some lives.

Keep some of those pretty girls prettier, keep the party going.

It isn't whether you have the stuff.

You've proven yourself.

But how are you going to take it to another level.

Maybe using some of that fast talk of yours to mess with their heads a little and get them thinking about other stuff.

Maybe get them thinking about the lives they could have if they weren't on this merry-go-round. I dunno.

Step #5. Test.

Try this approach in the situation and, as you improve your skill, notice how much your results improve.

Additional Advice

Communication skills are not based on tricks or memorized tech-niques. What we do in NLP is trying to get all of this "practice" into real practice, by working to make the skills move to the level of subconscious competence. Then, every opportunity to practice the skill becomes another brick on the road to mastery.

Instead of memorizing techniques, practice them in your imagination. When I just began studying these concepts, I went on a long imaginary journey every day. I practiced only in my mind, making up thousands of possible situations in which I would need to be persuasive and influential. What is so good about your imagination? You can slow the process down.

In real life, people are not going to wait for you to think about a presupposition that will help you build a double bind. They might also become suspicious if you use techniques that you have memorized. But they're going to be mesmerized if you're not using a technique consciously, if these ideas and concepts are expressed in your words without your intention to use them... as if they were always your natural way of communication.

ⵥ

149.

The Ambiguity Method

"The problem with communication ... is the illusion that it has been accomplished".

— George Bernard Show

CREDITS FOR THE CREATION of this NLP pattern belong to Milton H. Erickson, modeled by Richard Bandler and John Grinder.

Learn to use ambiguity for motivational and healing purposes. Milton Erickson was brilliant at using ambiguity to induce trance, and to guide the subconscious mind in its work during therapy. This pattern will focus on using ambiguity to induce light trance during TDS's. Do not try this exercise while operating any machinery or doing anything that could be dangerous, you may put yourself into a trance. If you are comfortable with hypnotic communication, you can try this on a partner for practice and get their feedback. You can also record your efforts and try them on yourself.

Overview: The Ambiguity Method

Step #1. Create an ambiguous statement pertaining to stages of hypnotic communication.

Step #2. Refine it to be more hypnotic.

Step #3. Engineer ambiguity for specific situations.

Step #4. Modify what you came up with to prime the person.

Step #1. Create an ambiguous statement pertaining to stages of hypnotic communication.

Write down or verbalize statements that would guide a person through hypnotic communication for at least the following stages: Body positioning, paying attention, going inward, focusing on an issue, developing a state, going deeper into relaxation, going into trance.

For example, for body positioning, here is an unambiguous statement: *"Please sit with your feet on the floor, your hands in your lap, and breath slowly."*

Made ambiguous, it could be: *"As you sit there, you can untangle your legs, finding a position that your mind prefers you to experience as it guides your hands to come to rest as they find you giving even more of your weight to the chair as it suspends you there in balance...now."*

Step #2. Refine it to be more hypnotic.

Practice this again, and emphasize ways of being ambiguous that will enhance the experience of relaxation and trance. Try various wordings.

Step #3. Engineer ambiguity for specific situations.

Try the same thing for a practical situation. This removes you and your agenda from causing the person to feel that there is anything to push against.

Step #4. Modify what you came up with to prime the person.

Add an element or two to the communication that will prime this person to act in the manner that you prefer.

Remember that priming is triggering a state that is conducive to a particular way of thinking or acting. That is different from a direct command. For example, *"I know most people's fondest memories are of the vacations they have been having with their families. They would never trade those memories away for any work memories, as they treasure them."*

In this case, we are not talking directly about him during our timeshare presentation. We are, however, priming our listeners regarding the many values of vacations, including family ties. Money is now less of an obstacle, especially if we have a well-orchestrated presentation with many such primes.

☙❧

150.

The Presupposition Method

"Words are, of course, the most powerful drug used by mankind".

— Rudyard Kipling

CREDITS FOR THE CREATION of this NLP pattern belong to Milton H. Erickson, modeled by Richard Bandler and John Grinder.

Learn to make your communication more persuasive with presuppositions. A presupposition is an assumption that your listener perceives from your communication. For example, a very common presupposition I used with clients in my hypnotherapy practice was, *"before you go deeper (into hypnosis), I would like you to notice how your breathing seems to be deeper…"*. That line had 2 presuppositions in it, that even if the client has consciously negated one, the other is still accepted. Milton Erickson was able to embed his communications with presuppositions that were often quite well hidden.

Overview: The Presupposition Method

Step #1. Select your presuppositions.

Step #2. Embed them in sentences.

Step #3. Create a conversational approach with the sentences and set ups.

Step #4. Practice on people.

Step #1. Select your presuppositions.

Imagine that you are about to encourage a trance state while in a conversational format.

Think of at least five things that you could presuppose (assume is a close synonym) about the person and their experience that you could leverage for relaxation, rapport, healing, and trance.

For example: *"...this allows you to more fully feel the relaxation spreading from your shoulders,"* (presupposing that the person is already relaxing and that it is spreading from their shoulders, making it possible to feel sensations that can be interpreted as relaxation and increase awareness there that will induce relaxation) or, at a higher logical level, *"As you go into your day, your subconscious will continue to heal you and build you,"* (presupposing that the subconscious has this agenda and is already healing and building).

Step #2. Embed them in sentences.

Create sentences that, as I showed in step one, include these presupposition. You get bonus points for preceding each sentence with a sentence or two that set up the presupposition to make it more stealthy.

For example, *"As you inhale, you can feel your shoulders spread very slightly, with your exhale allowing them to feel their natural weight. This allows you to more fully feel the relaxation spreading from your shoulders, into the weight of your hands, through the ends of your fingers."*

Step #3. Create a conversational approach with the sentences and set ups.

String these presupposition-bearing sentences together into a conversational approach to trance.

Step #4. Practice on people.

Try this on a willing participant, or record it and try it on yourself.

Observe your subjects for signs of trance.

Notice how your use of presuppositions can encourage what you presuppose to actually take place or become the basis for other behavior.

◑◐

151.

The Metaphor Method

*"The dead might as well try to speak to the living
as the old to the young".*

— Willa Cather

CREDITS FOR THE creation of this NLP pattern belong to Milton H. Erickson, modeled by Richard Bandler and John Grinder.

Practice using metaphors to achieve therapeutic ends. Metaphor is essentially the use of symbolic events or items to symbolize something else. The Wizard of Oz was a metaphor for the United States' debate about going off of the gold standard in the 1900's.

Kafka's Metamorphosis is a metaphor for the denial of self implicated in conformity to a harsh capitalist society. In coaching and psychotherapy, healing metaphors can bypass conscious filters and rally subconscious resources. Metaphors such as those in Little

---

Overview: The Metaphor Method

Step #1. Choose a situation that you can apply a healing metaphor to.

Step #2. Decide what is key to healing.

Step #3. Create your metaphor as a story situation.

Step #4. Complete the metaphor for healing.

Step #5. Practice the story.

Step #6. Tell the story.

Step #7. Test.

Annie Stories can be used to help children navigate developmental challenges and fears.

Step #1. Choose a situation that you can apply a healing metaphor to.

Think of a situation in your own or someone else's life that is creating fear or difficulty in adjusting. It can be an adult or child.

Step #2. Decide what is key to healing.

Jot down a core idea that would be healing or useful for that situation. Jot down some ideas that support it.

Step #3. Create your metaphor as a story situation.

Think of a story situation that resembles this, but does not directly say it. For example, a child who is afraid of the dark could be transformed into a story about prince who must get to the castle in order to become the next king, but he must pass through a dark forest that he is sure is full of goblins and witches.

Step #4. Complete the metaphor for healing.

Find a way to propel the story and reach a resolution with a healing meaning. For example, you could enthrall your child with the prince's travels through the dark forest, with his certainty that sounds he is hearing means he is about to be eaten by goblins or turned into a toad by witches.

He could have close calls with things that turn out to be birds and rabbits. (The metaphor is saying that those fears aren't really of bad things, in fact, they might be cute or harmless).

Step #5. Practice the story.

Practice telling the story until it feels fairly smooth

Step #6. Tell the story.

Tell the story to the person who needs to hear it.

Step #7. Test.

Notice if it has a positive impact on the person regarding the situation that they were having trouble with.

152.

Shared Resource

"If you have one true friend you have more than your share".

— Thomas Fuller

CREDITS FOR THE creation of this NLP pattern belong to Robert Dilts and Robert McDonald.

Improve the value of resourceful states by using various perceptual positions to experience and explore them. This pattern uses a novel fourth position by invoking a felt sense of sameness between people that results from having been through the other three perceptual positions.

We'll draw from the principles of spatial sorting, psycho-geography, and somatic syntax.

Overview: The Shared Resource Pattern

Step #1. Select a resourceful experience and express it in body movements.

Step #2. Face your partner and begin imitating their movements.

Step #3. Take on your partner's experience and movements.

Step #4. Compare and contrast this with your own movements.

Step #5. Facing the same directions, blend the two resource state movement patterns in a "we field."

Step #6. Repeat with another pair, but with "we fields."

Step #7. Test.

Step #1. Select a resourceful experience and express it in body movements.

Do this exercise in pairs the first time through. Choose a recent experience that you found to be resourceful.

Review it from first position (through your own eyes, etc.) Explore the body movements that somehow express that resourceful state.

Step #2. Face your partner and begin imitating their movements.

Face your partner and do this movement pattern. Now, continuing in first position, imitate your partner's body movements.

Step #3. Take on your partner's experience and movements.

Switch positions and go into second position, experiencing things through your partners eyes. Express your partner's movements as though you were them.

Notice any ways that this changes how you experience these movements.

Step #4. Compare and contrast this with your own movements.

From the third position (outside observer), sense what makes your partner's movements similar to and different from your own.

Step #5. Facing the same directions, blend the two resource state movement patterns in a "we field."

Go back to first position.

Turn to be side by side with your partner. Make your resource movements again.

Have your partner make their own version of movements.

Together, make small adjustments in your movements until you blend the two resource states through movement. What is it like to experience this shared space? We'll call it the fourth position, or a "we field."

Step #6. Repeat with another pair, but with "we fields."

The two of you are now to find another pair and repeat the pattern. This time, start with the movement that you created together.

Continue to expand these joinings until the entire group is experiencing this fourth position.

Step #7. Test.

Explore with the group what this "we field" is like.

Notice in the coming days and weeks any ways that this pattern has contributed to your ability to empathize, create rapport, and be intuitive.

☯

153.

The Dancing SCORE Pattern

"It's not what you're doing that's the problem, it's what you're doing when you're not doing what you're meant to be doing, that's the problem".

— Wyatt Woodsmall

CREDITS FOR THE creation of this NLP pattern belong to Judith DeLosier, based on the S.C.O.R.E model by R. Dilts & T. Epstein.

Solve problems by enhancing your intuition and body wisdom through movement. This pattern promotes the mind-body relationship in a way that accesses and mobilizes deep resources, creating a self-organizing pathway toward a resourceful and relevant state. In this pattern, we will think of a challenge as existing in a problem space.

The key elements that we will consider for this are in the acronym S.C.O.R.E., which stands for Symptoms, Causes, Outcomes, Resources, and Effects. We will ask you to express yourself in movement and dance, but we are talking about a personal form of expression for which there is no pressure to perform for anyone else. These are expressions that you find within yourself and express in whatever way you discover.

Overview: The Dancing SCORE Pattern

Step #1. Select a problem.

Step #2. Create your four spaces.

Step #3. Find a movement pattern expressing the symptoms.

Step #4. Find a movement pattern expressing the cause.

Step #5. Break state, the go to the Outcomes space, and find a movement pattern expressing the desired outcomes.

Step #6. Find a movement pattern expressing the effects of the desired outcomes.

Step #7. Moving through all spaces, discover a dance that integrates the movement from cause to effects.

Step #8. Discover a missing resource.

Step #9. Find a movement for the missing resource and integrate it into your movement expression.

Step #10. Repeat this to fully integrate the movement expression.

Step #11. Test.

Step #1. Select a problem.

Select a problem that you would like to solve.

Choose a problem that seems as though it will require an expanded frame or insight in order to be solved.

Step #2. Create your four spaces.

Go to a meta-position, and select a location for each of the following four items:

Cause,

Symptom,

Outcome,

Desired Effect.

Think of them as being in chronological order.

Remember that *Symptom* means the thing that tells you the problem is there.

Desired Effects refers to the long-term effects of the outcome.

Step #3. Find a movement pattern expressing the symptoms.

Step onto the *Symptom* space.

Access the symptom (problem) experience.

Find within yourself a pattern of movement that somehow expresses that experience.

Step #4. Find a movement pattern expressing the cause.

Step into the *Cause* space.

Discover how the feeling and movement associated with the *Symptom* space can guide you to a sense of the *Cause* of the *Symptom*.

Find the movements that express the *Cause* state.

Step #5. Break state, the go to the Outcomes space, and find a movement pattern expressing the desired outcomes.

Break state and move to the meta-position.

Step into the *Outcome* space.

Create a fully associated experience of the solution state; the state that you desire.

Discover and express the movements that express this state.

Step #6. Find a movement pattern expressing the effects of the desired outcomes.

Step into the *Desired Effect* space.
Explore how it feels to fully experience the results of your desired outcome.

Spend enough time to deeply experience this.

Step #7. Moving through all spaces, discover a dance that integrates the movement from cause to effects.

a. Step into the *Cause* location and slowly walk through all four spaces.

b. Especially notice how your body can intuitively connect the Symptom and Outcome locations.

c. Repeat this complete walk several times until you feel that the dance is a single dance that carries you from the *Cause* space to the *Desired Effect* space.

Step #8. Discover a missing resource.

Move out into a meta-position, and explore what feels like your dance is missing.

See if there is a sense of a missing resource that this feeling can bring your attention to.

Step #9. Find a movement for the missing resource and integrate it into your movement expression.

Go through your spaces, finding a movement expression of that missing resource, and add it to your dance. with this new dance.

Find a movement expression of that missing resource, and adding it to your dance.

Step #10. Repeat this to fully integrate the movement expression.

Repeat the movement through the spaces until it feels like a fully integrated personal movement expression.

Step #11. Test.

In the coming days, notice if new solutions occur to you, or if you spontaneously act them out in some way.

As you encounter challenging situations, explore how your way of being physically can express more of your resources in some way through body language or how you move your own internal sense of energy and emotion.

❧

154.

Advantageous NLP Beliefs

"If you hit every time, the target is either too big or too near".

— Tom Hirshfield

THE NLP presuppositions (or core beliefs) are the most important guidelines for learning and doing NLP, and for being successful in life. Some people have published are larger number than we have here, some have published less.

We feel that this list below is the best, most useful collection.

The word presupposition means something that you may not be able to prove, but that you base your behavior on. As a thinking person, you can see if there are exceptions to these rules, or situations where they don't apply.

Overview of NLP presuppositions:

1. The 'map' is not the 'territory'.

2. People respond according to their internal maps.

3. Meaning operates context-dependently.

4. Mind-and-body affect each other.

5. Individual skills function by developing and sequencing of rep systems.

6. We respect each person's model of the world.

7. Person and behavior describe different phenomena. We "are" more than our behavior.

8. Every behavior has utility and usefulness—in some context.

9. We evaluate behavior & change in terms of context and ecology.

10. We cannot not communicate.

11. The way we communicate affects perception & reception.

12. The meaning of communication lies in the response you get.

13. The one who sets the frame for the communication controls the action.

14. "There is no failure, only feedback."

15. The person with the most flexibility exercises the most influence in the system.

16. Resistance indicates the lack of rapport.

17. People have the internal resources they need to succeed.

18. Humans have the ability to experience one-trial learning.

19. All communication should increase choice.

20. People make the best choices open to them when they act.

21. As response-able persons, we can run our own brain and control our results.

1. The 'map' is not the 'territory'.

We base our actions on our mental map of the world. If you understand this, you understand that there are always ways to improve your map. People who are stuck in life don't know this. They get angry or passive when you talk about improving their view of the world.

Can you see how knowing that the map is not the territory can make you more flexible and adaptable? As in evolution, flexibility and adaptability are powerful traits for survival and satisfaction.

2. People respond according to their internal maps.

If you don't understand someone, you don't understand their mental map. You may understand what they should do, but you can only understand their internal map by learning about it. Can you imagine what kind of connection you will be able to make with people, and how much better you will react to people when you have all the curiosity and tools that come from this point of view?

3. Meaning operates context-dependently.

If you really want to understand what something means to someone, you have to understand the situation, that is, the context.

Context has many sides to it. You must understand a politician's motives to understand the real meaning of their speech. You must understand what a person has gone through in order to understand why they are reacting strongly to someone they hardly know.

If someone in an artist commune says they love you, it may mean something different than an "I love you" from your aunt. Think of the ways you can expand your view of the world and your understanding of human behavior by delving into context.

4. Mind-and-body affect each other.

We are not brains in jars, like in some science fiction movie. We don't just think with our brains, we think with our bodies. Science is revealing more about this all the time.

Successful leaders, sales people and others intuitively understand this. *Can you think of some ways you can use this knowledge to your advantage?* Some of the basic applications of this are the value of eating the right food, and getting good physical exercise. These have a great impact on your mind.

If you are trying to have a talk with an uncooperative teenager, see how they act if you take a walk with them. More advanced use of this know-how lies in fields such as body mind, or somatic, psychotherapy, participatory learning methods, and the use of evolutionary psychology in marketing, where primitive drives and instincts are brought into play.

5. Individual skills function by developing and sequencing of rep systems.

You have already gotten a taste of this powerful knowledge. The submodality techniques we tried are used to create many kinds of behavior change and success. Imagine what your life would be like if you applied one or more tools from a rich toolbox full of such methods every day. What experts or successful person would you most like to model using this insight?

6. We respect each person's model of the world.

You may not agree with everyone, but if you respect their model of the world, you can understand it and find ways to create more understanding, less conflict, and more good outcomes. Think of some of the people that you have reacted to too quickly or too harshly. People that you judged. Some of those situations caused you to lose opportunities.

Imagine what genuine interest and concern for people's models of the world can do for you in a world that is very diverse, political, and charged with sensitive issues? You can become a great navigator, and fare better than many people who are quite smart, but fail to understand this wisdom.

7. Person and behavior describe different phenomena. We "are" more than our behavior.

The idea that we are more than our behavior is a very profound idea. You could write many volumes about this from your own life once you unlock this insight. Let's just look at how deeply people are able to change, and why they change. Most people are on the verge of a very expanded way of being in the world, and don't even know it. We have no idea what any person's true potential or destiny are.

Whenever someone tells someone that they will not amount to anything, that person is failing to understand the truth of this proposition; the truth that we are more than our behavior.

In many places, a pattern of behavior or even a single act can define you. The idea of a human birth right, or inalienable rights that many constitutional governments are charged with supporting, is really a profound philosophical position that NLP expresses as well.

Whatever you have done wrong, learn from it, don't let it define you. Whatever your limitations are, get clear on how to move forward in harmony with your abilities and limits, don't just use will power to try harder, or sentence yourself to a life of shame.

You are bigger than that, whether you know it or not. Imagine the talent and energy that can be liberated in the world as this idea becomes better understood and more widely expressed.

8. Every behavior has utility and usefulness— in some context.

This idea can be very counter-intuitive. There are many behaviors that seem to make no sense, and are simply irritating and inconvenient at best, or criminal and threatening at worst. Milton Erickson, the famous psychiatrist and hypnotherapist that NLP has studied was a great model for this wisdom. He did something called utilization.

Often it involved finding the hidden power or motivation within the behavior that was the most easy to try to stop or ignore.

Do you know someone who does something that troubles you or otherwise seems to be a problem? Think about ways that the behavior might be used to support some kind of change, or how it may reveal motivations that you could somehow connect with a more effective behavior.

You can even take this approach with yourself. What kind of potentials might you release by having an attitude like that about yourself?

9. We evaluate behavior & change in terms of context and ecology.

NLP has been influenced by a very important approach called systems theory. The basic idea of systems theory is that we must consider how the parts of the world interact with each other.

When you make a change in one part, how does this cause a domino effect.

Systems theory applies to the human body, to families, organizations, ecology, nations, and the world. We could never do justice to systems theory in this course, but we will share this with you.

Consider the systems impact or, as we say, the ecological impact of any change you consider, or of any behavior you want to understand. It is an added dimension to behavior that gives you a larger and more interesting world, and gives you much more power for making change. It can also help to protect you from unexpected reactions from a system.

10. We cannot not communicate.

So true! Your clothes, your accent, your body language, subtle expressions that flit across your face, all communicate, all signal things to the people around you. We all size each other up all the time.

If someone tells you never to judge people, perhaps they mean not to limit that person or to be harsh, but you can't stop interpreting other's behavior and signals.

You do this from the most primitive parts of your brain that have radar for danger, to your more sophisticated abilities to determine who can offer the best relationships to you.

This is an important reason for NLP to exist. The more you can align your subconscious and conscious motives, the more your subtle behaviors will communicate the right message. One of the biggest ingredients for charisma is this alignment, or coherence.

11. The way we communicate affects perception & reception.

You don't just communicate a digital message. You send out your own collection of submodalities that affect how you are perceived, and even others' ability to perceive you accurately.

If you use conservative language to express liberal ideas or vice versa, peoples' filters will screen out the content of your message and just hear that you are conservative or liberal, unless they are very analytical types, and those are in the minority.

Even the analytical types will probably feel uncomfortable with you, despite hearing what you were actually saying. The will only be comfortable if they are in on the joke. As a communicator, part of your job is to know about your listeners filters.

What are the keys that will open their minds to what you have to say? The valuable lessons of NLP on creating rapport are a great contribution to this quest.

12. The meaning of communication lies in the response you get.

This is one of the most fundamental and early lessons to get from your study of NLP. Regardless of what you intended to say, the communication is what the other person heard. By carefully observing the other person's response, you can determine whether you have communicated effectively.

People who fail to take responsibility for this fail to communicate effectively. You could say that they don't care if they are broadcasting on the wrong station and nobody is hearing them.

Of course, you will not be able to do this if the person is purposely misunderstanding you. That is a tactic that some people use when they want to cast doubt on what you are saying or manipulate you.

But as a sensitive communicator, you will learn to tell the difference, and develop creative responses to that kind of thing. NLP is a wonderful art to help you deal with manipulative people.

13. The one who sets the frame for the communication controls the action.

Like our brains, communication doesn't exist in a vacuum. You can exert much more influence when you understand the frame around a communication. The frame consists of things like the assumptions about why the discussion is taking place, what the environment means about it, that sort of thing.

The presuppositions were covering here set the stage for NLP. Every communication comes in a package of presuppositions. Presuppositions can be constructive when they provide positive guidance. But they can cause harm, as they do when they serve to filter and bias propaganda. Instead of being a sitting duck, you can be proactive.

Before an important discussion, ask yourself what the frame will be if you do nothing. Consider how it may support or defeat your objectives. Then think about how that frame might be improved.

14. "There is no failure, only feedback."

This is a philosophy, not a scientific fact. As a philosophy, it is something you can live. If you turn your failures into learning experiences, you gain so many benefits, we can't list them all here.

But consider these: Instead of losing sleep and feeling ashamed, you will be inspired and focused; you will build confidence as you learn from your experiences. Instead of procrastinating and getting caught up in trivial matters, you will act on what is truly important to you.

Why? Because you will not fear failure. When postponing your destiny becomes more uncomfortable than the risks you take in pursuing success, then you are ready to live this philosophy.

15. The person with the most flexibility exercises the most influence in the system.

We have all seen the way inflexible people can only function in a certain culture or lifestyle. Take them out of their element, and they cannot adapt. Well, life is about change.

That means that you will need flexibility in order to adapt to change. Since you can depend on change, you must depend on your adaptive creativity. NLP stresses the importance of meta level thinking.

That is, looking at the situation from a higher level; not being caught up in the obvious. From a meta level, you can see how things are changing, and you can free yourself from rigid roles and seize upon opportunities that are invisible to everyone else.

A good place to start is to as yourself who you think you are; maybe in terms of your career. Then ask how that self-definition may be limiting your. As yourself how your world or your career field is changing and creating opportunities that adaptable people can benefit from.

16. Resistance indicates the lack of rapport.

This is especially important for sales people, consultants, coaches and psychotherapists. If your customer is resisting doing what is best, don't get mad, get rapport. As soon as you start seeing the person as resistant, you have locked onto your agenda and become inflexible.

Remember what we just said about flexibility. This is a perfect example. Not only do you want to use the NLP rapport-building skills in general, but in situations with resistance, you need to better understand their motives, their values, and their ecology.

Resistance often comes because the change you want to see would conflict with something you don't even know about.

This is why sales people qualify their customers. Part of qualifying a customer is to ask them how a product or service would or would not work in their lives. Often, people are resisting what they THINK you are trying to do, rather than what you ARE trying to do. This takes us back to the importance of framing.

If someone is quick to misjudge you, this is part of the frame. Once critical way to prevent or cure this kind of bad frame is rapport. Erase resistance from your vocabulary and focus on what is driving the person and on gaining rapport with them.

17. People have the internal resources they need to succeed.

This belief generates excellence, because when you believe in people's internal resources, you believe in your clients and your respect your competitors. This is a very powerful position.

With clients, one will dig deeper to find the creativity and doggedness that they need in order to become a master consultant or coach. With yourself, you will never give up. If you do not succeed, you will not collapse into failure, you will call upon your creativity.

This kind of creativity is the force that brings out your hidden resources. One of the greatest things about NLP is that is can help you surprise yourself in wonderful way.

18. Humans have the ability to experience one-trial learning.

You have seen people fail to learn the same life lesson over and over again. Perhaps you've seen them date or marry the wrong person time and again. People do this because they have not liberated the kind of insight and creativity that the NLP presuppositions encourage.

Living with a meta level view, living in a truly awake state, and living with inspiring objectives before you give you too much momentum to fall into the same hole over and over again.

Ask yourself about a negative life experience that you have had more than once. With that in mind, review the NLP presuppositions and I guarantee you, you will find several that can come to your aid. Failure is extinct when you liberate your learning potential.

19. All communication should increase choice.

When you pay attention to the frame of communication, and when you develop the learning and flexibility that NLP teaches, you become a master communicator. You develop the ability to expand choices. Hidden frames limit choices. Rigidity limits choices.

Failing to see people's inner resources limit choices. All of the presuppositions in some way expand choice-fulness. By infusing your communication with the lessons of NLP, you can expand your own and others' choices. Listen carefully to the next conversation you overhear.

There are probably various ways that one or both parties are limiting their choices. Ask yourself –

What you detect in that conversation that limits choice?

How can you do a conversation like that differently?

How can you knock down barriers to choice when you communicate?

20. People make the best choices open to them when they act.

Never take for granted that other people know what you know. They may have all the options that you have, but they don't know it. People make bad choices and limit themselves because they have not connected to the inner resources that will liberate them.

This applies to people who end up in jail, in dead-end careers, and in endless arguments. Don't get mad at them, especially if you are a supervisor or coach. Often, very simple and direct instruction and training is all that is needed. Other times, the person needs to get involved in something more psychological, like working with a successful NLP practitioner.

21. As response-able persons, we can run our own brain and control our results.

This is the most fundamental discovery that people make as they become truly conscious. Waking up to this choice gives you an entirely different fate. You have heard people who sound like juvenile delinquents. When they do something wrong, they always have someone to blame. When they are held accountable, everyone is being unfair to them.

Well, even mature adults fall into this thinking at times, as they do when they say that someone has made them feel a certain way. If you have learned to run your own brain, you have better things to do than complain about how someone made you feel.

You take that situation as a call to expand your choices; a call to experience a creative, confident, resourceful state when you are dealing with that person and their attitude; a call to know what your objectives really are in that situation.

You need to know what a truly great outcome would be, so that you can bring it about. That is about controlling your results. You may not have a magic wand, but you have something close to a magic wand when you are very clear about your ideal outcomes. People who lack this are rudderless ships, spending too much time complaining about their bad results and bad feelings.

No one needs to live like that. And you are learning many tools and perspectives that can take you light years beyond that existence, and into a far more successful way of being.

☙❧

155.

The D.V.P Pattern

"Some minds remain open long enough for the truth not only to enter but to pass on through by way of a ready exit without pausing anywhere along the route".

— Elizabeth Kenny

CREDITS FOR THE creation of this NLP pattern belong to Robert A. Yourell.

D.V.P stands for *Distillation* Plus *Vision* Plus *Passion*. This process allows you to take a cloud of reactions and ideas, and turn them into very tight talking points, like the ones politicians and sales people have, in order to communicate in a compelling way.

This is an excellent way to prepare for a situation in which you feel that you have too much to try to say to a manipulative person, or to many emotions to manage for clearer communication.

549

Overview: The D.V.P Pattern

Step #1. Select the situation, and fully express your thoughts about it.

Step #2. Repeat the thoughts with better organization and priority.

Step #3. Distill the thoughts by leaving out unnecessary detail.

Step #4. Distill the thoughts further.

Step #5. Continue distilling until you end up with a slogan.

Step #6. Practice improvising off of your talking points.

Step #7. Continue, but with more of a challenge.

Step #8. Add vision and passion.

Step #9. Have more practice sessions on this material in the coming days.

Step #10. Test.

Step #1. Select the situation, and fully express your thoughts about it.

Think of a situation such as those mentioned in the description of this pattern.

Run everything that you think about the situation through your mind, or write it down, or say it out loud by yourself or to a friend who can help you with the exercise.

Especially include those thoughts that you would like to communicate, whether or not you actually should.

Step #2. Repeat the thoughts with better organization and priority.

Do this again, but allow your thoughts, now that you have run them through your mind, to fall together in a more orderly fashion, with a better sense of your priorities.

Step #3. Distill the thoughts by leaving out unnecessary detail.

Do this again, but this time leave out any unnecessary details.

Step #4. Distill the thoughts further.

Do this again, but leave out more details that aren't absolutely necessary for you to say what is most important.

Step #5. Continue distilling until you end up with a slogan.

Keep doing this "distilling" process, until you have boiled it down to something that resembles an ad slogan, such as Apple's *"Think Different,"* or Dolly Madison's *"Nothing says lovin' like something in the oven."* It's okay to risk going to far, since you'll have no trouble beefing up the message with more details.

Step #6. Practice improvising off of your talking points.

Imagine the situation in which you will want to communicate your message.

At first, make it easy. After you are comfortable with this, try bringing out various aspects of your message, improvising off of the key points that you have boiled your message down to.

Remember to limit yourself to only the most important and compelling aspects.

Step #7. Continue, but with more of a challenge.

Imagine the person you need to communicate this to.

Have them try various manipulative gambits to throw you off. This is how they manipulate you and abuse their power, most likely.

Improvise from your key talking points, no matter what they say.

You probably know them, or people like them, well enough to imagine a good variety of distracting, intimidating, or simply irritating comments that they might make.

Step #8. Add vision and passion.

Get in touch with the positive vision and emotion that you have in connection with each talking point.

Really get in your mind the outcome and values behind the talking point, and how you really feel. You have positive emotions driving you to care enough to communicate about this.

Even if it was a negative situation and set of emotions such as being fed up with intimidation or other boundary crossings, you can work your way back to positive vision, such as respect for boundaries, human dignity, and productive relationships toward whatever your common goal is.

Be sure you are only connecting with the positive vision and the positive, inspiring emotions that flow from that connection.

Infuse your voice with this, and practice speaking from this emotional place.

Practice until it comes out in a smooth, compelling, grounded manner. If this is a challenge. It's good to sleep on it, since your subconscious will be working with this pattern in your sleep.

Step #9. Have more practice sessions on this material in the coming days.

Sleep will do wonders for this. After doing this pattern, your subconscious mind will be working to extend your intimacy with these talking points, and your ability to improvise in communicating from them.

Keep practicing in the coming days when you get a chance to fantasize, such as while doing dishes or driving.

Practice out loud now, because good muscle memory, and actually experiencing your own voice and vibration in this pattern builds your personal power and ability.

In between, listen to some of the great speeches by people who were good at putting compel-ling emotion and vision into their voices.

Step #10. Test.

As you take this skill into the real world, notice how people listen to you and respond to your vision, emotions and talking points.

Continue to use this pattern for other important communications. Any conflict or leadership situation is a good one for this pattern. Any sensitive communications with difficult people are good for practice.

Additional Advice

When you are practicing in your mind, you can show your subconscious mind that it can be confident.

For example, you can imagine the other person being just one in a crowd of a thousand listening to you up on a podium with a microphone. Then accept a *Nobel Peace Prize* after your speech.

When you hear ad slogans, think about how much work went into boiling down a rich message into it.

Notice how the commercials, and many nuances of the product and its presentation are aligned with this.

❧

156.

Belief Systems Dis-Integration

"There are two ways to slide easily through life: to believe every-thing or to doubt everything; both ways save us from thinking".

— Alfred Korzybski

CREDITS FOR THE creation of this NLP pattern belong to Robert Dilts.

Improve automatic reactions that come from multiple rep systems firing off a negative state. This pattern separates the parts of a negative synesthesia pattern so that it can be addressed.

Many problems come from this kind of reaction. Most people who lash out with hurtful words or violence discover that they are being controlled by impulses that cut across multiple rep systems. In this case, it is likely to include very strong non-verbal thoughts (auditory digital) that, when turned into words, become less powerful, as well as a hot rush of emotions (kinesthetic).

Overview: The Belief Systems Dis-Integration Pattern

Step #1. Select the situation and state.

Step #2. Clarify the verbal representation at the belief level.

Step #3. Identify all rep system material.

Step #4. Position the material according to eye accessing cues.

Step #5. Create a more effective response.

Step #6. Test

Step #1. Select the situation and state.

Pick a situation in which you have a rapid, automatic, negative reaction of some kind. The more irrational it is, the better.

Think of the most recent situation in which you rapidly experienced this negative state in a strong way.

Step #2. Clarify the verbal representation at the belief level.

Notice all the thoughts that you had immediately before, during, and after the incident.

Look for the thoughts that where most strongly related to the situation and your behavior.

Notice how they have a part in driving the behavior.

Look at the aspect of the thoughts that could best be described as beliefs. State them as beliefs. If you have trouble finding these beliefs, go to the next step and return here during the last step, and come back to this pattern a few times, as well.

Step #3. Identify all rep system material.

What happened in your mind during the incident? Notice what you saw, any visual representations your mind recalled or created, what you heard, any auditory material that you recalled or created, and what you felt, including any feelings that you recalled or created. Understand it fully.

Step #4. Position the material according to EAC.

Place each representation in its appropriate position in your field of awareness according to eye accessing cues.

Step #5. Create a more effective response.

Brainstorm until you have a more effective response. Imagine going through the situation again, but with the more effective response.

Notice anything that could make that response difficult, including any ecological issues and any rep system material that you have not positioned according to eye accessing cues.

Step #6. Test

As similar situations arise, notice how well you respond to them.

Repeat this exercise as needed to respond effectively to the situation.

157.

Criteria Installation

"Procrastination is the art of keeping up with yesterday".

— Don Marquis

CREDITS FOR THE creation of this NLP pattern belong to various contributors.

Clarify your values to bring more alignment to an area of your life that seems unclear. Resolve indecisiveness, procrastination, and waffling that stems from unclear or misaligned criteria.

Overview: The Criteria Installation Pattern

Step #1. Select a life area in which your values seem unclear.

Step #2. Create a hierarchy of criteria.

Step #3. Complete the continuum.

Step #4. Clarify the submodalities.

Step #5. Confirm the appropriate position and submodalities for each criterion.

Step #6. Review again, emphasizing the value and position of the criteria.

Step #7. Select the criterion to shift.

Step #8. Revise submodalities based on the final positions.

Step #9. Complete step #8.

Step #10. Future Pace.

Step #11. Test.

Step #1. Select a life area in which your values seem unclear.

Select a life area such as career, finances, or relationships, in which you feel that your decision-making or actions are not based on a firm foundation of values or criteria.

Step #2. Create a hierarchy of criteria.

a. Start by thinking of a trivial act that you could do but wouldn't bother to.

Ask what you would accomplish by refraining from this action.

Typically, you would save time. Be sure to state the criteria in positive terms.

b. Now ask what might get you to take this action anyway.

Note what you find important about this condition.

For example, if you said that you would stand on a chair because you needed to replace light bulb, you might feel that being able to see and function in your kitchen is more important than two minutes of time.

This pattern can be summarized so far as starting with a trivial act you would not do, citing the value that would prevent you from doing it, then stating the condition that would get you to do it.

At this point, you think of a condition that would reverse your stance.

c. Think of a condition that would stop you from doing it.

d. State the value that would apply.

For example, perhaps you would not replace the bulb if you had to meet an urgent deadline and didn't need to be in the kitchen for that.

The value might be the importance of maintaining your accounts, staying out of jail, or being on time for an appointment.

Try to summarize the value in one word, in addition to the brief statement of the value. For being on time, you might add, *"punctuality."*

e. Repeat this pattern.

Each time you state the criterion for your decision, come up with a condition that would get you to reverse your decision to do or not to do the action.

Then state the value behind that decision.

Step #3. Complete the continuum.

As you proceed, you are creating a continuum of criteria from least to most important.

Continue until you are certain you have identified the most important criteria of all. This will be one that you can't trump with any condition.

Step #4. Clarify the submodalities.

Explore the differences between the submodalities between the highest and lowest priority criteria.

Notice how you represent various values such as *"excellence,"* *"healing,"* and *"integrity."*

Pay attention to the analog submodalities that vary as you describe the criteria in all primary submodalities.

Step #5. Confirm the appropriate position and submodalities for each criterion.

For each criterion, decide whether you need raise or lower it, and where it should go on the scale.

Shift its submodalities to match those of the next lower criterion.

Code the criterion for the degree of importance it should have by adjusting the submodalities.

Step #6. Review again, emphasizing the value and position of the criteria.

From a meta-position, evaluate your hierarchy of values.

Ask how well these values serve you, and how well the function in their current sequence.

How well do they enable you to make resourceful decisions and experience peace of mind?

Note any criteria that you need to shift to another position, or change in any other way.

Step #7. Select the criterion to shift.

Determine which criterion you wish to shift. Determine where you want it to be.

Think about what sequence of values will move you ahead as you desire.

Step #8. Revise submodalities based on the final positions.

Gradually shift the criterion to the appropriate place on your continuum. Based on the importance that the criterion should have, apply the submodalities that you feel are appropriate.

Notice which submodalities appear in the criteria before and after it. Code it.

Step #9. Complete step #8.

Continue until you are satisfied that your value hierarchy will help guide you toward the most resourceful behaviors and decisions.

Step #10. Future Pace.

Imagine a situation in which your new criterion makes a differ-ence. Imagine yourself in that situation fully experiencing this.

Step #11. Test.

Notice over the coming days and weeks how accessible you find resourceful states for challenging situations.

☙❧

158.

Kinesthetic Criteria

"Don't fool yourself that important things can be put off till tomorrow; they can be put off forever, or not at all".

— Mignon McLaughlin, The Neurotic's Notebook

CREDITS FOR THE creation of this NLP pattern belong to various contributors. Start taking action by overcoming the criteria that get in the way.

Overview: The Kinesthetic Criteria Pattern

Step #1. Select a behavior that is desired but not taken.

Step #2. Identify the criteria for taking the desired action.

Step #3. Identify the criteria that stop the desired behavior.

Step #4. Generate higher-level criteria that support taking the desired action.

Step #5. Anchor the state.

Step #6. Imbue the lower levels with the positive state.

Step #7. Make an ecology check, adjusting as needed.

Step #8. Test.

Step #1. Select a behavior that is desired but not taken.

Identify a behavior the person says they want to do, but does not do for some reason.

Place it in location #1.

This can also be something they want to stop doing, such as smoking or biting nails or yelling at their kids.

Step #2. Identify the criteria for taking the desired action.

Have the person clarify the values and meta-outcomes behind their desire to take the action.

Ask why they want to take the action, and then, why that outcome itself is important to them. What you're looking for here is the 'toward' motivation. In this step they actually begin the change-work.

Place these in location #2.

Step #3. Identify the criteria that stop the desired behavior.

Solicit the criteria for not doing the behavior.

What stops them?

Identify the values and meta-outcomes that support NOT taking the desired action.

Put these in location #3.

Try to identify values that are at a higher level than those found in step #2. Remember that the hierarchy is set by the person you're working with, not by your own values hierarchy or logic.

We assume that such values or criteria exist, because they are overcoming the values that the person has for taking the desired action.

Step #4. Generate higher-level criteria that support taking the desired action.

Determine what higher-level criteria can override the criteria in location #3 in favor of taking the desired action.

For example, if position #3 values like relaxation are getting in the way of smoking cessation, ask what values are more important than that.

Come up with answers such as avoiding emphysema.

Step #5. Anchor the state.

Amplify the state associated with these overriding positive values and anchor it. You do not have to use a full anchoring procedure here; it is enough if you remind them of the state, ask them to enhance certain driver submodalities, and establish a kinesthetic anchor without explaining what an 'anchor' is.

Step #6. Imbue the lower levels with the positive state.

Hold the anchor and move into position #3 while in the state.

Continue in this state, moving to positions #2 and #1.

As the person walks through these positions have them come up with new, ideas for making sure that they take the desired action.

For each good idea, have them imagine carrying it out, and then adjust their submodalities to match those of the highest criterion from step #4.

Make every effort to ensure that the higher state is compelling as the person moves to these lower levels.

It is important to make these lower levels very rich with this positive state.

Step #7. Make an ecology check, adjusting as needed.

Check ecology as you future pace these creative ideas to see if you can make any additional adjustments.

Step #8. Test.

In the coming days and weeks, see how well this pattern has allowed the person to take the desired action.

⌒⌒

159.

The Spinning Icons Pattern

"My alphabet starts with this letter called yuzz. It's the letter I use to spell yuzz-a-ma-tuzz. You'll be sort of surprised what there is to be found once you go beyond 'Z' and start poking around!"

— Dr. Seuss

CREDITS for the creation of this NLP pattern belong to Nelson Zink and Joe Munshaw. Prevent or escape negative states. Solve problems and be creative. This pattern draws upon the power of imagery to create a valuable meta-state. This pattern has also been called "Synthesizing Generalizations."

Overview: The Spinning Icons Pattern

Step #1. Select a negative and positive state.

Step #2. Get a visual representation of the negative and positive states.

Step #3. Create a symbol for the negative state.

Step #4. Repeat for the positive state.

Step #5. Rotate the images around each other, accelerating to an extreme rate.

Step #6. Blend the images into one image.

Step #7. Tell a story.

Step #8. Test.

Step #1. Select a negative and positive state.

Identify two states.

One should be a state you are in, or sometimes find yourself in, that is not desirable. If this is your first time working with this pattern, choose a relatively "weak" state.

Once you get more comfortable work on the stronger, more disturbing, ones.

The other state should be a very desirable state that you might think of as an "antidote" to the negative state.

For example, you could take *"irritated easily when hearing a squeaky noise"* as the negative state, and its *"antidote"* state, *"hearing music in every seemingly inharmonic set of sounds".*

Step #2. Get a visual representation of the negative and positive states.

Access this negative state, and get a visual representation.

Notice where in your sensory field it exists, and explore its submodalities. Be certain to explore the driver submodalities in the major modalities, visual, kinesthetic and auditory. The driver submodalities will give you the most elegant path for the change-work to be successful.

Do the same for the positive state.

Step #3. Create a symbol for the negative state.

Have the person create an icon or symbol for the visual representations of the negative state.

You can ask the person to, *"Create a simple image that represents the negative state, such as a cartoon or icon."*

Step #4. Repeat for the positive state.

Do the same for the positive state.

Step #5. Rotate the images around each other, accelerating to an extreme rate.

Have the person begin to rotate the two icons around each other, as if they were two planets in each other's gravitational field.

The images will exchange locations and continue.

Have them gradually speed up until they reach an extreme speed.

Step #6. Blend the images into one image.

Have them allow the images to blend into a single image.

Ask the person to briefly describe the image. Do not get caught

THE BIG BOOK OF NLP TECHNIQUES

in too many details here, the idea is just to get the general feeling of the image in order to work with it elegantly.

Pace their description, but quickly move to the next step.

Step #7. Tell a story.

Begin telling a story.

Pick any story from your life or anywhere else that suits you. The purpose is to break state.

If you have additional skills such as those from Ericksonian language then use these advanced skills as appropriate.

Step #8. Test.

In the coming days and weeks, see how this process has make the positive state more accessible, and how well the pattern has reduced incidences of being in the negative state.

See whether the person has begun employing more creative ways of coping with situations that had been arousing the negative state, or more resourceful ways of preventing or getting out of the negative state.

Additional Advice

NLP, in general, is all about changing your state according to whatever is suitable and appropriate for the outcome at hand.

What I would advice you, especially at this point in the book, is to understand how this pattern works from a 3rd or 4th perceptual position. This is something that is extremely hard to explain in writing, and unfortunately many Neuro Linguistic Programming training programs are designed to certificate people, not to really train them in this art. Feel free to contact me for a recommendation on high quality NLP training programs. No, I'm not selling them, I had been in enough of those to learn to differentiate the good ones from the money-oriented ones.

☯

160.

Basic Belief Chaining

nown many troubles, but most of them have never happened"

— Mark Twain

S HIFT A BELIEF from an unresourceful one to a resourceful one.

Overview: The Basic Belief Chaining Pattern

Step #1. Get the somatic syntax.

Step #2. Use verbal reframes to assist with the shift.

Step #3. Attach reframes to each step.

Step #4. Practice the shift.

Step #5. Test.

Step #1. Get the somatic syntax.

a. Select a limiting belief and a resourceful alternative belief.

b. Identify steps between the two extremes of belief.

c. Walk through each of the steps from the limiting belief state to the resourceful belief state. Pay attention to the changes in kinesthetic sensations and body language that you experience from step to step.

Step #2. Use verbal reframes to assist with the shift.

Try several verbal reframes that help make the shift between these beliefs.

Notice which ones have the most positive impact in giving you a constructive and resourceful perspective.

Step #3. Attach reframes to each step.

Walk through the belief change steps, and decide which reframe is most useful at each step.

Step #4. Practice the shift.

Walk through the steps several times, experiencing the kinesthetics and belie frame that you have associated with each step.

Continue until you feel that the transition is easy and smooth.

Step #5. Test.

Over the coming days and weeks, notice any increased ease you experience in flexible thinking, and any increase in your use of positive frames and resourcefulness in your beliefs about any challenges that you experience.

☙❧

161.

Advanced Belief Chaining

nown many troubles, but most of them have never happened"

— Mark Twain

ARRY OUT THE Belief Chaining Pattern with a Guide and in a more advanced form.

Overview: The Advanced Belief Chaining Pattern

Step #1. Create four steps.

Step #2. Express the limiting belief from position one.

Step #3. Access a positive, resourceful and wise state from step location four.

Step #4. Return to location one.

Step #5. The Guide helps the Explorer experience position two.

Step #6. The Guide helps the Explorer experience position three.

Step #7. The Guide helps the Explorer experience position four.

Step #8. The Explorer shares what was learned.

Step #9. Test

Step #1. Create four steps.

Choose a location for each of the following steps:

1. Negative/unresourceful belief.

2. Somewhat negative/ unresourceful belief.

3. Somewhat positive negative/ unresourceful belief.

4. Positive/resourceful belief.

Step #2. Express the limiting belief from position one.

a. Both Explorer and Guide stand in the first step location, "negative/unresourceful belief."

b. The Explorer expresses the negative belief.

For example, *"I can't spend time with my family, because I always replay old behaviors that are really disturbing. I can't cope with them."*

c. The Guide goes to the second perceptual position, and identifies the positive intentions or presuppositions behind the belief.

For example, *"I value my emotional stability and the productivity that results from that. I value the people in my life who contribute in constructive ways to my development."*

Step #3. Access a positive, resourceful and wise state from step location four.

Explorer and Guide step into position four, "positive/resourceful belief" and, without attempting to create the positive belief, access a positive, resourceful and wise state.

Step #4. Return to location one.

Explorer and Guide return to location one, "Negative/ unresourceful belief."

Step #5. The Guide helps the Explorer experience position two.

a. The Guide steps to area two, "somewhat negative / unresourceful belief" and uses the positive presuppositions or intentions that were identified in order to produce a less negative belief. The belief must reflect the positive intentions or presuppositions.

For example, *"You are preventing contact with toxic people in order to avoid negative emotional states."*

Notice how this statement moves from "I can't" to an intention (*"You are preventing..."*), and from fate (*"I always..."*) to an active role, (*"In order to avoid..."*)

The frame is negative ("toxic people" and "negative emotional states") but is less negative than the original belief because it brings in intention and action, that is, an internal locus of control and a sense of a meaningful identity and need.

b. The Guide invites the Explorer to step into area two and experience this belief.

c. If the Explorer feels that the belief needs more work, then the Guide reworks the belief and tries again.

For example, the positive presupposition may need to be adjusted to more accurately reflect the motives of the Explorer. The Guide can step into area four to reinforce the positive state in order to be more effective.

Step #6. The Guide helps the Explorer experience position three.

a. The Guide steps into position three, "somewhat positive/resourceful belief" and creates a belief that crosses into being positive, and is based on the positive intentions and presuppositions of the Explorer.

For example, *"You are independently using the resources you have gained, including those from your family, to establish and maintain your boundaries in service of your emotional well being."*

b. The Guide invites the Explorer into the position to try out this belief.

c. If the belief needs improvement, the Explorer asks the Guide to rework it.

Step #7. The Guide helps the Explorer experience position four.

a. The Guide steps into position four, "positive/resourceful belief" and creates a positive belief that is based on the positive intentions and presuppositions of the Explorer.

For example, *"As your skill in using the resources you have gained, including those from your family, increases, you will expand the range of people that you can experience while fully benefiting from your boundaries and increasingly buoyant emotional well being."*

b. The Guide invites the Explorer into the position to try out this belief.

c. If the belief needs improvement, the Explorer asks the Guide to rework it.

Step #8. The Explorer shares what was learned.

The Explorer shares with the guide what lessons came from this experience.

Step #9. Test

Over the coming days and weeks, notice notice any increased ease you experience in flexible thinking, and any increase in your use of positive frames and resourcefulness in your beliefs about any challenges that you experience.

෴

162.

Gentling

"The mind that is wise mourns less for what age takes away; than what it leaves behind".

— William Wordsworth

CREDITS FOR THE creation of this NLP pattern belong to Robert Dilts.

Build your inner "good parent" experience by bringing your adult wisdom into your timeline.

Overview: The Gentling Pattern

Step #1. Imagine the three timelines.

Step #2. Create your resources.

Step #3. Give them to your grandparent.

Step #4. Experience this from the grandparent's position.

Step #5. Give them to your parent as the grandparent.

Step #6. Experience this from the parent's position.

Step #7. Give them to yourself as the parent.

Step #8. Experience this from your position as a baby.

Step #9. Return to the present with these gifts.

Step #10. Test.

Step #1. Imagine the three timelines.

Imagine three timelines.

One for yourself.

One for your parent (any of them).

One your grandparent.

Step #2. Create your resources.

Move to the third perceptual position, holding your awareness of your family system from a spiritual perspective and as part of a larger whole.

Think of resources or gifts that would benefit the family in the form of a blessing, metaphor and vision. It does not have to be the most amazing poem, but just a real statement of what you believe is the emotion that is missing the most.

Step #3. Give them to your grandparent.

Imagine that, borne on wisdom and gratitude from the future into the present, you can float back over your timeline to your grandparent's birth and early childhood.

Imagine holding and touching your grandparent as an infant, with the ethereal gentleness of a higher presence.

Offer your blessing and metaphor.

Step #4. Experience this from the grandparent's position.

Bringing your vision, move to second position, perceiving as your grandparent, and see yourself giving the vision to you as grandparent.

Imagine experiencing this gentle holding and nurturance.

Imagine receiving the blessing and metaphor.

Step #5. Give them to your parent as the grandparent.

Holding these resources and gifts in your heart as the grandparent, move up along the time line to the birth and infancy of your parent (your grandparent's child).

In your grandparent's position, gentle your parent passing on the blessing, metaphor and vision.

Use perceptual position #2 to make this transition as smooth and natural as possible.

Step #6. Experience this from the parent's position.

Associate into the perceptual position of your parent.

Imagine being held blessed and gentled, and receiving the metaphor and vision.

Step #7. Give them to yourself as the parent.

Hold these resources in your heart.

Now begin to float forward through your parent's timeline through your own birth and infancy.

From your parent's perceptual position, bless and gentle yourself, passing on the metaphor and vision.

Step #8. Experience this from your position as a baby.

Move back into your own perceptual position, but as a baby.

Imagine being held, blessed and gentled by your parent, receiving the metaphor and vision, and being held gently.

Step #9. Return to the present with these gifts.

As you continue ahead in your timeline, your timeline re-calibrates to these resources as you carry them through it.

The blessing, metaphor, vision, and nurturance create new memories and qualities to your timeline.

As you enter the present, you continue to have these gifts, knowing that they were passed down to you through countless generations.

Step #10. Test.

In the coming days and weeks, watch for signs that you are benefiting from these gifts.

☙❧

163.

Meta Transformation

"Not many people are willing to give failure a second opportunity. They fail once and it is all over. The bitter pill of failure is often more than most people can handle. If you are willing to accept failure and learn from it, if you are willing to consider failure as a blessing in disguise and bounce back, you have got the essential of harnessing one of the most powerful success forces".

— Joseph Sugarman

CREATE personality-wide changes by taking transformation to a meta level.

Overview: The Meta Transformation Pattern

Step #1. Select a behavior for transformation.

Step #2. Identify underlying intentions.

Step #3. Identify related outcomes.

Step #4. Identify meta-outcomes in the form of high states.

Step #5. Describe your ultimate transcendent meta-state.

Step #6. Step into your transcendent meta-state.

Step #7. Fully experience your meta-state.

Step #8. Experience this as a way of being in the world.

Step #9. Test.

Steps 1-4: Stepping Up.

Step #1. Select a behavior for transformation.

Choose a behavior for this pattern that you wish to change; one that is unpleasant or ineffective.

Step #2. Identify underlying intentions.

Determine what motives help to maintain this behavior.

Remember that these can be the motives of a part that has positive intentions, but that makes ineffective or unresourceful choices in pursuing those intentions.

Keep an eye out for results that have some indirect benefit, even though they are the less obvious outcomes of the behavior pattern (secondary gain).

Step #3. Identify related outcomes.

Repeat the following question until your answers begin to loop: *"What do you hope to accomplish, experience or have as a result of this behavior."*

Then begin asking, *"What do you want from this result, that is even more important to you?"* until you begin to loop.

Step #4. Identify meta-outcomes in the form of high states.

You are seeking meta-outcomes. You will know that you have identified them when the answers to these questions are states.

When you begin looping among high states, you have completed this part of the pattern.

Steps 5-9: Stepping Down

Step #5. Describe your ultimate transcendent meta-state.

Describe the state you would experience if you achieved all of the higher states stemming from your meta-outcomes.

Use all sense modalities, including self-talk.

Step #6.

Step into your transcendent meta-state.

Amplify the state as much as possible, and imagine stepping into this state as if you could step into the future where you have achieved your meta-outcomes.

Step #7. Fully experience your meta-state.

Continue to amplify your meta-state, experiencing it fully, as if you could absorb it into your body as pervasive energy.

Step #8. Experience this as a way of being in the world.

Return to your immediate life situation and future pace into your immediate future, with this meta-state pervading all that you are and do.

Experience how you express it in all your activities and way of being.

Step #9. Test.

In the coming days and weeks, discover how this experience alters how you experience your life, and how your behavior changes in the area of your life that had the undesired behavior pattern.

☙❧

164.

Re-Imprinting

"Learning doesn't work by osmosis"

— the author's university professor

UPGRADE YOUR deeper beliefs and your behaviors by changing the influence of role models. Improve the effect of negative role models, and create a stronger influence from positive role models. This pattern is called re-imprinting because many problems, including physical symptoms, learning disabilities, phobias and other problems are caused by influences that are active during key periods in our development (developmental windows).

This concept should not be used to deny genetic, toxic and other influences that form a direct biological basis for many such problems.

Step #1.

a. Choose the behaviors, symptoms or beliefs you wish to change. Unless you are a beginner, choose behaviors or beliefs that seem to be deeply ingrained.

b. Float up over your timeline and look toward the future.

c. Pay attention to the physical expression of your target as well as in the form of beliefs.

d. Walk backward slowly. Pause at each location that is relevant somehow to the target.

e. Continue back until you reach the earliest experience of the target (the initial imprint experience).

f. Access the state associated with this target and the experiences.

g. From that state, verbally express the beliefs that came from these experiences. h. Speak in first person, for example, "I do not deserve protection and compassion."

577

i. Move back in time to a point just before this first experience (the initial imprint experience).

j. Notice how this changes your state. You know that you have gone back far enough when you are in a very different state; one that has no sign of the imprint experiences or the beliefs that stem from them.

Step #2.

a. Float forward to the actual present, but stay in the observer (dissociated) position.

b. Looking back over your past timeline, notice how your imprinting experiences have affected your life; how they have helped generate the behaviors, symptoms or beliefs that you chose for this pattern, and any others that you can discover.

c. Talk to yourself, as if you were narrating a documentary about yourself, speaking in third person (he/she). Describe what you were just observing about your life.

d. Think about all this with positive intentions or secondary gain in mind. How have the behaviors, symptoms or beliefs that emerged from these experienced reflected an attempt, on some level, to cope with them.

Even if the results were bad, seek the underlying positive intention or presuppositions. You may get your best results by looking for subtle feelings connected with these things, and then putting words to those feelings.

If you discover that an irrational attitude has been strongly affecting your life, then you have found something especially important.

Remember that these attitudes can range from simple to complex.

They may show up in simple reactive measures such as avoiding responsibility or other fear-inducing experiences (because, for example, of an experience that lead you to believe that you would be harshly criticized any time you tried to do something).

On the other hand, they may manifest as more complicated ways of managing (or manipulating, more likely) other people in service of an agenda such as denial.

For example, *"I must carefully orchestrate interactions so that I am not exposed to any beliefs or ideas that would frame my pot consumption as a problem; my loss of motivation and mental clarity are not to be connected with that."*

Step #3.

a. Focus on any people that figured largely in these imprint experiences. Although we're talking about *"imprinting,"* your experiences may or may not actually involve other people in a significant way.

Pay special attention to any ways that you *"absorbed"* (modeled) another persons style or attitudes, so that you came to cope with certain situations in a characteristic, dysfunctional way.

b. For each person, associate into their perspective (the second perceptual position), and experience one or two of the most significant imprint experiences that they were involved in from their perspective.

Describe the experiences in their terms, using first person (I, me, my) language in their style as much as possible.

c. Step off of the timeline, into an objective position (third perceptual position), and determine the positive intentions behind their behavior.

Step #4.

Do the following for each person involved in your imprint experiences, if any:

a. Decide what resources that the person needed at those times, but did not have, but that you can contribute now in some way now.

b. Find a location on your timeline where you have had a very significant experience of being rich with these resources. (For example, a person dealing with drug use might recall being in a twelve step meeting that was very compelling and resulted in a period of drug avoidance and better functioning).

c. Step into that point on your timeline.

d. Amplify this rich state, and experience it as a kind of energy.

e. Anchor the state.

f. Imagine that you can transmit this resource back through your timeline to each person who needs it.

g. When you feel that you have made a good connection, float back to the imprint experience, and associate into the position of the person that received the resource.

h. Re-experience the imprint experience from their perspective, but with the resources actively in place. You can amplify the resource state in them by triggering the resource state.

i. Staying in this point on your timeline, move into your own perceptual position.

j. Notice how this experience has changed with the resources in place.

k. Experience how this upgraded experience stimulates beliefs and attitudes in you that are more resourceful.

l. Express this verbally in first person.

m. Do the previous two actions for each person that you identified as being significant in the imprinting experiences.

Step #5.

a. Move back to your present time, into an objective position.

b. Look back over the imprint experiences, and (as you did for the significant people), identify what resources would have been valuable to you during the imprint experiences.

c. Experience these resources and access the state that they inspire.

d. Anchor this state when it peaks.

e. With these resources, and in this state, float back to a point prior to your early imprint experience.

f. Transmit or give these resources to your younger self at that timeline point.

g. Imagine walking along your timeline from that point toward the present, and experiencing all the changes made by all the changes (re-imprinting) from this pattern.

Step #6. Test

In the coming days and weeks, notice any ways that this re-imprinting pattern has influenced the behaviors, symptoms or beliefs that you chose for this pattern.

Modeling Excellence With NLP

"Excellence is an art won by training and habituation. We do not act rightly because we have virtue or excellence, but we rather have those because we have acted rightly. We are what we repeatedly do. Excellence, then, is not an act but a habit."

— Aristotle

THIS is a short Overview of a few concepts in the area of NLP modeling. Once you decide you want to learn how to effectively model a skill get a hold of the book "Modeling Excellence With NLP – The Ultimate Guide".

In that book you will have step by step instructions with thorough examples, helpful assessment forms and needed documents to make your modeling project a successful one.

❧

Introduction To NLP Modeling

MODELING IS AN essential part of NLP. It is one of the seeds that gave birth to everything that now makes NLP what it is. The originators of NLP wanted to understand and teach excellence. Fields such as linguistics, psychology, and cybernetics helped them analyze highly effective people. Much of the early progress in NLP was breakthrough ideas on HOW to analyze the behavior, seeing things that were not even seen be the very people that they were studying.

A key to how NLP creates models for excellence is to recall an interesting definition of NLP, that it is "the study of the structure of subjectivity." This means that in brings together neurology, language, and programming as three key components of experience. Bandler had a great gift for modeling.

One of the key methods for modeling is to attempt to emulate the person you are modeling, but without any theories as to why they are successful. This causes you to perceive what you would have filtered out if you had gotten attached to a particular theory. Since you have experience in creating states, you will see that these masters create states within themselves to affect other people's states. Of course, you would expect them to generate states within themselves to harness their own creativity and skills, but masters understand, at least on an intuitive or subconscious level, that their state can help to influence the state and the behaviors of other people. This is a huge part of the power of people with interpersonal mastery, such as master psychotherapists.

We haven't delved into language patterns very much yet, and we certainly will. Language patterns can have a tremendous impact on people. Masters apply language patterns to themselves, and they also apply them to others in many ways.

You remember how important breaking state can be to an NLP pattern. There are language patterns to do that and much more, without the client having to necessarily understand and cooperate. This ability to move forward in a way that does not require conscious understanding and conscious cooperation is a great source of speed, efficiency, and power in NLP. If this sounds like it's just manipulation, consider these two things.

If a doctor gives you an antibiotic for an infection, do you have to consciously understand how it works to kill the infection, exactly what order it will go through the blood vessels, and how you will metabolize the end products of all this?

Do you have to consciously know how to beat your heart in order to maintain your circulation in order for the antibiotic to work? Of course not, your body and the drug take care of this for you.

People who sincerely want to succeed will universally approve of a method that works, even if they don't understand it every step along the way. The subconscious is much too powerful a resource

to neglect. What makes this even more efficient and powerful is that you are training your subconscious to use these skills on you and those you work with. The more you enjoy practicing these skills, the more you will gain momentum and abilities from your own deep well of creativity and intelligence.

This makes room for your conscious mind to concentrate on learning new things, and to have a reserve of conscious processing power so you can create new solutions for new challenges.

Did you notice that we just talked about neurology, or states, and linguistics, or language patterns?

As you know NLP stands for neuro-linguistic-programming. So the part that remains is programming. NLP studies how masters use neurology and language in order to create new, durable patterns in themselves and others. That is programming. It does not turn people into robots, it gives them new, successful choices that are available to them in a way that they can trigger.

A well-programmed behavior does not require a lot of will power or thought to act on, it is more like expressing yourself or singing a song that you already know very well. But, since NLP understand the magic of states and language patterns, these skills are much more powerful than mere steps in a manual.

If NLP had a slogan, it might be, "You CAN get there from here."

Speaking of powerful skills, one of the highly effective people that Bandler and Grinder studied was a famous therapist named Virginia Satir. When they told her what they felt were the active ingredients of her approach, she found it difficult to believe. In fact, it was kind of disturbing to her, because it seemed to take the humanity out of what she was doing.

She did not want to think of her self as applying technical skills that were effective on their own. But then, scientific exploration does not always flatter us. For example, there is a good body of research showing that experience does not increase the effectiveness of psychotherapists nearly as much as one might think. Certainly not as much as highly experienced therapists would like to think.

In order to test this, Satir attempted to model therapy without using the ingredients that Bandler and Grinder had brought to her attention.

Despite her heartfelt commitment and creativity as a therapist, this really hobbled her ability to conduct therapy. She was less able to gain rapport and involve clients in therapy. She was not getting the results she was used to. In the upcoming sections, we will tell you exactly what those active ingredients are, and we'll offer more from other models of excellence.

What is really interesting about this, as far as modeling is concerned, is that no matter what a trainer says about what makes them effective, you can use the universal principles of modeling from NLP to see even more.

NLP embraces not only what people think they are doing, but what they don't know they are doing. In NLP, this is called a meta-model. Creating the meta-model of language in therapy back in 1975 is how NLP really got its start in creating public interest.

The playwright Oscar Wilde said, "Success is a science; if you have the conditions, you get the result."

☙❧

The Key Elements of Modeling

As you have seen, NLP looks through various filters of perception in order to analyze. For example, when we looked at a client with a phobia, we used the logical levels for filtering our perception.

By filtering, we focus our awareness in order to analyze. As we get better at this filtering, we also get better at connecting the dots and seeing the big picture. This is part of gaining mastery, as we discussed in the NLP model of learning. Do you see how, piece by piece, we are building more and more understanding and skill as we use what we learned earlier in this book?

We are drawing on this knowledge in various ways. When you use a piece of knowledge in different ways and in different situations, that makes the learning much more valuable.

This is called generalization of learning, because you have an overall or general mastery of that knowledge. When learning is generalized, it is not limited to just one situation; it is flexible and allows for endless creativity.

As you can see, this book is modeling NLP as well as teaching it. Learning through experience, and modeling what is being taught are very important aspects of NLP philosophy.

To create a model of a person's excellent or successful behavior, the analyst starts by learning to elicit the strategy, or at least to understand how and when it is elicited. The analyst begins serving as a knowledge worker. That is, using observation and questioning to assemble the model.

Let's start observation – the observation of physiology.

A master of anything from sports to psychotherapy displays a unique physiology, that is, physiology that is part of their excellence strategy.

They have a certain way of breathing; of moving. They have a certain posture. It's easy to see how this would apply to a golfer or other athlete.

But how could breathing play an important role in a psychotherapist's effectiveness?

Breathing keeps them alive, you say? Of course, but I mean their pattern of breathing; how they influence their clients with their breathing pattern.

The answer to this question didn't make itself obvious. Even psychotherapists do not necessarily realize that they are using their body a certain way for a reason. Professionals who are very successful at establishing rapport with people use their own breathing as part of rapport-building. We will learn about this in the section on pacing that is coming up.

We also model by analyzing how the person creates their mental map of reality. What do they filter out? How do their values shape their behavior? Meta-programs and the NLP meta-model help with modeling as well. The simple way to put this is that we want to know what's going on in their heads.

In order to model excellence, we must know what strategies the excellent person is executing. Strategies, as you'll recall, are how people organize themselves internally and externally. In other words, how do they sequence events in their rep systems, and how do they sequence their behavior.

We can apply this kind of analysis to problem behaviors and painful states as well, in order to find the keys that allow escape from such states.

Consider these other helpful points.

When we model, we find out what really makes a difference. The rest may look important, but that doesn't mean that it is.

We also break the behavior down in to parts that have their own function. We also need to know of that part is there because of something about that successful person that only applies to certain people.

In using computers to analyze the strides of runners, researchers found that the runners had unique aspects to their strides. The researchers felt that if they tried to perfect the stride of the runners, they might be taking away something that accommodated for some unique structuring of the individual runner's body. The perfection might actually slow down the runner.

In analyzing a terrible airline crash, the assessment team learned that the pilot had a unique and non-essential way of working the tail of the plane that caused it to snap off in a high wind condition, and that lead to the fiery and fatal crash. This helped them understand that the tail was not defective.

We must also see what feedback the person seeks. Where does it come from? What adjustments does the person make based on what feedback?

A common way to do modeling is to imitate the excellent person. This helps us find out what is essential, because we can adopt or drop various behaviors, and we can pay attention to various kinds of feedback. We can also increase and decrease the intensity of various strategies.

❧

Once You Have a Model, What Do You Do With It?

As we have said, we use models of excellence in order to train others to achieve similar excellence. That can mean being a great chef, parent or anything else. We want to have a training design that is universal, in other words, anyone can learn from it. So the model does not exist as a finished product.

It must become a program for learning; a training. An important part of that training is the ability to train the trainers. The better they understand NLP and the NLP model of learning, the better they will perform.

❧

165.

Basic 2nd Position Modeling

"The promises of this world are, for the most part, vain phantoms; and to confide in one's self, and become something of worth and value is the best and safest course".

— Michelangelo

CREDITS FOR THE creation of this NLP pattern belong to various contributors.

Improve your ability to model excellence. For completing this pattern, you need four people. Designate one to be the Person Being Modeled, another as the Subject who interacts with the person, a Modeler, and an Observer.

Overview: The Basic 2nd Position Modeling Pattern

Step #1. Have the initial conversation.

Step #2. Have the Modeler stand in.

Step #3. Give feedback.

Step #4. Start a new conversation.

Step #5. Have the modeler stand in again.

Step #6. Provide feedback.

Step #7. Test.

Step #1. Have the initial conversation.

Have the Subject and the Person Being Modeled converse for about five minutes. Have the Person Being Modeled choose the topic.

Have the Modeler model the Person Being Modeled by going into second position, focusing on their most subtle muscle movements.

Step #2. Have the Modeler stand in.

Have the Modeler stand in for the Person Being Modeled, and continue the conversation with the Subject as though he or she were the Person Being Modeled.

Step #3. Give feedback.

Have the Person Being Modeled and the Observer give clear feedback and coaching to the Modeler as to how accurately he or she is imitating the Person Being Modeled.

Step #4. Start a new conversation.

Send the Modeler out of the room.

Have the Subject and the Person Being Modeled converse about a new subject for about five minutes.

The Subject chooses the subject this time.

Step #5. Have the modeler stand in again.

Have the Modeler return, and again stand in for the Person Being Modeled, continuing the conversation with the Subject.

The Subject tries to cover the same interaction topics in the conversation as much as possible for about five minutes.

Step #6. Provide feedback.

Have the Subject, Observer and the Person Being Modeled give the Modeler Step feedback on how well they matched the Person Being Modeled.

Step #7. Test.

Over the coming weeks and months, discuss how well the participants have been coming along in learning to model and establish rapport.

166.

2nd Position Intuitive Modeling

"People are like stained-glass windows. They sparkle and shine when the sun is out, but when the darkness sets in their true beauty is revealed only if there is light from within".

— Elisabeth Kübler-Ross

CREDITS FOR THE creation of this NLP pattern belong to various contributors.

Take more advanced steps in developing your ability to model.

You need three people for this pattern: the Person Being Modeled, and two Modelers.

Overview: The 2nd Position Intuitive Modeling Method

Step #1. Demonstrate the skill.

Step #2. Model the skill.

Step #3. Describe the internal state.

Step #4. Compare the results.

Step #5. Collaborate to describe the details of the skill.

Step #6. Test.

Step #1. Demonstrate the skill.

Have the Person Being Modeled exhibit a simple skill that can be modeled, such as some dance step or cultural gesture.

Step #2. Model the skill.

Have the Modelers enter a "not knowing" state from second position with A for a few minutes.

Step #3. Describe the internal state.

The two Modelers are to write down precisely what they suspect A is experiencing internally based on what they gathered from being in the second position.

Step #4. Compare the results.

Have the two Modelers compare and contrast their models.

Step #5. Collaborate to describe the details of the skill.

Have all three parties collaborate to describe the key elements of the skill.

Step #6. Test.

Over the coming weeks and months, discuss how well the participants have been coming along in learning to model and establish rapport.

Additional Advice

For a full step-by-step explanation and advice on the NLP modeling process, in a down to earth language, check out the book "NLP Modeling – The Ultimate Guide"

☙❧

167.

Basic 3rd Position Modeling

"You have brains in your head. You have feet in your shoes. You can steer yourself in any direction you choose. You're on your own. And you know what you know. You are the guy who'll decide where to go".

— Dr. Seuss

CREDITS FOR THE creation of this NLP pattern belong to various contributors.

Improve your capacity to model by using the third position. This pattern requires three people: The Person Being Modeled and two Modelers.

Overview: The Basic 3rd Position Modeling Method

Step #1. Demonstrate the skill.

Step #2. Gather information for modeling.

Step #3. Describe the internal state.

Step #4. Compare and contrast the models.

Step #5. Collaborate to describe the skill as a model.

Step #6. Test.

Step #1. Demonstrate the skill.

Have the Person Being Modeled engage in a skill.

Step #2. Gather information for modeling.

The Modelers gather information and demonstrations of the skill from the Person Being Modeled while they are in third position.

The modelers need to gather any helpful information from various levels, such as physiology, rep systems, language patterns, and meta-programs.

Step #3. Describe the internal state.

Have the modelers note what they think the Person Being Modeled is experiencing internally, based on what they have observed and collected.

Step #4. Compare and contrast the models.

Have the Modelers compare and contrast their models.

Step #5. Collaborate to describe the skill as a model.

Have all three parties collaborate to create a detailed description of the key elements of the skill.

Step #6. Test.

Over the coming weeks and months, discuss how well the participants have been coming along in learning to model and establish rapport.

☯

168.

Basic States Of Excellence Modeling

*"But that's always the way; it don't make no difference whether
you do right or wrong, a person's conscience ain't got no sense,
and just goes for him anyway. If I had a yaller dog that didn't
know no more than a person's conscience does I would pison
him. It takes up more room than all the rest of a person's insides,
and yet ain't no good, nohow".*

— Mark Twain, Huck Finn

CREDITS FOR THE creation of this NLP pattern belong to various contributors.

Model states of excellence. This pattern requires three people: The Person Being Modeled and two Modelers.

Overview: The Basic States Of Excellence Modeling Method

Step #1. Demonstrate a pattern of excellence.

Step #2. Model the Person Being Modeled.

Step #3. Model with how and why questions.

Step #4. Demonstrate an opposite state.

Step #5. Repeat steps two and three.

Step #6. Compare and contrast.

Step #7. Test.

Step #1. Demonstrate a pattern of excellence.

Have the Person Being Modeled enter a state of excellence.

Step #2. Model the Person Being Modeled.

Have the first Modeler explicitly model the Person Being Modeled from second position.

Step #3. Model with how and why questions.

Have the second Modeler explicitly model the Person Being Modeled.

Have them ask why questions to elicit beliefs, values, meta-programs, meta-outcomes, and have them ask how questions to elicit goals, and T.O.T.E.S. (evidences and operations).

Step #4. Demonstrate an opposite state.

Have the first Modeler choose an experience which is the oppo-site of the state of excellence being modeled, such as a stuck state.

Step #5. Repeat steps two and three.

Have the two Modelers repeat steps two and three.

Step #6. Compare and contrast.

Have the Modelers compare and contrast their models of what the Person Being Modeled has demonstrated, as well as its opposite, and to explore what is similar and different in these descriptions.

Step #7. Test.

Over the coming weeks and months, discuss how well the participants have been coming along in learning to model and establish rapport.

❦

The NLP Meta-Model

"But behavior in the human being is sometimes a defense, a way of concealing motives and thoughts, as language can be a way of hiding your thoughts and preventing communication."

— Abraham Maslow

Introduction

THE NLP META model of language creates questions that clear up deletions, generalizations, and distortions in speech. Done wrong, these are called violations of well-formed syntax. In grammar, syntax means the proper order of words in a sentence. In NLP, syntax means the proper laying out of concepts in speech.

The NLP meta model is important for everyone to know, because these violations of well-formed syntax cause all sorts of problems, from everyday relationship problems to tremendous political problems. But by asking meta-model questions that clear up these violations, we also clear up our thinking. They also help us see when another person's thinking is affected by these violations, so that we can be more in control of our own mental maps; our own sense of reality. With the meta-model, we are much less vulnerable to manipulation.

Here is part of a speech with a lot of deletion:

Back in the day, they started our country so everybody could be free. Now everybody's fighting and it could all go down the toilet.

That was a little vague. Who started our country? Free in what way? What is the fight he's talking about? What could all go down the toilet; what does that really mean? Now here's that piece as written by Abraham Lincoln:

Four score and seven years ago our fathers brought forth, upon this continent, a new nation, conceived in Liberty, and dedicated to the proposition that all men are created equal.

Now we are engaged in a great civil war, testing whether that nation, or any nation so conceived, and so dedicated, can long endure.

Now that was a lot more specific. But let's say that instead of a speech, it was a paper about constitutional law. When the word liberty came up, it would require a lot more explaining. What exactly is liberty, and for who, and what are the circumstances? Needless to say, around the world, countless court cases, government documents, and materials from civil rights activists expand on the meaning of liberty every year.

The meta-model helps us analyze speech by showing us the difference between two kinds of structure: deep structure and surface structure. Surface structure is what you say, and deep structure is all that you know that is relevant. For example, if I say I can't get a decent salad in this town, I might mean that the salads they serve are too high in calories. I might mean that I have only been to three restaurants in my neighborhood in order to form this opinion.

That would be part of my deep structure. If you don't know my deep structure, you might use your own. Let's say my friend likes a salad with lots of croutons soaking of a lot of oily salad dressing, and plenty of chunks of cheese and bacon.

My friend would send me to a restaurant with that kind of salad. I'd be horrified by all the calories and wonder what my friend could have been thinking. Well, if we had both used the meta-model, we would have known what each other was thinking. The whole thing would have been cleared up in a matter of seconds.

The other thing about deep structure is that at it's deepest, it is a collection of sensory representations that come together a lot like a chemical reaction. They bubble up and come together to form thoughts, opinions, and decisions. Then we put those thoughts, opinions and decisions into words. That's when we have the surface structure.

Those words cannot possibly contain all the impressions that led you to speak the words. This is why you must have habits, or strategies, for deleting, generalizing, and distorting them into something that you can say efficiently; something that will make sense and not take too long to say.

People who are very manipulative will hide the deep structure in bad deletions, generalizations, and distortions in order to be manipulative. If someone wants their government to be based on their religion, but they know that would not be popular, they can delete the bible and creationism, and distort it into something that sounds scientific, such as intelligent design.

This way, they can pursue a religious agenda that gets by some people. In the United States, high courts know how to ask meta-model-like questions in order to analyze legal arguments. When they did this in the case of intelligent design, they stopped certain schools from forcing their science teachers to say that intelligent design was science. The science teachers were very relieved to know that someone was paying attention and asking the right questions.

If someone's girlfriend starts accusing them of looking at other women, and becomes very jealous, meta-model questions may reveal that the girlfriend didn't really have evidence, but her mind subconsciously collected some impressions that led to the jealousy.

The deep structure may have really been a need to escape some internal pain and to get more attention. Accusing someone of something definitely gets their attention. Unfortunately, in addition to badly formed syntax, the accusation also creates attention that is not very rewarding, and may even stress the relationship to the breaking point.

If the boyfriend uses the meta-model, the girlfriend may begin to see that she was really in need of something else. If the boyfriend knows Neuro Linguistic Programming, he will give her attention that does not reinforce her jealous behavior, but instead helps to create a constructive relationship. However, if the boyfriend does not have constructive strategies, and his deep structure references negative experiences, he may just get angry and act superior.

Here, I'll give you meta-model questions for all the major types of syntactical violations, that is, poorly formed syntax.

☙❧

599

169.

Generalizations

GENERALIZATIONS happen when someone translates some experiences into a rule that applies to all similar experiences. Bigotry is an example we gave earlier. Sometimes generalizations can go by without being noticed.

If someone says, *"Everybody at the party hated me!"* you might ask, *"Who else did they hate?"* If she says, *"Everyone had friends there, they just were mean to me,"* you know she is unaware of anyone else feeling uncomfortable there.

If you asked, *"Oh, so they were sorry to see you arrive and glad to see you go,"* she might start thinking of exceptions and reveal one, even though she seems to be attached to the idea that everyone hated her.

This means that her poor syntax just opened up to a more accurate internal map, that is, she realized that there were exceptions to her generalization.

Now she has a resource: the knowledge that there are people that appreciate her.

☯

170.

Universal Quantifiers

UNIVERSAL QUANTIFIERS ARE an all or nothing kind of generalization.

If someone says, *"Every time I do someone a favor, it ends up biting me in the rear,"* you might ask, *"I wonder what it is about you that makes that happen every time, I mean, you know, since that doesn't happen every time to anybody else."* Your friend might come up with an insight like, *"Well,* *your right, I need to quit trying to help people who are so out of control, because it spills into the lives of anybody who connects with them."*

In this case, he found a universal source that gave the universal quantifier at least some truth. In this case, that could be better than finding the exceptions to his generalization.

❧

171.

Lost Performatives

Lost performatives make a rule without anybody having responsibility for it.

If a girl gets a cut on her face, and a nurse says, *"Now you'll never win a beauty pageant,"* then you have a kind of cloud of lost performatives. One is that she should care about winning beauty pageants.

Another is the implication, not a direct statement, but the implication that people will think she is ugly for the rest of her life.

Another is in the nurse's tone of voice, which is telling the girl that it is her fault. You had to be there to hear that part. If you consider the culture of the region where this happened, it is also connected with the idea that she won't find a man to love her.

Let's just take the main one, which is that she should care about winning beauty pageants.

You might respond to that with, *"You idiot, she's just an impressionable, vulnerable, wonderful, young girl with infinite potential, and she's too bright to waste her time running around with bimbos who try to be beauty queens. I'm going to get your fired for being such a twisted human being."* But that's pretty confrontative.

How about this one: *"Who is it who thinks she should care about winning beauty pageants?"*

❧❧

602

172.

Modal Operators

MODAL operators make a *must* out of a preference. Albert Ellis, the developer of rational emotive therapy focused on this one a great deal. People cause themselves a lot of suffering with modal operators, because, when the "must" is not achieved, they feel like some horrible injustice has taken place. It distracts them from finding creative solutions and enjoying life as it is.

If a client says, *"I must have that woman, but she likes my friend,"* you might say, *"It sounds like something really awful will happen if you don't get her. Tell me about that."*

He might say, *"Well, that is the really awful thing. If I don't get her, that will be really awful."*

You might say, *"So if you didn't get her, you will be in a really bad way emotionally, really broken hearted."*

To which he might say, *"Yes, I couldn't handle it."*

Now you can go in for the exception, asking, *"I wonder how many months it would take before you got your sense of humor back."* His subconscious mind would have to have an incredible amount of restrictive control over him to keep him from clicking into exceptions.

You could add fuel to this. *"I suppose you'd know that from how you've handled a broken heart in the past."*

Witty quotes charm us because they toy with our internal syntactical violations. Consider this quote from Oscar Wilde, "There is only one thing in life worse than being talked about, and that is not being talked about."

☙☙

173.

Deletions

Deletions happen when the speaker leaves something out. When a person is being too vague or manipulative, deletion may be the culprit.

If someone says, *"What a lousy day,"* you could ask, *"What's lousy about it."* If he says he has lice, you now know he really DID mean it was a lousy day, since that's how the word "lousy" got its start. Unless you need to know where he got the lice, that's probably more information than you really needed to know.

Simple deletions are those where information is simply left out. You can't talk for long without making numerous simple deletions. After all, if you included all the details, it would take a long time and you'd get a reputation as a crashing bore; so deletions are a necessary part of everyday speech.

Unspecified nouns and verbs are deletions that leave you wondering what thing or action the person is talking about.

If a powerful local criminal says, *"I'd hate to see what happens to your family, if you don't pay us to take care of your nice restaurant in our part of town,"* you'd say, *"how much do I pay and to whom do I write the check? Oh, I mean, do you take unmarked bills?"*

Maybe that wasn't such a good example. How about if someone tells your friend, *"I was driving and here I am with this bad head wound."* While he's taking his friend to the hospital, he might say, *"but what happened?"* Maybe it wasn't a car accident. Was he attacked? Was he being vague because he's hiding something, or is he being vague because the head injury affected his brain? If so, then we could say that the deep structure is the injury itself. Let's hope it isn't TOO deep. But seriously, it is important to remember that deep structure includes everything from manipulation to psychological defenses to pure physiology.

Let's try one more, a nice plain one. Your employee says, *"We'll be a little late delivering to the buyer this month."* You might ask, *"How late, exactly?"* With the information you need, you'll know whether it's an emergency, and how to handle the buyer. Otherwise you could really be blind-sided. Employers and other leaders often get a watered-down version of bad news from their staffs. That is a good time to trot out your meta-model questions.

∞

174.

Lack of Referential Index

LACK OF REFERENTIAL index is a deletion where there's an unspecified party or an unknown "they".

If someone tells you, *"Everybody knows you're a liar,"* you could say, *"Who on earth would say something like that about someone like me?"*

That kind of backs the person into a corner, challenging them to disclose their sources. Maybe someone does think that you're a liar or that you lied about something, but how could everyone think that? Has this person been telling stories behind your back?

At the very least, your meta-model question shows them that you can't be intimidated by such a cheap shot.

If you say, *"Everyone knows everyone is a liar,"* then they are put in a position to say that you are some kind of special liar that makes everyone talk about you. The more specific the person is, the more flimsy they will sound, until their statements collapse because the evidence is weak.

If the person says, *"Well, the attorney general thinks so, and I have a warrant to search your office and home,"* the-e-e-n maybe you should go to the Cayman Islands where all your secret money is stashed, and decide where you want to live from now on.

175.

Comparative Deletions

COMPARATIVE deletions happen when the speaker fails to say what they are comparing something to.

If a sales person tells you, *"This motorcycle gets fifty percent better gas mileage!"* you'll want to know, *"Better than what, my skate board?"*

☙❧

176.

Distortions

DISTORTIONS are based on real sensory data, but they twist it in some way to create the wrong conclusion. If it's extreme enough, it's a delusion in psychological language.

If someone says, *"A white care followed me all the way to the gas station, someone must be obsessed with me and stalking me,"* you might wonder if the driver of the white care was going to the same gas station.

Coincidences are distorted all the time. When someone hears about two occurrences of something, like a business closing in town, and turns it into a pattern, they might say, *"Can you be-lieve it, the whole down is going out of business. I'm moving to Brussels."*

You could say, *"I'm moving to Brussels because six new businesses opened. That means we'll be overrun in no time! Two of them were opened by Pakistanis, lets go before there's no one left who speaks English."*

Maybe that would be a little too sarcastic. You'd better know this person well before you get too carried away with what you are learning, or else you'll end up alone, and bitter, homeless and freezing. Whoops, I just made one of those distortions.

☙❧

177.

Nominalization

NOMINALIZATION happens when we transform a verb or adjective into a noun. It also has to be something that isn't a real thing in the world. In other words, you couldn't put it into a wheel barrel. In fact, come to think of it, nominalization is, in itself, a nominalization.

It's a noun that isn't an actual, real-world object. Some other examples include: accuracy, righteousness, superiority, excellence, and destiny.

You can see nominalization happen in old philosophy and old psychology texts quite a bit. That's odd, because philosophers have published material critical of this for centuries.

Nominalization gets really bad when a number of nominalizations, or a chain of them, are discussed as though they were definite, real, understood things. When people do this, they come to all sorts of weird conclusions.

Here's an example. Someone said that atheists believe in a dog-eat-dog world. The deep structure that went on in their mind went something like this. Atheist equals evolution. Evolution equals Darwinism. Darwinism equals social Darwinism. Social Darwinism equals survival of the fittest, which equals no compassion for those in need, a dog-eat-dog world.

But social Darwinism is a political philosophy that only got Darwin's name attached to it because it resembled natural selection, which is a part of the theory evolution.

On each side of that weak link, the chain contains fairly good generalizations. Most atheists believe in evolution. Social Darwinists believe in a dog-eat-dog world. But those two chains are only linked by a completely irrelevant nominalization.

The verb "to evolve" becomes a noun, evolution. Then, that noun gets attached to social Darwinism only because Darwin discovered evolution. The jump to social Darwinism is only possible because of word play. This is what we mean when we say that people live in a fantasy world because of acting like words are real things.

But there is often a hidden agenda behind nominalization.

People who are not very intro-spective may not even realize that they are pursuing an agenda. The person who said atheists are dog-eat-doggers wanted so badly to feel superior to non-believers, that he came up with this as a re-sponse to research showing that atheist doctors were doing more for poor people than religious ones.

Outside of NLP, a word for *nominalization* is reification.

☙❧

v

178.

Mind Reading

Mind reading is an irritating distortion. This happens when someone decides they know what you are thinking. For some reason, it's usually something pretty bad.

If you tell them they are projecting, they probably won't understand. If you tell them what you are really thinking, they may actually argue with you, as if they know what you're thinking and you don't. If they think you're lying, what more can you say?

So you see how irritating this distortion is. If your boss tells you that you asked for the day off so you could sell company secrets to the competition, that's a pretty extreme example. You might want to look for another job, or get his boss to look at your boss' mental health. But most examples are more subtle.

Let's say you have a friend that you have seen a good deal, and you have done some nice favors for. It's someone you care about quite a bit, and really enjoy. But let's say you didn't come to their party, and now he's upset that you don't really care about him.

You know that he is wrong, and you know that when he feels better, he'll realize that he's wrong. This means you don't have to take it personally. If he hasn't been drinking, you might say something like, *"Exactly, if I cared about you, I wouldn't have let that bus crash into my car, or I would at least have left the hospital against doctors orders to get to your party. The IV bag would have been a good conversation piece."*

But really, as a good friend, you want him to know that you had something that you couldn't reschedule, whether it was an accident, a final exam, or anything else.

❧

611

179.

Cause and Effect Distortions

CAUSE AND EFFECT distortions can be sneaky. This happens when someone thinks they know what causes something, simply because the two things happened together. It's like the rooster thinking that crowing makes the sun come up. He must be right. It happens every time.

People do that a lot with their emotions. They'll say someone made them angry, as if they have no responsibility for their emotions. Everyone understands what they mean, but people can go too far with this.

If they do it to manipulate people, as in emotional blackmail, then you might want to say something, like, *"Even I am amazed at the power I have over your every emotion."* Or you could simply restate that you are doing what you do for perfectly good reasons and let them sort it out. After all, if you don't give attention to emotional manipulation, and you DO pay attention to their mature, appropriate behavior, you will probably have a better time, and they will respect themselves more. It's good to bring the best out in others.

You could say that this is meta to the meta level, because when you produce a strategy that serves your personal well-being or higher values, then you have gone beyond coming up with cute responses to show other people that they are illogical.

You have taken things to another level. It is understanding and using the meta-level that is important, not having a lot of snappy come backs that could alienate people. This section is to build your understanding, not make you think you need to be sarcastic or directly confrontative all the time in real life.

☙❧

180.

Presuppositions

PRESUPPOSITIONS are the hidden ideas in a statement.

If someone asks you if you have stopped beating your spouse, they are presupposing that you beat your spouse. And that's assuming that you have one to beat. You could say, *"You should know, or haven't you spoken with your mother lately?"* but we wouldn't advise that. Maybe you could say, *"I never started, but I hear it's hard to stop once you start, have you considered a support group?"*

☙❧

181.

Complex Equivalence

COMPLEX EQUIVALENCE connects two ideas that don't belong together.

For example, if your client is too upset about an argument with her son, she might say, *"I can't believe I told him he was lazy, now he'll be traumatized forever."*

You could respond with questions about the kind of stresses that he has survived, and how he was recovered from them, maybe even how they have helped to build his character. You could discuss ways to get over the argument and build better agreements about his responsibilities and the consequences of good and bad behavior.

You could talk about how to create more consistent rules at home and how this benefits everyone.

One of the best says to help with complex equivalence, is to supportively approach the issue from several factual and positive directions, as in the example above.

☙❧

How to Use the Meta-Model for Therapeutic Purposes?

THE creators of motivational interviewing have created two very helpful elements that can be used in meta model responses that are quite therapeutic, and that protect the therapeutic relationship between a therapist and client. Coaches can use this as well.

This approach causes the client to make progressive, mature statements instead of the therapist. This eliminates resistance, and creates healing momentum within the client.

The first technique is what we call negative spotlighting. When a person says something that violates well-formed syntax, you can exaggerate this to highlight it so that the other person will model their world more effectively.

For example, if a drug addict says, *"I don't need to be a purist. I can have some cocaine once in a while."* You can say, *"So you are now totally in control of cocaine."*

If the person has been in a recovery program, they know this is ridiculous. They have to say something like, *"Well, uh, I guess that's just the addiction talking."*

Notice that the other person said it, not you. You only used the motivational interviewing technique to mirror back what they said in a way that they could not support.

Although the practitioner's statement is kind of an exaggeration, it is not done with the least bit of sarcasm. It has to be done in a completely straight-faced and gentle manner. It is said in a factual tone. Not, *"Oh, so you think you can control cocaine now, huh?"* It's a flat statement of fact. *"So, you are now totally in control of cocaine."* You say it smoothly and plainly, maybe even a little like it's new information.

This way, the client can correct you and enlighten you. That tells the client that he is insightful and has something to contribute. It gives the client the experience of coming to his own conclusions, and a sense of controlling his own thoughts to change his direction in a positive way. This creates more flexibility in the client's thinking.

This is very helpful because now the client owns the more enlightened statement; they do not feel compelled to resist you, because you are not trying to shove it down their throat. Any time you feel like you are pushing a client or customer, you could probably benefit from a motivational interviewing technique. The original book on this is called Motivational Interviewing.

The other motivational interviewing technique that is a great meta model response, we call positive spotlighting. Here, you highlight something very constructive or adaptive that the client says.

This reinforces the constructive way of thinking, and gives them credit. If the person says, *"I realized that my wife left me because I was abusing drugs,"* you could say, *"You have the kind of insight that shows real courage in the face of a tremendous loss."* Isn't that much better than saying, *"So you're finally realizing what a schmuck you've been!"*

This positive approach reinforces the best qualities of the person and creates hope and strength that could make the difference between sobriety and relapse, perhaps even life and death.

This is not to say that you bear total responsibility for every choice a client, customer, or employee makes, but I say it to remind you of what an important contribution you can make to people's lives when you learn the powerful insights and methods of Neuro Linguistic Programming.

The Milton-Model

"Every person's map of the world is as unique as their thumbprint. There are no two people alike. No two people who understand the same sentence the same way... So in dealing with people, you try not to fit them to your concept of what they should be".

— Milton H. Erickson

EARLY IN THE development of Neuro Linguistic Programming, the developers modeled a famous hypnotherapist and physician named Dr. Milton H. Erickson. He is quite legendary in the field of psychotherapy, especially in clinical hypnosis.

৩৯

Why Use Hypnosis in NLP?

First please understand that hypnosis offers much more than the stereotypes you may have run across. Hypnosis doesn't just happen on a stage where you make someone act like a chicken, and it is not just making someone sle-e-e-py and programming them to stop smoking.

Because NLP is about modeling, NLP has drawn several important things from hypnosis. The language and methods that Erickson used has value on various forms of persuasion and stress management, as well as treating mental health issues. Much of it has nothing to do with going into deep trances.

৩৯

Milton Erickson

Milton H. Erickson, MD lived from 1901 to 1980. He was a psychiatrist who provided medical hypnosis and family therapy. People love to tell the many stories about his unconventional and innovative methods as a psychotherapist.

The book **Uncommon Therapy**, by Jay Haley has many fascinating stories about his work, and was a best-selling book.

He pioneered brief therapy methods, and even coined the term "brief therapy".

He achieved his results by blending together numerous things he knew about, like systems theory, behavior modification, and the subconscious mind. He saw the subconscious mind as being a creative, solution-generating force all on its own.

Much of his work was about bringing subconscious resources into play for therapeutic purposes. People often had no idea what he did or how he did it, but experienced tremendous improvements in their lives and symptoms.

He had a big impact on psychotherapy beginning in the 1950's.

When he was seventeen, Erickson contracted polio, and nearly died. Recovery was very difficult. Regaining his ability to move, and dealing with chronic pain led him to use various psychological and trance techniques. Because his resulting intense interest in psychology, he got a degree in psychology while he was in medical school.

Erickson also credited his dyslexia, tone deafness, and color blindness with causing him to pay attention to communication patterns that other people overlooked.

Because of Erickson's reputation in hypnosis, Gregory Bateson and Margaret Mead had him analyze films of trance states in Bali. Later Bateson consulted with him on communication patterns. It was through Bateson that Erickson met Bandler, Grinder, and Jay Haley.

After this, Bandler and Grinder began modeling Erickson.

☙☙

Your Subconscious

The subconscious mind contains everything in your mind that you are not aware of. Some of these things are easy to become aware of.

Stop and listen to the sounds around you that you weren't aware of until…now.

Some of these things you can directly influence, like if your fidgeting without knowing it and someone asks you to stop. You can even influence some of them indirectly, like when you learn relaxation or stress management, and lower your heart rate or brain-waves.

This brings up an interesting point.

Where should you draw the boundary between the subconscious mind and the mechanics of the body, such as the electric impulses and chemical reactions that regulate the heartbeat?

Since NLP has evolved into a holistic approach, it thinks of the body and mind as an interplay or an entity, not as two things with a definite line between them. The mind can have extraordinary effects on the body.

Countless research studies have shown this. NLP has hundreds of patterns, far more than you could possibly need to be an effective practitioner, that can alter your state. There's even one for allergies. All aspects of you are connected. This point of view empowers you.

And please remember that we used the word *"influence."* There's no reason to feel guilty if you get sick, as if you have total control over every aspect of your body. We call NLP a practice because you can learn and improve your use of NLP over your entire lifetime. Some people get carried away, like a person who said not to talk about personal growth using the word growth, because that would give you cancer. That's definitely getting carried away.

They probably said that because subtle word choices can have a big effect on how people perform. You are learning a lot of powerful language patterns in this book. Words will become your allies in creating powerful skills for a more fulfilling life.

Among its many jobs, the subconscious mind decides what needs to become conscious, what you can do subconsciously, and what your mental filters can dispose of. Neuro-psychologists have even found a physical area of the brain that serves to filter your sensory impressions. It allows you to focus on what you need to do, but if it detects possible danger, it directs your attention to it.

The subconscious mind performs many such tasks, so a lot of our behavior gets shaped by things we don't think about. But you could say that since you have a subconscious mind you have a responsibility and an art form, because the subconscious mind can shape our behavior in unwanted ways as well.

Just as animal trainers shape the behavior of tigers, dogs, and dolphins in complicated ways, our behavior has been shaped without our knowledge.

Our patterns of experience, our temperament, and even programming by commercial advertisers influence us. The subconscious can actually put up barriers to awareness in the form of psychological defenses,

NLP provides the antidote. It puts the tools of behavior change in your hands to use according to your values. It helps you restore awareness where you need it. And better yet, it can be a lot of fun to use NLP, and it can create plenty of inspiration in your life.

This can get people into a lot of hang ups, avoiding things that they would be better off dealing with. NLP can make it easier for people to be assertive and proactive in their lives, because it can open up a positive pathway to action.

This way, the subconscious mind does not busy itself so much putting up obstacles or defenses. The anxiety gets reduced, and the person becomes reconnected with their joys, passions, and higher values. When people switch on this way, they are much more successful and attractive.

What is Hypnosis?

It is difficult to define hypnosis, because it can take various forms, and even experts have varying definitions. A good working definition is that hypnosis is a state of inner absorption that can include intense focus or free reverie. Hypnosis is distinguished from a trance state in that it is guided by the hypnotist, usually for therapeutic purposes.

Stage hypnosis may involve actual hypnosis, or participants acting out impulses while on the spot to be entertaining.

An amusing dialog that would go one between Bandler and Grinder on the question of the definition of hypnosis, was a debate over whether everything was hypnosis or nothing was really hypnosis. This was not only a way of making important points about hypnosis, but also inducing hypnosis in the audience as a teaching technique.

A key point was that trance is really a matter of degree, and all communication influences your mind by creating artificial experiences of some kind.

There are two sources of confusion here. One is that influencing the subconscious mind is not necessarily hypnosis. That's because sub-liminal influence and hypnosis are not the same thing. The other is that NLP has drawn things from hypnosis that do not involve trance or hypnot-ic phenomena, or may only involve brief periods of light trance.

☙

Defining A Trance

In trance, the person is not conscious in the typical sense. At most, the person is conscious of being observant, and fairly free of thoughts and judgments, or of a stream of thoughts or reverie, car-rying him away from the present moment.

This state allows a hypnotist to have more influence on the sub-conscious mind, because the con-scious mind is not able to get in the way and subvert solutions that are not acceptable for some reason.

This may sound like it would cause a problem with the person's ecology, but when a serious prob-lem resolves through the sub-conscious, the persons conscious mind tends to go along. This is be-cause the conscious mind, though normally acting as a gate keeper, is only taking that role as the result of subconscious adaptations.

Once the subconscious is aligned and using the right re-sources, the conscious mind no longer acts out the subconscious problems.

This does not mean that hyp-nosis can easily change a well-thought-out or deeply ingrained opinion or a tradition. Hypnosis is for things that do not have a strong conscious structure, but rather, it is for dysfunctional patterns with subconscious roots.

The conscious mind may ap-pear to be the cause, but that is only because the conscious cre-ates pretexts for subconscious mo-tivations in order to preserve for a person a coherent sense of iden-tity. In other words, the conscious mind takes credit, but it is not re-ally the cause.

Trance is not an either-or phenomenon; we are in various degrees of trance all the time. We range from being very clear-headed and responsive to our environment in general, to drift-ing into a mild reverie, to drifting into a daydream, to drifting off altogether.

You do not have to go through a formal induction process in order to experience hypnosis. Erickson was famous for creating and utilizing trance through conversational hypnosis.

☙❧

Experiencing Rapid Trances

You can have a brief trance experience that you ARE aware of right now, and you can come out of it right away as well.

If you are driving or doing anything dangerous such as cutting vegetables, skip past this for later. Otherwise, control this experience by sitting or lying down, and participating in a manner that you find comfortable, such as by becoming aware of how your shoulders gently expand as you exhale, and feel their natural weight as you exhale.

This allows you to experience the relaxation that occurs s you exhale, such as how the surface you are on presses up to suspend you in space. This makes it easier to sense how other muscles can allow your full weight into the surface, including the gentle expansion of the back of your neck.

I know that you sometimes think about the healthy things that you do, even the ones that you do more or less consistently, and so it isn't much more to think of how you would like to look twenty years from now.

Your imagination allows you to create an ideal image in some way. You can see yourself in very desirable activities, and enjoying the attention of other witty, active people. Your subconscious mind can continue creating these excellent conditions as you go through your life, enjoying other activities like studying Neuro Linguistic Programming.

Yes, you can take this creativity with you as a background program that creates your excellent life. To begin, notice your environment, it's sounds and feelings. And as you look through your eyes, the colors around you. As this creates more alertness in you, you can take a breath and stretch, fully restoring your alertness and connection with your environment.

☙❧

Conversational Hypnosis

Erickson championed the idea NLP called conversational or covert hypnosis. Instead of setting up a formal induction and requiring the patient to concentrate in some fashion, Erickson would produce trance in his patients through normal-seeming interaction.

In the hypnosis field, this is called naturalistic hypnosis. Bandler and Grinder modeled this mysterious and provocative approach.

Since the patient may not be aware that it is taking place, and may not even remember it, it can be called covert hypnosis. They were fascinated with the idea that the power of the subconscious mind could be utilized in what appeared to be such an off-hand method.

෪෪

Benefits Of The Milton Model

As we mentioned, there are various benefits from hypnosis as practiced by Milton Erickson, and there are still more benefits that NLP derived from Erickson's work that are not necessarily hypnosis; at least they do not involve prolonged trance states.

Because of its diverse elements and flexibility, the Milton model can be used in some fashion in nearly all communication challenges. These include persuasion, sales, psychotherapy, rapport-building, braking a state, creating brief and useful trance states, stress management and self-hypnosis.

We will look at a whole tool box full of Milton model techniques, including something called transderivational search.

As you'll recall, rapport-building is very important in NLP, be-cause it supports all communication. Erickson's abilities in this area, largely based on rapid trance induction are key parts of NLP.

෪෪

Transderivational Search

Transderivational search, which we will call TDS, is a little like a search you can do on a computer, except that it is looking for even vague matches. To do this, something called fuzzy logic is used.

The human mind is great at fuzzy logic. In fact, it is so good at it that it may come up with vague matches and give them more power than it should. This gives even fairly inept Tarot card readers a great deal of credibility as the mind of the person whose cards are being read makes sense out of what the reader is saying. The mind comes up with various memories and situations that match the general statements of the reader. This can be a very convincing experience.

Nonetheless, we really do need our TDS abilities. We make decisions by assembling related sensory information, and we need TDS in order to assemble them and derive a decision. It is TDS that gives us the ability to work quickly with incredibly large amounts of life experience, and it is TDS that gives us flexibility in our responses that no present day machine can approach.

One of the useful things about TDS from an NLP point of view is that it generates a brief trance state while it occurs. Stage psychics actually generate repeated brief trance states in their subject, and then kindle the trance into a focused, involved, and credulous, that is, easy belief, state.

You can see this in some sales presentations as well. Psychotherapists may use this to help clients become more open minded, but the therapist may have no idea they are doing this.

৩।৩

182.

Meta-Model Violations

ERICKSON'S WORK goes completely against the direction of the NLP meta-model. While the meta-model gets at more specific knowledge, Erickson's work takes people to higher levels of abstraction, to values that are more general. He used a great deal of vague language that was extraordinarily good at shaping the states and directing the resources of his patients.

You can find all of the meta-model violations sprinkled throughout the text of Erickson's hypnotic work. As you learn the patterns of the Milton model that follow, you will see that they contain strategic meta-model violations.

☙❧

183.

Pacing Current Experience

WE HAVE TALKED quite a bit about rapport building, and pacing was a key part of that. Pacing the breath, that is, breathing at the same rate as someone else, is an example. What you say is also a really important resource for pacing. When you pace a person's current experience, you are simply bringing their experience into what you are saying somehow. This makes what you are saying more invisible and trustworthy at the same time. It creates a kind of momentum that gives power to other things you will say.

For example, "As you feel the surface you are on, and hear the sound of my voice, the relaxation you're starting to feel allows you to take an easy, slow breath."

⚭

184.

Pacing and Leading

ONCE YOU have done enough pacing, the person is ready for you to not merely MATCH their state with pacing, but to LEAD them into whatever state is necessary for what you are doing. As in the previous example, where we insert an easy, slow breath, we are encouraging deeper relaxation.

Notice that we don't tell the person to relax, we cultivate a state of relaxation by supporting the physiology of relaxation.

Better yet, we are pacing and leading at the same time, because we timed the easy slow breath with one that was already taking place in the other person. That means that that was just the beginning of leading, where we are punching up the awareness of the state that we want to increase.

This is called **kindling**, where an existing state is reinforced and supported so that it will become dominant and rise above the other states that are, in a sense, competing for dominance in the person.

As the state increases, your leading can become increased as well, as with the statement, "As your relaxation deepens, the remaining muscles that feel some tension can absorb this relaxation, making your inhale seem to fill more of your body.

∞

627

185.

Linking Words

ERICKSON USED WORDS called conjunctions, words such as "and" in pacing and leading. He linked the pacing with the leading in a way that made it all seem to belong together, and this gave his leading commands a lot of impact. Consider this example. *"As you experience this training, and wonder how >>you will apply it successfully, you hear the sound of my voice providing the information so that >>you can enjoy mastery."*

The pacing was that you experience this training, and that you wonder how successful you'll be. This last bit about wondering can inspire a transderivational search for anything you are wondering and any ways that this training may make you feel challenged.

Brining up any doubts that you have about yourself and then em-bedding the command that *"you will apply it successfully"* is a mild anchor collapse as well as trance reinforcer.

Nonetheless, the statement that "you are wondering" is also pacing your actual experience. Then I said *"you hear the sound of my voice providing the information"* which is still pacing. I finished with *"so that you can enjoy mastery."* Giving the purpose of the information doesn't seem like leading, but as you probably noticed, it is really a command to enjoy mastery.

That is leading disguised as a simple statement about information.

As you can tell, we are not only training you on a simple technique, but showing you how you can blend several techniques together. With experience, NLP practitioners' skills become so multilayered that they rely on their subconscious minds to do most of the work.

When they listen to transcripts of their own work, they can be surprised to hear how many techniques they are actually using at the same time. I say this because you can trust that this will happen for you as well. Remember that Milton Erickson had some very serious impairments, including pain and dyslexia, as well as delayed development because of polio. Yes, he was very bright, but there are plenty of people who have learned these techniques who aren't particularly bright. Not that I would say who they are.

ော

186.

Disjunction

DISJUNCTION IS A lot like linking, but it makes a contrast or choice while it slips in an embedded command or leading statement.

For example, *"I don't know whether you will give your full attention to this section, or think of some other useful information from your experiences, or even relax and learn while in a deeply relaxed state."*

In this example all three options are desirable. But it starts out as if I would say, *"I don't know whether you will give your full attention or not."*

Of course, the implied "not" can bring up any feelings of resistance or self doubt about one's ability to focus and pay attention. Now we have some transderivational search contributing to the trance and open-mindedness.

But we also have the unexpected shift into a very different statement. This kind of unexpected shift can also contribute to trance, instead of simply causing alertness, because the wording continues to simply take the form of choices that more or less pace the person's experience.

The actual choices that follow, of drawing from experience or learning while in trance aren't actually much of a contrast with the first option of paying attention, are they. Instead, they do utilization. Utilization of the mind wandering. Why not remind the subconscious, if it is going to wander, to bring up useful experiences, or to learn while the conscious mind is distracted?

You can try this with volunteers among your friends, telling them that you'd like them to tell you if they notice you giving them three choices that aren't exactly choices. It can be a game and they can learn with you.

☙❧

187.

Implied Causes

THIS TECHNIQUE is a little like the previous ones, by pacing and leading using a simple connection. Implied Causes is a technique that uses words that imply that one thing will lead to another.

I might say, *"As you take in all this information, you can know that your mind will digest it into useful wisdom in time. Knowing you have a subconscious mind gives you time to relax and enjoy learning."*

That doesn't really exactly make sense, does it. You have whatever time you have, knowing you have a subconscious mind doesn't actually give you time.

But I created an implied cause there, and it was intended to help the student of NLP learn more effectively by being more relaxed about it. Since people can feel anxiety as they learn, that can make them really enjoy the contrast of relaxing into learning that will occur over a period of time. Now there's an implied cause.

That anxiety will make you relax. Let me say part of that again; see how that worked as an implied cause. *"Since people can feel anxiety as they learn, that can make them really enjoy the contrast of relaxing into learning."*

The words that usually occur in implied causes are since, when, while, as, after, often, before, during, following, and throughout. Before you learn through relaxation, you might want to sit in an even more comfortable position. When you become aware of the sounds around you, you can realize that your relaxation is a powerful force for focus and learning.

While you are hearing these examples of implied causes, your subconscious mind has been busy creating understanding that your conscious mind do whatever it wants to as you learn even more.

෧෨

188.

Tag Questions

TAG QUESTIONS are phrases like, "can't you?" that are added to the end of a statement. They help the statement get by the conscious mind by occupying the mind with the tag question. Since the question elicits some transderivational searching, it also helps with the trance.

Drug companies do something like this in their advertising in order to make the information about side effects of drugs less notice-able. That is an unfortunate use of a valuable tool.

Here are some example statements with tag questions: As you think of these successes, you can let your mind go to early memories of success, can't you? You have memories of special things you can do, do you not? And this strong foundation of early learning and success is part of how you feel, isn't it?

❦

189.

Double Binds

IN DOUBLE BINDS that are thera-peutic or motivational, you give the person a choice between two forms of the very same pre-supposition.

For example, you might say, *"These memories of success can come up with your help, or run through your subconscious on their own, I don't know which one your subconscious will choose."*

As you can see, we added a vague statement of uncertainty about your subconscious choosing one of the options.

This reduces the sense of co-ercion, generates some trans-derivational search for increased trance, and makes the sense of having options less stress-ful. It's part of using language in a way that feels less like working though information, and more like floating.

෨෯

190.

Embedded Commands

EMBEDDED commands are statements that are inserted into larger sentences.

You may notice embedded commands more and more as you hear them in this training. Did you hear the ones I just used? I said, *"notice embedded commands more and more,"* and I said, *"hear them in this training."*

Listen as I say the whole sentence again, "You may notice embedded commands more and more as you hear them in this training." You heard them this time, didn't you? As you >>practice this technique, you will >>find yourself able to >>use embedded commands in many situations.

☙❧

191.

Analogue Marking

ERICKSON would change the way he said the embedded commands that he was sending into the subconscious.

This marked them in a way that was not too obvious, but helped them function as influential entities all on their own. >>You can do this when >>you speak persuasively to >>influence others.

∞

192.

Utilization

UTILIZATION IS a technique that has opened up entirely new vistas in mental health treatment and personal life.

Utilization happens when you turn an existing resource into a tool for a meaningful purpose.

Where this can be surprising is when things that seem very negative or inappropriate are used, or repurposed. Often, the negative behavior is just a dysfunctional attempt to get a good outcome, as when a child misbehaves because it gets them some attention.

When Erickson was working at a mental hospital, there was a patient there who claimed to be Jesus Christ. The patient spent quite a bit of time rubbing his hands together while he was spaced out.

It also happens that the hospital had a wood shop where patients could do projects. One day,

Erickson approached the patient and said, *"Sir, I understand you are a carpenter."* Since Jesus is well-known to have been a carpenter, Erickson knew that the patient would have to say yes, that he was a carpenter.

Erickson got him to cooperate with having sand paper and a wood block attached to his hands so that instead of merely rubbing his hands together, he would sand the block of wood. In time, this sensory experience created familiarity, and his skills and interest became stronger. In time, this patient, who had seemed to be a hopeless case, was making furniture.

So what was it that Erickson utilized?

He utilized the two most serious symptoms, symptoms that most other professionals would have attempted to eliminate; the delusion of being Jesus, and the long periods of being spaced out and uselessly rubbing his hands together.

Erickson used these symptoms to link the patient with valuable resources: identity, motivation, engagement, and experience, as well as the real-world resource of the wood shop.

The next time you are concerned, disturbed, or just irritated by something that someone else is doing, put your creative hat on and see what creative forms of utilization you can come up with. Do brainstorming with other people who are also concerned for even more ideas and practical ways to put them into action. You can do utilization with difficult or troubled children as well.

ᘓᘔ

193.

Nesting

ESTING means that an idea is contained within another. That can happen in the form of a story that occurs within a another story. The purpose is to enhance trance and open-mindedness. It makes the metaphors or teaching elements of the story more powerful.

"When I was learning hypnosis, one of my teachers told us about when he was in Italy, and he was seeing so much art and architecture, and learning so much, that he had a dream where he was in a big Catholic church, and Mother Mary came down into the church on this sunbeam that glistened and radiated through the huge, beautiful and colorful stained glass window. She told him about giving birth, and the exquisite joy that she felt being part of history and a new movement that promised to make a better world, that the pain of childbirth and the humbleness of her surroundings could not compare with the kindness of her people."

This is about the memories as told by someone in a dream as told by someone in another country in a story about my training. That is four levels deep. My story (recalling training), the trainers story (being in Italy), the dream (of the big church) and another story (Mother Mary's recollections).

The story served as a container for metaphors about making changes in one's life despite the discomfort that can be part of that. The metaphor was of childbirth.

☙❧

194.

Extended Quotes

EXTENDED quotes are a type of nesting where you have nested quotations.

The example I just gave is a rich version of extended quotes, because each layer involves someone talking. The story was four levels, but involved only one nested quote, which was the trainer telling us what Mary said. Even a simple version can enhance trance.

Although hearing something third or fourth hand should mean it has less credibility, filling someone's mind with credible or interesting people can have the opposite effect of making something more believable and desirable.

᠊ᢀ᠊

195.

Spell Out Words

SPELLING out an important word draws the person's attention to it, and promotes t-r-a-n-c-e.

∽∽

196.

Conversational Postulate

WHEN someone asks you if you can pass the salt, they are actually asking you to pass the salt, but they're being nice about it. NLP calls this a conversational postulate. In hypnosis, this avoids creating resistance, and it generates a subconscious drive to act on the question.

Here are some examples.

"Can you imagine doing that?"

"Would you invite that area to relax?"

"How easily can you let your subconscious mind do this for you?"

You can use this structure in day-to-day business. *"Are you prepared to use us as a vendor?"* wouldn't exert a magic mind power over a potential customer, but it would be part of a persuasive communication pattern and attractive bid to the customer.

❧

197.

Selectional Restriction Violations

IN the course of eliciting a state or creating a metaphor, you can ascribe feelings to things. This is called selectional restriction violation. Doing this not only furthers the metaphor, or supports the state, but it also contributes to trance and open-mindedness.

"Your lower back would like to absorb and store all that extra agitation you have been feeling, and create a balanced sense of your energies."

"What if your media player could tell you about all the wisdom and ideas for success that it will ever hold."

"The cactus lives peacefully in the arid desert."

☙❧

198.

Ambiguities

Part of Erickson's approach to working with trance states, was to take advantage of the opportunities afforded by ambiguity.

The double meaning of a vague phrase can contribute to trance, because of the transderivational searching that results.

The double meanings also can draw the attention toward a theme, but subconsciously, and can encourage a state be bringing up related material.

☙

199.

Phonological Ambiguities

You can take advantage of similarities of sound between words in creating ambiguity.

Phonological ambiguity is uncertainty created by similar-sounding words. Can you be a good support about this? (Sounds like good sport.) Relaxing from your head on down to your sole-s of your feet. (Sounds like down to your soul, spelled s-o-u-l instead of s-o-l-e.)

☯

200.

Syntactic Ambiguities

You can create ambiguity through violations of syntax. Now we're talking about actual grammar syntax, meaning word order.

Syntax ambiguity means that the meaning of the statement is not readily clear because the syntax does not do the job it normally does of clarifying meaning.

You can easily create examples by taking a participle, that is, an –ing word, and a verb. For example, "Deeply comforting psychotherapy clients cause success."

What do you think, am I saying that clients become successful by developing comforting personalities? Or is it that learning to self-sooth creates success through greater emotional stability? Or is it simply that when you comfort them, this leads to success?

Add to that that the *-ing* word, "comforting", could be a verb or an adjective. Consider all the transderivational searching packed into that simple, short sentence. And as for state elicitation, all three of these interpretations have to do with comfort and success, and the pathway to success.

If you want the client to develop a state and mental direction that is about that, then this technique should help create those things.

☙

645

201.

Scope Ambiguities

I N scope ambiguities, you wonder what part of the sentence applies to what other part.

For example, *"When you are talking quietly with your child and your husband at ease to talk more openly..."* Does this mean she is talking quietly with her child and her husband, and SHE is becoming more open, or is it the husband who is becoming more open?

I'll say it again, *"When you are talking quietly with your child and your husband at ease to talk more openly..."* This could be part of a session intended to help her become ready for her husband to be more honest with her. In any case, consider how this ambiguity creates transderivational searching for meaning, and primes a state and interest in a topic.

☙❧

202.

Punctuation Ambiguities

You can create transderivational searches with punctuation ambiguities.

One form is to blend sentences.

For example, *"As you sense some of the excitement of learning physically sensing calm alertness"* is a sentence where the word "physically" does double duty in the middle of two clauses, one about physically sensing excitement, and the other about physically sensing calm alertness.

You can also add improper pauses like… this… as you experience… transderivational searching causing… you to try mind reading. These pauses can help you pace the person's breath as well. Another punctuation ambiguity is created by not providing the end of the… As you do a transderivational search, into which I blend a new idea.

☙❧

203.

Metaphors

THE subconscious is always looking for solutions, but our defenses and traumas can keep us from connecting the dots.

We have evolved to digest our daily experience through REM sleep, but traumatic and other anxiety-provoking material can prevent REM sleep from doing its job.

However it is that we become stuck, one of the solutions to being stuck lies in the art of metaphor.

Metaphor means creating a story or idea that symbolizes something. For example, you might write a story about a famous event in history, but change the characters into various mythological or magic characters. Many of the most famous stories are actually metaphors for what was going on politically at the time they were written. Many more are love stories that resemble our own love lives in vari-

ous ways. That's why we can relate to them.

But Erickson contributed a great deal to using metaphor for healing. Metaphor bypasses the conscious mind, and helps the subconscious process issues that are stuck.

Metaphors can help us process things that we did not process on our own.

The book Little Annie Stories is a wonderful collection of metaphorical stories to tell children that is intended to help them deal with difficult issues like bed wetting. The book **My Voice Will Go With You: The Teaching Tales of Milton H. Erickson, M.D.** is an excellent addition to the library of anyone interested in the Milton model and metaphor.

One way to begin building metaphors is to read collections of them, that is why I recommended those books. Of course there are others. You can begin building metaphors by picking a challenging issue, and changing it into a story about animals.

Whatever the challenge is, turn it into something that has a similar emotional significance.

For example, if the challenge is about regaining self esteem after a failure, the story could be about the animals going to a dried up watering hole, and going on a search for water.

The thing that makes a metaphor healing, is that there is some kind of healing message embedded in the story. In the water metaphor, the animals going on a quest for water is like someone not being stuck in low self esteem, and going for new opportunities.

Being thirsty didn't stop the animals, it drove them on. Having a failure doesn't stop people, it drives them to build the needed skills and seek new challenges. So the water is the metaphor for success and self esteem at the same time.

Since people have parts, as we have learned. Different characters in the story can match different parts. One of the animals could say, "It's hopeless, there's no point in going on, we must stay here and hope for rain." The ensuing dialogue could be a message to the subconscious to turn the voice of hopelessness into a voice for motivation.

☯

The Satir Model

*"I am Me. In all the world, there is no one else exactly like me.
Everything that comes out of me is authentically mine, because
I alone chose it — I own everything about me: my body, my feelings, my mouth, my voice, all my actions, whether they be to others or myself. I own my fantasies, my dreams, my hopes, my fears.
I own my triumphs and successes, all my failures and mistakes.
Because I own all of me, I can become intimately acquainted with
me. By so doing, I can love me and be friendly with all my parts.
I know there are aspects about myself that puzzle me, and other
aspects that I do not know — but as long as I am friendly and loving to myself, I can courageously and hopefully look for solutions
to the puzzles and ways to find out more about me. However I
look and sound, whatever I say and do, and whatever I think and
feel at a given moment in time is authentically me. If later some
parts of how I looked, sounded, thought, and felt turn out to be
unfitting, I can discard that which is unfitting, keep the rest, and
invent something new for that which I discarded. I can see, hear,
feel, think, say, and do. I have the tools to survive, to be close to
others, to be productive, and to make sense and order out of the
world of people and things outside of me. I own me, and therefore, I can engineer me. I am me, and I am Okay".*

— Virginia Satir

Introduction

Virginia Satir was one of the first family therapists. Like Erickson, she was modeled for NLP purposes, and her work is one of the three fundamental models of

NLP. She was born in 1916 and became a noted psychotherapist. Her best known books were Conjoint Family Therapy and Peoplemaking in which she describes her family therapy work to a popular audience. Satir wrote the book Changing With Families: A Book About Further Education for Being Human with Bandler and Grinder.

She developed the Virginia Satir

Change Process Model through clinical studies. This model has also been applied to organizational change.

❀

Satir categories

Satir found that people fell into five categories, each of which had its own body language, attitude, and communication patterns. They are the Blamer, Placater, Computer, Distracter and Leveler. NLP has incorporated these styles into its trainings.

204.

The Blamer

BLAMER's externalize blame, and appear to be always ready to place the blame in a harsh or judgmental way. When things go wrong, the blamer starts blaming. The blamer also pushes their thoughts and feelings onto everyone else. In NLP, you may see blamers referred to as skunks, because they spray their criticism outward.

Blamers, like all the categories, have their own body language. When they're in blaming mode, they point their finger at people and have a firm, controlling style of body language. They tend to use confusion tactics to make it easier to get the blame to stick without too much resistance from others.

They do this with meta-model violations such as over-generalizing, connecting ideas that don't belong together, and making claims for which there is no proof. Blamers can end up being pretty lonely, because their behavior is alienating. They do best with very like-minded people and stay at peace with them by focusing their blame on the same people or groups. This forms a kind of bond.

Inside, the blamer may not be nearly as confident and secure as they appear. Blaming can serve to compensate for vulnerabilities such as the fear of judgement, and feeling so small as to need to align with a larger authority that justifies being blaming in service of that larger authority.

Blamers generally blame in the name of a system such as family, church, employer or political cause.

As an employer or supervisor, they may blame in the name of profit. Blame can be a strategy for office politics.

Blamers use general statements, complex comparisons and missing proofs to confuse the other person, and then place the blame. Such people usually end up alone, since nobody wants to be at the receiving end of the blame.

⊛

205.

The Placater

THE placater is also one for displacing blame, but they do it more diplomatically. The placater is much more concerned about how people view them, so much of their behavior is an escape from conflict or unwanted attention or blame.

A blamer will fight fire with fire, but a placater blows the fire onto someone else's house and shares their neighbor's upset over the fire department being slow to arrive. Their body language tends to be palms facing up and shoulders shrugging, they may tend to slouch.

Placaters hide their approach with meta-model violations such as cause and effect, modal operators and unspecified verbs.

They may get your sympathy with a poor-me attitude.

When there is conflict, they go into hiding, at least by becoming noncommittal.

Placaters may be found firmly sitting on the fence.

☙❧

206.

The Computer

THE computer style can be pretty unemotional. They cover up possible emotions with extra words. They may sound academic or scientific. When someone else becomes emotional, they act like they are trying to become a counter-weight, by acting even more cool, calm, and collected.

Computers hide from their own feelings and invalidate other's feelings, because they have not learned to cope with feelings, whether the feelings are their own or someone else's.

Neuro Linguistic Programming training materials have referred to them as Mr. Cool, or Mr. Spock, a science fiction character from a planet where everyone aspired to be perfectly logical. They may tend to fold their arms, especially when things get too personal for them, and they are often seen in a neutral posture.

Some fit the nerd stereotype, and may be physically awkward or make gestures that are a bit eccentric or *un-self-conscious*. It may seem like they are drawing their energy up into their head, and that their body mostly serves to support their brain.

In relationships, the computer can harm the intimacy by being too far removed. Many computer style people are considered to have an autism spectrum diagnosis such as *Asperger syndrome*.

In terms of meta-model patterns, computers hide out by using generalizations and omitting references.

❦

207.

The Distracter

THERE is another style that can be a chameleon.

They are seen as a mix of blamer, computer, and placater. But there is a common thread that runs through their style, and that is to manipulate through distraction.

They may induce confusion or simple fatigue in the other person.

They train others not to hold them accountable by making it very difficult to have a straight conversation with them. They are intuitive about escalating the distraction as needed.

They can be quite exasperating, especially if they are not very socially skilled or if they are cognitively impaired. They may tend to gesture a great deal in an attempt to communicate their thoughts and emotions with their body, but subconsciously, this can serve to further fill up other people with excess stimuli for adding to the confusion.

From a meta-model point of view, they switch topics too much, overgeneralize, and omit references.

❦

208.

The Leveler

INALLY, there is the leveler. The leveler has high congruence and does not blanch at being factual. They do not over-dramatize, so if there is blaming to do, they are objective and fair about it. When confronted by the other styles, the most evolved levelers have a special ability to stay in touch with reality and their own agenda and self-interest.

If they upset anyone, it's because their style interferes with manipulation by the other styles. What upsets people more than someone getting in the way of their attempts to manipulate?

The leveler may have their hands facing down, as if they are trying to calm things down and encourage level-headedness. This is because they often end up in a mediator role because of their own level-headedness. Their ability to see both sides of an argument makes them good mediators.

⊗⊘⊗

209.

Utilizing Flexibility

An important part of the Satir model is that people need to develop flexibility in their styles, so that they are not locked into one. With more flexibility, people can adapt to more situations, and can solve more interpersonal problems. They can certainly create less personal problems with that flexibility.

So while the leveler sounds like the best style, it can be a problem if it is the only style you are comfortable in. A good mediator knows that having various styles can make the difference between success and failure in a negotiation. The same holds true for anyone, really.

For example, being a blamer may help knock someone off of a stuck position, because it is a real state interrupt. It may help level the playing field when someone else is being too high-handed.

☙❧

210.

Category Rapport-Building

ONE properly, you may actually win the respect of a blamer by acting like a blamer, but this is advanced. You have to be in that style without putting the blamer on the defensive, so pacing the blamer style means adopting that kind of critical attitude and intensity WITHOUT causing the blamer to feel that they must fight with you or otherwise defend their vulnerability.

Being upset about the same thing as the blamer is an excellent strategy. Remember that after pacing comes leading. The blamer is much more open to your input once rapport has been established.

The problem for most people is that they are too shaken up or angry to want to establish rapport with a blamer. Since blamers may hold a lot of power in an organization, this can be a fatal mistake. It's best to see it as an opportunity to practice NLP rather than to practice your vulnerability. Which to you love more?

You can gain rapport with a placater pretty easily, since they really crave attention and understanding. The trick is to get them connected with their real responsibilities without losing them. Starting with their higher values, that is, at a more general or abstract level and working down into the specifics is an excellent strategy.

Distracters are more open to rapport-building than you might think. As with most rapport-building, you must start out being non-threatening. Being non-threatening with a Satir category means not directly confronting the way the style acts as a defense against internal vulnerabilities.

In the case of the distracter, you do not rub their face in whatever it was they were trying to distract you from. As an Neuro Linguistic Programming practitioner, you are getting used to juggling different ideas and even using confusion as a technique yourself.

The trick with the distracter is to lock firmly onto the facts and position and agenda that are important to you, and then take a detour. Go all over the place with the distracter, but keep dropping in points about how it is in the best interest of the distracter to do what must be done. It's a bit like breaking a horse.

While the distracter tends to fatigue others, you are fatiguing the distracter because all their efforts keep bringing them back to the same spot, your agenda. On one level, you are pacing them, on another, you are kindling a state of compliance.

Add Ericksonian language to the free-wheeling conversation and you will be the distracter master.

Since levelers respect other levelers, and your NLP skills help you see both sides to any debate, you will have the easiest time establishing rapport and understanding with the leveler. If there is a disagreement, make sure that you have good mastery of the facts and good knowledge of the agendas of the players in the situation.

Of course, you can use everything you had already learned about rapport-building. But now you know even more. By learning about the Satir categories, you know not only more about what to do, but also about what to avoid doing.

But if you aren't sure where to start in an interaction, being the leveler is best. That's because the leveler always understands their side of the issue. The only concern is that the leveler may be persuaded by the other side.

This creates an incentive for the person you are talking to to want to create rapport.

If they are not skilled, or if they are stressed, they may fall into their more un-evolved category style, but that means that they will be more obvious as to what category they belong to.

You will be able to take your cues from there. It is very important to remember that when you see someone in a more stereotypical or manipulative or irrational state, that may not be where they are most of the time, so don't limit yourself by assuming that what you see is all you will be dealing with in the future. People who see this have an easier time bringing out the best in people. This makes their lives a lot easier.

Meta Programs

"I personally believe we developed language because of our deep inner need to complain".

— Jane Wagner

Introduction To The NLP Meta-Programs

LESLIE Cameron Bandler and her collaboration first developed the meta-programs model in NLP with Richard Bandler. Later on, Wyatt Woodsmall, another famous NLP developer, further developed it. We've heard of other people in the history of NLP contributing to the development of the meta-programs model, but without concrete evidence. Surely many people, experimenting practitioners and participants alike, have given their outputs for the creation of this model.

Meta-programs allow you to really understand human behavior, to learn how the person's mind is processing reality and therefore producing a certain outcome. People's behavior may sometimes seem random, spasmodic and thoughtless, but under the surface the factors influencing even a mood change are quite complex and intriguing. The next time another person snaps at you, as if they were trying to "get to you," step back and, instead of participating in the emotional roller-coaster, try to guess their meta-programs.

Meta-programs are deep structure tendencies that drive automatic behaviors and thought patterns. The meta-programs are related to all levels of a person's mind management. They relate to personality, decision-making, beliefs, values, dynamic relationships to self and others, emotions, true memories, false memories, and so on.

Meta-programs describe functions on a continuum. They do not describe personality traits, though

661

they relate to personality. In essence, the meta-programs do not come to portray what a person IS, but how that person functions at a given moment in time in a specific context or situation (preferably, the moment you're communicating with them).

In other words, it is not "the way I am," but it's "the way I do it." My identity is not a noun ("I am") but a continuing and dynamic process ("my current strategies"). If you say, "I am a failure," you're generalizing too much; if you say, "I failed in math 3 times in the past year," you're already taking a new perspective on those 3 events. The meta-programs are not necessarily going to show you how to succeed in math, but they are going to show you how your deep structured neurology is working perfectly, but not always towards the outcomes you envision for yourself.

Meta-programs are changeable, manageable and predictable. The person you're trying to analyze might express the same meta-program distinction, in both extremes, given different contexts and situations. People are complex, so even if you've easily identified a meta-program distinction in someone, it does not mean that this person will hold and cherish it for a long time. It is bound to change.

What you define by working with the meta-program model is the "how," not the "is." The person you're analyzing is not a mismatcher, he's a person who's currently using the mismatch strategy, and if you change the theme or topic of your conversation, he might become a very extreme matcher! This makes the meta-programs model much more interesting and usable, because you don't need to tag people or memorize their attributes, you need to constantly shift your communication with them, according to your own outcomes, to their current influencing meta-programs and the context in which you both participate.

The meta-programs offer much more than just random analysis of people's tendencies in given contexts. The meta-programs allow you to also discover ways by which you can stop behaving in a certain way and install new ways, or strategies, for "working differently." If you find that you tend to see things in black and white terms, that may be useful in some contexts, but certainly not in your relationship with your spouse; not if you want a nurturing and loving marriage. With your spouse, you would want to hold a continuum as your perception. You would want to see all shades of gray and understand him or her from multiple viewpoints. If you only see things as "good" or "bad," every little thing about them might bother you too much. If they're late, or the dinner gets cold, or the kids didn't make it to a game because of a Yoga class, or whatever else, you might over-generalize merely because of a tiny Perception Category meta-program!

However, you do want to keep the black and white extreme when it comes to traffic rules, right? You do want to stop at a stop sign every time, drive under the maximum allowed speed and certainly never drive after drinking alcohol. These are black and white Perception Category situations, in which the Continuum would be ineffective or even dangerous. Surely you can't argue with a policeman and say, "but there aren't any other cars around" after crossing a red light. Policemen do not care about the gray area, they want the law to be followed as is.

How Does A Meta-Program Work?

Meta-programs exist to make us more efficient. When you work with a familiar workflow, you "chunk up" and perform faster and better each time. A meta-program is kind of a set of instructions that your mind has gotten used to. In our modern and ultra-fast world, making prompt decisions is a necessity. A meta-program exists to perform even when your conscious mind is overloaded and stressed. Knowing meta-programs can help you tremendously to understand and predict other people's behaviors, and your own.

One of the most crucial elements to successful living is really just getting along with people, and especially getting along with people who can or should contribute to your achievable outcomes. Although the meta-programs can be used effectively in persuasion settings, like sales or therapy, they also serve us in other important ways.

The meta-programs give us a way to better understand another person's model of the world. We get to "read" and interpret reality through their processing preferences. As with the example I gave a few paragraphs ago, if you know that your spouse is categorizing her perception on a continuum, seeing all shades of gray, you can use language to communicate with her more effectively. You can still express your "extreme" black or white perception, but you would do so by acknowledging her way of seeing things first. Why? Because you want your relationship to work and improve, not to deteriorate because of lack of communication. And what is lack of communication if not ignoring each other's model of the world?

This is why we try to understand each other; we want to relate. Relationships are a crucial factor in any human's life (in fact, in almost any species), because there aren't many men or women who live on a deserted island. We have to communicate in order to survive, to propagate, to experience shared joy, to learn and grow and so on. There is no way around it. Either you work hard on your communication skills, or you are not going to get far on your outcomes.

When you and another person can't understand each other, you both feel misunderstood, frustrated and disconnected. Even if you discover the differences between you, you still need to come to agreement (in relevant contexts). How would you do that if you can't understand where each other is coming from and how you got there?

One of NLP's basic presuppositions, or advantageous beliefs, is that you are responsible for the results of your communication with another person. So if you and I are talking, for example, it is your responsibility to make me understand your point. The opposite is also true. As I am communicating with you, it is my responsibility to help you understand my point. Don't think of it as a shared responsibility, think of it as the responsibility of the person who's trying to convey his or her message to others.

When you try to explain your ideas, you need to use an effective approach. This requires being in a frame of mind in which you take the responsibility for your communication. Then you are in a good position to accept and even appreciate the differences between us, and then utilize what you know to get me to understand your message.

At this point I'd like to remind you of a commonly used NLP pattern: the Physiomental State Interruption pattern. In order to interrupt a person's state of mind, use the opposite extreme of a meta-program you recognize in their language. If the wife from the example above is a "gray zone" advocate, send messages implicitly as black and white perception. "I love X more than anything" or "I hate X more than anything" are two examples of a Black and white style of thinking.

Using the opposite preference of a specific meta-program is a sure way to get a person agitated or a bit angry at you. But it will also break the state, and you can always smile as if you meant it as a joke, change the topic and you're off on another conversational atmosphere.

The benefit of using meta-programs, among others, is that instead of assuming and predicting another person's thoughts and behaviors, in an ineffective way, you're actually aiming for the right ones. You can never really understand what's going on in another person's mind. Each one of us is a complex individual with a whole lot of memories and experiences that comprise a unique identity. You can't "figure out" a person, you can only assume a close guess, more or less.

Another key related to meta-programs, and NLP in general, is that each person is trying to impose his or her model of the world on the rest of us. Unless you're a well-trained NLP enthusiast, you're seeing the world through your own perceptual filters and consider it to be the only reality. You would see bad people and good people, comfortable situations and stressful events, misfortune and greed, and so on. But if you wish to master NLP, this facade is not going to fool you anymore.

You will no longer tag people for any reason. You'd be exploring their map of the world instead of judging them according to yours. You would have more curiosity and agility to help you learn HOW a person is functioning and not WHY are they "not working well."

One of the hardest stages I had to go through as a practitioner is when I received a phone call from a parole officer, asking me to work with a convicted ex-prisoner who was just released after a sentence of several years for abusing his wife. I really had to grow inside to accept such a client. I always thought that a perpetrator of a crime should keep paying so he or she won't forget to stop themselves the next time. Meeting this person has changed my way of thinking. He really needed help and he was willing to do anything and everything to "become normal," as he said. I changed my mind, accepted him, and that was one event I remember well because from then on, I started being curious about every person's HOW, regardless of the outcome.

The meta-programs are real, and you can observe them in any person. The reason that they are real lies in the essence of communication with self and communication with others. There are two modes of communication, verbal and non verbal. When it comes to your communication with yourself, you can speak to yourself (internal voice, self talk) and that's verbal communication, or you can imagine pictures or movies (mental visualization) or simply have a "feeling" or intuition, and these are non-verbal communication formats. When you communicate with other people, again you could speak to them verbally (auditory digital), or you could express non-verbally through your physiology.

At this point you still get to have control, more or less, on what you're expressing. But this is just a false sense of control. In reality, you can consciously manage around 7 items or bits of information, more or less, simultaneously. Everything else that you express, verbally and non-verbally, comes from your subconscious mind. Needless to say, your subconscious mind does not know how to lie and does not have the same objectives as your conscious mind or conscious thought process.

The subconscious mind has made it easier on itself by producing patterns. These are neurologi-cal connections, a kind of blue-print for processing, reprocessing and reproducing information. Your mind is accessing these blueprints all the time to know how to react to stimuli, how to make a decision, how to relate to the world, and so on.

These blueprints are also context-dependent. Accessing a blueprint to make a decision makes it feel "right," as a kind of intuition that relaxes you and makes you feel like you've made the best choice. And even if you have made the worst decision ever, it was still the best one your mind could produce at that given moment. You always do your best, satisfying some sort of subconscious need, even when it seems like a part of you is against improvement.

People who do not engage in studying these ideas, either investing time in acquiring knowledge from psychology or from NLP, are usually blind to these blueprints. The most they know is, that there are habits that control their thoughts and actions, but they usually claim nonsense such as, "that's just the way I am" or "I am just screwed up like this."

Meta-programs are habitual, true, but they are also easy to

change. Merely by recognizing a tendency in your actions or thoughts, in a specific context, reminds you of it the next time you have a similar experience. Taking the example above, if you know that your wife is a "gray-zone" perceptual categorizer, the next time you two argue you will alread have the tools to calm down the emotional storm within you, think logically for a moment, and then reconstruct your words by taking a "middle ground" approach. You need to explain what you have to say in terms that exist in a "Continuum" style of thinking and not in your habitual black and white. This is not to say that you're wrong thinking in either/or terms, this is to say that if you want your wife to understand you, it is your responsibility to express yourself in the formats that her model of the world is working with. And no, you cannot just send her to an NLP seminar and then drop the whole deal on her.

There is another aspect to blueprint blindness. People usually think that everyone else is either working the same way they are, or they are unbearable or just strange! The fact is, that if you take the list of meta-programs and start questioning people, you will find many differences in thinking and decision-making between each and every one of the people you interview.

People are blind not only to their own blueprints, but also to everyone else's. Unless you study communication or psychology or NLP, there is a very high chance that you would find it really hard to "figure out" a person.

The meta-programs model works in such a way that you need to step out of your model of the world and observe objectively the blueprints another person is working with. Most of these blueprints are subconscious, so it makes no use to ask a person which perceptual category he's in at the moment or whether or not he chunked down a certain message you gave him. Observe! Open your eyes, ears and whatever else you need to gather knowledge objectively. The other person will offer you verbal information (auditory digital) or non-verbal information (visual external), both of which you can use. The more useful one, of course, would be the non-verbal communication, because it is easy to lie with words, but your body language usually speaks the truth. When you observe meta-programs try not to judge the content you're hearing. The "story" is not important as much as the format of it.

How to Learn and Practice the Meta-Programs

There are many meta-programs. In this book I will list the ones that I find to be the most interesting and influential. In order to learn so many distinctions, you would need to work, first of all, slowly and methodically. Yes, of course, go ahead and read them all, no one is going to stop you. But when you go out there, to the real world, and start to practice recognizing and applying meta-programs distinctions, take them one at a time. In fact, I would recommend that you consciously work with only one meta-program a week.

The reason is that your mind needs time to process these ideas and concepts, and since you're also applying them in numerous social situations, your mind needs to "push" them down to become unconscious competencies. To prevent overwhelm and possible failure, work slowly. It will benefit you later on when you master the meta-programs.

I also suggest that you not apply the meta-programs on everyone in every situation. This is something that new NLP learners mistakenly engage in. They apply everything they learn, on everyone, all the time and everywhere.

This is not healthy. Nothing in excess can be healthy. Stay "normal." Applying NLP 24/7 will make you a control-freak or some kind of a zombie. Now, to make it clear, I'm talking about consciously practicing the skills of Neuro Linguistic Programming. If something has become a part of you, if you do not need to "think about it" to make it work. But if you go out there, consciously trying to apply NLP on everything and everyone, you will find yourself exhausted, frustrated and with many annoyed relatives. Separate practice times from reality times. When you practice, engage with everything you can as an NLP practitioner. When you live your life, give NLP a rest. You will find that the skills you're practicing will naturally flow into your everyday actions and thoughts, so you really do not need to force this process.

Most important, remember that people's actions do not match their identity. You are not defined by your random actions. Everything you do and think about is context dependent, and every blueprint you recognize in yourself or in other people, might change drastically given different circumstances. In other words, respect your own model of the world and respect other people's models of the world. Reality is shared but not perceived the same by everyone.

As I wrote above, the meta-programs are distinguishable on a continuum. There is a sliding scale for most of them. Estimate more or less how far to an extreme a person's tendency is. You cannot be 100% accurate, but you can hit the right mark close enough. You can use the numerical grading system (1 to 10) or percentages (1-100%), or you can imagine it graphically, as I do, like an empty rectangle being filled with a color according to intensity.

When recognizing meta-programs in other people avoid the judgement. It would be counter-productive for you if you start estimating the "good" or "bad" in their preferences. There are no "right" or "wrong" tendencies, but "useful" or "non-useful," and again even this estimation is context-dependent.

Do not expect the meta-programs you elicit in others to be consistent. Even when you come across the same context, a meta-program can change drastically. People evolve, even when they are not aware of it. Any experience, big or small, can modify a person's meta-program. To use the meta-program model practically, you treat every interaction like a first one and re-work the meta-programs accordingly.

Finally, have fun! Exploring another person's map of the world is an exciting endeavor. Get curious and stay curious and delighted about other people. You will enjoy social interactions, you will become much more attractive to everyone, and your groupies (every person has some) will grow and grow. Your influence abilities will definitely increase and strengthen, and your days will not seem like carbon copies of each other anymore. NLP can, and should in my opinion, be practiced in a state of joy.

Perception and Interest Styles Meta Programs

View:

Global (Seeing the forest for the trees, big picture)
vs.
Details (detailed view, specific).

Boundary Locus:

Internal (how I feel, think, etc.)
vs.
External (what you're doing, what's happening).

Person locus:

Self (me, number one, narcissism)

vs.
Other (you, empathy, codependency).

Distinction:

Match or sameness (how these things are similar or overlap, what they have in common)
vs.
Mismatch or difference (how they are distinct, different, in contrast, unique).

Arousal hierarchy:

The type of thing that the person finds most interesting to notice or value, can be listed in order of that person's level of interest or sequence of noticing when in a new situation.

People
vs.
Activities
vs.
Location
vs.
Things
vs.
Information
(other categories can be added as needed)

Arousal sub-hierarchies:

Same as arousal hierarchy, but for categories within the arousal hierarchy item.

Example for *People*: dynamics, power hierarchy position or class, motivations, usefulness, threat, individual personality characteristics, sophistication or capacity (e.g. psychological, occupational, emotional, social, motivational).

Behavior Styles Meta Programs

Immediacy:

Proactive (acting in advance, being prepared)
vs.
Reactive (in the moment, immediacy, emergency)

Personal style:

Similar to Mayers Briggs.
Assertive vs. *Passive*.
Judgmental vs. *Open perception*.
Thinking and Logical vs. *Intuitive*.
Active vs. Complacent.
Invasive vs. Tolerant
Concerned vs. *Indifferent*.

Developmental issues:

Developmental delays
vs.
Age-appropriate maturity (in specific areas of living such as handling authority), physical, thinking (cognitive), and emotional impairments that can affect development (such as a mental health diagnosis

which can be mild, moderate or severe).

Outcomes Alignment Styles Meta Programs

Outcome locus:

Towards (what I want, eagerness) vs.
Away from (avoiding what I reject or fear, loathing or concern)

Time locus:

Far vs. *Distant,*

Past vs. *present* vs. *future* (thoughts and reference points tend to be there)

Convincer patterns and learning preferences:

Being convinced of something or learning something most efficiently through reading, observing, doing, experiencing, etc.

McClelland's motivational preferences:

Power vs. *Popularity* vs. *Performance*

Additional Resources

DURING the couple of years of research for The Big Book I came across, or created, quite a lot of educational resources, mostly on Neuro LInguistic Programming. Please note, that the links below were available during the last revision before printing the book, so if any of them is not accessible anymore look it up on Google.com.

Resourceful Websites

BigBookOfNLP.com

The Big Books' home page. You can read my blog there, with a whole lot of free articles, additional chapters that didn't make it to this volume, downloads, advice, and join the biggest most affectionate international NLP community online. I do not sell produces or services through the site or use any "affiliate" linking.

૭/૭

NLPWeekly.com

I started a blog back in 2004, and called it NLP Weekly. After a year it became a full online magazine and shortly after a real international NLP community.

૭/૭

YouTube.com/nlptv

Youtube is simply the best. In our channel, NLPtv, we provide dozens of free educational videos, obviously on NLP and Hypnosis. Subscribe to our channel and also get some news and more free videos by private messages.

૭/૭

FaceBook.com

FaceBook is the largest social networking website, and I really admire its clean design and almost ad-free interface. You can meet new NLP colleagues, find practice groups in your area and join our

FaceBook.com group – search for "Shlomo 'Vaknin" or "NLP Weekly".

Patterns Originators And NLP Authors – Official Sites

Richard Bandler – RichardBandler. com
John Grinder – JohnGrinder.com
Robert Dilts – NLPU.com
Tad&AdrianaJames–NLPCoaching. com
Michael Hall – NeuroSemantics.com
Steve Andreas – SteveAndreas.com
Kevin Hogan – KevinHogan.com
Charles Faulkner – NLPCo.com
Anne Linden – AnneLinden.com

❧

On My Bookshelf – NLP & Hypnosis

My Voice Will Go With You: The Teaching Tales of Milton H. Erickson, M.D.

By: Sidney Rosen (Editor).
ISBN-13: 978-0393301359

Patterns of the Hypnotic Techniques of Milton H. Erickson, M.D

By: Richard Bandler, John Grinder.
ISBN-13: 978-1555520526

Patterns of the Hypnotic Techniques of Milton H. Erickson, M.D., Vol. 2

By: John Grinder, Judith Delozier, Richard Bandler
ISBN-13: 978-1555520533

Uncommon Therapy: The Psychiatric Techniques of Milton H. Erickson, M.D.

By: Jay Haley
ISBN-13: 978-0393310313

Beliefs: Pathways to Health and Wellbeing

By: Robert Dilts
ISBN-13: 978-1555520298

Sleight Of Mouth

By: Robert Dilts
ISBN-13: 978-0916990473

The Spirit Of NLP

By: Michael L. Hall
ISBN-13: 978-1899836048

The Structure of Magic II: A Book About Communication and Change (Book 2)

By: John Grinder, Richard Bandler.
ISBN-13: 978-0831400491

Time Line Therapy and the Basis of Personality

By: Tad James, Wyatt Woodsmall.
ISBN-13: 978-0916990213

Presenting Magically: Transforming Your Stage Presence with NLP

By: Tad James, David Shephard.
ISBN-13: 978-1899836529

Training Trances: Multi-Level Communication in Therapy and Training

John Overdurf, Julie Silverthorn.
ISBN-13: 978-1555520694

Frogs into Princes: Neuro Linguistic Programming

By: John Grinder, Richard Bandler, Steve Andreas.
ISBN-13: 978-0911226195

NLP: The New Technology of Achievement

By: NLP Comprehensive, Steve Andreas, Charles Faulkner.
ISBN-13: 978-0688146191

The User's Manual For The Brain / Michael Hall

By: Michael L. Hall, Bob Bodenhamer.
ISBN-13: 978-1899836321

Sourcebook of Magic: A Comprehensive Guide to NLP Change Patterns

By: Michael L. Hall, Barbara P. Belnap.
ISBN-13: 978-1904424253

Mindworks: An Introduction to Nlp: the Secrets of Your Mind Revealed

By: Anne Linden
ISBN-13: 978-1845900861

NLP Workbook: A Practical Guide to Achieving the Results You Want

By: Joseph O'Connor
ISBN-13: 978-0007100033

Awaken the Giant Within : How to Take Immediate Control of Your Mental, Emotional, Physical and Financial Destiny!

By: Anthony Robbins
ISBN-13: 978-0671791544

Unlimited Power : The New Science Of Personal Achievement

By: Anthony Robbins
ISBN-13: 978-0684845777

Appendix A:

Modalities Abbreviations

V – Visual

Ve – Visual external (physical perception of sight)

Vi – Visual internal (imagery, mind's eye)

A – Auditory

Ae – Auditory external (physical perception of sound)

Ai – Auditory internal (inner voice, thoughts)

At – Auditory tonal (tone, sound, music)

Ad – Auditory digital (the words)

Adi – Auditory digital internal (self talk)

K – Kinesthetic (physical sensations)

Kv – Kinesthetic visceral (inside feeling, e.g. 'butterflies" or warm stomach)

Kt – Kinesthetic tactile / touch, skin sensation

Ke – Kinesthetic perceptions – emotions

O – Olfactory

G – Gustatory

Appendix B:

The Submodalities

I N this section we introduce the most common submodalities, their characteristics and expected influence.

Visual Submodalities

Movie/Still Picture

Is the thought being represented by a still picture, such as a photograph, or by a moving picture, a mental movie?

Most people I worked with report that a photograph is less emotional than a mental movie. In a mental movie, you can see the event happening again, whether you're in it or not (watching from the side); you could hear the words being said and feel the tension in the event.

A mental still picture is most often used to understand a concept or to remember a visual object, such as a face or a name or a date.

Color/Black & White

Is the thought being represented as black and white still picture/movie, or is it in color? The continuum here, obviously, would be how strong the colors are, for example, or if it's a black and white imagery, are there shades of grey or complete distinction between the 2 colors?

Location Above/Below

When you think inside your head, there's always a location where you can point out towards the image you're making up. If you keep your head straight and consider your field of vision to be the "screen", where is that picture/movie located on the screen? Is it above your eye level, forcing you to look up? Is it below your eye level? Is it exactly at that point?

Location Left/Right

The same as with Above/Below, where on that continuum stands your picture/movie. Normally, the image or movie itself, as a whole, won't be running around – it works quite the same as with your TV. It would be hard for you to watch it if someone would move it left and right constantly. So on your field of vision, the Screen, where is that picture or movie? How far to the left, how far to the right?

Light Intensity – Driving Submodality

For most, if not all, the people I worked with, this specific submodality proved itself to be one of the strongest. When one specific submodality drives so much change in an emotional response, we call it a "driving submodality".

It means, that when you change that submodality (yes, you can change them, I'll show you how), and move it on its continuum, it creates a new emotional response to that image you're working with.

Light intensity means – how dark or how bright is the image/movie. Is it dim? Is it brighter than "reality"? Is it too dark to notice some important details?

It works the same as in the film industry. You would notice, that in order to grab your attention to a specific item, the director would distort or dim the background and will sharpen the image of that item... Yes, you know it already! They do that in advertising all the time...

Perhaps because it IS a driving submodality, which "drives" us to drive our cars and take their product for a test-drive... Ok, enough word-games with the word "drive". Let's drive forward...

Size – Driving Submodality

Yes, this one is another very important and effective submodality. Size matters! Don't believe the girl who says it isn't. If she can't see it... Alright, we'll focus on your mind for now...

Size in terms of visual modality is measured in relation to your field of vision. Is that picture / movie "bigger than life" size?

Is it small and compact?

Can you look above it, below it, around it?

Is it "in your face", preventing you from noticing actual sensations from the outside world? Is it too small to realize what's going on exactly?

Change Of Focus

It could have been a part of the Intensity modality, but it also has an effect of its own. If your actual physical vision is blurry, you get anxious. You might even become a bit paranoid. It works the same with your mental images or movies.

If you think of something important, and it becomes blurry, you will experience the same emotions as if these were your eyes that got blurry.

Change of focus also changes the way you pay attention to that specific scenario. You might suddenly ignore it completely just to deal with that "vision issue". Or you may become really obsessed about making it clearer. And that can cost you in energy, time and relationships.

For example, you might burst at someone you care about, just because they "draw a picture" for you, mentally, which is unclear. They spoke in words that only they can make clear meaning of (you know, women are excellent in that skill – and luckily for all of us, they use it well to educate their men).

And that unclear image drives you crazy, because you want to understand, you want to be able to solve it... you want to be a good friend/father/lover, etc.

Speed Of Thought

The rate of images is also important. A movie is nothing more than slightly changed images, presented in light speed, to create the illusion of movement. Of course, this submodality only refers to the internal movie and not to a picture which does not present any action.

Speed is action potential. It is also quite a strong submodality, although it works much better when the Size of the movie is also large. Small fast movies are not so effective.

We use speeding up for motivation and slowing down for relaxation or analysis. For example, if you imagine yourself riding on a roller coaster (remember that distinction?), as if you are there in that cabin – but the only difference is that it is all in slow motion. You see the movie "turn pages", the picture running slowly, like in the old movies (with the black and white strip in between them)… that's not so scary suddenly. It's even boring! How could a roller coaster, first person experience, be so emotionless and boring? If it's too slow to drive your emotions.

We call this submodality "Speed Of Thought" because there are so many useful ways you can use it to benefit your life instantly. In our seminars we teach our students to do it automatically (since most of our thinking is in patterns, anyway), and their results are amazing. All the way from creativity sparks, motivational boosts, anger management, addiction busting and so much more. Again, if you feel you want to grab this set of tools and own it for real, give us a call or drop us an email; we'll make it happen for you too.

Discrimination By Changing Focus

We will talk about the master operative filters soon, but for now this specific submodality is quite a strong one. By discriminating details in your mental picture or movie, you actually create a whole new meaning.

A great example is one that I also give in my seminars: 2 people go to the same Christmas party but have 2 different opinions of how good it was. The first person was focusing on the happy faces of people around him while the other person was focusing on the tiny red wine stain on his white shirt… the first had a great time while the second spent the same time thinking about the red stain.

Even though the party was going on around them in the same manner, since they shared the same time, location and social interactions – the only difference was the discrimination each of them used by focusing on a specific detail of the experience.

Later on, if you ask them both how did they enjoy the party (considering you're not the host, so they don't have to lie to you), how do you think each of them will react?

Changing your focus by discriminating details and zoning in on one specific, even if it's only "in your mind", changes your experience.

Panoramic Frame

This submodality represents a continuum between a picture or movie which resides in a frame, just as if you were watching a movie on your television screen (which must have a frame) or glancing in a picture on your wall which might also have a (wooden?) frame.

For most people I've met, the difference in the experience is that they consider the panoramic type (the movie or picture stretched on your field of vision without a distinct border) to be more "realistic" and the framed type to be more metaphoric. In addition, I did notice that many people use the framed mental picture or movie for planning the future and the panoramic for most of their memories.

If you do that differently, though, there is nothing wrong with that! I will be happy to hear your discoveries in this subject of Submodalities.

Dimensions

Another very distinctive feature of a mental image is the number of dimensions it occupies. I like to compare this to the cartoons I watched when I was a child (ok, I'm still watching some, but so do you!).

The continuum of the dimensions submodality lies between a two-dimension and a three-dimension picture or movie. Disney's cartoons from the 50's, such as the older Micky Mouse, were made in a 2D world. They were flat on the page, and while watching the movie, you could tell there's only one flat dimension they live in. They didn't seem to have a depth inside the picture, even if they used different sizes for creating that illusion.

The three dimensional cartoon, however, did have a whole lot of depth. You get the illusion that there's not only one stretched canvas from left to right, but as if there's a world going inward and outwards towards you as the viewer. Many cartoons today are made in 3D.

683

This submodality is usually dominant when you explore subjects you are bored about and feel no excitement what-so-ever. You might find, that you think of "math" or "history" or "your wife's make up routine" as being black and white, still picture, framed... and 2D! Well, that's one boring thought right there!

Now take these features and make one of your other more exciting memories the same. You would lose the excitement. So don't do that, we are here to enhance your experience, not to make you dull.

Perspective

"Let's look at it from another side, shall we?"

"You need to take a more global view on this one..."

"If you saw this from MY side..."

We use perspectives all the time, numerous times a day. You can't really get through your day without using a whole lot of different perspectives.

And here's a clue – the perspective you use to think and visualize a situation might be crucial for the understanding and conclusions you would make. Perspectives, in many cases, are the ones you use to make decisions.

You change your mind when you change your perspective. We have all had those arguments, when we finally were brave enough to look at the situation from our rival's point of view... and we felt they were right. We were wrong because we took a certain perspective which was not congruent with reality.

There are many useful ways for you to explore the visual submodality Perspectives. You could choose, for example, to take the Global view, as if you're a bird flying up there and seeing it all from above... you could get out of your own body (mentally, of course) and go around your mate's shoulders and see the interaction from that perspective.

You might decide to take a more distant point of view, a closer, a higher, a lower one... whatever creative perspective you can come up with – the more angels you use to look at a serious situation, the more choices and information you get.

Visual Triggers

This is not a specific sub-modality but it is an inner visual stimulation and it is quite important for our subject of memory management. Visual triggers are what we call "Anchors". It could be anything from your experience – it could be a face or features of a face, for example.

I had a client who was attacked in her childhood, and ever since she has a very strong reaction towards people who share the same facial characteristics as her attacker.

A complete stranger who had nothing to do with her past could be getting some hatred (and disturbing) looks from her, just because he had the same type of nose, same facial hair arrangement, same eye patterns, etc.

Anchors are very important simply because of two reasons: one, you have registered in your mind numerous anchors (literally, millions); and second, many of those anchors trigger subconscious processes that can change your emotions, your thoughts and your decisions, without any conscious awareness.

Auditory Submodalities

Self Talk Vs. Other People's Voices

The voice you hear inside your head, whether it is your own voice or someone else's (even imaginary or generic) voice.

Actual Content

We put less emphasis on content since the words you use are not as important as the form in which you express them. But the syntax your choose for your words can describe a lot of your internal experience.

Emotional Expression

The emotion that is obvious through the voice; angry voice and sexy voice do not sound the same.

Volume

How high, how low, how strong – weak voice doesn't cause as much effect as a strong voice.

Tonality

The tonality of your voice.

Tempo/Speed Of Speech

The tempo or speed of your voice.

The Source Location

From which point in space the voice is originating from?

Harmonic/Disharmony

Is it a pleasant "rhythmic" voice or is the speech full with breaks and "umm" or "ehh"? yes, we do that on the inside as well.

Regular/Irregular

Hearing Dracula's voice or Clinton's voice is not equal. Does the voice has an irregular distracting quality or is it "normal"?

Inflections

This one is also related to content and context – in which points of the text does the voice change a quality? Is there a reason?

Length/Duration

For which periods of time do you hear that voice? Does it use long sentences or short ones?

Key Words

Also related to content but these are key words, kind of digital "anchors", that trigger an emotional reaction in you. For example, for many people the syntax "nine eleven" drives a whole set of very strong emotions. It would be a different reaction for a New York citizen and a Taliban militant…

Kinesthetic Submodalities

Temperature

Perhaps the most frequently noticed submodality – our temperature rise when we're excited and lowers when we are bored. We use terms like "hot blooded" or "cold bitch" to describe behaviors.

Since all behavior is a result of thoughts, and most thoughts are the conclusion of memories… you feel what you think due to what you remember, and that has an effect on your perceived body temperature.

Your actual physiological temperature (normally at 37C) might not change at all although you may feel "hot" or "frozen" inside.

Texture

Our world is experienced mostly in 3D. Texture as a kinesthetic submodality is the fabric of that memory – what do you sense it could be if you touched it? Rough? Smooth? Bumpy?

Level Of Flexibility

That is also a mental attitude and not only a visible piece of information. Could you change the movement of emotion you feel inside or is it too rigid and "out of your control"? Road rage is often described as total lack of flexibility in a specific context and time frame.

Vibration

Should I really add more?

Pressure

When you remember a memory, it might cause a certain pressure in your body, usually felt above the eyes or on the lower lip (notice that many people who spend time in emotional day fantasies, their lips are swollen and their lower lip especially is dropped).

Tension

Tension is felt similar to pressure but it is a definite uncomfortable feeling that causes the desire to "release the tension". Also tension can be described by location in the body.

Movement

Emotions move. Emotion can be described as energy in motion. At most times, if you feel a strong emotion it does not just lay there motionless. It moves around, up and down, left and right, in crosses, in circles, in half-moon circles or an infinite spiral…

If you feel the movement, you can also find a pattern. In NLP seminars we work a lot with this submodality, since it is a very effective modal to gain control over fears and phobias.

Breathing

The breathing pattern is a kinesthetic submodality. How deep, from where to where, how low or shallow is your breathing?

Weight

Here we don't refer to your body's weight, but to the "weight" of the experience. Does it feel "heavy"? "Unbearable"? or "Light"?

Confined

We can also define some feelings as "confined", which means they are not only manageable and light-weighted, but we can block them to a specific location, usually between our hands. These are the kind of emotional experiences that we can turn on and turn off almost on cue, without being overwhelmed. Sadly enough, in most cases we found that "love" or "passion" get confined while "rage" and "anger" are not.

Change Of Size Or Shape

That is related to the Movement Submodality, since sometimes as the sensation moves through your body (or beyond it) it might change its size and shape accordingly. You may be able to "confine" it if it's a foot ahead of you and felt as less than length of shoulders.

Direction

Where did it go? Where is it going? From where?

Triggers

Just as certain words can trigger emotions, also a certain touch can be an "anchor" for an emotional roller-coaster. It is physically observable in rape victims, when a certain movement and touch can send them into a trance and a fearful internal experience in less than a brief second.

NLP Contributors

The proper credits to the right people...

Unfortunately, the Neuro Linguistic Programming field has known its share of "credits-theft". One lucky person has shared a strategy, and another has stolen the originator credit from him. We have seen many law-suits and a whole lot of a heartache in the past 20 years. We want it to stop.

We did our best here to research the quite complex NLP history and give the right credits to the people who have originated these patterns and techniques. Most NLP enthusiasts know only a few names of actual contributors, although they use their ideas on a daily basis.

We might have mistakes here, though! So please, if you do find those, let us know about them. We will fix them in future editions of the book and in our website.

Appendix C:

Logical Levels

Dilts' logical levels, from the higher, overriding levels, to the lower ones:

<Insert Image "logical-levels.jpg">

Spirit or strategic vision – Belief in higher purpose or values that give meaning to identity.

Identity – Sense of self that fosters values and beliefs.

Values and beliefs – Higher level of internal resources that drive decisions and how you apply your skills and knowledge.

Skills and knowledge – Fundamental internal resources for behavior.

Behavior – Physical actions and patterns, including habits and the power of behavior modification principles.

Environment – The context and how it stimulates, guides, facilitates and limits behavior.

Bibliography

Alpha Leadership: Tools for Business Leaders Who Want More from Life, Anne Deering, Julian Russell, and Robert Dilts, 2002

An Insiders Guide to Sub Modalities, Will Macdonald and Richard Bandler, 1989

An Introduction to NLP Neuro-Linguistic Programming : Psychological Skills for Understanding and Influencing People, Joseph O'Connor, 1998

Awaken the Giant Within : How to Take Immediate Control of Your Mental, Emotional, Physical and Financial Destiny!, Anthony Robbins, 1992

Beliefs: Pathways to Health and Wellbeing, Robert Dilts, Tim Hallbom, and Suzi Smith, 1990

Changing Belief Systems With NLP, Robert Dilts, 1990

Change Your Mind-And Keep the Change : Advanced NLP Submodalities Interventions, Connirae Andreas, Steve Andreas, Michael Eric Bennett, and Donna Wilson, 1987

Dynamic Learning, Robert B. Dilts and Todd A. Epstein, 1995

Encyclopedia of Systemic Neuro-Linguistic Programming and NLP New Coding, Robert B. Dilts and Judith A. Delozier, 2000

Frogs into Princes: Neuro Linguistic Programming, Richard Bandler, John Grinder, Steve Andreas, and John O. Srevens, 1979

From Coach to Awakener, Robert Dilts, 2003

Get the Life You Want: The Secrets to Quick and Lasting Life Change with Neuro-Linguistic Programming, Richard Bandler, 2008

Giant Steps : Author Of Awaken The Giant And Unlimited Power, Anthony Robbins, 1997

Heart of the Mind – Engaging Your Inner Power to Change with Neuro-Linguistic Programming, Connirae Andreas and Steve Andreas, 1989

Jay Haley On Milton H. Erickson, Jay Haley, 1993

Magic In Action, Richard Bandler, 1982

Mindworks: An Introduction to Nlp: the Secrets of Your Mind Revealed, Anne Linden, 1998

Manage Yourself, Manage Your Life: Vital Nlp Techniques for Personal Well-Being and Professinal Success, Ian McDermott and Ian Shircore, 1999

Modeling With NLP, Robert Dilts, 1998

My Voice Will Go With You: The Teaching Tales of Milton H. Erickson, M.D., Sidney Rosen, 1991

Neuro-Linguistic Programming: Volume I (The Study of the Structure of Subjective Experience), Robert Dilts, 1980

NLP at Work, Second Edition: How to Model What Works in Business to Make It Work for You (People Skills for Professionals), Sue Knight, 2002

NLP: The New Technology Of Achievement, NLP Comprehensive & Charles Faulkner & Steve Andreas, 1996

NLP Workbook: A Practical Guide to Achieving the Results You Want, Joseph O'Connor, 2001

Patterns of the Hypnotic Techniques of Milton H. Erickson, M.D. (Volume I), Richard; Grinder, John Bandler, 1975

Patterns of the Hypnotic Techniques of Milton H. Erickson, M.D., Vol. 2, John Grinder, Judith Delozier, and Richard Bandler, 1997

Persuasion Engineering, Richard Bandler and John LA Valle, 1996

Presenting Magically: Transforming Your Stage Presence with NLP, Tad James and David Shephard, 2001

Personality Selling : Using NLP and the Enneagram to Understand People and How They Are Influenced, Albert J. Valentino, 1999

Precision: A New Approach to Communication : How to Get the Information You Need to Get Results, Michael McMaster and John Grinder, 1993

Reframing: Neuro-linguistic Programming and The Transformation of Meaning, Richard Bandler and John Grinder, 1982

Roots Of Neuro Linguistic Programming, Robert Dilts, 1983

Skills for the Future: Managing Creativity and Innovation, Robert Dilts and Gino Bonissone, 1993

Sleight Of Mouth: The Magic Of Conversational Belief Change, Robert Dilts, 2006

Sourcebook of Magic: A Comprehensive Guide to NLP Change Patterns, Michael L. Hall & Barbara P. Belnap, 2001

Strategies of Genius, Volume One, Robert Dilts, 1994

Strategies of Genius, Volume Two, Robert Dilts, 1994

Successful Selling With NLP: Powerful Ways to Help You Connect with Customers, Joseph O'Connor, 2001

Success Mastery With NLP/Cassettes, Charles Faulkner, 1994

The Enneagram and NLP: A Journey of Evolution, Anne Linden and Murray Spalding, 1994

The Spirit Of NLP, L. Michael Hall, 2001

The Structure of Magic: A Book About Language and Therapy (Structure of Magic), Richard Bandler and John Grinder, 1975

The Structure of Magic II: A Book About Language and Therapy (Book 2), Richard Bandler and John Grinder, 1975

The Wisdom of Milton H. Erickson: The Complete Volume, Ronald A. Havens, 2005

Tools of the Spirit, Robert Dilts and Robert McDonald, 1997

Training With NLP, Joseph O'Connor, 1994

Training Trances: Multi-Level Communication in Therapy and Training, John Overdurf and Julie Silverthorn, 1995

Trance-Formations: Neuro-Linguistic Programming and the Structure of Hypnosis, John Grinder and Richard Bandler, 1981

Transforming Your Self: Becoming Who You Want to Be, Steve Andreas, 2002

Turtles All the Way Down: Prerequisites to Personal Genius, John Grinder and Judith Delozier, 1995

Uncommon Therapy: The Psychiatric Techniques of Milton H. Erickson, M.D., Jay Haley, 1993

Unlimited Power : The New Science Of Personal Achievement, Anthony Robbins, 1997

User's Manual for the Brain, Vol. II: Mastering Systemic NLP, L. Michael Hall and Bob G. Bodenhamer, 2003

Using Your Brain–For a Change: Neuro-Linguistic Programming, Richard Bandler, 1985

Virginia Satir: the Patterns of Her Magic, Steve Andreas, 1999

Visionary Leadership Skills: Creating a World to Which People Want to Belong, Robert B. Dilts, 1996

Begin!

This book was meant to be "tortured", not to stay smooth, shiny and new. Use it and abuse it. Write comments and case studies or experiences in and between patterns. Cut out the Overview sections and use them as cue cards, so you won't have to carry the book around. Highlight the ideas that inspire you the most. This is *not* the holy bible; this is a purely practical workbook, so make it work for you.

Once you get results from the concepts and methods in this book, please let me know about it. My direct email is – **editor@bigbookofnlp. com**.

I normally get around 50 or so new emails a day, but I promise you that I'll respond personally as soon as I can. If it is something urgent, if you're stuck with a client or need an advice on an issue that is not discussed in the book, write the word "Urgent for Shlomo" in the subject of your email. You can (or should?) also join our international NLP community at BigBookOfNLP.com.

Thank you again for choosing The Big Book Of NLP Techniques.

1908437